The Manager's Bookshelf

The Manager's Bookshelf

A Mosaic of Contemporary Views

Third Edition

Jon L. Pierce
University of Minnesota, Duluth

John W. Newstrom
University of Minnesota, Duluth

HarperCollins*Publishers*

Acquisitions Editor: *Melissa A. Rosati*
Project Coordination and Text Design: *Monotype Composition Company, Inc.*
Cover Design: *Kay Petronio*
Compositor: *ComCom, Inc.*
Printer and Binder: *R. R. Donnelly & Sons Company*
Cover Printer: *The Lehigh Press, Inc.*

The Manager's Bookshelf: A Mosaic of Contemporary Views, Third Edition

Library of Congress Cataloging-in-Publication Data
The Manager's bookshelf : a mosaic of contemporary views / [collated
  by] Jon L. Pierce, John W. Newstrom — 3rd ed.
      p.   cm.
  Includes bibliographical references and index.
  ISBN 0-06-500707-7
  1. Management literature—United States.   I. Pierce, Jon L. (Jon
Lepley)   II. Newstrom, John W.
HD70.U5M32   1992
658—dc20   92-36884
                                              CIP

    94 95 9 8 7 6 5 4 3

In memory of snowshoe treks, the search for firewood,
never-ending manuscript revisions,
and the eternal delight of sunrises over Lake Gichigami (Gitchee Gumee).

Contents

Preface

RESOURCES FOR THE INFORMED ORGANIZATIONAL CITIZEN

The 1980s were marked by an intense fascination with and an explosion in the number of books published on the topic of management, managers, and organizations. Bookstores around the country featured a larger number of management books than ever before, and many found themselves on, or close to, the "best-sellers" list. The early 1990s suggest that this trend is continuing.

The third edition of *The Manager's Bookshelf: A Mosaic of Contemporary Views* was prepared for both managers and management students. A significant number of individuals in both of these groups do not have sufficient time to read each of these books, yet many people find themselves involved in conversations where someone else refers to vision, self-directed workteams, or superleadership. We believe that a laudable goal for all students of management as well as managers is to remain current in their understanding of the views being expressed about organizational and management practices. To help you become a better-informed organizational citizen, we prepared *The Manager's Bookshelf,* which introduces you to more than thirty recently popular management books.

The Manager's Bookshelf: A Mosaic of Contemporary Views, as a book of readings, does not express the views of one individual on the management of organizations, nor does it attempt to integrate the views of several dozen authors. Instead, *this book is a collage.* It provides you with insights into many aspects of organizational management from the perspectives of a diverse group of management writers, including some highly popular individuals like Peter Drucker, Douglas McGregor, Warren Bennis, Michael Porter, Edward Lawler, Thomas Peters, and Rosabeth Kanter. Through this collection we will introduce you to the thoughts, philosophy, views, and experiences of a number of authors whose works have captivated the attention of today's business community.

This book contains a rich array of pieces. From a topical perspective there are inclusions which focus on ethics, global perspectives, participative practices, environmental trends, organizational culture, managing diversity, strategy, entrepreneurship, and managerial/leadership styles. This collection includes the views of a variety of individuals—some practitioners, some philosophers, some management consultants, and some management educators. The selections reflect a wide variety in terms of their tone and tenor, for critics have characterized some of the authors' works as passionate, academic, hollow, and insightful.

The nature and source of the ideas expressed in this collection are diverse. Some inclusions are prescriptive in nature, while others are descriptive; some are philosophical, while others report on personal and/or organizational experiences; some of these works represent armchair speculation, while others are based upon empirical study. Finally, the selections take a variety of forms. Some of the readings are excerpts extracted from the original book, some of the readings are articles written by the book's author in which part of the author's philosophy on management is revealed, and some of the inclusions are descriptive summaries of popular books that have been specially prepared for inclusion in *The Manager's Bookshelf.*

This collage can provide you with some useful insights, stimulate your thinking, and spark some dialogue with your colleagues about the management of today's organizations. We hope that these readings will prompt you to question both yourself and your peers about the viability of many of the ideas expressed by these authors regarding the practice of organizational management. If these goals are met, our purpose for assembling this collection will be realized.

Acknowledgments

We would like to express our sincere and warm appreciation to several colleagues who read and prepared summaries of the contemporary books contained in this edition of *The Manager's Bookshelf.* Their efforts made this edition possible.

We would also like to express our appreciation to friend and colleague Larry L. Cummings (University of Minnesota, Minneapolis) for his "reflections on the role of the best-sellers" that is contained in the epilogue to our book. We thank Larry for taking the time to reflect upon and update the insightful observations that he prepared for the earlier editions.

Summaries were prepared by:

INTRODUCTION
Diane Dodd-McCue, University of Richmond—Kilmann's *Managing Beyond the Quick Fix*
MANAGEMENT PARADIGMS
Robert Marx, University of Massachusetts, Amherst—Quinn's *Beyond Rational Management* and Bolman and Deal's *Reframing Organizations*
HIGH-PERFORMING ORGANIZATIONS
Jean Grube, University of Wisconsin, Madison—Argyris' *Overcoming Organizational Defenses*

Dorothy Marcic, Metropolitan State University, Minneapolis—Senge's *The Fifth Discipline*

ORGANIZATIONAL STRATEGY

Thomas A. Kolenko, Kennesaw State College—Leavitt's *Corporate Pathfinders*

Sara A. Morris, Old Dominion University—Porter's *Competitive Advantage*

MOTIVATION

Gayle Porter, The Ohio State University—McGregor's *The Human Side of Enterprise*

Charles C. Manz, Arizona State University—Blanchard and Johnson's *The One Minute Manager*

Mark J. Martinko and **Sherry Moss,** Florida State University—LeBoeuf's *The Greatest Management Principle in the World*

EMPOWERMENT AND PARTICIPATION

Constance Campbell, Georgia Southern University—Byham's *Zapp! The Lightning of Empowerment*

Charles C. Manz, Arizona State University and **Henry P. Sims, Jr.** University of Maryland—Manz and Sims' *SuperLeadership*

Sally Riggs Fuller, University of Wisconsin, Madison—Lawler's *High-Involvement Management*

LEADERSHIP

James R. Meindl, State University of New York, Buffalo—Gardner's *On Leadership*

Philip Anderson, University of St. Thomas—Zaleznik's *The Managerial Mystique*

Jim Laumeyer, Minnesota Department of Transportation—Conger's *The Charismatic Leader*

MANAGING DIVERSITY

Stephen A. Rubenfeld, University of Minnesota, Duluth—Morrison, et al's *Breaking the Glass Ceiling*

Linda E. Parry, University of Minnesota, Duluth—Loden and Rosener's *Workforce America!*

PREPARING FOR THE TWENTY-FIRST CENTURY

Robert Heller, University of Minnesota, Duluth—Reich's *The Work of Nations*

Thomas A. Kolenko, Kennesaw State College—Toffler's *Powershift: Knowledge, Wealth, and Violence at the Edge of the Twenty-First Century*

Richard S. Blackburn, University of North Carolina, Chapel Hill—Vaill's *Managing as a Performing Art*

INNOVATION AND ORGANIZATIONAL CHANGE

Kim Stewart, University of Denver—Belasco's *Teaching the Elephant to Dance*

Robert C. Ford, University of Alabama, Birmingham—Kanter's *When Giants Learn to Dance*

Ann Wiggins Noe, University of Minnesota, Minneapolis—Peters' *Thriving on Chaos*

ORGANIZATIONAL DECLINE & RENEWAL

Linn Van Dyne, University of Minnesota, Minneapolis—Meyer and Zucker's *Permanently Failing Organizations*

Stephen A. Rubenfeld, University of Minnesota, Duluth—Pascale's *Managing on the Edge*

Warren Candy, Minnesota Power—Beer, et al's *The Critical Path to Corporate Renewal*

MANAGING QUALITY IN CUSTOMER-DRIVEN ORGANIZATIONS

William B. Gartner, Georgetown University and **M. James Naughton,** Expert-Knowledge Systems, Inc.—Deming's *Out of the Crisis*

Gregory R. Fox, University of Minnesota, Duluth—Carlzon's *Moments of Truth*

Robert C. Ford, University of Alabama, Birmingham—Albrecht and Zemke's *Service America!*

Susan Zacur, University of Baltimore—Band's *Creating Value for Customers*

ETHICS AND MANAGEMENT

Cynthia A. Lengnick-Hall, Wichita State University—Blanchard and Peale's *The Power of Ethical Management*

Sara A. Morris, Old Dominion University—Freeman and Gilbert's *Corporate Strategy and the Search for Ethics*

GLOBAL DIMENSIONS

Michael Bisesi, University of Houston—Ouchi's *Theory Z: How American Business Can Meet the Japanese Challenge*

Robert Wharton, University of Minnesota, Duluth—Ohmae's *The Borderless World*

We would also like to express our appreciation to a number of individuals who provided us with a great deal of assistance and support during the preparation of this book. Many of our management colleagues took the time and effort to contribute to this book by carefully reading and preparing a description of one of the selected books. Many of these individuals wanted to offer their personal opinions, offer their endorsements and/or criticisms, and surface elements of their own philosophies, but they stuck to their task. To them we express our thanks for their time, energy, and commitment to furthering management education. To Professor Larry Cummings we express our gratitude for his reflections on these popular management books and contributions to the book's epilogue. To those who reviewed our proposal for this third edition and a draft of the final manuscript, we appreciated your recommendations: Gregory Fox, University of Minnesota, Duluth; Cynthia Fukami, University of Denver; Debra Arvanites, Villanova; Grant Learned, Defiance College; Don Plymale, Indiana University; Dale Finn, University of Massachusetts at Amherst; Bernard Lynch, Baruch College; David F. Summers, West Texas State University; Diane Dodd-McHugh, University of Richmond. To Jean Jacobson and Connie Johnson, who patiently prepared the manuscript, we want to say "thank you" for helping us once again meet our tight deadlines. We especially appreciate the continued project commitment and the assistance that we have received from Debra Reigert, Pamela Wilkie, and Melissa Rosati, at HarperCollins.

Jon L. Pierce

John W. Newstrom

About the Editors

Jon L. Pierce is Professor of Management and Organization in the School of Business and Economics at the University of Minnesota, Duluth. He received his Ph.D. in management and organizational studies at the University of Wisconsin, Madison. He is the author of more than sixty papers which have been published or presented at various professional conferences. His publications have appeared in the *Academy of Management Journal, Academy of Management Review, Journal of Management, Journal of Occupational Behavior, Journal of Applied Behavioral Sciences, The Personnel Administrator,* and *Organizational Behavior and Human Decision Processes.* His research interests include sources of psychological ownership, employee ownership systems, and organization-based self-esteem. He has served on the editorial review board for the *Academy of Management Journal, Journal of Management,* and *Business Insights.* He is the coauthor of four other books: *Alternative Work Schedules, Management, Windows into Management* (with John W. Newstrom), and *Managing.*

John W. Newstrom is Professor of Human Resource Management in the School of Business and Economics at the University of Minnesota, Duluth. He completed his doctoral degree in management and industrial relations at the University of Minnesota, and then taught at Arizona State University for several years. He is the author of over seventy articles and professional papers, and his work has appeared in publications such as *Personnel Psychology, California Management Review, Journal of Management, Academy of Management Journal,* and *The Journal of Occupational Behavior.* He has served on the editorial review boards for the *Academy of Management Review, Academy of Management Journal, The Personnel Administrator, Human Resource Development Quarterly,* and *The Journal of Management Development.* He is the coauthor of ten other books, including *Organizational Behavior: Human Behavior at Work,* 9th ed. (with Keith Davis) and *Transfer of Training* (with Mary Broad). His primary research interests lie in the areas of transfer of training, alternative work schedules, and self-managing teams.

Introduction

Part One contains three pieces. The first, "Understanding and Using the Best-Sellers," prepared by the editors of *The Manager's Bookshelf,* provides insight into why such a large number of management-oriented books have found themselves in the downtown bookstores, on our coffee tables, and on the bookshelves of those who manage today's organizations. Pierce and Newstrom discuss the rationale for this mosaic of contemporary views on organizations and management, and they provide you with insight into the nature and character of *The Manager's Bookshelf: A Mosaic of Contemporary Views.* They challenge you to read and reflect upon this collection of thoughts and experiences. They invite you to debate the ideas and philosophies that are presented here. They encourage you to let these contemporary management books stimulate your thinking, to motivate you to look more systematically into the science of organizations and management, and to provide you with the fun of learning something new.

As a result of their concern that these contemporary books will be seen as "quick and dirty" cures for organizational woes, Pierce and Newstrom encourage you to read Ralph H. Kilmann's *Managing Beyond the Quick Fix.*

Several years ago Ralph Kilmann, in his book *Beyond the Quick Fix:*

Managing Five Tracks to Organizational Success, attempted to provide us with a valuable message, one that should serve as the backdrop to your consumption and assessment of the myriad of purported "one minute" cures for organizational problems and for the management of today's complex organizations. Kilmann encourages you to stop perpetuating the myth of organizational and management simplicity, and to develop a more complete and integrated approach to the management of today's complex organizations. In *Managing Beyond the Quick Fix,* Kilmann showcases his framework for understanding and managing organizational success by using his integrated five-track approach: culture, management skills, team building, strategy-structure, and reward systems. After describing the five tracks, he offers an account of Eastman Kodak's successful implementation of the five-track program. Ralph H. Kilmann is a Professor of Business Administration and Director of the Program in Corporate Culture at the University of Pittsburgh.

Management guru Peter Drucker, in *The New Realities,* addresses a comprehensive array of topics in the social superstructure: economics, politics, society, education, and social organizations. Although the book addresses Drucker's concerns for the knowledgeable worker, an information-based organization, and the need for dramatic educational changes, he is perhaps most quoted when commenting on the state of management today and its needs in the future. Specifically, Drucker lays out seven essential principles defining management. He concludes that it is truly a liberal art, because it is the practice and application of fundamental knowledge and wisdom. *Business Week* (September 28, 1987) referred to Peter F. Drucker as the "Dr. Spock of Business." For generations of managers, Peter F. Drucker probably is "the most read, most listened-to, and most enduring guru of professional management" (pp. 61–65). Since 1971 he has been a Professor of Social Sciences at Claremont Graduate School in California.

Reading 1

Understanding and Using the Best-Sellers

Jon L. Pierce and John W. Newstrom

In the past, a large number of books treating various aspects of management have been in high demand at local bookstores. Several business books have sold millions of copies, led by *Iacocca, The One Minute Manager, Trump: The Art of the Deal,* and *In Search of Excellence.* Some of these books have stayed on "best-seller" lists for many weeks. What are the reasons for their popularity? What is the reason for their continued popularity as we move through the decade of the 1990s? One insight comes from Frank Freeman of the Center for Creative Leadership, who suggested simply that we are living in the "business decade."[1] Corporate America, he says, is back in good standing with the public, and there has been a resurgence of pride and hope in the business community.

We've all heard stories about the success of foreign organizations. We have continued to watch bigger and bigger portions of our markets being dominated by foreign-owned and controlled organizations. And we have witnessed more and more of America being bought up by foreign interests. There is, therefore, a tremendous thirst for *American* success stories. In essence, the public is receptive and the timing is right for the sale of popular management books at bookstores everywhere.

A second reason for the upsurge in management books stems from another form of competition. Many management consultants, fighting for visibility, have written books they hope will become "best-sellers."[2] Through the printed word they hope to provide a unique take-home product for their clients, communicate their management philosophies, gain wide exposure for themselves or their firms, and occasionally profit handsomely.

Third, the best-sellers also provide an optimistic message to a receptive market. In difficult economic times, managers may be as eager to swallow easy formulas as sick patients are to drink their prescribed medicine. Sensing this, the authors of the best-sellers (and of many other books with lesser records) often claim, at least implicitly, to present managers with an easy cure for their organizational woes or with an easy path to personal success.

Fourth, we are witnessing an increased belief in and commitment to

3

proactive organizational change. An increasing number of managers are reject-ing the notion that "if it ain't broke, don't fix it," and instead they are adopting a bias toward action instead of this status quo orientation. These managers are seriously looking for and experimenting with different approaches toward orga-nizational management. Many of the popular books are providing managers with insights into new and different ways of managing.

In their search for the "quick fix," generations of American managers have adopted a series of organizational management concepts, such as management by objectives (MBO), job enlargement, job enrichment, flextime, and a variety of labor-management participative schemes.[3] Each has been widely heralded, frequently implemented, and sometimes later abandoned and replaced by another emerging management technique. As a consequence of this manage-rial tendency to embrace ideas and then soon discard them, many viable mana-gerial techniques have received a tarnished image. For example, many of the Japanese participative management systems that are being copied by American managers today found their way into the garbage cans of an earlier generation of American managers. With the demand for quick fixes there is a ready market for new, reborn, and revitalized management ideas. We encourage you to read Ralph Kilmann's views on the quick fix that follow in this opening part.

We alert you to this managerial tendency to look for "new" solutions to current organizational problems. The rush to resolve problems and take advan-tage of opportunities frequently leads to the search for simple remedies for complex organizational problems. Yet very few of today's organizational prob-lems can be solved with any single approach. High-involvement management, intrapreneurship, and corporate culture advocated in today's generation of popular management books are likely to join the list of "tried and abandoned" solutions to organizational woes. We especially hope that the "quick fix" ap-proach to organizational problem solving that characterizes the management style of many will *not* be promoted as a result of this mosaic of today's popular business books.

RATIONALE FOR THIS BOOK

The business world has been buzzing with references to terms like vision, competitive advantage, transformational and charismatic leaders, high-involve-ment (commitment) management, networks, high tech/high touch, the "excel-lent" companies, and corporate cultures. On the negative side, these new terms feed the management world's preoccupation with quick fixes and the perpetua-tion of management fads. On the positive side, many of these concepts may serve as catalysts to the further development of sound management philoso-phies and practices.

In earlier decades a few books would occasionally enter the limelight (e.g., *Parkinson's Law, The Peter Principle, My Years With General Motors, The Money Game*), but for the most part they did not generate the widespread and prolonged popularity of the current generation of business books. Moreover, many weren't written in the readable style that makes most of the contemporary books so easy to consume.

Managers seem to find the current wave of books not only interesting, but enjoyable to read. For example, a small survey by the Center for Creative Leadership found that a significant number of managers who participated in a study of their all-around reading selections chose one or more *management* books as their favorite! Of the 179 business or management books identified in total, *In Search of Excellence* accounted for more than half of the books that were read by managers.[4] The point is that many of the "popular" management books *are* being read by managers—probably because the books are often supportive of their present management philosophies! Many managers report that these books are insightful, interestingly presented, and seemingly practical. Whether or not the prescriptions in these books have had (or ever will have) a real and lasting impact on the effective management of organizations remains to be determined.

Despite the best-sellers' overall popularity, some managers don't read *any* current management books, and many other managers have only read a very limited number of them, or small parts of a few books.† Similarly, many university students studying management may have heard about these books but have not read them. *The Manager's Bookshelf: A Mosaic of Contemporary Views* presents perspectives from (but not a criticism of) a number of those popular management books. *The Manager's Bookshelf* was prepared for two audiences: the managers who are interested in the ideas presented in many of the popular management books but don't have time to read them in their entirety, and the students of management who want to be well-informed as they prepare for entry into the work world. Reading about the views expressed in many of the best-sellers will expand the knowledge level of both groups, enabling them to fit in better (at least conversationally) with their managerial colleagues. Although reading the three dozen samplers contained herein can serve as a useful introduction to this literature, the samplers should not be viewed as a substitute for immersion into the original material, nor do they remove the need for further reading of the more substantive management books and professional journals.

As your editors, we are strong advocates of both managers and students being "informed organizational citizens." Therefore, we believe that it is important for you to develop an awareness and an understanding of what is being *written* about organizations and management. To achieve that end we believe that it is also important for you to become aware of what is being *read* by the managers who surround you, some of which is contained in these popular books, and much of which is contained in more traditional management books as well as professional and scientific journals.[5]

---

†Those of you who incorporate these types of management books in your management training programs might find the following article useful: "The potential role of popular business books in management development programs," by J. W. Newstrom and J. L. Pierce in *Management Development Review,* 1989, 8, 2, 13–24.

CONTENTS OF THE BEST-SELLERS

What *topics* do these best-selling books cover, what is their *form,* and what is their *merit?* Although many of the authors cover a wide range of topics and others may not have a clear focus, there are a number of "boxes" into which many seem to fall. Some have attempted to describe the more successful and unsuccessful companies and identify what made them effective or failures. Others focus on "micro" issues in leadership, motivation, or ethics. Other books have turned their attention toward broad questions of corporate strategy and competitive tactics for implementing strategy.

In terms of form, many contain apparently simple answers and rather trite prescriptions. Others are built around literally hundreds of spellbinding anecdotes and stories. Some have used interviews of executives as their source of information. Still others have adopted the parable format for getting their point across. As a group they are rich in their diversity of presentational style.

Judging the merits of best-sellers is a difficult task (and one that we will leave for readers and management critics to engage in). Some critics have taken the extreme position of calling these books "intellectual wallpaper" and "business pornography." Certainly, labels like this, justified or not, should encourage readers to be cautious. A better perspective is provided by an assessment of the *sources* of many of the books, which are often anecdotal in nature. In other words, much of the information in these best-sellers stems from the experiences and observations of a single individual and is often infused with the subjective opinions of that writer. Unlike the more traditional academic literature, these books do not all share a sound scientific foundation. Requirements pertaining to objectivity, reproducibility of observations, and tests for reliability and validity have not guided the creation of much of the material that is being communicated in these books. As a consequence, the authors are at liberty to say whatever they want (and often with as much passion as they desire!).

Unlike authors who publish research-based knowledge, authors of best-sellers do not need to submit their work to a panel of reviewers who then critically evaluate the ideas, logic, and data that are being presented. The authors of these popular management books are able to proclaim as sound management principles virtually anything that is intuitively acceptable to their publisher and readers. Therefore, readers need to be cautious consumers. The ideas presented in these books need to be compared critically with the well-established thoughts from more traditional sources of managerial wisdom.

NATURE OF THIS BOOK

This is the third edition of *The Manager's Bookshelf.* The first edition was published in 1988; the second in 1990. There are many books included in the third edition that were not previously summarized, representing approximately a sixty percent revision. *The Manager's Bookshelf* provides a comprehensive introduction to many of the major best-sellers in the management field during recent years. It is important to identify the nature of the selections contained here, and to indicate how they were selected for inclusion.

The selections consist of two types: excerpts of original material, and summaries provided by a panel of reviewers. In some cases, the editors of this book felt it was important to provide the reader not only with the main ideas presented by the author of a best-seller, but also with the *flavor* (style or nature) of the author's approach. In some cases, permission was obtained to excerpt directly a chapter from the original book, especially when the chapter was the keystone presentation of the author's major theme. In other cases, the author's original thoughts and words were captured by selecting an article (representing part of the book) that the author had written for publication in a professional journal. Here again the reader will see the author's ideas directly, though only sampled or much condensed from the original source.

The other major format chosen for inclusion was a comprehensive *summary* of the best-seller prepared by persons selected for their relevant expertise, interest, and familiarity. These summaries are primarily descriptive, designed to provide readers with an overall understanding of the nature of the book. These summaries are not judgmental in nature, nor a reflection of the authors' management philosophy.

Determination of what constituted a "best-seller" worthy of inclusion was easy in some cases and more difficult in others. From the hundreds of books available for selection, the ones included here were rated highly on one or more of these criteria:

1. *Market acceptance:* Several books have achieved national notoriety by selling hundreds of thousands of copies, and occasionally over a million
2. *Provocativeness:* Some books present thought-provoking viewpoints that run counter to "traditional" management thought
3. *Distinctiveness:* A wide variety of topical themes of interest to organizational managers is presented
4. *Representativeness:* In an attempt to avoid duplication from books with similar content, many popular books were excluded
5. *Author reputation:* Some authors (e.g., Peter Drucker, Edward Lawler III) have a strong reputation for the quality of their thinking and the insights that they have historically generated, and therefore some of their newer products were included.

AUTHORS OF THE BEST-SELLERS

It is appropriate for a reader to inquire of a best-seller, "Who is the author of this book?" Certainly the authors come from varied backgrounds. Some have previously developed a respected academic and professional record and have subsequently integrated their thoughts into book form. Others have spent their entire careers working in a single organization and now share their reflections from that experience base.

Some of the authors have been described as self-serving egotists who have little to say constructively about management—but who do say it with a flair and passion such that reading their books may be very exciting! Some books are seemingly the product of armchair humorists who set out to entertain their readers with tongue in cheek. Other books on the best-seller charts have been written with the aid of a ghostwriter (that is, by someone who takes information that has been provided by another and then converts it into the lead author's story). In summary, it may be fascinating to read the "inside story" as told by the CEO of a major airline or oil conglomerate, but the reader still has the opportunity and obligation to challenge the author's credentials for making broad generalizations from that experience base.

CONCLUSIONS

We encourage you to read and reflect on this collection of thoughts from the authors of today's generation of management books. We invite you to expand and enrich your insights into management as a result of learning from this set of popular books. We challenge you to question and debate the pros and cons of the ideas and philosophies that are presented by these authors. We hope you will ask when, where, how, and why these ideas are applicable. Examine the set of readings provided here, let them stimulate your thinking, and in the process, learn something new. You'll find that learning can be fun!

NOTES

1. Freeman, Frank, "Books That Mean Business: The Management Best Sellers." *Academy of Management Review,* 1985, 345–350.
2. Carroll, Dan, "Management Principles and Management Art." Paper presented to the Academy of Management annual meeting, Chicago, Illinois, August, 1986.
3. "Business Fads: What's In—And Out." *Business Week,* January 20, 1986.
4. Freeman, "Books That Mean Business."
5. See, for example, a report on executive reading preferences by Marilyn Wellemeyer in "Books Bosses Read," *Fortune,* April 27, 1987.

Reading 2

Managing Beyond the Quick Fix

Ralph H. Kilmann

Summary prepared by Diane Dodd-McCue

Diane Dodd-McCue is an Assistant Professor of Management at the University of Richmond, Virginia. Her writings have appeared in *Journal of Management, Business Horizons, Journal of Management Education, Personnel, Academy of Management Review,* and other academic publications. Dr. Dodd-McCue's current research interests include the impact of gender, family, and job structure on professionals' perceived stress, retention of women in accounting, and corporate responses to child and elder care needs. She received her D.B.A. in organizational theory from the University of Kentucky.

Understanding "the essence" of organizational activity—success—demands a fully integrated, holistic program and patience. Organizations can be revitalized, but only by rejecting the myth of simplification. Quick fixes—simple solutions to complex problems—will not produce lasting change.

Managers must don a new world view. Viewing the world as a complex hologram best captures the dynamic complexity of contemporary life because it emphasizes the interconnectedness of the open system. Through the holographic lens organizational problems, now seen as complex and interrelated, demand multiple problem-solving approaches. For multiple approaches to success, breadth of knowledge and information are needed. Participative management, coupled with the contributions of internal and external consultants, is the only way to combine expertise with commitment. However, even with these implementations long-term success is doomed without *top management's commitment to an integrated program of planned change.*

The holographic approach goes far beyond the "quick fix" programs often adopted by firms today. It accents a five-track formula for managing an organization successfully. Each of the five tracks—culture, management skills, team

Reprinted, by permission of the publisher, from *Management Review,* November 19 American Management Association and adapted from *Beyond the Quick Fix: Managing Five Tracks to Organizational Success* (San Francisco: Jossey-Bass, 1984.) © 1984 Ralph H. Kilman. All rights reserved.

building, strategy-structure, and reward systems—will be briefly described. Then, to illustrate this approach in action, an account of Eastman Kodak's successful implementation of the five-track program is included. In this discussion theoretical concepts and recommendations come to life in an extensive "real world" laboratory.

THE FIVE TRACKS

The five tracks to organizational success comprise an all-encompassing program. Implementing each of the tracks requires a participative effort among managers, consultants, and organizational members. In planning the integrated program, scheduling within and across tracks demands coordination, sharing, and flexibility.

The Culture Track

The *Culture Track* emphasizes establishing trust, information sharing, and adaptiveness. To achieve these culture-change objectives, the organization needs to survey actual norms, establish desired norms, identify and close the culture gap, and sustain culture change.

There are four types of cultural norms—task support, task innovation, social relationships, and personal freedom. *Task support norms* focus on information sharing, helping other groups, and efficiency concerns; extreme examples include "supporting others" as opposed to "them versus us." *Task innovation norms* emphasize creativity and innovation and reflect the organization's stance on status quo versus change. *Social relationships norms* suggest the extent to which socializing and mixing work with pleasure are condoned or even encouraged. *Personal freedom norms* reflect the organization's norms for self-expression, the exercise of personal discretion, and self-satisfaction. Each of these four types of cultural norms can be characterized across two dimensions: technical or human, short term or long term.

An adaptive culture is imperative for all other improvement efforts beyond the quick fix for two reasons. First, an adaptive culture allows managers to accept their shortcomings and learn how to address tough, complex problems. Second, the openness of an adaptive culture allows organizational members to participate in the team-building efforts which are critical to improvement. Only in an adaptive culture can efforts in the remaining tracks proceed successfully.

The Management Skills Track

The *Management Skills Track* builds on the assumption that a variety of skills—conceptual, analytic, administrative, social, and interpersonal—are vital in successfully managing complex problems. Problem management involves sensing problems, defining problems, deriving solutions, implementing solutions, and evaluating outcomes. Further complicating the problem management process is the psychological baggage managers bring with them to the process.

Among the management skills needed is *assumption analysis,* a systematic method of addressing the most difficult aspects of problem management, problem definition and solution implementation. Assumption analysis involves categorizing the assumptions that underlie conclusions in light of certainty and importance. Through a series of integrated group and individual exercises managers can evaluate whether their assumptions represent fantasy and habit, or reality and choice. Nested in an organizational culture of openness and trust, managers can be comfortable altering faulty assumptions to lay the groundwork for dealing with the complexity of their new holographic world.

The Team-Building Track

The *Team-Building Track* emphasizes infusing new cultures and skills throughout the organization. At this third stage in the organization-improvement program, the culture and management skills tracks have been addressed. The Team-Building Track provides an arena for the organization to capitalize on its new and emerging adaptive culture and its members' new and improved talents.

The Team-Building Track focuses on three areas: managing troublemakers, team building, and interteam building. Successful implementation within the Team-Building Track creates a (positive) domino effect. If troublemakers curtail their disruptive behavior, others will feel more comfortable and free to express themselves. If work groups evolve into effective teams, they will manage their work-related setbacks more effectively. If interconnected work groups become cooperative teams, difficult organizational problems that span traditional group boundaries will be managed successfully.

At this stage managers should take notice: successes within the first three tracks have yet to be translated into formally documented systems. Only at this point is the organization ready to face the gritty issues of the strategy-structure and reward system tracks.

The Strategy-Structure Track

The *Strategy-Structure Track* addresses how the organization can align objectives, tasks, and people, and develop written statements specifying where an organization is going and how it will get there. For the Strategy-Structure Track process a **Problem Management Organization (PMO)** is created, which is a diverse collection of organizational members from varying levels and areas in the organization who spend part of their time away from their formal responsibilities addressing complex organizational issues.

The Strategy-Structure Track proceeds from classifying and synthesizing strategic assumptions, to strategy formation, to operationalizing strategies through structure. Particular attention is given to making the structure succeed: (1) those assigned to work units are given the resources needed to translate plans into action; and (2) sequential and reciprocal interdependencies ("more costly task flows") are grouped *within* subunits.

The Reward System Track

The *Reward System Track* aims high: to motivate high performance and sustain all previous improvements. Addressing the organization's reward system assumes that the organization moving is the "right" direction, with the "right" strategies and the "right" resources. A good reward system also provides employees with an opportunity to experience intrinsic rewards. If the other tracks have been implemented successfully, employees would be working within an open, trusting environment where their contributions are valued; they would have refined skills that lead to their job successes and are recognized by others; they are contributing members in effective teams; and their jobs and groupings are designed to allow them some autonomy and to see the results of their efforts. Thus, the formal reward system can then focus on ways to extrinsically reward these desirable behaviors and outcomes.

How implementation of the Reward System Track unfolds is again a function of a Program Management Organization (PMO), although the desired membership may include different individuals than PMO members from the Strategy-Structure Track PMO. A broad representation of different perspectives from different areas within the organization is desired because what is being rewarded—desired performance—may vary across subunits. With this attempt to create a synthesized reward system, the "final" reward system usually is marked by five characteristics:

1. The entire organization is guided by a unified policy of performance-based evaluations and rewards.
2. Within this holistic framework, autonomous subunits have the freedom to tailor a subunit-specific reward system to fit their needs.
3. Even with subunit-specific reward systems, similarities surface: measures for short and long term evaluations, schedules for adjustments, recognition of individual and group contributions, formulas for superior rewards.
4. Relevant business information (i.e., financial, marketing, human resource, manufacturing) is needed and must be accessible to organizational members; this information is vital if they are to make well-informed decisions about how they can achieve high levels of performance, and hence high levels of reward.
5. Each subunit offers a wide range of intrinsic and extrinsic rewards to satisfy their employees' needs and personalities.

In summary, the Reward System Track ties together the Kilmann program and marks the point at which the program has gone the full circle. The improvement program has progressed from the early tracks, which have required external consultants to provide needed resources, to this final stage, during which the program has been internalized and formalized by the organization.

THE EASTMAN KODAK EXPERIENCE

The Five Tracks Come Alive

The previous discussion presented the complete organizational success program, one track at a time. However, given a holographic view of organizations, it is unrealistic to evaluate the program without attempting to fit these inter-related pieces into an integrated whole. Fortunately Eastman Kodak provided this opportunity, using its 125-member Market Intelligence (MI) group as the target.

Kodak's program was conceived in 1984, the brainchild of Vince Barabba, who headed this division. Barabba, brought into Kodak with a mandate to develop the corporate function of market intelligence, was familiar with the five-track program and sympathetic to the idea of managing beyond the quick fix.

Although the five-track program demands patience and commitment, the Kodak experience initially raced along. The key ideas were presented to top managers; then fifty members of the MI organization and twenty-five key external stakeholders were interviewed. From these interviews emerged an initial diagnosis of organizational problems, with emphasis on their links to the five tracks and a schedule of implementing the five tracks, plus a *shadow track*. The *shadow track* was a special steering committee that included Barabba, the three directors of MI divisions, and an additional director who was responsible for coordinating program logistics. The shadow track's role was to monitor the entire program and do whatever was necessary to ensure its success.

All 125 members of MI participated in the first three tracks, although employees were separated by job level for the culture and skills tracks. The culture track and skills track both involved a series of monthly workshops scheduled on alternate weeks over a three-month period. The team-building track, which marked the first time natural work groups would be united during the improvement program, involved inter- and intra-group workshops begun a few months later. The strategy-structure track, undertaken by a PMO of fifteen members representing all levels and areas of Kodak's MI worked to develop a recommended plan. The reward system track, steered by a different PMO, was slated to initiate its work thereafter and complete it six months later.

The culture and skills building tracks got off to a timely start but soon participants began complaining that they could no longer attend the workshops because of time demands. At this point some members of the shadow track suggested canning the improvement program altogether. In a compromise move the workshops were rescheduled to include a working lunch, and one skills-building workshop was refocused on time management. This near-derailment proved a blessing in disguise.

Targeting time management as a skills workshop topic brought several issues out on the table. Participants confronted "time-wasters" and "time-gaps" much like they had confronted culture. Their new-found openness and ability to communicate were evidenced both within and between work groups.

The Team-Building Track began as scheduled. A participant from each group served as a process observer for each group and provided feedback at the end of each session. During the workshops participants analyzed *team-gaps,* the difference between actual and desired dimensions of work-group functioning, and sought solutions for narrowing these gaps.

A demanding workload for MI members led to a two-month delay for the Strategy-Structure Track. Even with a continuing heavy workload, the PMO developed and presented its recommendations for strategy-structure changes to the shadow track on schedule. Among the major recommendations of the PMO were: (1) defining the function of the MI group as *business intelligence,* and renaming it accordingly; (2) defining the role of the MI group to include providing Kodak decision makers not only information but also the *implications* of the information; (3) enhancing the organization's "people" orientation through enhanced employee orientation, mentoring, and increased opportunities for employee participation. Within one year the majority of these recommendations were implemented, often without any modifications.

Implementation of the final track—reward system—was delayed because of the increased work load and resistance by several members of the shadow track to relinquish their prerogative to manage the reward system. Further complications also surfaced. Leadership of the MI unit changed; Barabba, the continuing program sponsor, left Kodak and was replaced by an insider who also affirmed his support of the program. Kodak issued corporate mandates that all divisions were required to design a Special Recognition Plan and that all divisions were to postpone recommendations for improving the formal rewards system until after a corporate-wide revamping was completed. Thus, the focus of the Reward System Track was limited to only one aspect of the reward system: special recognitions.

Even with these changes and limitations the Reward System Track presented its recommendations for the Special Recognition Plan to the shadow track on schedule. The plan was approved and implemented without modifications. Key characteristics of the plan included a committee to oversee implementation, no limits on employee eligibility for rewards, and endorsement of any combination of tangible, informal, or cash rewards deemed appropriate.

The Story Revisited

Follow-up observations tend to validate the success of the fully-integrated five-track program.

First, the organizational culture had extinguished employee class difference. Prior to the program, employees had been identified by salary and managerial/non-managerial labels; now the fundamental and equal contributions of different types of employees were valued.

Second, there was corporate-wide respect for Business Research, and not just by top executives. Prior to the program market intelligence personnel had been criticized for their lack of "street smarts"; now they were respected because they effectively provided information and analysis on its implications with greater knowledge of the consumer.

Third, the program had become so well ingrained into Business Research that employees hired *after* the program could recognize its outcomes even though they were unfamiliar with the separate tracks leading to those outcomes. For example, new employees commented on the warm nurturing culture, the participative, team-oriented work environment, and their qualified, articulate coworkers. Although they voiced dissatisfaction with Kodak's overall reward system, they pointed to the Special Recognition Award system as a timely celebration of excellent performance.

Kodak's experience at a completely integrated program—managing beyond the quick fix—had proved a worthwhile experience for members and consultants. Top management's commitment to the five-track program had not wavered, even in the midst of increased workloads, personnel changes, and pressures for bottom-line results. The five-track implementations had continued to focus on the evolving needs of the organization even though the original implementation schedule had undergone extensive revision. But, most significantly, the organization's ongoing adaptability had shown the program's effectiveness at creating an organization devoted to the basics needed to create and maintain success: vibrance and relevance for the key stakeholders.

Reading 3

The New Realities

Peter F. Drucker

When Karl Marx was beginning work on *Das Kapital* in the 1850s, the phenomenon of management was unknown. So were the enterprises that managers run. The largest manufacturing company around was a Manchester cotton mill employing fewer than three hundred people and owned by Marx's friend and collaborator Friedrich Engels. And in Engels's mill—one of the most profitable businesses of its day—there were no "managers," only "charge hands" who, themselves workers, enforced discipline over a handful of fellow "proletarians."

Rarely in human history has any institution emerged as quickly as management or had as great an impact so fast. In less than one hundred fifty years, management has transformed the social and economic fabric of the world's developed countries. It has created a global economy and set new rules for countries that would participate in that economy as equals. And it has itself been transformed. Few executives are aware of the tremendous impact management has had. Indeed, a good many are like M. Jourdain, the character in Molière's *Bourgeois Gentilhomme,* who did not know that he spoke prose. They barely realize that they practice—or mispractice—management. As a result, they are ill-prepared for the tremendous challenges that now confront them. The truly important problems managers face do not come from technology or politics; they do not originate outside of management and enterprise. They are problems caused by the very success of management itself.

To be sure, the fundamental task of management remains the same: to make people capable of joint performance through common goals, common values, the right structure, and the training and development they need to perform and to respond to change. But the very meaning of this task has changed, if only because the performance of management has converted the workforce from one composed largely of unskilled laborers to one of highly educated knowledge workers.

THE ORIGINS AND DEVELOPMENT OF MANAGEMENT

Eighty years ago, on the threshold of World War I, a few thinkers were just becoming aware of management's existence. But few people even in the most advanced countries had anything to do with it. Now the largest single group in the labor force, more than one third of the total, are people whom the U.S. Bureau of the Census calls "managerial and professional." Management has been the main agent of this transformation. Management explains why, for the first time in human history, we can employ large numbers of knowledgeable, skilled people in productive work. No earlier society could do this. Indeed, no earlier society could support more than a handful of such people. Until quite recently, no one knew how to put people with different skills and knowledge together to achieve common goals. Eighteenth-century China was the envy of contemporary Western intellectuals because it supplied more jobs for educated people than all of Europe did—some twenty thousand per year. Today, the United States, with about the same population China then had, graduates nearly a million college students a year, few of whom have the slightest difficulty finding well-paid employment. Management enables us to employ them.

Knowledge, especially advanced knowledge, is always specialized. By itself it produces nothing. Yet a modern business, and not only the largest ones, may employ up to ten thousand highly knowledgeable people who represent up to sixty different knowledge areas. Engineers of all sorts, designers, marketing experts, economists, statisticians, psychologists, planners, accountants, human-resources people—all working together in a joint venture. None would be effective without the managed enterprise.

There is no point in asking which came first, the educational explosion of the last one hundred years or the management that put this knowledge to productive use. Modern management and modern enterprise could not exist without the knowledge base that developed societies have built. But equally, it is management, and management alone, that makes effective all this knowledge and these knowledgeable people. The emergence of management has converted knowledge from social ornament and luxury into the true capital of any economy.

Not many business leaders could have predicted this development back in 1870, when large enterprises were first beginning to take shape. The reason was not so much lack of foresight as lack of precedent. At that time, the only large permanent organization around was the army. Not surprisingly, therefore, its command-and-control structure became the model for the men who were putting together transcontinental railroads, steel mills, modern banks, and department stores. The command model, with a very few at the top giving orders and a great many at the bottom obeying them, remained the norm for nearly one hundred years. But it was never as static as its longevity might suggest. On the contrary, it began to change almost at once, as specialized knowledge of all sorts poured into enterprise. The first university-trained engineer in manufacturing industry was hired by Siemens in Germany in 1867—his name was Friedrick von Hefner-Alteneck. Within five years he had built a research department. Other specialized departments followed suit. By World War I the standard functions of a manufacturer had been developed: research and engineering, manufacturing, sales, finance and accounting, and a little later, human resources (or personnel).

Even more important for its impact on enterprise—and on the world economy in general—was another management-directed development that took place at this time. That was the application of management to manual work in the form of training. The child of wartime necessity, training has propelled the transformation of the world economy in the last forty years because it allows low-wage countries to do something that traditional economic theory had said could never be done: to become efficient—and yet still low-wage—competitors almost overnight.

Adam Smith reported that it took several hundred years for a country or region to develop a tradition of labor and the expertise in manual and managerial skills needed to produce and market a given product, whether cotton textiles or violins. During World War I, however, large numbers of unskilled, pre-industrial people had to be made productive workers in practically no time. To meet this need, businesses in the United States and the United Kingdom began to apply the theory of scientific management developed by Frederick W. Taylor between 1885 and 1910 to the systematic training of blue-collar workers on a large scale. They analyzed tasks and broke them down into individual, unskilled operations that could then be learned quite quickly. Further developed in World War II, training was then picked up by the Japanese and, twenty years later, by the South Koreans, who made it the basis for their countries' phenomenal development.

During the 1920s and 1930s, management was applied to many more areas and aspects of the manufacturing business. Decentralization, for instance, arose to combine the advantages of bigness and the advantages of smallness within one enterprise. Accounting went from "bookkeeping" to analysis and control. Planning grew out of the "Gantt charts" designed in 1917 and 1918 to plan war production; and so did the use of analytical logic and statistics, which employ quantification to convert experience and intuition into definitions, information, and diagnosis. Marketing evolved as a result of applying management concepts to distribution and selling. Moreover, as early as the mid-1920s and early 1930s, some American management pioneers such as Thomas Watson, Sr., at the fledgling IBM, Robert E. Wood at Sears, Roebuck, and George Elton Mayo at the Harvard Business School, began to question the way manufacturing was organized. They concluded that the assembly line was a short-term compromise. Despite its tremendous productivity, it was poor economics because of its inflexibility, poor use of human resources, even poor engineering. They began the thinking and experimenting that eventually led to "automation" as the way to organize the manufacturing process, and to teamwork, quality circles, and the information-based organization as the way to manage human resources. Every one of these managerial innovations represented the application of knowledge to work, the substitution of system and information for guesswork, brawn, and toil. Every one, to use Frederick Taylor's term, replaced "working harder" with "working smarter."

The powerful effect of these changes became apparent during World War II. To the very end, the Germans were by far the better strategists. Having much shorter interior lines, they needed fewer support troops and could match their opponents in combat strength. Yet the Allies won—their victory achieved by management. The United States, with one fifth the population of all the other belligerents together, had almost as many men in uniform. Yet it produced more war matériel than all the others taken together. It managed to transport the stuff to fighting fronts as far apart as China, Russia, India, Africa, and Western Europe. No wonder, then, that by the war's end almost all the world had become management-conscious. Or that management emerged as a recognizably distinct kind of work, one that could be studied and developed into a discipline—as happened in each country that has enjoyed economic leadership during the postwar period.

After World War II we began to see that management is not *business* management. It pertains to every human effort that brings together in one organization people of diverse knowledge and skills. It needs to be applied to all third-sector institutions, such as hospitals, universities, churches, arts organizations, and social service agencies, which since World War II have grown faster in the United States than either business or government. For even though the need to manage volunteers or raise funds may differentiate non-profit managers from their for-profit peers, many more of their responsibilities are the same— among them defining the right strategy and goals, developing people, measuring performance, and marketing the organization's services. *Management worldwide has become the new social function.*

MANAGEMENT AND ENTREPRENEURSHIP

One important advance in the discipline and practice of management is that both now embrace entrepreneurship and innovation. A sham fight these days pits "management" against "entrepreneurship" as adversaries, if not as mutually exclusive. That's like saying that the fingering hand and the bow hand of the violinst are "adversaries" or "mutually exclusive." Both are always needed and at the same time. And both have to be coordinated and work together. Any *existing* organization, whether a business, a church, a labor union, or a hospital, goes down fast if it does not innovate. Conversely, any *new* organization, whether a business, a church, a labor union, or a hospital, collapses if it does not manage. Not to innovate is the single largest reason for the decline of existing organizations. Not to know how to manage is the single largest reason for the failure of new ventures.

Yet few management books paid attention to entrepreneurship and innovation. One reason was that during the period after World War II when most of these books were written, managing the existing rather than innovating the new and different was the dominant task. During this period most institutions developed along lines laid down clearly thirty or fifty years earlier. This has not changed dramatically. We have again entered an era of innovation, and it is by no means confined to "high tech" or to technology generally. In fact, social innovation—as this book tries to make clear—may be of greater importance and have much greater impact than any scientific or technical invention. Furthermore, we now have a "discipline" of entrepreneurship and innovation (see my *Innovation and Entrepreneurship,* 1986). It is clearly a part of management and rests, indeed, on well-known and tested management principles. It applies to both existing organizations and new ventures, and to both business and non-business institutions, including government.

THE LEGITIMACY OF MANAGEMENT

Management books tend to focus on the function of management inside its organizations. Few yet accept its social function. But it is precisely because management has become so pervasive as a social function that it faces its most serious challenge. To whom is management accountable? And for what? On what does management base its power? What gives it legitimacy?

These are not business questions or economic questions. They are *political* questions. Yet they underlie the most serious assault on management in its history—a far more serious assault than any mounted by Marxists or labor unions: the hostile takeover. An American phenomenon at first, it has spread throughout the non-Communist developed world. What made it possible was the emergence of the employee pension funds as the controlling shareholders of publicly owned companies. The pension funds, while legally "owners," are economically "investors"—and, indeed, often "speculators." They have no interest in the enterprise and its welfare. In fact, in the United States at least they are "trustees," and are not supposed to consider anything but immediate pecuniary gain. What underlies the takeover bid is the postulate that the enterprise's sole function is to provide the largest possible *immediate* gain to the shareholder. In the absence of any other justification for management and enterprise, the "raider" with his hostile takeover bid prevails—and only too often immediately dismantles or loots the going concern, sacrificing long-range, wealth-producing capacity to short-term gains.

Management—and not only in the business enterprise—has to be accountable for performance. But how is performance to be defined? How is it to be measured? How is it to be enforced? And to *whom* should management be accountable? That these questions can be asked is in itself a measure of the success and importance of management. That they need to be asked is, however, also an indictment of managers. They have not yet faced up to the fact that they represent power—and power has to be accountable, has to be legitimate. They have not yet faced up to the fact that they matter.

WHAT IS MANAGEMENT?

But what is management? Is it a bag of techniques and tricks? A bundle of analytical tools like those taught in business schools? These are important, to be sure, just as thermometer and anatomy are important to the physician. But the evolution and history of management—its successes as well as its problems—teach that management is, above all else, a very few, essential principles. To be specific:

1. Management is about human beings. Its task is to make people capable of joint performance, to make their strengths effective and their weaknesses irrelevant. This is what organization is all about, and it is the reason that management is the critical, determining factor. These days, practically all of us are employed by managed institutions, large and small, business and non-business. We depend on management for our livelihoods. And our ability to contribute to society also depends as much on the management of the organizations in which we work as it does on our own skills, dedication, and effort.

2. Because management deals with the integration of people in a common venture, it is deeply embedded in culture. What managers do in West Germany, in the United Kingdom, in the United States, in Japan, or in Brazil is exactly the same. How they do it may be quite different. Thus one of the basic challenges managers in a developing country face is to find and identify those parts of their own tradition, history, and culture that can be used as management building blocks. The difference between Japan's economic success and India's relative backwardness is largely explained by the fact that Japanese managers were able to plant imported management concepts in their own cultural soil and make them grow.

3. Every enterprise requires commitment to common goals and shared values. Without such commitment there is no enterprise; there is only a mob. The enterprise must have simple, clear, and unifying objectives. The mission of the organization has to be clear enough and big enough to provide common vision. The goals that embody it have to be clear, public, and constantly reaffirmed. Management's first job is to think through, set, and exemplify those objectives, values, and goals.

4. Management must also enable the enterprise and each of its members to grow and develop as needs and opportunities change. Every enterprise is a learning and teaching institution. Training and development must be built into it on all levels—training and development that never stop.

5. Every enterprise is composed of people with different skills and knowledge doing many different kinds of work. It must be built on communication and on individual responsibility. All members need to think through what they aim to accomplish—and make sure that their associates know and understand that aim. All have to think through what

they owe to others—and make sure that others understand. All have to think through what they in turn need from others—and make sure that others know what is expected of them.

6. Neither the quantity of output nor the "bottom line" is by itself an adequate measure of the performance of management and enterprise. Market standing, innovation, productivity, development of people, quality, financial results—all are crucial to an organization's performance and to its survival. Non-profit institutions, too, need measurements in a number of areas specific to their mission. Just as a human being needs a diversity of measures to assess his or her health and performance, an organization needs a diversity of measures to assess its health and performance. Performance has to be built into the enterprise and its management; it has to be measured—or at least judged—and it has to be continuously improved.

7. Finally, the single most important thing to remember about any enterprise is that results exist only on the outside. The result of a business is a satisfied customer. The result of a hospital is a healed patient. The result of a school is a student who has learned something and puts it to work ten years later. Inside an enterprise, there are only costs.

Managers who understand these principles and function in their light will be achieving, accomplished managers.

MANAGEMENT AS A LIBERAL ART

Thirty years ago, the English scientist and novelist C. P. Snow talked of the "two cultures" of contemporary society. Management, however, fits neither Snow's "humanist" nor his "scientist." It deals with action and application; and its test are results. This makes it a technology. But management also deals with people, their values, their growth and development—and this makes it a humanity. So does it concern with, and impact on, social structure and the community. Indeed, as everyone has learned who, like this author, has been working with managers of all kinds of institutions for long years, management is deeply involved in spiritual concerns—the nature of man, good and evil.

Management is thus what tradition used to call a liberal art—"liberal" because it deals with the fundamentals of knowledge, self-knowledge, wisdom, and leadership; "art" because it is practice and application. Managers draw on all the knowledges and insights of the humanities and the social sciences—on psychology and philosophy, on economics and history, on the physical sciences and ethics. But they have to focus this knowledge on effectiveness and results—on healing a sick patient, teaching a student, building a bridge, designing and selling a "user-friendly" software program.

For these reasons, management will increasingly be the discipline and the practice through which the "humanities" will again acquire recognition, impact, and relevance.

PART
TWO

Management Paradigms

Management consultants comment that the management philosophy reflected by the notion "If it ain't broke, don't fix it," needs to be discarded if organizations are going to survive the decade of the 1990s and enter the twenty-first century as viable and competitive social systems. In its place, Peters argues, is the need for the philosophy which espouses "If it ain't broke, fix it anyway"—reasoning which, if working today, in highly turbulent environments, will most likely be short-lived. In order to make this change, managers need to make a major paradigm shift. The three books summarized in this section of *The Manager's Bookshelf* have as their theme issues pertaining to management and changing management paradigms.

Joel Barker has defined a paradigm as a set of rules and regulations that establishes boundaries and tells people how to be successful within them.[1] Managers are urged to be *aware* of their paradigms, test and *adapt* them to new conditions, and constantly seek new ones.

Robert E. Quinn, in *Beyond Rational Management: Mastering the*

---

[1]Barker, Joel Arthur, *Future Edge: Discovering the New Paradigms of Success*. New York: William Morrow and Company, Inc., 1992.

Paradoxes and Competing Demands of High Performance, contends that the successful manager of the future cannot find answers to critical organizational questions in one-dimensional frameworks offered by such theories as Theory Y and Theory Z. The successful manager, who may have thrived as a professional engineer employing rational approaches and technical skills, will have to find a way to deal with the irrational world of organizational politics and employee morale.

Quinn, who is Professor of Organization Studies and Public Administration at the State University of New York, Albany, introduces the idea of a *master manager,* outlines how one can be developed, and lays out the master manager's journey to excellent performance. In particular, the master manager must acquire the ability to apply flexibly (and live with) competing values systems.

Lee G. Bolman and Terrence E. Deal's book, *Reframing Organizations: Artistry, Choice, and Leadership,* focuses on ways of becoming a more versatile manager and artistic leader. They approach these issues by focusing their attention on structure, human resources, political, and symbolic frames for bringing major leadership and organizational change.

Lee Bolman is a Lecturer on Education at the Harvard Graduate School of Education, and Terrence Deal is Professor of Education at the Peabody College at Vanderbilt University. They also serve as codirectors of the National Center for Educational Leadership.

Edgar H. Schein is the Sloan Fellow Professor of Management in the Sloan School of Management at the Massachusetts Institute of Technology (MIT). In his book *Organizational Culture and Leadership,* Schein attempts to develop a definition of "culture" that focuses on valid assumptions about how to perceive, think, feel (and presumably act) that get passed along to new employees. Managers tend to develop and perpetuate their implicit theories of organization and organizational process. "This is the way things are done around here" not only tends to reflect the culture of the organization, but it also reflects the dominant management paradigm.

Beyond Rational Management: Mastering the Paradoxes and Competing Demands of High Performance

Robert E. Quinn

Summary prepared by Robert Marx

Robert Marx is Associate Professor of Management at the University of Massachusetts in Amherst. He received his doctorate in clinical psychology from the University of Illinois. His research efforts have focused on the problem of skill retention following management development programs. He has published on the topic of relapse prevention.

THE JOURNEY FROM NOVICE TO MASTER MANAGER

There is hardly a consultant, social scientist, or practicing manager who does not have an opinion about what makes a master manager. The search for answers to this critical question wanders through a veritable dictionary of management panaceas exploring everything from the danger of Type A behavior[1] to the promise of theories Y[2] and Z.[3] These prescriptive models offer novice managers widely varying responses to a myriad of managerial problems.

The master manager, however, has learned that these prescriptive approaches are "one-dimensional bromides"[4] that explain only a small part of the managerial arena. Master managers recognize that organizations are "gyrating in constant chameleonic flux."[5] Behavioral consistency and logic, when overused, fail to cope effectively with such pervasive change. Master managers must develop the capacity to use *contradiction and paradox*. The real world

Robert E. Quinn, *Beyond Rational Management*, San Francisco: Jossey-Bass, 1988.

of organizations is not characterized by stable, predictable patterns that easily lend themselves to structured, analytical solutions. The higher levels of managing occur in complex dynamic systems that include change, ambiguity, and contradiction.

An engineer who has thrived professionally by solving complex technical problems may begin the journey to management mastery with a simplistic technical approach to management success. However, the rational technical skills that worked so well solving engineering problems are based on a set of assumptions that are unlikely to work well in the irrational world of organizational politics and employee morale.

The master manager must learn to use contradictory paradoxical frames that respond to existing circumstances. Unfortunately, such abilities do not come easily or naturally to most individuals. Because people develop a set of values and a world view from which they take action, contradictory perspectives may appear initially to be wrong or evil. The entrepreneur excels at innovation and seizing the moment. Development of the formal systems necessary to *maintain* the innovation are seen as unimportant by the novice manager. Conversely, the keeper of the systems sees the entrepreneur as a "loose cannon" who must be brought under control before an entire operation is blown to bits. Master managers transcend several competing values and assumptions. They see no contradiction in loose cannons and secure systems operating in tandem. The path from novice to master manager crosses many streams of thought and acknowledges how each one contributes to the flow of organizational life.

Research has shown that master managers have greater cognitive complexity than novices, thus allowing for more discrimination of cues and greater differences in responses to situations.[6] Master managers also evolve to higher levels of ego development.[7]

Whereas novice managers are likely to function at the technician stage of ego development characterized by a high degree of logic, bureaucracy, and detail orientation, master managers reach the strategist stage generating new orders, delighting in paradoxes, and understanding "the uniqueness of each individual and situation."[8]

The path to mastery evolves from the *novice stage* where facts and rules dominate[9] to the *advanced beginner stage* where experience becomes critical. Just as a novice chess player begins by learning the rules and experiencing exceptions in play, so does the evolving manager. With the *competence stage* comes the ability to appreciate the complexity of the task and to take risks that go beyond rational analysis. The *proficiency stage* brings with it "flow," pattern recognition, and intuitive moves that indicate a holistic view of the game or the workplace. The chess masters and master managers evolve to the *expert stage* where they have transcended the rules and personal styles and can deal with existing contradictions. The master manager can simultaneously function at the level of detail and vision, task and person, coach and politician, and with this flexibility achieves a high level of productivity.

ACHIEVING EXCELLENCE THROUGH PARADOX

The master manager's journey to excellent performance must proceed through a dynamic cycle of events called the *transformational cycle*. The cycle begins with the *initiation phase*, where the person has a desire to improve and is willing to take risks to explore the unknown. Fear of failure can end the cycle, but high performers see failure as a stepping-stone. "Contrary to rational-technical thinking, the initiation of action under conditions of risk is an important step to begin performance."[10] The *uncertainty phase* is entered once the new action is taken. This uncertainty is epitomized by a youngster learning to ride a two-wheel bike. As she tries to keep the bike upright, a natural response is to stop pedaling and manage the impending fall. If she can overcome the fear and keep pedaling, the bike will stay upright and "excellence" will be experienced. As she begins to gain control over the bike, the youngster experiences the *transformation phase*. Here the risk of falling has been challenged and supplanted with a new set of accomplishments. The child and parents feel the excitement and exhilaration of the moment. Then the *routinization phase* sets in. She "knows" how to ride. There is little risk, but logical, systematic practice prevail. Sustaining excellence is difficult over the long term. Risk and intuition that led to transformation and exhilaration must yield to control and rationality to consolidate gains. The master manager does not forget to repeat the risk-taking behavior that brought her to new levels of exhilaration and transformation.

THE COMPETING VALUES MODEL: REDEFINING ORGANIZATIONAL EFFECTIVENESS AND CHANGE

It is inherently difficult for people to think in contradictory ways. Bateson[11] describes the natural tendency of Western thought to be "schismogenic," where one value is chosen *over* another, eliminating contradiction and paradox. Schismogenic thinking thus eliminates competing positive values from consideration because they are not logically consistent with the "best" choice.

Rather than be trapped in any single set of values and assumptions about organizational life, master managers can tolerate several competing sets of assumptions simultaneously. They may be purposive in temporarily choosing to solve a specific management problem. Yet they are not schismogenic or *stuck* in any single frame.

The ways that managers process information culminate in strong predispositions and values that determine what they believe good managers should do. Often managers are unaware of these underlying values, but they become "emotionally held moral positions" about what "good" managers do. Unfortunately, these deeply held positions are only effective part of the time. Instead of remaining consistent and logical and clinging to a single set of values, it is frequently advantageous to see problems from a contradictory set of values.

Indeed, master managers must free themselves from "their preferred way of seeing and behaving"[12] and learn to balance a set of competing values. The competing values model makes explicit the contradicitons that managers must constantly live with. Organizations must be adaptable and at the same time be stable. They must emphasize the value of people, while maintaining productivity.

The competing values framework, displayed in Figure 1, is scaled along two bipolar axes, which yield four quadrants. The vertical axis measures the degree of control exerted by the organization. High control is exemplified by values that support centralization, hierarchy, and integration, which allow the organization to maintain stable procedures and develop plans. High flexibility at the other pole of the axis is exemplified by decentralization, self-management, and differentiated action, which allows the organization to respond quickly to changing circumstances and avoid the dysfunctional elements of bureaucracy.

The horizontal axis measures the degree of internal versus external emphasis of the organization. The external emphasis is exemplified by an orientation toward competition, growth, and response to the world outside the organization. The internal emphasis is exemplified by values oriented toward maintaining the sociotechnical systems within the organization. It focuses on internal structure, information systems, clear job descriptions, morale, and decision-making.

Each of the four competing values is based on a mode of information processing. As presented here, each perspective comprises a combination of two factors: (a) flexible or tight controls and (b) external or internal forces. Thus the commonality and contrast of each of the competing values' orientations can be seen within an integrated framework. Effective managers recognize the delicate blend of contradictory perspectives necessary for effective organizational problem solving. The four cells include the *human relations, internal process, open systems,* and *rational goal* perspectives.

Human Relations Perspective

This cell combines the values of internal emphasis and flexibility. The approach prefers long time lines and low certainty. The primary information of importance is that of process, where the nature of human interaction is observed. Organizations emphasizing process are often managed as a team. The prevailing concern in this culture is for members of the organization. Commitment and morale are maintained by openness, participation, and discussion. Human resources are valued, and training, autonomy, and delegation are commonplace. Career management, fair salaries, incentives, and matching jobs to the skill of the individual are concrete expressions of this value system. This culture emphasizes the importance of understanding the needs of employees. However, when used to the extreme this perspective can be perceived as the irresponsible country club where human relations criteria are emphasized to the point of encouraging laxity and negligence.

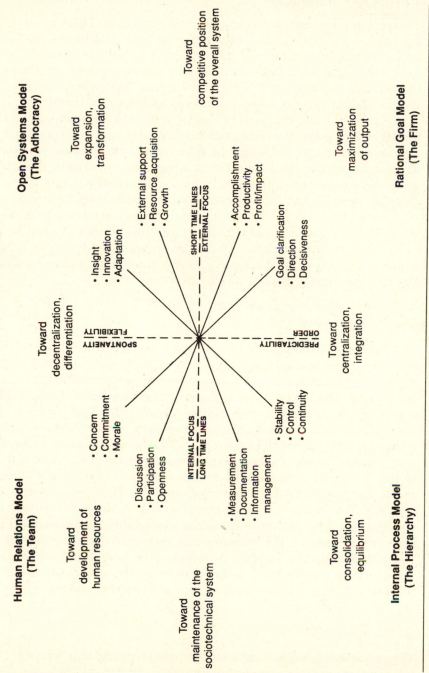

Figure 1 Competing Values Framework: Culture

Human Relations Model
(The Team)

Open Systems Model
(The Adhocracy)

Internal Process Model
(The Hierarchy)

Rational Goal Model
(The Firm)

Toward
development of
human resources

Toward
maintenance of the
sociotechnical system

Toward
decentralization,
differentiation

Toward
expansion,
transformation

Toward
competitive position
of the overall system

Toward
maximization
of output

Toward
centralization,
integration

Toward
consolidation,
equilibrium

• Concern
• Commitment
• Morale

• Discussion
• Participation
• Openness

• Measurement
• Documentation
• Information
  management

• Insight
• Innovation
• Adaptation

• External support
• Resource acquisition
• Growth

• Accomplishment
• Productivity
• Profit/impact

• Goal clarification
• Direction
• Decisiveness

• Stability
• Control
• Continuity

FLEXIBILITY
SPONTANEITY

PREDICTABILITY
ORDER

INTERNAL FOCUS
LONG TIME LINES

SHORT TIME LINES
EXTERNAL FOCUS

Source: Figure 6, p. 51, Robert Quinn, *Beyond Rational Management: Mastering the Paradoxes and Competing Demands of High Performance.* San Francisco: Jossey-Bass, 1988. Used with permission.

The Internal Process Perspective

This model represents the values of internal focus and high control. The internal process approach processes information with long time lines and high certainty. It emphasizes rational problem-solving and perpetuation of the status quo. Organizations based on this information processing style are often managed as bureaucracy.[13] This model works "best when the task to be done is well understood and when time is not an important factor."[14]

The prevailing concerns of this value system are maintaining the hierarchy, which provides the organization with the stability and continuity to make effective long-range decisions. In this framework, information management and documentation allow for efficient integration. An organization that emphasizes these values has an accessible and comprehensive data base. There are clear job descriptions, role expectations, and procedures for resolving conflicts over unclear procedures. This culture emphasizes an internally organized company. However, when used to the extreme this perspective can be perceived as the "frozen bureaucracy," where the organization becomes atrophied as a result of excessive measurement and documentation and everything is done "by the book" regardless of its effectiveness.

Open Systems Perspective

The values of flexibility and an external focus define the third quadrant. This perspective organizes information along short time lines and low certainty. The open systems approach seeks risk, variation, intuitive thought, and a future orientation. The system is always open to new feedback. Organizations based on this information processing style are organized as "adhocracies," preferring organic matrix forms that are easily modified. The adhocracy functions well when the task is not well understood, and when quick completion is essential.

The prevailing concerns of this value system are expansion and adaptation to the changing business environment. Readiness to make decisions is viewed as the key to growth and resource acquisition. The open systems perspective is designed to produce in a competitive market through constant innovation and change. This culture emphasizes adaptability to the marketplace. However, when used to the extreme this perspective can be perceived as the "tumultuous anarchy," where the emphasis on insight and innovation result in disastrous experimentation, political expediency, and an obsession with competitive advantage at the expense of continuity and control over work.

Rational Goal Perspective

This model combines the values of external focus and high control. The prevailing concerns of this value system are productivity and efficiency. The rational goal approach organizes information along short time lines and high certainty, and requires short-term goals and rapid decision-making. Organizations based on this information processing style are often managed as "firms" with the emphasis on the bottom line. These are achieved through planning, goal setting, goal clarification, and direction. The rational goal perspective values the control inherent in planning and goal setting and builds in feedback systems to modify procedures when goals are not accomplished. This culture emphasizes the maximization of output in a competitive environment. However, when used to the extreme, this perspective can be perceived as the "oppressive sweatshop," where the emphasis on productivity and effectiveness yield perpetual exertion, and eventual burnout, and limited opportunity for individual differences and employee input.

Each of these four perspectives represents an important set of values that yield an entirely different set of managerial activities. The team-oriented manager would emphasize the needs of the individual, while the firm-oriented manager would emphasize goal accomplishment. Master managers see these contrasting value orientations as complementary rather than competing. They learn to play each of these roles as necessary in the changing environment, avoiding schismogenic thought and appreciating the strengths and weaknesses of each perspective.

THE FRAMEWORK AS A DIAGNOSTIC TOOL

This framework can be used to diagnose organizational problems and suggest appropriate interventions. For example, a fast-growing high tech firm used the competing values framework to diagnose that it had become very good at functioning in the open systems model by adapting rapidly to a changing marketplace. However, the internal process model, which should provide a system for decision-making, was sorely neglected. The firm had bought flexibility at the cost of internal integrity.[15] The human relations model, which champions cohesiveness and morale, also suffered because of the extreme external emphasis of this firm. Strategies were developed to emphasize competing values to bring the firm into balance and renew its creative thrust.

Because values change in organizations over time, new emphases must be adopted. The competing values framework explains how different values may be emphasized during various stages of organizational growth. Organizations move through four distinct transitional stages, each of which requires a different values emphasis. The *entrepreneurial stage* of an organization is typified by innovation and creativity and fits the open systems model. The *collectivity stage* follows with a strong emphasis on informal communication, commitment, and a sense of family. Focusing human motivation and energy is a strength of the human relations model. As the organization matures during the *formalization stage*, organizational stability and efficiency of productivity become paramount. The internal process model provides necessary rules and procedures, while the rational goal model highlights goal accomplishment and productivity. In the fourth stage, *elaboration of structure*, the organization turns its emphasis toward the external environment to renew itself or expand. Otherwise it risks stagnation beneath a structure that is static in nature and unresponsive to the changing environment.

Failure to recognize the changes in culture as a firm develops can spell disaster. Don Burr of People Express used his creativity to build a dynamic organization that was creative and humanistic. However, when confronted with the formalization stage requiring policies, procedures, and coordination, he could not adapt. Burr's inability to emphasize internal stabilization represented a failure to utilize competing values and transcend his personal style.[16]

By contrast, Bill Gates of Microsoft (now the world's second largest software firm) survived a similar formalization crisis by bringing in professional managers who understood how to create internal stability. Gates was able to maintain his own entrepreneurial and technological focus, while simultaneously maintaining a secure infrastructure. By not perceiving the need to formalize a competing, either-or value, Gates was able to move from one set of values to another. Effective managers of today must understand how to manage change. The competing values model offers a powerful tool.

APPLICATIONS OF THE COMPETING VALUES MODEL: THE ROLES OF LEADERSHIP

While many models of leadership recommend espousing one leadership style over another, the competing values model recognizes the importance of avoiding either-or considerations. It simply asks what leadership skills are needed to manage specific organizational concerns. This model identifies eight leadership roles and integrates them with the four competing values perspectives:

The open systems model supports leadership activities that are creative and risk-taking, externally oriented, and flexible. Leaders operating from this perspective function in the *innovator role,* envisioning the future and risking needed change. The *broker role* requires political astuteness in order for an individual to serve as an effective external liaison to acquire needed resources.

The rational goal model encourages leadership activities that are competitive and structured, with goal orientation and productivity of greatest importance. The *producer role* requires task orientation and understanding of how to motivate employees to accomplish stated goals. The *director role* emphasizes defining and designing goals, roles, and tasks for high-output performance.

The internal process model focuses on leadership activities that develop necessary internal stability. This conservative, structured approach includes the *monitor role,* which controls and analyzes information to facilitate logical problem solving, and the *coordinator role,* which maintains continuity through careful planning and organizing, linking the performance of producers with the evaluation of the monitors.

The human relations model highlights leadership activities that emphasize interpersonal collaboration. The leadership style is supportive and based on people's need for affiliation. The *facilitator role* develops group cohesion and participative decision making, and mediates conflict. The *mentor role* develops people through skill building, availability, and trust.

Each of the four perspectives has perceptual biases about the assumptions and roles of leadership. The cautious, stable approach of the internal process perspective contrasts starkly with the risk-taking predilection of the open systems approach. However, the competing values models asks managers to move from the either-or schismogenic position of the novice to the both/and frame of mind of the master manager.

A preliminary study of effective and ineffective managers[17] suggests that *balance* is the key. Ineffective managers scored below average on all eight leadership roles or emphasized only one or two at the expense of others. Effective managers were above average on five or more roles, thus allowing flexibility in leadership behavior despite a few weak areas.

TRANSFORMING MANAGEMENT STYLES

The journey from novice to master manager requires diagnosing and confronting one's weak quadrants. Such transformations require taking risks and dealing with fear of the unknown or of the underdeveloped side of oneself. Such transformations can take place *spontaneously* when a manager in crisis discovers that old strategies won't solve new problems. In one example, a manager indoctrinated in the hierarchical approach to leadership found that when a crisis required him to set up task forces to solve problems, motivation, trust, and performances unexpectedly improved dramatically. Leadership activities previously associated with "bad management" suddenly proved their worth. Out of the chaos came a valuable lesson about balancing polarities.

Transformation can also occur through *self-examination.* Managers can learn about themselves through self-assessment, feedback from peers and subordinates, and maintaining a journal. Using the competing values framework and its related assessment instruments, managers can become more aware of their prevailing value systems and develop change strategies for improving weak areas.

The journey from novice to master manager requires a balance between logical, purposive behavior, and holistic, intuitive flow. Managers get stuck by being too predisposed to values in a given quadrant. What has started out as a positive value becomes negative when it is overused. When managers get in trouble they often continue to do whatever they have been doing, only harder. The competing values framework allows managers to dismantle polarities. It makes available to master managers both ends of the continuum and the middle as well. It provides a meaningful framework to help managers respond to change in their organizations and to risk change within themselves.

NOTES

1. Friedman, M., and R. H. Rosenman, *Type A Behavior and Your Heart.* New York: Alfred Knopf, 1974.
2. McGregor, D., *Human Side of Enterprise.* New York: McGraw-Hill, 1960.
3. Ouchi, W. G., *Theory Z: How American Business Can Meet the Japanese Challenge.* Reading, MA: Addison-Wesley, 1981.
4. Quinn, R. E., *Beyond Rational Management: Mastering The Paradoxes and Competing Demands of High Performance.* San Francisco: Jossey-Bass, 1988, p. 3.
5. Ibid., p. xiv.
6. Streufert, S. and R. W. Swezey, *Complexity, Managers and Organizations.* Orlando, FL: Academic Press, 1986.
7. Torbert, W. R., *Managing the Corporate Dream: Restructuring for Long-Term Success.* Homewood, IL: Dow Jones-Irwin, 1987.
8. Quinn, p. 7.
9. Dreyfus, H. L., S. E. Dreyfus, and T. Albanasion, *Mind Over Machine: The Power of Human Intuition and Expertise in the Era of the Computer.* New York: Free Press, 1986.
10. Quinn, p. 18.
11. Bateson, G., *Mind and Nature.* New York: Bantam Books, 1979.
12. Quinn, p. 90.
13. Weber, M., *Theory of Social and Economic Organization.* Translated by A. M. Henderson and T. Parsons. London: Oxford University Press, 1921.
14. Quinn, p. 39.
15. Quinn, p. 53.
16. Hackman, J. R., "The Transition That Hasn't Happened." In J. R. Kimberly and R. E. Quinn (eds.), *Managing Organizational Transitions.* Homewood, IL: Dow Jones-Irwin, 1984.
17. Quinn, R. E., S. R. Faerman, and N. Dixit, "Perceived Performance: Some Archetypes of Managerial Effectiveness and Ineffectiveness." Working paper, Institute for Government and Policy Studies, Department of Public Administration, State University of New York at Albany, 1987.

Reading 2

Reframing Organizations: Artistry, Choice, and Leadership

Lee G. Bolman and Terrence E. Deal

Summary prepared by Robert Marx

Robert Marx is an Associate Professor of Management at the University of
Massachusetts at Amherst. He is the coauthor of *Management Live! The Video
Book.* Marx was the 1991 recipient of the Bradford Outstanding Educator
Award from the Organizational Behavior Teaching Society in recognition of his
excellence in teaching.

THE POWER OF REFRAMING

In this century, our society has evolved from a simple, local lifestyle where
people could manage their own affairs to a global, technologically sophisticated
world dominated by large, complex organizations. These new organizations
have proliferated because they have been enormously successful at producing
a wide range of goods and services, including better health care, education, and
communication linkages. Yet, for all their successes, there are flaws in these
large companies and government organizations.

Indifferent salespersons, meaningless work, contradictory and unethical
policies, and shoddy products represent the price paid for creating these unwieldy groups of people that comprise organizations. Despite the best efforts
to improve these organizations through new management techniques, the use
of consultants, and government interventions, organizations still do more of the
same, handling problems the "only way"[1] they could be handled. *Managers and
leaders must be able to expand their repertoire of ideas to handle the complex
problems of organizations.* They must be able to "reframe" their thinking.

THE FOUR FRAMES

"The truly effective leader will need multiple tools, the skill to use each of them,
and the wisdom to match frames to situations."[2]

Based on insights from research and experience working with many organizations and managers, four perspectives or frames have emerged. Each frame views the world from a particular set of values and basic assumptions. They are:

The Structural Frame

Based on rational systems theory, the structural frame emphasizes the rational aspect of organizational life. The organization is viewed as a machine whose parts must be run and maintained efficiently. Organizations create structures to fit their environment and technology. Formal roles, clear rules, and responsibilities are necessary for efficient functioning. When problems arise, reorganizing is the primary method for restoring equilibrium.

The Human Resources Frame

Based on theories of human behavior from the psychological sciences, the human resources frame views the organization as a family. People are the heart of the organization and they have needs and feelings which must be understood and addressed. There must be a good fit between the organization's structure and the needs of its people. That is, people must be able to get the job done and feel good about what they're doing. When problems arise, communication and support are required.

The Political Frame

Based on theories of power, the political frame sees the organization as a jungle where different interest groups compete for scarce resources. Conflict is a part of everyday life in organizations because each interest group has its own agenda. Effective managers must understand how to build power bases and coalitions and manage conflict as productively as possible. When problems arise, power may be concentrated in the wrong places and negotiating may be required.

The Symbolic Frame

Based on anthropological theory, the symbolic frame emphasizes the meaning of organizational activity. It views the organization as a theater, in which stories, rituals, and myths make up a culture which helps to give employees a sense of shared values and mission. The symbolic frame considers the importance of history and tradition in building a strong culture that employees can believe in. Problems may develop when symbols lose their meaning. The culture may be improved by developing meaningful rituals, traditions, and visions.

Taken one by one, each frame offers its own perspective on a problem and each frame provides a set of ideas and techniques that managers can employ in order to enhance organizational efficiency and effectiveness. For example, an executive trying to reduce turnover among middle managers might receive the following suggestions from consultants representing each of the four frames.

"As your firm has grown, managers' responsibilities have probably become blurred and overlapping. When reporting relationships are confused, you get stress and conflict. You need to restructure." (Structural)

"You are probably neglecting your managers' needs for autonomy and for opportunities to participate in important decisions. You need an attitude survey to pinpoint the problems." (Human Resource)

"Your real problem is that you have been ignoring the realities of organizational politics. The union has too much power and top management has too little. No one knows how to deal with conflict. There's turf protection everywhere. You have to bring politics out of the closet and get people to negotiate." (Political)

"Your company has never developed a strong value system, and growth has made the situation worse. Your managers don't find any meaning in their work. You need to revitalize your company's culture." (Symbolic)[3]

Each of these suggestions is based on a different frame and would result in very different courses of action. However, managers who adhere too tightly to one frame that is most consistent with their professional training or personal values are *unnecessarily limiting themselves to a single tool for solving organizational problems* that are complex, changing, and ambiguous.

Some problems in organizations have little to do with rational and quantitative analysis, but are caused by poor interpersonal communication. Other problems are essentially based on a cloudy picture of the organization's mission and values and have little to do with power and influence. All managers must develop self-awareness of their prevailing frames and their blind spots, and they must develop the ability to view complex organizational activities through *each of the four frames* from a multiple perspectives point of view. Managers must be able to think and act in more than one way and to ask new questions that will reveal creative possibilities for effective action.

GETTING ORGANIZED: THE STRUCTURAL FRAME

The structural frame inquires about the best way to structure the organization given the goals that it is pursuing. This frame is based upon the work of Frederick Taylor and a German sociologist, Max Weber. Taylor introduced time and motion studies as a way to determine scientifically the most efficient way for a laborer to complete a task. Weber introduced the concept of bureaucracy as a rational approach to structuring organizations.

McDonald's and Harvard University are both highly successful organizations, yet each has a radically different structure that is designed to fit its circumstances. All organizations, for example, have goals, boundaries, levels of authority, and procedures, yet they differ widely on how these structural characteristics appear.

McDonald's is highly centralized. Most decisions are made at the top and efforts are made to ensure conformity, so that a "Big Mac" tastes the same at McDonald's franchises all over the world.

Harvard is highly decentralized, with each school of the University controlling its own destiny. Unlike the McDonald's employees, who have little discretion about how they carry out their tasks, Harvard faculty have enormous autonomy over what they research and how they run their classes. People therefore expect a predictable product from McDonald's but a unique learning experience from a Harvard professor.

Organizations such as McDonald's, which have highly specific and easily measurable goals such as profitability, growth, and market share, are able to structure themselves tightly through written procedures and detailed checklists. Harvard's teaching and research goals are much less routine and predictable. Producing knowledgeable students and "important research" are rather diffuse goals that require a more decentralized and loosely connected structure.

Organizations change their structure to fit a changing environment. A simple structure that worked with a boss and a small number of employees will likely give way to a machine bureaucracy for routine tasks or a professional bureaucracy for more creative activities. Divisional forms serve specific areas or products within the larger organization while ad hocracy and matrix structures are helpful for adapting to a rapidly changing, turbulent environment.

Groups and teams must grapple with the same kinds of design questions that face the large organization. Likewise, it has been shown that the structure of the group may need to change significantly over the group's life as the group develops and different tasks are required.

When the structural frame is overutilized by the manager, adherence to the rulebook and established procedures may interfere with creative input. Management may be cold and impersonal. Good ideas may not be implemented because of insufficient power and influence. Work may be done without a clear set of values or mission.

When the structural frame is underutilized, the organization may not be designed in a manner that optimizes output. Role confusion and unclear job descriptions may result in repeated conflict. An appropriate emphasis on structure will help the organization cope with these problems.

PEOPLE AND ORGANIZATION: THE HUMAN RESOURCE FRAME

The human resource frame is grounded in psychological theories of human behavior, including the work of Maslow, McGregor, and Argyris. This frame "starts from the premise that people's skills, insights, ideas, energy and commitment are an organization's most critical resource. Organizations, however, can be so alienating, dehumanizing, and frustrating that human talents are wasted and human lines are distorted."[4] This frame assumes that organizations exist to serve human needs, and a good fit between the individual and the organization benefits both. People find meaningful work, and organizations receive people's talents and commitment.

Numerous strategies have been developed to improve human resource management. These activities generally involve listening more closely to the ideas of employees and allowing them a voice in how their work is carried out. These interventions include management training, job enrichment, participative management, survey feedback, organization development consultation, and self-managed work teams.

When managers overuse the human resource frame, they may focus too heavily on resolving problems by open communication and support while overlooking structural flaws that may precipitate such conflict. Overuse of this frame may also fail to give proper acknowledgment of the role of power and authority in dealing with competitive issues. Overuse of the human resources frame may result in an overly optimistic view that all organizational issues can be resolved through consensus and collaborative activities.

Underuse of the human resource frame may be seen in organizations which have not bothered to ask what the needs and aspirations of their workers are. Such organizations may not experience the increased creativity, commitment, and communication from employees who feel that they are heard and supported.

POWER, CONFLICT, AND COALITIONS: THE POLITICAL FRAME

The tragic explosion of the space shuttle Challenger with seven astronauts aboard was in part caused by political forces which created a context for conflict and power plays among individuals and groups.

The procedure had always been clear. Before any space vehicle could be launched, NASA and their contractors had to prove that it was safe to fly. But on the night of January 27, 1986, Morton Thiokol senior managers overruled the no-launch decision by their engineers; the next day seven astronauts were killed and the nation's space program was in a shambles. Technically, the record cold temperature on the launch pad had caused the "O-rings" to fail, thus allowing hot gases to escape. Further investigation revealed that the decision-making process had changed significantly since NASA's early days when decisions were made on the lowest possible level. Clearly the evolution of NASA since the heady days of the Apollo moon landing had changed the structure of the organization so that the people making the important decisions were getting farther and farther away from the people getting their hands dirty.

In addition to these structural problems, the human resource view of NASA showed an organization whose morale had diminished since the days of generous funding and national commitment to push back the frontiers of space. The fit between the organization's needs and the needs of its employees had eroded. The space pioneers of the early years had given way to the shuttle program's "box car in space."[5] But correcting the structural and human resource problems in the space program may not have prevented the tragedy of the space shuttle Challenger.

The political forces in Washington, in NASA, and in Morton Thiokol (the contractor responsible for the O-rings) collectively overruled the advice of technical experts and put the space shuttle in harm's way.

The political frame views organizations as living political arenas that house a complex variety of individual and group interests. Because of competition for scarce resources (time, money, positions), conflict is inevitable in organizations and members of different coalitions must know how to bargain and negotiate for their positions.

In the Challenger case there were many political forces that affected the decision-making process.

NASA ran the space program because a complex coalition of Congress, the White House, the media, and the public supported them. Crista McAuliffe, the teacher-in-space, was aboard the Challenger because having an ordinary citizen as a member of the crew built public support for the program.

The president intended to mention the launch of the Challenger in his State of the Union speech to Congress and to a national TV audience, but Morton Thiokol engineers recommended against the launch for valid scientific reasons. However, corporate executives feared that more delays would put their lucrative government contract in jeopardy. Similarly, NASA managers were aware that NASA's credibility was slipping, deemed the engineering data inconclusive, and recommended the launch.

On the night before the fateful launch, a coalition of managers from NASA and Morton Thiokol brought together by the dwindling space budget combined forces to overrule the scientists, who in the end had made the right recommendation.

The political frame focuses on situations of scarce resources and incompatible preferences and thus the collision of different needs. If a group of graduate students, for example, wants the university to become more democratic and responsive to their needs, while the faculty wishes to tighten controls and standards, the political theorist might emphasize how each group articulates its preferences and mobilizes the power to get what it wants. The structural view assumes that some solutions are better than others and urges rational problem-solving methods to reach a discussion. The human resource approach seeks a win-win outcome of this conflict where the needs of both groups are shared and an integrative solution is reached. For the political manager, scarcity and conflict are enduring facts of organizational life, and they are less optimistic than the structural- and human-resource-oriented managers of achieving the "best" or "win-win" resolutions.

The political frame is focused on the use of power and the tactics of conflict. Power can come from authority, expertise, control of rewards and punishments, alliances and networks, control of agendas, control of meetings and symbols, and personal power. Most managerial jobs are characterized by an imbalance where responsibility seems to be larger than the authority to get things done. As a consequence, other forms of power (e.g., reward) must be enlisted to manage effectively.

Within the political frame, conflict is not necessarily seen as something bad and to be avoided. Therefore, its focus is not always on the resolution of conflict, as is often the case for the human resource and structural frames. The political frame asserts that conflict has benefits, such as encouraging innovative approaches to problem solving, challenging the status quo, and reducing complacency. Because conflict is not going to disappear, the political frame asks how groups and individuals can make the best use of it. To use the political frame effectively, managers must understand the strategy and tactics of conflict. According to the political frame, not only do the authorities have power, but there are many in the organization who have different forms of power. Those who get and use power best see their ideas implemented. The use of power does not need to be destructive. Constructive use of power is necessary to create effective organizations.

Managers who underutilize the political frame may be ignoring an enduring reality of organizational life. The political perspective can be a powerful antidote to the rationality of the structural frame.

Overuse of the political frame can be equally restrictive. The political frame can be cynical and pessimistic, overestimating the inevitability of conflict and understating the potential for rational analysis and interpersonal collaboration.

ORGANIZATIONAL CULTURE AND SYMBOLS: THE SYMBOLIC FRAME

When Martin Luther King spoke to the huge throng that participated in the march on Washington in August 1963, he said to them, "I have a dream." In that memorable speech, Dr. King spoke with conviction and passion about American values. He included many of the most cherished symbols of our country. His speech included "My country 'tis of thee, sweet land of liberty," and other songs and phrases uttered daily in every school in our land. He reminded his listeners of the basic values and principles that our country was founded upon when its first settlers sought refuge from political persecution nearly two centuries earlier.

The symbolic frame emphasizes the symbolic aspect of the human experience. It departs from the rational, linear view of organizations and recognizes the importance of culture, rituals, stories, and metaphors. Just as the earliest tribal rituals may have required a youngster at puberty to kill a lion and be circumcised, large corporations have their modern-day versions of initiation rituals.

In a strong culture, the message to newcomers will be "you are different and not yet one of us." The newcomer (in this example, a woman) may say "I know this place is hostile to women and I expect that to change." In this symbolic interchange, newcomers have a part to play by bringing new ideas and perspectives into the organization. At the same time, old-timers act as a force for cohesion, stability and the wisdom of the past.[6]

The basic assumption of the symbolic frame is that what is important about any event is not what happened, but *what it means to people.* Because organizations are so complex, it is often hard to know what is happening and why it is happening. With such uncertainty and ambiguity, it is difficult to analyze rationally the causes of problems and their solutions. People create symbols to reduce confusion and provide direction in their lives. The core values of McDonald's, the golden arches, and the stories of its founder, Ray Kroc, give direction to franchise holders. The history and rituals of Harvard University offer professors and students a common set of values from which to work.

In Martin Luther King's memorable "I have a dream" speech, he was able to articulate how a set of values based on our country's history could serve as a vision for our future. A more structural Dr. King might have spoken about "I have a plan" while a human resource or political leader would have emphasized feelings and coalition-building. But in that moment, he chose to reach people with his vision. Managers who understand the importance of the symbolic frame appreciate the power of rituals, ceremonies, and stories, and they use them to articulate a set of shared values called *culture.*

The symbolic frame views the organization as theater. For example, the structure of an organization may be seen as more than the structural view, which emphasizes the network of interdependent roles and linkages that are determined by goals, technology and environment. To the symbolic manager, the structure may be more like a stage design and props that make the organization look credible to its audience. For example, because of their elusive goals and underdeveloped technologies, schools have symbols of effectiveness and modern appearance. Certified teachers, American flags, and computers are part of the props. The schools achieve legitimacy by maintaining an appearance "that conforms to the way society thinks they should look."[7]

There are two faces of the symbolic perspective. Symbols can be used to camouflage or distort. The certified teacher may be incompetent. The corporation that states "People come first" may have an abysmal record in dealing with people. Managers who emphasize vision and charisma may be inept at enacting their vision. The symbolic frame is on dangerous ground when symbols are not congruent with reality. On the other hand, *symbols offer order and predictability in an ambiguous and uncertain world.* When the space shuttle Challenger exploded, killing its precious crew, people engaged in rituals to help them deal with their collective loss. In this way the symbolic frame can give meaning and hope to organizational activities that defy explanation in more rational terms.

INTEGRATING FRAMES FOR EFFECTIVE PRACTICE

While each of the frames emphasizes a different slice of organizational life, each one alone serves only as an incomplete map of a complex terrain. Each frame has a unique comparative advantage. For example, the structural frame will be most salient under conditions of stable authority, clear goals, and well-developed technologies. Human resource issues are likely to become prominent in an organization where employee motivation is important but problematic, and when resources are abundant. When goals and values are in conflict, resources are scarce, and the distribution of power is unstable, the political frame is likely to stand out. The symbolic frame is likely to be important under conditions of high ambiguity and inadequate information.

Taken together, the frames remind us that people and organizations try to behave in rational ways, but they are also affected by their needs and biases. They are adaptable but not infinitely so. They often will be dealing with scarce resources, and the importance of power and politics cannot be underestimated. Finally, the symbolic frame reminds us that we attribute meaning to organizational events. It is only in this multiple-perspective mode that we can begin fully to understand organizational activity at the level of complexity that is experienced by managers.

Multiple-perspective managers are able to interpret the same event in many different ways. A simple meeting can, for example, be a formal occasion for making decisions. Besides this structural interpretation, it can serve human resource needs by being an occasion for sharing feelings and building commitment to an idea. Meetings can serve as occasions to gain power and win points, and they can symbolically reaffirm values or transform the culture. Managers who can apply all of these frames and diagnose which perspectives are being used by the meeting's participants are likely to be more effective than those limited to a single perspective.

REFRAMING CHANGE

Modern organizations are being buffeted by powerful external forces that threaten the status quo.

Globalization requires organizations to enter new markets, adapt to new cultures, and reorganize their management structure. New technologies introduce new production and communication strategies. Deregulation in the airline and communications fields has forced these industries to shift from a service emphasis to a marketing emphasis. Demographic shifts have meant a changing workplace which is more diverse and multicultural, resulting in a sense of loss for some members.

The four frames can help managers anticipate the impact of change and act in ways to reduce resistance to change. The four approaches to change may look like this:

1. *Structural*—Change alters existing structural arrangements, causing confusion and ambiguity. Formal patterns and policies need to be realigned.
2. *Human Resource*—Change causes people to feel incompetent and powerless to handle new situations and behaviors. Training and psychological support are necessary when employees feel insecure.
3. *Political*—Change causes conflict and creates winners and losers. Managers must create arenas where issues can be negotiated.

4. *Symbolic*—Change creates loss of meaning and purpose. When attachments to symbols are severed, transition rituals are required and new symbols created.

"A fully effective change requires attention to all four issues: structure, needs, conflict, and loss. Changes in one frame inevitably reverberate through the others and the frame that is ignored is very likely to be the one that distorts or undermines the effort."[8]

REFRAMING LEADERSHIP: LEADERS AS ARCHITECTS, CATALYSTS, ADVOCATES, AND PROPHETS.

Many current views of leadership have been based on oversimplified models. Each of the frames offers a different perspective on how leaders might behave when they are effective and ineffective.

Effective leaders are more likely to have the skills to lead from a multiple perspectives framework, and they are more likely to know which frame might be the most appropriate fit for the situation at hand. Effective leaders can develop rational systems but avoid leading too heavily by the rules. They can support and empower people but avoid abdicating their leadership role. Effective leaders are able to build coalitions and advocate for their constituents, but use power fairly and judiciously. They can inspire others by giving meaning to their experience and by communicating a vision, but they can avoid the use of hollow symbols and balance their vision with concrete action.

ARTISTRY, CHOICE, AND LEADERSHIP

The best managers and leaders understand their prevailing frames and know how those frames both benefit and limit their effectiveness. Wise leaders know how to build teams that can provide leadership across all four frames as the situation requires. They will be able to create a balance between core values and elastic strategies. They can be dramatically explicit about their core values and beliefs but apply frames flexibly in pursuit of their mission.

In a world of constant change, leaders of complex organizations will need the ability to see new possibilities and to discover choices, even when options seem severely constrained. The ability to reframe their thinking can give them new power and new skills.

NOTES

1. Bolman, Lee G., and Terrence E. Deal, *Reframing Organizations: Artistry, Choice, and Leadership.* San Francisco CA: Jossey-Bass, 1991. p. 4.
2. Bolman and Deal, p. 12.

3. Bolman and Deal, p. 10.
4. Bolman and Deal, p. 120.
5. Bolman and Deal, p. 184.
6. Bolman and Deal, p. 249.
7. Bolman and Deal, p. 275.
8. Bolman and Deal, p. 402.

Organizational Culture and Leadership

Edgar H. Schein

The purpose of this article is to define the concept of organizational culture in terms of a dynamic model of how culture is learned, passed on, and changed. As many recent efforts argue that organizational culture is the key to organizational excellence, it is critical to define this complex concept in a manner that will provide a common frame of reference for practitioners and researchers. Many definitions simply settle for the notion that culture is a set of shared meanings that make it possible for members of a group to interpret and act upon their environment. I believe we must go beyond this definition: even if we knew an organization well enough to live in it, we would not necessarily know how its culture arose, how it came to be what it is, or how it could be changed if organizational survival were at stake.

The thrust of my argument is that we must understand the dynamic evolutionary forces that govern how culture evolves and changes. My approach to this task will be to lay out a formal definition of what I believe organizational culture is, and to elaborate each element of the definition to make it clear how it works.

ORGANIZATIONAL CULTURE: A FORMAL DEFINITION

Organizational culture is the *pattern of basic assumptions* that a *given group* has *invented, discovered, or developed in learning to cope* with its *problems of external adaptation and internal integration,* and that have *worked well enough to be considered valid,* and, therefore, to be *taught to new members* as the correct way to *perceive, think, and feel* in relation to those problems.

1. PATTERN OF BASIC ASSUMPTIONS

Organizational culture can be analyzed at several different levels, starting with the *visible artifacts*—the constructed environment of the organization, its architecture, technology, office layout, manner of dress, visible or audible behavior patterns, and public documents such as charters, employee orientation materials, stories (see Figure 1). This level of analysis is tricky because the data are easy to obtain but hard to interpret. We can describe "how" a group constructs its environment and "what" behavior patterns are discernible among the members, but we often cannot understand the underlying logic— "why" a group behaves the way it does.

To analyze *why* members behave the way they do, we often look for the *values* that govern behavior, which is the second level in Figure 1. But as values are hard to observe directly, it is often necessary to infer them by interviewing key members of the organization or to content analyze artifacts such as documents and charters.[1] However, in identifying such values, we usually note that

Figure 1 The Levels of Culture and Their Interactions

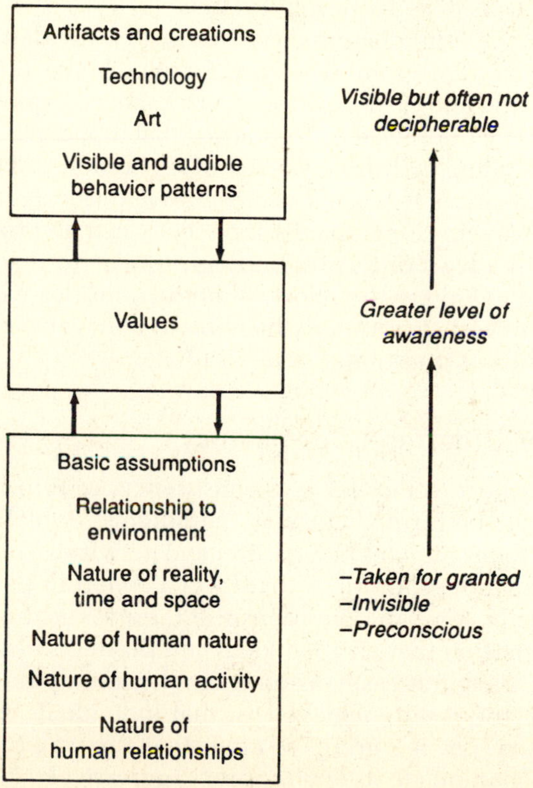

Artifacts and creations

Technology

Art

Visible and audible behavior patterns

Visible but often not decipherable

Values

Greater level of awareness

Basic assumptions

Relationship to environment

Nature of reality, time and space

Nature of human nature

Nature of human activity

Nature of human relationships

—Taken for granted
—Invisible
—Preconscious

they represent accurately only the manifest or *espoused* values of a culture. That is they focus on what people *say* is the reason for their behavior, what they ideally would like those reasons to be, and what are often their rationalizations for their behavior. Yet, the underlying reasons for their behavior remain concealed or unconscious.[2]

To really *understand* a culture and to ascertain more completely the group's values and overt behavior, it is imperative to delve into the *underlying assumptions,* which are typically unconscious, but which actually determine how group members perceive, think, and feel.[3] Such assumptions are themselves learned responses that originated as espoused values. But, as a value leads to a behavior, and as that behavior begins to solve the problem which prompted it in the first place, the value gradually is transformed into an underlying assumption about how things really are. As the assumption is increasingly taken for granted, it drops out of awareness.

Taken-for-granted assumptions are so powerful because they are less debatable and confrontable than espoused values. We know we are dealing with an assumption when we encounter in our informants a refusal to discuss something, or when they consider us "insane" or "ignorant" for bringing something up. For example, the notion that businesses should be profitable, that schools should educate, or that medicine should prolong life are assumptions, even though they are often considered "merely" values.

To put it another way, the domain of values can be divided into (1) ultimate, nondebatable, taken-for-granted values, for which the term "assumptions" is more appropriate; and (2) debatable, overt, espoused values, for which the term "values" is more applicable. In stating that basic assumptions are unconscious, I am not arguing that this is a result of repression. On the contrary, I am arguing that as certain motivational and cognitive processes are repeated and continue to work, they become unconscious. They can be brought back to awareness only through a kind of focused inquiry, similar to that used by anthropologists. What is needed are the efforts of both an insider who makes the unconscious assumptions and an outsider who helps to uncover the assumptions by asking the right kinds of questions.[4]

Cultural Paradigms: A Need for Order and Consistency

Because of the human need for order and consistency, assumptions become patterned into what may be termed cultural "paradigms," which tie together the basic assumptions about humankind, nature, and activities. A cultural paradigm is a set of interrelated assumptions that form a coherent pattern. Not all assumptions are mutually compatible or consistent, however. For example, if a group holds the assumption that all good ideas and products ultimately come from individual effort, it cannot easily assume simultaneously that groups can be held responsible for the results achieved, or that individuals will put a high priority on group loyalty. Or, if a group assumes that the way to survive is to conquer nature and to manipulate its environment aggressively, it cannot at the same time assume that the best kind of relationship among group members is one that emphasizes passivity and harmony. If human beings do indeed have a cognitive need for order and consistency, one can then assume that all groups will eventually evolve sets of assumptions that are compatible and consistent.

To analyze cultural paradigms, one needs a set of logical categories for studying assumptions. Table 1 shows such a set based on the original comparative study of Kluckhohn and Strodtbeck.[5] In applying these categories broadly to cultures, Kluckhohn and Strodtbeck note that Western culture tends to be oriented toward an active mastery of nature, and is based on individualistic competitive relationships. It uses a future-oriented, linear, monochronic concept of time,[6] views space and resources as infinite, assumes that human nature is neutral and ultimately perfectible, and bases reality or ultimate truth on science and pragmatism.

In contrast, some Eastern cultures are passively oriented toward nature. They seek to harmonize with nature and with each other. They view the group as more important than the individual, are present- or past-oriented, see time as polychronic and cyclical, view space and resources as very limited, assume that human nature is bad but improvable, and see reality as based more on revealed truth than on empirical experimentation.

In this light, organizational culture paradigms are adapted versions of broader cultural paradigms. For example, Dyer notes that the GEM Corpora-

---

Table 1. BASIC UNDERLYING ASSUMPTIONS AROUND WHICH CULTURAL PARADIGMS FORM

---

1.   **The Organization's Relationship to Its Environment.** Reflecting even more basic assumptions about the relationship of humanity to nature, one can assess whether the key members of organization view the relationship as one of dominance, submission, harmonizing, finding an appropriate niche, and so on.

2.   **The Nature of Reality and Truth.** Here are the linguistic and behavioral rules that define what is real and what is not, what is a "fact," how truth is ultimately to be determined, and whether truth is "revealed" or "discovered"; basic concepts of time as linear or cyclical, monochronic or polychronic; basic concepts such as space as limited or infinite and property as communal or individual; and so forth.

3.   **The Nature of Human Nature.** What does it mean to be "human" and what attributes are considered intrinsic or ultimate? Is human nature good, evil, or neutral? Are human beings perfectible or not? Which is better, Theory X or Theory Y?

4.   **The Nature of Human Activity.** What is the "right" thing for human beings to do, on the basis of the above assumptions about reality, the environment, and human nature: to be active, passive, self-developmental, fatalistic, or what? What is work and what is play?

5.   **The Nature of Human Relationships.** What is considered to be the "right" way for people to relate to each other, to distribute power and love? Is life cooperative or competitive; individualistic, group collaborative, or communal; based on traditional lineal authority, law, or charisma; or what?

---

tion operates on the interlocking assumptions that: (1) ideas come ultimately from individuals; (2) people are responsible, motivated, and capable of governing themselves; however, truth can only be pragmatically determined by "fighting" things out and testing in groups; (3) such fighting is possible because the members of the organization view themselves as a family who will take care of each other. Ultimately, this makes it safe to fight and be competitive.[7]

I have observed another organization that operates on the paradigm that (1) truth comes ultimately from older, wiser, better educated, higher status members; (2) people are capable of loyalty and discipline in carrying out directives; (3) relationships are basically lineal and vertical; (4) each person has a niche that is his or her territory that cannot be invaded; and (5) the organization is a "solitary unit" that will take care of its members.

Needless to say, the manifest behaviors in these two organizations are totally different. In the first organization, one observes mostly open office landscapes, few offices with closed doors, a high rate of milling about, intense conversations and arguments, and a general air of informality. In the second organization, there is a hush in the air: everyone is in an office and with closed doors. Nothing is done except by appointment and with a prearranged agenda. When people of different ranks are present, one sees real deference rituals and obedience, and a general air of formality permeates everything.

Nonetheless, these behavioral differences make no sense until one has discovered and deciphered the underlying cultural paradigm. To stay at the level of artifacts or values is to deal with the *manifestations* of culture, but not with the cultural essence.

2. A GIVEN GROUP

There cannot be a culture unless there is a group that "owns" it. Culture is embedded in groups, hence the creating group must always be clearly identified. If we want to define a cultural unit, therefore, we must be able to locate a group that is independently defined as the creator, host, or owner of that culture. We must be careful not to define the group in terms of the existence of a culture, however tempting that may be, because we then would be creating a completely circular definition.

A given group is a set of people (1) who have been together long enough to have shared significant problems, (2) who have had opportunities to solve those problems and to observe the effects of their solutions, and (3) who have taken in new members. A group's culture cannot be determined unless there is such a definable set of people with a shared history.

The passing on of solutions to new members is required in the definition of culture because the decision to pass something on is itself a very important test of whether a given solution is shared and perceived as valid. If a group passes on with conviction elements of a way of perceiving, thinking, and feeling, we can assume that that group has had enough stability and has shared enough common experiences to have developed a culture. If, on the other hand, a group has not faced the issue of what to pass on in the process of socialization, it has not had a chance to test its own consensus and commitment to a given belief, value, or assumption.

The Strength of a Culture

The "strength" or "amount" of culture can be defined in terms of (1) the *homogeneity* and *stability* of group membership and (2) the *length* and *intensity* of shared experiences of the group. If a stable group has had a long, varied, intense history (i.e., if it has had to cope with many difficult survival problems and has succeeded), it will have a strong and highly differentiated culture. By the same token, if a group has had a constantly shifting membership or has been together only for a short time and has not faced any difficult issues, it will, by definition, have a weak culture. Although individuals within that group may have very strong individual assumptions, there will not be enough shared experiences for the group as a whole to have a defined culture.

By this definition, one would probably assess IBM and the Bell System as having strong cultures, whereas, very young companies or ones which have had a high turnover of key executives would be judged as having weak ones. One should also note that once an organization has a strong culture, if the dominant coalition or leadership remains stable, the culture can survive high turnover at lower ranks because new members can be strongly socialized into the organization as, for example, in elite military units.

It is very important to recognize that cultural strength may or may not be correlated with effectiveness. Though some current writers have argued that strength is desirable,[8] it seems clear to me that the relationship is far more complex. The actual content of the culture and the degree to which its solutions fit the problems posed by the environment seem like the critical variables here, not strength. One can hypothesize that young groups strive for culture strength as a way of creating an identity for themselves, but older groups may be more effective with a weak total culture and diverse subcultures to enable them to be responsive to rapid environmental change.

This way of defining culture makes it specific to a given group. If a total corporation consists of stable functional, divisional, geographic, or rank-based subgroups, then that corporation will have multiple cultures within it. It is perfectly possible for those multiple cultures to be in conflict with each other, such that one could not speak of a single corporate culture. On the other hand, if there has been common corporate experience as well, then one could have a strong corporate culture on top of various subcultures that are based in subunits. The deciphering of a given company's culture then becomes an empirical matter of locating where the stable social units are, what cultures each of those stable units have developed, and how those separate cultures blend into a single whole. The total culture could then be very homogeneous or heterogeneous, according to the degree to which subgroup cultures are similar or different.

It has also been pointed out that some of the cultural assumptions in an organization can come from the occupational background of the members of the organization. This makes it possible to have a managerial culture, an engineering culture, a science culture, a labor union culture, etc., all of which coexist in a given organization.[9]

3. INVENTED, DISCOVERED, OR DEVELOPED

Cultural elements are defined as learned solutions to problems. In this section, I will concentrate on the nature of the learning mechanisms that are involved.

Structurally, there are two types of learning situations: (1) positive problem-solving situations that produce positive or negative reinforcement in terms of whether the attempted solution works or not; and (2) anxiety-avoidance situations that produce positive or negative reinforcement in terms of whether the attempted solution does or does not avoid anxiety. In practice, these two types of situations are intertwined, but they are structurally different and, therefore, they must be distinguished.

In the positive problem-solving situation, the group tries out various responses until something works. The group will then continue to use this response until it ceases to work. The information that it no longer works is visible and clear. By contrast, in the anxiety-avoidance situation, once a response is learned because it successfully avoids anxiety, it is likely to be repeated indefinitely. The reason is that the learner will not willingly test the situation to determine whether the cause of the anxiety is still operating. Thus all rituals, patterns of thinking or feeling, and behaviors that may originally have been motivated by a need to avoid a painful, anxiety-provoking situation are going to be repeated, even if the causes of the original pain are no longer acting, because the avoidance of anxiety is, itself, positively reinforcing.[10]

To fully grasp the importance of anxiety reduction in culture formation, we have to consider, first of all, the human need for cognitive order and consistency, which serves as the ultimate motivator for a common language and shared categories of perception and thought.[11] In the absence of such shared "cognitive maps," the human organism experiences a basic existential anxiety that is intolerable—an anxiety observed only in extreme situations of isolation or captivity.[12]

Secondly, humans experience the anxiety associated with being exposed to hostile environmental conditions and to the dangers inherent in unstable social relationships, forcing groups to learn ways of coping with such external and internal problems.

A third source of anxiety is associated with occupational roles such as coal mining and nursing. For example, the Tavistock sociotechnical studies have shown clearly that the social structure and ways of operation of such groups can be conceptualized best as a "defense" against the anxiety that would be unleashed if work were done in another manner.[13]

If an organizational culture is composed of both types of elements—those designed to solve problems and those designed to avoid anxiety—it becomes necessary to analyze which is which if one is concerned about changing any of the elements. In the positive-learning situation, one needs innovative sources to find a better solution to the problem; in the anxiety-avoidance situation, one must first find the source of the anxiety and either show the learner that it no longer exists, or provide an alternative source of avoidance. Either of these is difficult to do.

In other words, cultural elements that are based on anxiety reduction will be more stable than those based on positive problem solving because of the nature of the anxiety-reduction mechanism and the fact that human systems need a certain amount of stability to avoid cognitive and social anxiety.

Where do solutions initially come from? Most cultural solutions in new groups and organizations originate from the founders and early leaders of those organizations.[14] Typically, the solution process is an advocacy of certain ways of doing things that are then tried out and either adopted or rejected, depending on how well they work out. Initially, the founders have the most influence, but, as the group ages and acquires its own experiences, its members will find their own solutions. Ultimately, the process of discovering new solutions will be more a result of interactive, shared experiences. But leadership will always play a key role during those times when the group faces a new problem and must develop new responses to the situation. In fact, one of the crucial functions of leadership is to provide guidance at precisely those times when habitual ways of doing things no longer work, or when a dramatic change in the environment requires new responses.

At those times, leadership must not only insure the invention of new and better solutions, but must also provide some security to help the group tolerate the anxiety of giving up old, stable responses, while new ones are learned and tested. In the Lewinian change framework, this means that the "unfreezing stage" must involve both enough disconfirmation to motivate change and enough psychological safety to permit the individual or group to pay attention to the disconfirming data.[15]

4. PROBLEMS OF EXTERNAL ADAPTATION AND INTERNAL INTEGRATION

If culture is a solution to the problems a group faces, what can we say about the nature of those problems? Most group theories agree it is useful to distinguish between two kinds of problems: (1) those that deal with the group's basic survival, which has been labeled the primary task, basic function, or ultimate mission of the group; and (2) those that deal with the group's ability to function as a group. These problems have been labeled socioemotional, group building and maintenance, or integration problems.[16]

Homans further distinguishes between the *external system* and the *inter-*

nal system and notes that the two are interdependent.[17] Even though one can distinguish between the external and internal problems, in practice both systems are highly interrelated.

External Adaptation Problems

Problems of external adaptation are those that ultimately determine the group's survival in the environment. While a part of the group's environment is "enacted," in the sense that prior cultural experience predisposes members to perceive the environment in a certain way and even to control that environment to a degree, there will always be elements of the environment (weather, natural circumstances, availability of economic and other resources, political upheavals) that are clearly beyond the control of the group and that will, to a degree, determine the fate of the group.[18] A useful way to categorize the problems of survival is to mirror the stages of the problem-solving cycle as shown in Table 2.[19]

The basic underlying assumptions of the culture from which the founders of the organization come will determine to a large extent the initial formulations of core mission, goals, means, criteria, and remedial strategies, in that those ways of doing things are the only ones with which the group members will be familiar. But as an organization develops its own life experience, it may begin to modify to some extent its original assumptions. For example, a young company may begin by defining its core mission to be to "win in the marketplace over all competition," but may at a later stage find that "owning its own niche in the marketplace," "coexisting with other companies," or even "being a silent partner in an oligopolistic industry" is a more workable solution to survival. Thus for each stage of the problem-solving cycle, there will emerge

Table 2. PROBLEMS OF EXTERNAL ADAPTATION AND SURVIVAL

Strategy:	Developing consensus on the *primary task, core mission, or manifest latent functions of the group.*
Goals:	Developing consensus on *goals,* such goals being the concrete reflection of the core mission.
Means for Accomplishing Goals:	Developing consensus on the *means to be used* in accomplishing the goals—for example, division of labor, organization structure, reward system, and so forth.
Measuring Performance:	Developing consensus on the *criteria to be used in measuring how well the group is doing against its goals and targets*—for example, information and control systems.
Correction:	Developing consensus on *remedial or repair strategies* as needed when the group is not accomplishing its goals.

Source: Reprinted, by permission of the publisher, from "The Role of the Founder in Creating Organizational Culture," by Edgar H. Schein, *Organizational Dynamics,* Summer 1983. © 1983 Periodicals Division, American Management Associations. All rights reserved.

solutions characteristic of that group's own history, and those solutions or ways of doing things based on learned assumptions will make up a major portion of that group's culture.

Internal Integration Problems

A group or organization cannot survive if it cannot manage itself as a group. External survival and internal integration problems are, therefore, two sides of the same coin. Table 3 outlines the major issues of internal integration around which cultural solutions must be found.

While the nature of the solutions will vary from one organization to another, by definition, every organization will have to face each of these issues and develop some kind of solution. However, because the nature of that solution will reflect the biases of the founders and current leaders, the prior experiences of group members, and the actual events experienced, it is likely that each organi-

Table 3. PROBLEMS OF INTERNAL INTEGRATION

Language:	*Common language and conceptual categories.* If members cannot communicate with and understand each other, a group is impossible by definition.
Boundaries:	Consensus on *group boundaries and criteria for inclusion and exclusion.* One of the most important areas of culture is the shared consensus on who is in, who is out, and by what criteria one determines membership.
Power & Status:	Consensus on *criteria for the allocation of power and status.* Every organization must work out its pecking order and its rules for how one gets, maintains, and loses power. This area of consensus is crucial in helping members manage their own feelings of aggression.
Intimacy:	Consensus on *criteria for intimacy, friendship, and love.* Every organization must work out its rules of the game for peer relationships, for relationships between the sexes, and for the manner in which openness and intimacy are to be handled in the context of managing the organization's tasks.
Rewards & Punishments:	Consensus on *criteria for allocation of rewards and punishments.* Every group must know what its heroic and sinful behaviors are; what gets rewarded with property, status, and power; and what gets punished through the withdrawal of rewards and, ultimately, excommunication.
Ideology:	Consensus on *ideology and "religion."* Every organization, like every society, faces unexplainable events that must be given meaning so that members can respond to them and avoid the anxiety of dealing with the unexplainable and uncontrollable.

Source: Reprinted, by permission of the publisher, from "The Role of the Founder in Creating Organizational Culture," by Edgar H. Schein, *Organizational Dynamics,* Summer 1983. © 1983 Periodicals Division, American Management Associations. All rights reserved.

zational culture will be unique, even though the underlying issues around which the culture is formed will be common.[20]

An important issue to study across many organizations is whether an organization's growth and evolution follows an inherent evolutionary trend (e.g., developing societies are seen as evolving from that of a community to more of a bureaucratic, impersonal type of system). One should also study whether organizational cultures reflect in a patterned way the nature of the underlying technology, the age of the organization, the size of the organization, and the nature of the parent culture within which the organization evolves.

5. ASSUMPTIONS THAT WORK WELL ENOUGH TO BE CONSIDERED VALID

Culture goes beyond the norms or values of a group in that it is more of an *ultimate* outcome, based on repeated success and a gradual process of taking things for granted. In other words, to me what makes something "cultural" is this "taken-for-granted" quality, which makes the underlying assumptions virtually undiscussable.

Culture is perpetually being formed in the sense that there is constantly some kind of learning going on about how to relate to the environment and to manage internal affairs. But this ongoing evolutionary process does not change those things that are so thoroughly learned that they come to be a stable element of the group's life. Since the basic assumptions that make up an organization's culture serve the secondary function of stabilizing much of the internal and external environment for the group, and since that stability is sought as a defense against the anxiety which comes with uncertainty and confusion, these deeper parts of the culture either do not change or change only very slowly.

6. TAUGHT TO NEW MEMBERS

Because culture serves the function of stabilizing the external and internal environment for an organization, it must be taught to new members. It would not serve its function if every generation of new members could introduce new perceptions, language, thinking patterns, and rules of interaction. For culture to serve its function, it must be perceived as correct and valid, and if it is perceived that way, it automatically follows that it must be taught to newcomers.

It cannot be overlooked that new members do bring new ideas and do produce culture change, especially if they are brought in at high levels of the organization. It remains to be settled empirically whether and how this happens. For example, does a new member have to be socialized first and accepted into a central and powerful position before he or she can begin to affect change? Or does a new member bring from the onset new ways of perceiving, thinking, feeling, and acting, which produce automatic changes through role innovation?[21] Is the manner in which new members are socialized influential in determining what kind of innovation they will produce?[22] Much of the work on innovation in organizations is confusing because often it is not clear whether the elements that are considered "new" are actually new assumptions, or simply new artifacts built on old cultural assumptions.

In sum, if culture provides the group members with a paradigm of how the world "is," it goes without saying that such a paradigm would be passed on without question to new members. It is also the case that the very process of passing on the culture provides an opportunity for testing, ratifying, and reaffirming it. For both of these reasons, the process of socialization (i.e., the passing on of the group's culture) is strategically an important process to study if one wants to decipher what the culture is and how it might change.[23]

7. PERCEIVE, THINK, AND FEEL

The final element in the definition reminds us that culture is pervasive and ubiquitous. The basic assumptions about nature, humanity, relationships, truth, activity, time, and space cover virtually all human functions. This is not to say that a given organization's culture will develop to the point of totally "controlling" all of its members' perceptions, thoughts, and feelings. But the process of learning to manage the external and internal environment does involve all of one's cognitive and emotional elements. As cultural learning progresses, more and more of the person's responses will become involved. Therefore, the longer we live in a given culture, and the older the culture is, the more it will influence our perceptions, thoughts, and feelings.

By focusing on perceptions, thoughts, and feelings, I am also stating the importance of those categories relative to the category of *overt behavior*. Can one speak of a culture in terms of just the overt behavior patterns one observes? Culture is *manifested* in overt behavior, but the idea of culture goes deeper than behavior. Indeed, the very reason for elaborating an abstract notion like "culture" is that it is too difficult to explain what goes on in organizations if we stay at the descriptive behavioral level.

To put it another way, behavior is, to a large extent, a joint function of what the individual brings to the situation and the operating situational forces, which to some degree are unpredictable. To understand the cultural portion of what the individual brings to the situation (as opposed to the idiosyncratic or situational portions), we must examine the individual's pattern of perceptions, thoughts, and feelings. Only after we have reached a consensus at this inner level have we uncovered what is potentially *cultural*.

The Study of Organizational Culture and Its Implications

Organizational culture as defined here is difficult to study. However, it is not as difficult as studying a different society where language and customs are so different that one needs to live in the society to get any feel for it at all. Organizations exist in a parent culture, and much of what we find in them is derivative from the assumptions of the parent culture. But different organizations will sometimes emphasize or amplify different elements of a parent culture. For example, in the two companies previously mentioned, we find in the first an extreme version of the individual freedom ethic, and in the second one, an extreme version of the authority ethic, *both* of which can be derived from U.S. culture.

The problem of deciphering a particular organization's culture, then, is more a matter of surfacing assumptions, which will be recognizable once they have been uncovered. We will not find alien forms of perceiving, thinking, and feeling if the investigator is from the same parent culture as the organization that is being investigated. On the other hand, the particular pattern of assumptions, which we call an organization's cultural paradigm, will not reveal itself easily because it is taken for granted.

How then do we gather data and decipher the paradigm? Basically, there are four approaches that should be used in combination with one another:

1. Analyzing the Process and Content of Socialization of New Members By interviewing "socialization agents," such as the supervisors and older peers of new members, one can identify some of the important areas of the culture. But some elements of the culture will not be discovered by this method because they are not revealed to newcomers or lower members.

2. Analyzing Responses to Critical Incidents in the Organization's History By constructing a careful "organizational biography" from documents, interviews, and perhaps even surveys of present and past key members, it is possible to identify the major periods of culture formation. For each crisis or incident identified, it is then necessary to determine what was done, why it was done, and what the outcome was. To infer the underlying assumptions of the organization, one would then look for the major themes in the reasons given for the actions taken.

3. Analyzing Beliefs, Values, and Assumptions of "Culture Creators or Carriers" When interviewing founders, current leaders, or culture creators or carriers, one should initially make an open-ended chronology of each person's history in the organization—his or her goals, modes of action, and assessment of outcomes. The list of external and internal issues found in Tables 2 and 3 can be used as a checklist later in the interview to cover areas more systematically.

4. Jointly Exploring and Analyzing with Insiders the Anomalies or Puzzling Features Observed or Uncovered in Interviews It is the *joint inquiry* that will help to disclose basic assumptions and help determine how they may interrelate to form the cultural paradigm.

The insider must be a representative of the culture and must be interested in disclosing his or her *own* basic assumptions to test whether they are in fact cultural prototypes. This process works best if one acts from observations that puzzle the outsider or that seem like anomalies because the insider's assumptions are most easily surfaced if they are contrasted to the assumptions that the outsider initially holds about what is observed.

While the first three methods mentioned above should enhance and complement one another, at least one of them should systematically cover all of the external adaptation and internal integration issues. In order to discover the underlying basic assumptions and eventually to decipher the paradigm, the fourth method is necessary to help the insider surface his or her own cultural assumptions. This is done through the outsider's probing and searching.[24]

If an organization's total culture is not well developed, or if the organization consists of important stable subgroups, which have developed subcultures, one must modify the above methods to study the various subcultures.[25] Furthermore, the organizational biography might reveal that the organization is at a certain point in its life cycle, and one would hypothesize that the functions that a given kind of culture plays vary with the life-cycle stage.[26]

Implications for Culture Management and Change

If we recognize organizational culture—whether at the level of the group or the total corporation—as a deep phenomenon, what does this tell us about when and how to change or manage culture? First of all, the evolutionary perspective draws our attention to the fact that the culture of a group may serve different functions at different times. When a group is forming and growing, the culture is a "glue"—a source of identity and strength. In other words, young founder-dominated companies need their cultures as a way of holding together their organizations. The culture changes that do occur in a young organization can best be described as clarification, articulation, and elaboration. If the young company's culture is genuinely maladaptive in relation to the external environment, the company will not survive anyway. But even if one identified needed changes, there is little chance at this stage that one could change the culture.

In organizational midlife, culture can be managed and changed, but not without considering all the sources of stability which have been identified above. The large diversified organization probably contains many functional, geographic, and other groups that have culture of their own—some of which will conflict with each other. Whether the organization needs to enhance the diversity to remain flexible in the face of environmental turbulence, or to create a more homogeneous "strong" culture (as some advocate) becomes one of the toughest strategy decisions management confronts, especially if senior management is unaware of some of its own cultural assumptions. Some form of outside intervention and "culture consciousness raising" is probably essential at this stage to facilitate better strategic decisions.

Organizations that have reached a stage of maturity or decline resulting from mature markets and products or from excessive internal stability and comfort that prevents innovation[27] may need to change parts of their culture, provided they can obtain the necessary self-insight. Such managed change will always be a painful process and will elicit strong resistance. Moreover, change may not even be possible without replacing the large numbers of people who wish to hold on to all of the original culture.

No single model of such change exists: managers may successfully orchestrate change through the use of a wide variety of techniques, from outright coercion at one extreme to subtle seduction through the introduction of new technologies at the other extreme.[28]

SUMMARY AND CONCLUSIONS

I have attempted to construct a formal definition of organizational culture that derives from a dynamic model of learning and group dynamics. The definition highlights that culture: (1) is always in the process of formation and change; (2) tends to cover all aspects of human functioning; (3) is learned around the major issues of external adaptation and internal integration; and (4) is ultimately embodied as an interrelated, patterned set of basic assumptions that deal with ultimate issues, such as the nature of humanity, human relationships, time, space, and the nature of reality and truth itself.

If we are to decipher a given organization's culture, we must use a complex interview, observation, and joint-inquiry approach in which selected members of the group work with the outsider to uncover the unconscious assumptions that are hypothesized to be the essence of the culture. I believe we need to study a large number of organizations using these methods to determine the utility of the concept of organizational culture and to relate cultural variables to other variables, such as strategy, organizational structure, and ultimately, organizational effectiveness.

If such studies show this model of culture to be useful, one of the major implications will be that our theories of organizational change will have to give much more attention to the opportunities and constraints that organizational culture provides. Clearly, if culture is as powerful as I argue in this article, it will be easy to make changes that are congruent with present assumptions, and very difficult to make changes that are not. In sum, the understanding of organizational culture would then become integral to the process of management itself.

NOTES

1. See J. Martin and C. Siehl, "Organizational Culture and Counterculture: An Uneasy Symbiosis." *Organizational Dynamics,* Autumn 1983, pp. 52–64.
2. See C. Argyris, "The Executive Mind and Double-Loop Learning," *Organizational Dynamics,* Autumn 1982, pp. 5–22.
3. See: E. H. Schein, "Does Japanese Management Style Have a Message for American Managers?" *Sloan Management Review,* Fall 1981, pp. 55–68; E. H. Schein, "The

Role of the Founder in Creating Organizational Culture," *Organizational Dynamics,* Summer 1983, pp. 13–28.

4. See R. Evered and M. R. Louis, "Alternative Perspectives in the Organizational Sciences: 'Inquiry from the Inside' and 'Inquiry from the Outside.' " *Academy of Management Review* (1981):385–395.

5. See: F. R. Kluckhohn and F. L. Strodtbeck, *Variations in Value Orientations* (Evanston, IL: Row Peterson, 1961). An application of these ideas to the study of organizations across cultures as contrasted with the culture of organizations can be found in W. M. Evan, *Organization Theory* (New York: John Wiley & Sons, 1976), ch. 15; Other studies of cross-cultural comparisons are not reviewed in detail here. See for example: G. Hofstede, *Culture's Consequences* (Beverly Hills, CA: Sage Publications, 1980); G. W. England, *The Manager and His Values* (Cambridge, MA: Ballinger, 1975).

6. See E. T. Hall, *The Silent Language* (New York: Doubleday, 1969).

7. W. G. Dyer, Jr., *Culture in Organizations: A Case Study and Analysis* (Cambridge, MA: Sloan School of Management, MIT, Working Paper #1279-82, 1982).

8. See: T. E. Deal and A. A. Kennedy, *Corporate Culture* (Reading, MA: Addison-Wesley, 1982); T. J. Peters and R. H. Waterman, Jr., *In Search of Excellence* (New York: Harper & Row, 1982).

9. See: J. Van Maanen and S. R. Barley, "Occupational Communities: Culture and Control in Organizations" (Cambridge, MA: Sloan School of Management, MIT, November 1982); L. Bailyn, "Resolving Contradictions in Technical Careers," *Technology Review,* November-December 1982, pp. 40–47.

10. See R. L. Solomon and L. C. Wynne, "Traumatic Avoidance Learning: The Principles of Anxiety Conservation and Partial Irreversibility," *Psychological Review* 61, 1954, p. 353.

11. See D. O. Hobb, "The Social Significance of Animal Studies," in *Handbook of Social Psychology,* G. Lindzey, ed. (Reading, MA: Addison-Wesley, 1954).

12. See E. H. Schein, *Coercive Persuasion* (New York: Norton, 1961).

13. See: E. L. Trist and K. W. Bemforth, "Some Social and Psychological Consequences of the Long-Wall Method of Coal Getting," *Human Relations,* 1951, pp. 1–38; I.E.P. Menzies, "A Case Study in the Functioning of Social Systems as a Defense against Anxiety," *Human Relations,* 1960, pp. 95–121.

14. See: A. M. Pettigrew, "On Studying Organizational Cultures," *Administrative Science Quarterly* (1979): 570–581; Schein (Summer 1983), pp. 13–28.

15. See: Schein (1961); E. H. Schein and W. G. Bennis, *Personal and Organizational Change through Group Methods* (New York: John Wiley & Sons, 1965).

16. See: A. K. Rice, *The Enterprise and Its Environment* (London: Tavistock, 1963); R. F. Bales, *Interaction Process Analysis* (Chicago, IL: University of Chicago Press, 1950); T. Parsons, *The Social System* (Glencoe, IL: The Free Press, 1951).

17. See G. Homans, *The Human Group* (New York: Harcourt Brace, 1950).

18. See: K. E. Weick, "Cognitive Processes in Organizations," in *Research in Organizational Behavior,* ed. B. Staw (Greenwich, CT: JAI Press, 1979), pp. 41–74; J. Van Maanen, "The Self, the Situation, and the Rules of Interpersonal Relations," in *Essays in Interpersonal Dynamics,* W. G. Bennis, J. Van Maanen, E. H. Schein, and F. L. Steele (Homewood, IL: Dorsey Press, 1979).

19. See E. H. Schein, *Process Consultation* (Reading, MA: Addison-Wesley, 1969).

20. When studying different organizations, it is important to determine whether the deeper paradigms that eventually arise in each organizational culture are also unique, or whether they will fit into certain categories such as those that the typological schemes suggest. For example, Handy describes a typology based on Harrison's

work that suggests that organizational paradigms will revolve around one of four basic issues: (1) personal connections, power, and politics; (2) role structuring; (3) tasks and efficiency; or (4) existential here and now issues. See: C. Handy, *The Gods of Management* (London: Penguin, 1978); R. Harrison, "How to Describe Your Organization," *Harvard Business Review,* September-October 1972.

21. See E. H. Schein, "The Role Innovator and His Education," *Technology Review,* October-November 1970, pp. 32–38.

22. J. Van Maanen and E. H. Schein, "Toward a Theory of Organizational Socialization," in *Research in Organizational Behavior,* Vol. 1, ed. B. Staw (Greenwich, CT: JAI Press, 1979).

23. Ibid.

24. See Evered and Louis (1961).

25. See M. R. Louis, "A Cultural Perspective on Organizations," *Human Systems Management* (1981):246–258.

26. See: H. Schwartz and S. M. Davis, "Matching Corporate Culture and Business Strategy," *Organizational Dynamics,* Summer 1961, pp. 30–48; J. R. Kimberly and R. H. Miles, *The Organizational Life Cycle* (San Francisco: Jossey-Bass, 1961).

27. See R. Katz, "The Effects of Group Longevity of Project Communication and Performance," *Administrative Science Quarterly* (1962):27, 81–194.

28. A fuller explication of these dynamics can be found in my forthcoming book on organizational culture.

THREE

High-Performing Organizations

Most organizations don't want merely to survive; they want to be effective, or even excellent, at what they do. To do so requires a prior definition of success, and this often encourages the managers of an organization to examine their competitors for comparative models (benchmarks). The assumption is that if they can identify the organizational characteristics that allow others to succeed, perhaps these attributes can be transplanted (or adapted) to facilitate their own success. There is, therefore, considerable interest across a wide variety of organizations and management groups in what "high-performing organizations" actually do and what the guiding principles are.

The three books in this section concern themselves with issues pertaining to organizational effectiveness. High-performing organizations, according to Peters and Waterman, tend to be characterized by a set of key attributes (e.g., a bias toward action, productivity improvement through people, simple form, and lean staff). Argyris suggests to us that these organizations have learned about the importance of overcoming defensiveness and the maintenance of the status quo. They have gotten to this place by placing an emphasis on learning, competence, and justice. The importance of organizational learning is also emphasized by Senge.

While working as partners for McKinsey & Company (a management consulting firm), Thomas J. Peters and Robert H. Waterman, Jr., conducted research that led their to their book *In Search of Excellence.* The result of their study of management practices in several dozen companies in six industries led to the identification of eight attributes that were practiced consistently and appeared to be related to organizational success.

Chris Argyris' book *Overcoming Organizational Defenses* portrays ways of overcoming the defenses that tend to slow down change and inhibit the organization's ability to significantly improve performance. Shifting from established tradition which focuses on morale, loyalty, and satisfaction as the foundation for the achievement of organizational excellence, Argyris argues that a more realistic base for excellence may come from an emphasis placed upon learning, competence, and justice. Chris Argyris is on the Business and Education faculties at Harvard University.

Peter M. Senge is the Director of the Systems Thinking and Organizational Learning Program at MIT's Sloan School of Management. His book *The Fifth Discipline: The Art and Practice of the Learning Organization* emphasizes the importance of organizations developing the capacity to engage in effective learning. Senge identifies and discusses a set of disabilities that are fatal to organizations, especially those operating in rapidly changing environments. The fifth discipline—systems thinking—is presented as the cornerstone for the learning organization. Personal mastery, mental models, shared vision, and team learning are presented as the core disciplines and the focus for building the learning organization.

Reading 1

In Search of Excellence

Thomas J. Peters and
Robert H. Waterman, Jr.

What makes for excellence in the management of a company? Is it the use of sophisticated management techniques such as zero-based budgeting, management by objectives, matrix organization, and sector, group, or portfolio management? Is it greater use of computers to control companies that continue to grow even larger in size and more diverse in activities? Is it a battalion of specialized MBAs, well-versed in the techniques of strategic planning?

Probably not. Although most well-run companies use a fair sampling of all these tools, they do not use them as substitutes for the basics of good management. Indeed, McKinsey & Co., a management consultant concern, has studied management practices at thirty-seven companies that are often used as examples of well-run organizations and has found that they have eight common attributes. None of those attributes depends on "modern" management tools or gimmicks. In fact, none of them requires high technology, and none of them costs a cent to implement. All that is needed is time, energy, and a willingness on the part of management to think rather than to make use of management formulas.

The outstanding performers work hard to keep things simple. They rely on simple organizational structures, simple strategies, simple goals, and simple communications. The eight attributes that characterize their managements are:

- A bias toward action.
- Simple form and lean staff.
- Continued contact with customers.
- Productivity improvement via people.
- Operational autonomy to encourage entrepreneurship.
- Stress on one key business value.
- Emphasis on doing what they know best.
- Simultaneous loose-tight controls.

Reprinted from Thomas J. Peters, "Putting Excellence into Management," *Business Week,* July 21, 1980, by special permission, © 1980 by McGraw-Hill, Inc.

Although none of these sounds startling or new, most are conspicuously absent in many companies today. Far too many managers have lost sight of the basics—service to customers, low-cost manufacturing, productivity improvement, innovation, and risk-taking. In many cases, they have been seduced by the availability of MBAs, armed with the "latest" in strategic planning techniques. MBAs who specialize in strategy are bright, but they often cannot implement their ideas, and their companies wind up losing the capacity to act. At Standard Brands Inc., for example, Chairman F. Ross Johnson discovered this the hard way when he brought a handful of planning specialists into his consumer products company. "The guys who were bright [the strategic planners] were not the kinds of people who could implement programs," he lamented to *Business Week.* Two years later, he removed the planners.

Another consumer products company followed a similar route, hiring a large band of young MBAs for the staffs of senior vice-presidents. The new people were assigned to build computer models for designing new products. Yet none of the products could be manufactured or brought to market. Complained one line executive: "The models incorporated eighty-three variables in product planning, but we were being killed by just one—cost."

Companies are being stymied not only by their own staffs but often by their structure. McKinsey studied one company where the new product process required 223 separate committees to approve an idea before it could be put into production. Another company was restructured recently into 200 strategic business units—only to discover that it was impossible to implement 200 strategies. And even at General Electric Co., which is usually cited for its ability to structure itself according to its management needs, an executive recently complained: "Things become bureaucratic with astonishing speed. Inevitably when we wire things up, we lose vitality." Emerson Electric Co., with a much simpler structure than GE, consistently beats its huge competitor on costs—manufacturing its products in plants with fewer than 600 employees.

McKinsey's study focused on ten well-managed companies: International Business Machines, Texas Instruments, Hewlett-Packard, 3M, Digital Equipment, Procter & Gamble, Johnson & Johnson, McDonald's, Dana, and Emerson Electric. On the surface, they have nothing in common. There is no universality of product line: Five are in high technology, one is in packaged goods, one makes medical products, one operates fast-food restaurants, and two are relatively mundane manufacturers of mechanical and electrical products. But each is a hands-on operator, not a holding company or a conglomerate. And while not every plan succeeds, in the day-to-day pursuit of their businesses these companies succeed far more often than they fail. And they succeed because of their management's almost instinctive adherence to the eight attributes.

BIAS TOWARD ACTION

In each of these companies, the key instructions are *do it, fix it, try it.* They avoid analyzing and questioning products to death, and they avoid complicated procedures for developing new ideas. Controlled experiments abound in these companies. The attitude of management is to "get some data, do it, then adjust it," rather than to wait for a perfect overall plan. The companies tend to be tinkerers rather than inventors, making small steps of progress rather than conceiving sweeping new concepts. At McDonald's Corp., for example, the objective is to do the little things regularly and well.

Ideas are solicited regularly and tested quickly. Those that work are pushed fast; those that don't are discarded just as quickly. At 3M Co., the management never kills an idea without trying it out; it just goes on the back burner.

These managements avoid long, complicated business plans for new projects. At 3M, for example, new product ideas must be proposed in less than five pages. At Procter & Gamble Co., one-page memos are the rule, but every figure in a P&G memo can be relied on unfailingly.

To ensure that they achieve results, these companies set a few well-defined goals for their managers. At Texas Instruments Inc., for one, a typical goal would be a set date for having a new plant operating or for having a designated percent of a sales force call on customers in a new market. A TI executive explained: "We've experimented a lot, but the bottom line for any senior manager is the maxim that more than two objectives is no objective."

These companies have learned to focus quickly on problems. One method is to appoint a "czar" who has responsibility for one problem across the company. At Digital Equipment Corp. and Hewlett-Packard Co., for example, there are software czars, because customer demand for programming has become the key issue for the future growth of those companies. Du Pont Co., when it discovered it was spending $800 million a year on transportation set up a logistics czar. Other companies have productivity czars or energy czars with the power to override a manufacturing division's autonomy.

Another tool is the task force. But these companies tend to use the task

HOW 10 WELL-RUN COMPANIES PERFORMED IN 1979

| | Millions of dollars | | Percent | |
	Sales	Profits	Return on sales	Return on equity
IBM	$ 22,862.8	$ 3,011.3	14.8 %	21.6 %
Procter & Gamble	10,080.6	615.7	5.6	19.3
3M	5,440.3	655.2	12.2	24.4
Johnson & Johnson	4,211.6	352.1	6.5	19.6
Texas Instruments	3,224.1	172.9	5.1	19.2
Dana	2,789.0	165.8	6.1	19.3
Emerson Electric	2,749.9	208.8	7.5	21.5
Hewlett-Packard	2,361.0	203.0	8.2	18.1
Digital Equipment	2,031.6	207.5	9.7	19.7
McDonald's	1,937.9	188.6	8.7	22.5
BW composite of 1,200 companies			5.1	16.6

force in an unusual way. Task forces are authorized to fix things, not to generate reports and paper. At Digital Equipment, TI, HP, and 3M, task forces have a short duration, seldom more than ninety days. Says a Digital Equipment executive: "When we've got a big problem here, we grab ten senior guys and stick them in a room for a week. They come up with an answer and implement it." All members are volunteers, and they tend to be senior managers rather than junior people ordered to serve. Management espouses the busy-member theory: "We don't want people on task forces who want to become permanent task force members. We only put people on them who are so busy that their major objective is to get the problem solved and to get back to their main jobs." Every task force at TI is disbanded after its work is done, but within three months the senior operations committee formally reviews and assesses the results. TI demands that the managers who requested and ran the task force justify the time spent on it. If the task force turns out to have been useless, the manager is chided publicly, a painful penalty in TI's peer-conscious culture.

SIMPLE FORM AND LEAN STAFF

Although all ten of these companies are big—the smallest, McDonald's, has sales in excess of $1.9 billion—they are structured along "small is beautiful" lines. Emerson Electric, 3M, J&J, and HP are divided into small entrepreneurial units that—although smaller than economies of scale might suggest—manage to get things done. No HP division, for example, ever employs more than 1,200 people. TI, with ninety product customer centers, keeps each notably autonomous.

Within the units themselves, activities are kept to small, manageable groups. At Dana Corp., small teams work on productivity improvement. At the high-technology companies, small autonomous teams, headed by a product "champion," shepherd ideas through the corporate bureaucracy to ensure that they quickly receive attention from the top.

Staffs are also kept small to avoid bureaucracies. Fewer than 100 people help run Dana, a $3 billion corporation. Digital Equipment and Emerson are also noted for small staffs.

CLOSENESS TO THE CUSTOMER

The well-managed companies are customer driven—not technology driven, not product driven, not strategy driven. Constant contact with the customer provides insights that direct the company. Says one executive: "Where do you start? Not by poring over abstract market research. You start by getting out there with the customer." In a study of two fast-paced industries (scientific instruments and component manufacturing), Eric Von Hippel, associate professor at Massachusetts Institute of Technology, found that 100 percent of the major new product ideas—and eighty percent of the minor new product variations—came directly from customers.

At both IBM and Digital Equipment, top management spends at least 30 days a year conferring with top customers. No manager at IBM holds a staff job for more than three years, except in the legal, finance, and personnel departments. The reason: IBM believes that staff people are out of the mainstream because they do not meet with customers regularly.

Both companies use customer-satisfaction surveys to help determine management's compensation. Another company spends twelve percent of its research and development budget on sending engineers and scientists out to visit customers. One R&D chief spends two months each year with customers. At Lanier Business Products Inc., another fast growing company, the twenty most senior executives make sales calls every month.

Staying close to the customer means sales and service overkill. "Assistants to" at IBM are assigned to senior executives with the sole function of processing customer complaints within 24 hours. At Digital Equipment, J&J, IBM, and 3M, immense effort is expended to field an extraordinarily well-trained sales force. Caterpillar Tractor Co., another company considered to have excellent management, spends much of its managerial talent on efforts to make a reality of its motto, "24-hour parts delivery anywhere in the world."

These companies view the customer as an integral element of their businesses. A bank officer who started his career as a J&J accountant recalls that he was required to make customer calls even though he was in a financial department. The reason: to ensure that he understood the customer's perspective and could handle a proposal with empathy.

PRODUCTIVITY IMPROVEMENT VIA CONSENSUS

One way to get productivity increases is to install new capital equipment. But another method is often overlooked. Productivity can be improved by motivating and stimulating employees. One way to do that is to give them autonomy. At TI, shop floor teams set their own targets for production. In the years since the company has used this approach, executives say, workers have set goals that require them to stretch but that are reasonable and attainable.

The key is to motivate all of the people involved in each process. At 3M, for example, a team that includes technologists, marketers, production people, and financial types is formed early in a new product venture. It is self-sufficient and stays together from the inception to the national introduction. Although 3M is aware that this approach can lead to redundancy, it feels that the team spirit and motivation make it worthwhile.

Almost all of these companies use "corny" but effective methods to reward their workers. Badges, pins, and medals are all part of such recognition programs. Outstanding production teams at TI are invited to describe their successes to the board, as a form of recognition. Significantly, the emphasis is never only on monetary awards.

AUTONOMY TO ENCOURAGE ENTREPRENEURSHIP

A company cannot encourage entrepreneurship if it holds its managers on so tight a leash that they cannot make decisions. Well-managed companies authorize their managers to act like entrepreneurs. Dana, for one, calls this method the "store manager" concept. Plant managers are free to make purchasing decisions and to start productivity programs on their own. As a result, these managers develop unusual programs with results that far exceed those of a division or corporate staff. And the company has a grievance rate that is a fraction of the average reported by the United Auto Workers for all the plants it represents.

The successful companies rarely will force their managers to go against their own judgment. At 3M, TI, IBM, and J&J, decisions on product promotion are not based solely on market potential. An important factor in the decision is the zeal and drive of the volunteer who champions a product. Explains one executive at TI: "In every instance of a new product failure, we had forced someone into championing it involuntarily."

The divisional management is generally responsible for replenishing its new product array. In these well-managed companies, headquarters staff may not cut off funds for divisional products arbitrarily. What is more, the divisions are allowed to reinvest most of their earnings in their own operations. Although this flies in the face of the product-portfolio concept, which dictates that a corporate chief milk mature divisions to feed those with apparently greater growth potential, these companies recognize that entrepreneurs will not be developed in corporations that give the fruits of managers' labor to someone else.

Almost all these companies strive to place new products into separate startup divisions. A manager is more likely to be recognized—and promoted—for pushing a hot new product out of his division to enable it to stand on its own than he is for simply letting his own division get overgrown.

Possibly most important at these companies, entrepreneurs are both encouraged and honored at all staff levels. TI, for one, has created a special group of "listeners"—138 senior technical people called "individual contributors"—to assess new ideas. Junior staff members are particularly encouraged to bring their ideas to one of these individuals for a one-on-one evaluation. Each "contributor" has the authority to approve substantial startup funds ($20,000 to $30,000) for product experimentation. TI's successful Speak'n'Spell device was developed this way.

IBM's Fellows Program serves a similar purpose, although it is intended to permit proven senior performers to explore their ideas rather than to open communications lines for bright comers. Such scientists have at their beck and call thousands of IBM's technical people. The Fellows tend to be highly skilled gadflies, people who can shake things up—almost invariably for the good of the company.

The operating principle at well-managed companies is to do one thing well. At IBM, the all-pervasive value is customer service. At Dana it is productivity improvement. At 3M and HP, it is new product development. At P&G it is product quality. At McDonald's it is customer service—quality, cleanliness, and value.

STRESS ON A KEY BUSINESS VALUE

At all these companies, the values are pursued with an almost religious zeal by the chief executive officers. Rene McPherson, new dean of Stanford University's Graduate School of Business but until recently Dana's CEO, incessantly preached cost reduction and productivity improvement—and the company doubled its productivity in seven years. Almost to the day when Thomas Watson Jr. retired from IBM he wrote memos to the staff on the subject of calling on customers—even stressing the proper dress for the call. TI's ex-chairman Patrick Haggerty made it a point to drop in at a development laboratory on his way home each night when he was in Dallas. And in another company, where competitive position was the prime focus, one division manager wrote 700 memos to his subordinates one year, analyzing competitors.

Such single-minded focus on a value becomes a culture for the company. Nearly every IBM employee has stories about how he or she took great pains to solve a customer's problem. New product themes even dominate 3M and HP lunchroom conversations. Every operational review at HP focuses on new products, with a minimum amount of time devoted to financial results or projections—because President John Young has made it clear that he believes that proper implementation of new-product plans automatically creates the right numbers. In fact, Young makes it a point to start new employees in the new-product process and keep them there for a few years as part of a "socialization" pattern. "I don't care if they do come from the Stanford Business School," he says. "For a few years they get their hands dirty, or we are not interested." At McDonald's the company's values are drummed into employees at Hamburger U., a training program every employee goes through.

As the employees who are steeped in the corporate culture move up the ladder, they become role models for newcomers, and the process continues. It is possibly best exemplified by contrast. American Telephone & Telegraph Co., which recently began to develop a marketing orientation, has been hamstrung in its efforts because of a lack of career telephone executives with marketing successes. When Archie J. McGill was hired from IBM to head AT&T's marketing, some long-term employees balked at his leadership because he "wasn't one of them," and so was not regarded as a model.

Another common pitfall for companies is the sending of mixed signals to line managers. One company has had real problems introducing new products despite top management's constant public stress on innovation—simply because line managers perceived the real emphasis to be on cost-cutting. They viewed top management as accountants who refused to invest or to take risks, and they consistently proposed imitative products. At another company, where the CEO insisted that his major thrust was new products, an analysis of how he spent his time over a three-month period showed that no more than 5 percent of his efforts were directed to new products. His stated emphasis therefore was not credible. Not surprisingly, his employees never picked up the espoused standard.

Too many messages, even when sincerely meant, can cause the same problem. One CEO complained that no matter how hard he tried to raise what he regarded as an unsatisfactory quality level he was unsuccessful. But when McKinsey questioned his subordinates, they said, "Of course he's for quality, but he's for everything else, too. We have a theme a month here." The outstanding companies, in contrast, have one theme and stick to it.

STICKING TO WHAT THEY KNOW BEST

Robert W. Johnson, the former chairman of J&J, put it this way: "Never acquire any business you don't know how to run." Edward G. Harness, CEO at P&G, says, "This company has never left its base." All of the successful companies have been able to define their strengths—marketing, customer contact, new product innovation, low-cost manufacturing—and then build on them. They have resisted the temptation to move into new businesses that look attractive but require corporate skills they do not have.

SIMULTANEOUS LOOSE-TIGHT CONTROLS

While this may sound like a contradiction, it is not. The successful companies control a few variables tightly, but allow flexibility and looseness in others. 3M uses return on sales and number of employees as yardsticks for control. Yet it gives management lots of leeway in day-to-day operations. When McPherson became president of Dana, he threw out all of the company's policy manuals and substituted a one-page philosophy statement and a control system that required divisions to report costs and revenues on a daily basis.

IBM probably has the classic story about flexible controls. After the company suffered well-publicized and costly problems with its System 360 computer several years ago—problems that cost hundreds of millions of dollars to fix—Watson ordered Frank T. Cary, then a vice-president, to incorporate a system of checks and balances in new-product testing. The system made IBM people so cautious that they stopped taking risks. When Cary became president of IBM, one of the first things he did to reverse that attitude was to loosen some of the controls. He recognized that the new system would indeed prevent such an expensive problem from ever happening again, but its rigidity would also keep IBM from ever developing another major system.

By sticking to these eight basics, the successful companies have achieved better-than-average growth. Their managements are able not only to change but also to change quickly. They keep their sights aimed externally at their customers and competitors, and not on their own financial reports.

Excellence in management takes brute perseverance—time, repetition, and simplicity. The tools include plant visits, internal memos, and focused systems. Ignoring these rules may mean that the company slowly loses its vitality, its growth flattens, and its competitiveness is lost.

Reading 2

Overcoming Organizational Defenses

Chris Argyris

Summary prepared by Jean A. Grube

Jean A. Grube is a Lecturer in Management at the University of Wisconsin, Madison, where she received her Ph.D. Her current research interests include organizational commitment, stress and coping behaviors, and organizational change.

Managers have long focused on morale, satisfaction, and loyalty as foundations for the achievement of organizational excellence. A more realistic base for excellence may come from organizational members' *learning* (how to detect and correct organizational errors), *competence* (solving problems such that they remain solved and increase the members' ability to solve future problems), and *justice* (promoting values about organizational health that are applicable to all organizational members). These are the underpinnings for *Overcoming Organizational Defenses*.

Although the concept of organizational defenses is not a new one, approaches to understanding how and why such defenses develop have historically focused primarily on *first-order errors*—those caused by "not knowing." This book is directed at understanding how organizational defenses develop from *second-order errors*—those errors that humans actively design and produce.

We need to examine managerial activities that belie sound management practice (puzzles) and how they result from defensive reasoning. It is important to understand how and why defensive reasoning develops in organizational members, and which activities are used to routinize defensiveness and ensure its survival in organizations. Interestingly, the usual help procedures (e.g., consulting practices and organizational surveys) actually compound the problem. Specific advice for dealing with organizational defensiveness (Model II) is needed. New mindsets about management are needed if Model II theories-in-use are to survive in organizations. Organizational defenses and their potential contribution to the "ethical pollution" in organizations must be examined continually.

PUZZLES

The actions of modern management are characterized by *puzzles* that depict weaknesses of modern management behavior. Individuals engage in activities that produce and proliferate errors, even when the results run counter to what they say they want and to what they believe reflects sound management. If organizational players are free to choose activities and elect to choose those that are contrary to good management, then defensive reasoning must be taking place.

According to Argyris, *defensive reasoning* occurs when individuals: (1) hold premises the validity of which is questionable yet they think it is not; (2) make inferences that do not necessarily follow from the premises yet they think they do; and (3) reach conclusions that they believe they have tested carefully yet they have not because the way they have been framed makes them untestable. Defensive reasoning is caused by programs in individuals' heads that are skillfully deployed to deal with errors that are embarrassing or threatening. Utilization of these mental managerial programs results in the creation of organizational defense routines, and activities used to protect the defensive routines emerge as a self-sealing device.

To understand how and why organizational members develop these programs, one must consider the issue of skilled incompetence.

HUMAN THEORIES OF CONTROL: SKILLED INCOMPETENCE

Skilled incompetence has its origins in the fact that human beings seek to be in control of their actions because they feel good when they are able to produce intended results. When faced with situations that could lead to lack of control (i.e., embarrassing or threatening conditions), people look for guidelines to direct their actions. Two programs that exist in the minds of individuals serve as guidelines. The first program, *espoused theories of action,* is comprised of the beliefs and values people hold about how to manage their lives. The second program, *theories-in-use,* contains rules people use to manage their beliefs.

Most people follow a *Model I* theory-in-use which directs them to achieve unilateral control, to win, and to suppress negative feelings. Such theories-in-use are learned at an early age and are supported by such social virtues as caring, helping, and respecting others. Model I action strategies include selling, persuading, and face-saving. Some of these strategies are counterproductive. For example, people tell "little white lies" to salvage another person's pride (face-saving). This requires people to (1) bypass the errors others make, and act as if they are not making errors because one can only save another's face by not revealing what is happening; (2) make the bypass undiscussable, because errors cannot be bypassed successfully if others discuss it, and (3) make the undiscussability of the undiscussable also undiscussable. Consequently, important thoughts and feelings are not communicated honestly and fully by organizational members. This pattern leads to misunderstandings and distortions making it unlikely that managers or others will be able to detect and correct errors. Ironically, Model I strategies require great skill at doing counterproductive things (e.g., it is difficult to change the mind of an individual without upsetting him or her) and hence are illustrated by the term *skilled incompetence.*

Although such strategies are counterproductive, they are repeated because they have become automatic, spontaneous, and taken for granted by organizational members. Furthermore, such actions are supported by a society that sees giving approval, offering praise, and deferring to others as virtues. Skilled incompetence becomes even more counterproductive when routinized in organizations.

ORGANIZATIONAL DEFENSIVE ROUTINES

Because most individuals' actions are guided by Model I theories-in-use, these activities become organizational norms. Subsequently, *organizational defensive routines* (actions or policies that are established to protect individuals or segments of the organization from experiencing embarrassment or threat) develop. Managers and other organizational members construct the framework for these defensive routines in accordance with Model I: (1) messages are crafted that contain inconsistencies, and yet, individuals act as if the messages are not inconsistent; (2) the inconsistencies of the message are made undiscussable; (3) the undiscussability of the undiscussable is also made undiscussable.

Defenses present a "double bind" for many organizational members. They recognize that organizational performance will suffer if they are not able to discuss errors. However, they find it difficult to change defensive routines because "opening this can of worms" invokes more defensive routines, thus worsening the situation. So they continue to massage the truth, which serves to reinforce and proliferate defenses. The actions becoming self-fulfilling and self-sealing.

How do individuals live with this "double bind"? Many do not, which may be the most fundamental cause of burnout and turnover in upper level management. Others rely on fancy footwork in order to live with their inconsistencies.

FANCY FOOTWORK AND MALAISE

To deal with the "double bind," some organizational members use *fancy footwork* (actions that permit them to ignore inconsistencies in their actions, deny that inconsistencies exist, or place the blame on other people). Eventually, a sense of malaise develops in which members recognize that fancy footwork permeates the organization but feel helpless to change it. There are three symptoms associated with *organizational malaise*. First, members seek and find fault with the organization but do not accept responsibility for correcting its failures. Second, individuals begin to accentuate and magnify negative aspects of the organization. In fact, they find pleasure in doing so because it helps them to justify their own distancing and helplessness behaviors. Finally, people espouse values that everyone knows cannot be implemented. Because they are never implemented they eventually lose credibility.

The result of skilled incompetence, organizational defensive routines, fancy footwork, and malaise is an *organizational defensive pattern (ODP)*. ODP is generic to all human organization and, unfortunately, traditional techniques are ineffective in reducing its effects.

SOUND ADVICE: IT COMPOUNDS THE PROBLEM

If executives who want to deal with ODP followed the advice of the "best and the brightest," they would find themselves in trouble for a variety of reasons. Management consultants, for instance, rarely deal with ODP. When they do, the advice is too abstract to be of help. The vast majority of leadership books focus on "espoused theories" and, therefore, offer little in the way of correcting the actual behaviors that are guided by theory-in-use. Similarly, problems occur when solutions are sought through organizational surveys, because respondents reply based on their espoused theories of action.

Another problem with advice is that it can reinforce errors and organizational defensive routines. For example, management literature advises that feedback be obtained in a manner that allows subordinates not to worry about negative consequences of being honest. However, the very act of using a third "trusted" party reinforces that subordinates cannot be honest with their supervisors in situations that may be threatening or cause embarrassment. Actions like these further justify defensive routines.

For advice to be implementable or enactable, it must possess certain characteristics. First, it must show *causality* (engaging in this behavior will produce these results). Second, advice must be *concrete* (this is exactly what must be done). Finally, the advice must *make explicit the values* that govern the suggested actions (this action is suggested so that I can monitor the outcome of my decision). Conventional advice does not meet these criteria.

REDUCING THE ORGANIZATIONAL DEFENSE PATTERN

If traditional techniques are ineffective, what should managers do to reduce ODP? The answer lies in double-loop learning.

Model I theory-in-use is characterized as a *single-loop model* because it focuses on the presenting problem (symptom) and does not direct attention to the cause. Consequently, it is only a matter of time before the problem resurfaces. To correct ODP, the initial values that governed the actions that led to errors must be changed. This is termed *double-loop learning*. To sustain double-loop learning, an organization's managers must develop a culture that rewards individuals who learn how to divorce themselves from Model I actions that contribute to ODP. In essence, a new theory-in-use model *(Model II)* must be taught.

To learn new actions for handling situations that are embarrassing or threatening, organizational members must first see how they presently deal with problems under such conditions. Next, the individuals must be shown how these actions are counterproductive. Third, individuals are taught how to use Model II as a theory-in-use and are encouraged to practice this step. Finally, these three steps are repeated for each new problem that arises.

The values governing Model II theory-in-use are valid information, informed choice, and responsibility for evaluating the quality of choice implementation. The actions that flow from Model II are those that invite inquiry into one's stated position and minimize face-saving behaviors. Model II assumes that productive reasoning is occurring; individuals make clear to others what premises and inferences they are using, they develop conclusions that others can test, and they actively look for inconsistencies in their own logic and invite others to do the same. This necessarily means that members must openly deal with organizational defensive routines, fancy footwork, and malaise. Otherwise, Model II theory-in-use cannot survive.

MAKING THE NEW THEORY OF MANAGING HUMAN PERFORMANCE COME TRUE

There are other compelling reasons why Model II theory-in-use must become a reality in organizations. Over the last twenty years, a new theory of managing human performance has evolved. It focuses on employee energy and initiative that can be tapped through the experience of psychological success. It emphasizes the need for commitment and involvement over more traditional values of unilateral control, dependency, and submissiveness. However, some suggest that this new management approach will bring with it new contradictions and dilemmas. Furthermore, some learning through trial and error will naturally occur as managers shift away from a more traditional view of managing employees. This implies that embarrassing and threatening situations will occur which invites ODP to develop. Unless a Model II theory-in-use is utilized, it is difficult to envision how nontraditional management practices can survive.

GETTING FROM HERE TO THERE

How can managers move organizational members from Model I to Model II? Several modes can facilitate the transition. Although there are variations, all modes have features in common. An organizational member writes a case that depicts a particular problem and how he or she responded. Guided by professionals, other participants review the case and offer insights into how the actions contributed to ODP and what corrective actions are available. A six-step procedure can help individuals overcome organizational defenses.

1. Diagnose the problem.
2. Connect the diagnosis to the actual behavior of participants.
3. Show participants how their behavior creates organizational defenses.
4. Help them change their behavior.
5. Change the defensive routine that reinforced the old behavior.
6. Develop new organizational norms and culture that reinforce the new behavior.

UPPING THE ANTE

Some managers are able to ignore or deny the existence of ODP because the building of, and negative consequences associated with, these defenses is an insidious process. Additionally, managers introduce activities that attempt to minimize the likelihood of embarrassment or threat. One such activity is to objectify methods for monitoring actions of the organization in order to minimize the effects of the human element. However, since humans have to implement the systems, such "correcting" methods ultimately fail. Another strategy is to create greater tolerance for embarrassment and threat in organizational members through the development of involvement and internal commitment (the nontraditional management practice). The assumption is that individuals who are more involved and committed will show more initiative for detecting and correcting errors. The problem with such an approach is that it is difficult to use as a foundation for a major organizational strategy, and it does not take into account the ingenious ways that members seek to protect themselves when they encounter situations of threat or embarrassment.

For new management practices to be successful, a new mindset is necessary. There are four activities that will promote the mindset needed to foster new management approaches. First, members must stop taking for granted what is taken for granted (i.e., they must learn to examine more carefully what they assume is obvious). Second, members must make learning as sacred as they make other activities or policies (e.g., such as the policy of face-saving). Third, members must evaluate how they contribute to ODP and accept individual responsibility for reducing defenses in the organization. Finally, members must come to understand that productive reasoning is as critical for human problems as it is for those technical in nature.

ETHICS AND THE ORGANIZATIONAL DEFENSES PATTERN

Many have cited openness and trust as critical to ethical behavior in organizations. By engaging in cover-up behaviors, organizational members may unknowingly be contributing to the "ethical pollution" in organizations. The solution lies within each manager as each must learn to manage and accept responsibility for his or her own actions and help the organization develop rewards for this self-responsible behavior.

The Fifth Discipline

Peter Senge

Summary prepared by Dorothy Marcic

Dorothy Marcic is Professor of Management in the graduate program at Metropolitan State University in Minneapolis, where she teaches organizational behavior and strategy. In addition, she has conducted over 350 training programs for managers. Her doctorate is from the University of Massachusetts in Amherst and she is the author of 12 books, including *Organizational Behavior: Experiences and Cases* and *Management International*, both from West Publishing.

Learning disabilities can be fatal to organizations, causing them to have an average life span of only 40 years—half a human being's life. *Organizations need to be learners, and often they aren't.* Somehow some survive, but never live up to their potential. What happens if what we term "excellence" is really no more than mediocrity? Only those firms which become learners will succeed in the increasingly turbulent, competitive global market.

LEARNING DISABILITIES

There are seven learning disabilities common to organizations.

Identification with One's Position   American workers are trained to see themselves as what they do, not who they are. Therefore, if laid off, they find it difficult, if not impossible, to find work doing something else. Worse for the organization, though, is the limited thinking this attitude creates. By claiming an identity related to the job, workers are cut off from seeing how their responsibility connects to other jobs. For example, one American car had three assembly bolts on one component. The similar Japanese make had only one bolt. Why? Because the Detroit manufacturer had three engineers for that component, while a similar Japanese manufacturer had only one.

External Enemies   This belief is a result of the previously-stated disability. External enemies refers to people focusing blame on anything but themselves or their unit. Fault is regularly blamed on factors like the economy, the weather, or the government. Marketing blames manufacturing, and manufacturing blames engineering. Such external fault-finding keeps the organization from seeing what the real problems are, and prevents them from tackling the real the issues head-on.

The Illusion of Taking Charge   Being proactive is seen as good management—doing something about "those problems." All too often, though, being proactive is a disguise for reactiveness against that awful enemy out there.

The Fixation on Events   Much attention in organizations is paid to events— last month's sales, the new product, who just got hired, and so on. Our society, too, is geared toward short-term thinking, which in turn stifles the type of generative learning that permits a look at the real threats—the slowly declining processes of quality, service or design.

The Parable of the Boiled Frog   An experiment was once conducted by placing a frog in boiling water. Immediately the frog, sensing danger in the extreme heat, jumped out to safety. However, placing the frog in cool water and slowly turning up the heat resulted in the frog getting groggier and groggier and finally boiling to death. Why? Because the frog's survival mechanisms are programmed to look for sudden changes in the environment, and not to gradual changes. Similarly, during the 1960s, the U.S. auto industry saw no threat by Japan, which had only four percent of the market. Not until the 1980s when Japan had over twenty-one percent of the market did the Big Three begin to look at their core assumptions. Now with Japan holding about thirty percent share of the market, it is not certain if this frog (U.S. automakers) is capable of jumping out of the boiling water. Looking at gradual processes requires slowing down our frenetic pace and watching for the subtle cues.

The Delusion of Learning from Experience   Learning from experience is powerful. This is how we learn to walk and talk. However, we now live in a time when direct consequences of actions may take months or years to appear. Decisions in R & D may take up to a decade to bear fruit and their actual consequences may be influenced by manufacturing and marketing along the way. Organizations often choose to deal with these complexities by breaking themselves up into smaller and smaller components, further reducing their ability to see problems in their entirety.

The Myth of the Management Team   Most large organizations have a group of bright, experienced leaders who are supposed to know all the answers. They were trained to believe there are answers to all problems and they should find them. People are rarely rewarded for bringing up difficult issues or for looking at parts of a problem which make it harder to grasp. Most teams end up operating below the lowest IQ of any member. What results are "skilled incompetents"—people who know all too well how to keep *from* learning.

SYSTEMS THINKING

There are five disciplines required for a learning organization: personal mastery, mental models, shared vision, team learning, and systems thinking. The fifth one, systems thinking, is the most important. Without systems thinking, the other disciplines do not have the same effect.

The Laws of the Fifth Discipline

Today's problems result from yesterday's solutions.   A carpet merchant kept pushing down a bump in the rug, only to have it reappear elsewhere, until he lifted a corner and out slithered a snake. Sometimes fixing one part of the system only brings difficulties to other parts of the system. For example, solving an internal inventory problem may lead to angry customers who now get late shipments.

Push hard and the system pushes back even harder.   Systems theory calls this compensating feedback, which is a common way of reducing the effects of an intervention. Some cities, for example, built low-cost housing and set up jobs programs, only to have more poor people than ever. Why? Because many moved to the cities from neighboring areas so that they, too, could take advantage of the low-cost housing and job opportunities.

Behavior gets better before it gets worse.   Some decisions actually look good in the short term, but produce *compensating feedback* and crisis in the end. The really effective decisions often produce difficulties in the short run, but create more health in the long term. This is why behaviors such as building a power base or working hard just to please the boss come back to haunt you.

The best way out is to go back in.   We often choose familiar solutions, ones that feel comfortable and not scary. But the effective ways often mean going straight into what we are afraid of facing. What does *not* work is pushing harder on the same old solutions (also called the "what we need here is a bigger hammer" syndrome).

The cure can be worse than the disease.   The result of applying non-systematic solutions to problems is the need for more and more of the same. It can become addictive. Someone begins mild drinking to alleviate work tension. The individual feels better and then takes on more work, creating more tension and a need for more alcohol, and the person finally becomes an alcoholic. Sometimes these types of solutions only result in shifting the burden. The government enters the scene by providing more welfare and leaves the host system weaker and less able to solve its own problems. This ultimately necessitates still more aid from the government. Companies can try to shift their burdens to consultants, but then become more and more dependent on them to solve their problems.

Faster is slower.   Every system, whether ecological or organizational, has an optimal rate of growth. Faster and faster is not always better. (After all, the tortoise finally did win the race.) Complex human systems require new ways of thinking. Quickly jumping in and fixing what *looks* bad usually provides solutions for a problem's symptoms and not for the problem itself.

Cause and effect are not always related closely in time and space. *Effects* here mean the symptoms we see, such as drug abuse and unemployment, while *causes* mean the interactions of the underlying system which bring about these conditions. We often assume cause is near to effect. If there is a sales problem, then incentives for the sales force should fix it, or if there is inadequate housing, then build more houses. Unfortunately, this does not often work, for the real causes lie elsewhere.

Tiny changes may produce big results; areas of greatest leverage are frequently the least obvious.   System science teaches that the most obvious solutions usually don't work. While simple solutions frequently make short-run improvements, they commonly contribute to long-term deteriorations. The *non-*obvious and *well-focused* solutions are more likely to provide leverage and bring positive change. For example, ships have a tiny trim tab on one edge of the rudder that has great influence on the movement of that ship, so small changes in the trim tab bring big shifts in the ship's course. However, there are no simple rules for applying leverage to organizations. It requires looking for the structure of what is going on rather than merely seeing the events.

You can have your cake and eat it too—but not at the same time. Sometimes the most difficult problems come from "snapshot" rather than "process" thinking. For example, it was previously believed by American manufacturers that quality and low cost could not be achieved simultaneously. One had to be chosen over the other. What was missed, however, was the notion that improving quality may also mean eliminating waste and unnecessary time (both adding costs), which in the end would mean lower costs. Real leverage comes when it can be seen that seemingly opposing needs can be met over time.

Cutting the elephant in half does not create two elephants.   Some problems can be solved by looking at parts of the organization, while others require holistic thinking. What is needed is an understanding of the boundaries for each problem. Unfortunately, most organizations are designed to prevent people from seeing systemic problems, either by creating rigid structures, or by leaving problems behind for others to clean up.

There is no blame.   Systems thinking teaches that there are not outside causes to problems; instead, you and your "enemy" are part of the same system. Any cure requires understanding how that is seen.

THE OTHER DISCIPLINES

Personal Mastery

Organizations can learn only when the individuals involved learn. This requires personal mastery, which is the discipline of personal learning and growth, where people are continually expanding their ability to create the kind of life they want. From their quest comes the spirit of the learning organization.

Personal mastery involves seeing one's life as a creative work, being able to clarify what is really important, and learning to see current reality more clearly. The difference between what's important, what we want, and where we are now produces a "creative tension." Personal mastery means being able to generate and maintain creative tension.

Those who have high personal mastery have a vision which is more like a calling, and they are in a continual learning mode. They never really "arrive." Filled with more commitment, they take initiative and greater responsibility in their work.

Previously, organizations supported an employee's development only if it would help the organization, which fits in with the traditional "contract" between employee and organization ("an honest day's pay in exchange for an honest day's work"). The new, and coming, way is to see it rather as a "covenant," which comes from a shared vision of goals, ideas, and management processes.

Working towards personal mastery requires living with emotional tension, not letting our goals get eroded. As Somerset Maugham said, "Only mediocre people are always at their best." One of the worst blocks to achieving personal mastery is the common belief that we cannot have what we want. Being committed to the truth is a powerful weapon against this, for it does not allow us to deceive ourselves. Another means of seeking personal mastery is to integrate our reason and intuition. We live in a society which values reason and devalues intuition. However, using both together is very powerful and may be one of the fundamental contributions to systems thinking.

Mental Models

Mental models are internal images of how the world works, and they can range from simple generalizations (people are lazy) to complex theories (assumptions about why my co-workers interact they way they do). For example, for decades the Detroit automakers believed people bought cars mainly for styling, not for quality or reliability. These beliefs, which were really unconscious assumptions, worked well for many years, but ran into trouble when competition from Japan began. It took a long time for Detroit even to begin to see the mistakes in their beliefs. One company which managed to change its mental model through incubating a business worldview was Shell.

Traditional hierarchical organizations have the dogma of organizing, managing and controlling. In the new learning organization, though, the revised "dogma" will be values, vision and mental models.

Hanover Insurance began changes in 1969 designed to overcome the "basic diseases of the hierarchy." Three values espoused were:

1. *openness*—seen as an antidote to the dysfunctional interactions in face-to-face meetings
2. *merit,* or making decisions based on the good of the organization—seen as the antidote to decision-making by organizational politics
3. *localness*—the antidote to doing the dirty stuff the boss doesn't want to do.

Chris Argyris and colleagues developed "action science" as a means for reflecting on the reasoning underlying our actions. This helps people change the defensive routines which lead them to skilled incompetence. Similarly, John Beckett created a course on the historical survey of main philosophies of thought, East and West, as a sort of "sandpaper on the brain." These ideas exposed managers to their own assumptions and mental models, and provided other ways to view the world.

Shared Vision

A shared vision is not an idea. Rather it is a force in people's hearts, a sense of purpose which provides energy and focus for learning. Visions are often exhilarating. Shared vision is important because it may be the beginning step to get people who mistrusted each other to start working together. Abraham Maslow studied high-performing teams and found that they had shared vision. Shared visions can mobilize courage so naturally that people don't even know the extent of their strength. When John Kennedy created the shared vision in 1961 of putting a man on the moon by the end of the decade, only fifteen percent of the technology had been created. Yet it led to numerous acts of daring and courage.

Learning organizations are not achievable without shared vision. Without that incredible pull toward the deeply felt goal, the forces of *status quo* will overwhelm the pursuit. As Robert Fritz once said, "In the presence of greatness, pettiness disappears." Conversely, in the absence of a great vision, pettiness is supreme.

Strategic planning often does not involve building a shared vision, but rather announcing the vision of top management, asking people to, at best, enroll, and, at worst, to comply. What Senge talks of is gaining commitment from people. This is done by taking a personal vision and building it into a shared vision. In the traditional hierarchical organization, compliance is one of the desired outcomes. For learning organizations, commitment must be the key goal. Shared vision, though, is not possible without personal mastery, which is needed to foster continued commitment to a lofty goal.

Team Learning

Bill Russell of the Boston Celtics wrote about being on a team of specialists whose performance depended on one another's individual excellence and how well they worked together. Sometimes that created a feeling of magic. He is talking about *alignment,* where a group functions as a whole unit, rather than as individuals working at cross purposes. When a team is aligned, its energies are focused and harmonized. They do not need to sacrifice their own interests. Instead, alignment occurs when the shared vision becomes an extension of the personal vision. Alignment is a necessary condition to empower others and ultimately empower the team.

Never before today has there been greater need for mastering team learning, which requires mastering both dialogue and discussion. *Dialogue* involves a creative and free search of complex and even subtle issues, while *discussion* implies different views being presented and defended. Both skills are useful, but most teams cannot tell the difference between the two. The purpose of dialogue is to increase individual understanding. Here, assumptions are suspended and participants regard one another as on the same level. *Discussion,* on the other hand, comes from the same root word as *percussion* and *concussion* and involves a sort of verbal ping-pong game whose object is winning. Although this is a useful technique, it must be balanced with dialogue. A continued emphasis on winning is not compatible with the search for truth and coherence.

One of the major blocks to healthy dialogue and discussion is what Chris Argyris calls *defensive routines.* These are habitual styles of interacting that protect us from threat or embarrassment. These include the avoidance of conflict (smoothing over) and the feeling that one has to appear competent and to know the answers at all times.

Team learning, like any other skill, requires practice. Musicians and athletes understand this principle. Work teams need to learn that lesson as well.

OTHER ISSUES

Organizational politics is a perversion of truth, yet most people are so accustomed to it, they don't even notice it anymore. A learning organization is not possible in such an environment. In order to move past the politics, one thing needed is openness—both speaking openly and honestly about the real and important issues, and being willing to challenge one's own way of thinking.

Localness, too, is essential to the learning organization, for decisions need to be pushed down the organizational hierarchy in order to unleash people's commitment. This gives them the freedom to act.

One thing lacking in many organizations is time to reflect and think. If someone is sitting quietly, we assume they are not busy and we feel free to interrupt. Many managers, however, are too busy to "just think." This should not be blamed on the tumultuous environment of many crises. Research suggests that, even when given ample time, managers still do not devote any of it to adequate reflection. Therefore, habits need to be changed, as well as how we structure our days.

PART
FOUR

Organizational Strategy

Many of the authors in this book have suggested that organizations can benefit by defining their own standard of effectiveness, especially after examining other successful firms. An organization's external environment has a powerful influence on organizational success and needs to be monitored for significant trends and influential forces. In addition, effective executives need to recognize when internal changes are necessary to adapt to the external environment.

The two readings in this section are designed to stimulate thinking about strategic management through a focus on the management and leadership of the internal environment, and the management of the organization relative to its external context.

Taken collectively, these two readings suggest that organizations can (and should) proactively *take control of their destinies.* One way of doing this is by articulating and following a set of organizational strategies and plans that can systematically guide them into the future and help deal with current affairs. In effect, managers are urged to have a master plan that defines their mission, identifies their unique environmental niche, builds on their strengths, and adapts to changing needs.

The two authors whose work is summarized here are Harold J. Leavitt, the Walter Kilpatrick Professor of Organizational Behavior in the Graduate School of Business at Stanford University, and Michael E. Porter, Professor in the Harvard Business School.

Harold J. Leavitt contends that today's leaders lack creativity and a visionary sense of purpose. Instead, they assume a rational, analytical, and control-oriented management style. In his book, *Corporate Pathfinders: Building Vision and Values into Organizations,* Leavitt looks into the leadership styles and forms of management that will be needed to cope effectively with the future. Pathfinding, problem solving, and implementing represent three different managerial thinking styles. According to Leavitt, the effective manager is capable of moving across these three styles as situational demands dictate. Along with advocating leadership flexibility, development of a pathfinding approach to leadership is a major focus of Leavitt's work.

Michael Porter's book, *Competitive Advantage: Creating and Sustaining Superior Performance,* received the 1986 George R. Terry book award. (*Competitive Advantage* is a follow-up to Porter's earlier book *Competitive Strategy;* he also is the author of *Competitive Advantage of Nations.*) Porter argues that firms will receive above-average profits by synthesizing and applying their unique strengths effectively within their industry. They can do this either through creating a cost advantage, or by differentiating a product or service from that of their competitors. The key, which some firms seemingly ignore, is to link strategy formulation successfully with strategy implementation. Porter encourages managers to study their industry in depth, to select a source of competitive advantage, to develop a set of strategies that adapt the firm to its external environment, and to draw on their executive leadership talents.

Corporate Pathfinders: Building Vision and Values Into Organizations

Harold J. Leavitt

Summary by Thomas A. Kolenko

Thomas A. Kolenko is an Associate Professor of Management at Kennesaw State College, where he teaches organizational behavior and human resource management. He received his Ph.D. from the University of Wisconsin, Madison, after several management positions within General Motors Corporation. His research and consulting interests have been focused in the areas of person-job matching, strategic human resource planning, and executive self-management.

Today's executives and the aspiring leaders of tomorrow can profit personally and professionally from an awareness of three critical thinking styles and how these influence managerial effectiveness and success. American managers must learn to balance *pathfinding, problem solving,* and *implementation* thinking styles in order to be effective in the competitive business world. Leavitt contends that we must be able to describe adequately and understand our managerial thinking styles and patterns or we will be handicapped in our ability to lead others effectively in organizational settings.

Leavitt provides a concise integration of three streams of leadership thought that have guided managerial action for decades. The richness of this contribution lies in its straightforward discussion of how CEOs think and how they have been taught to think. Following the currently popular "transformational" approach to personal leadership, Leavitt contends that today's leaders lack creativity and a visionary sense of purpose. Instead, they focus and rely on rational, analytical, and control-oriented leadership styles.

The corporate pathfinder style is clearly championed as the leadership

---

Harold J. Leavitt, *Corporate Pathfinders,* Homewood, IL: Dow Jones-Irwin, 1986.

style capable of maximizing employee effort and organizational commitment. Leavitt begins by investigating the complexity of the management process and its requisite cognitive components. From this foundation, pathfinders and pathfinding needs are developed as leadership tools for the 1990s. Last, the scope and role of a pathfinder's influence is extended to the organizational level by discussing the development and maintenance of pathfinding cultures over time.

MANAGEMENT PROCESS MIX

According to Leavitt, the management process is composed of three different managerial thinking styles: pathfinding, problem solving, and implementing. These three components represent an integrative perspective for addressing the functions of the executive. Effective managers are seen as flexible and capable of moving across the three styles depending on the characteristics and requirements of the situation.

PATHFINDERS

Pathfinding is the critical focus of this book. This major function depends on the leader's ability to clarify a mission within an organization based on his or her beliefs, sensitivity to values, and aesthetics. The spotlight here is on vision, purpose, and direction. In business, pathfinders have typically been entrepreneurs and company founders.

Pathfinding is defended as the leadership style most responsible for innovation, risk taking, and the development of competitive advantage in organizations. The pathfinding style is also asserted to be congruent with our heritage as Americans. However, a total pathfinding focus can invite anarchy, whenever the practical and realistic options are ignored.

If pathfinders are to become the key managerial types for the 1990s, how can organizations nurture this dimension in their leadership ranks? Can pathfinding be taught in business schools? Where should pathfinding exist within an organization's structure—at all levels and by all managers, or only in designated creativity zones or positions? These questions summarize Leavitt's agenda for developing an understanding of the powerful force this style exerts on the overall managerial process. Pathfinding is clearly portrayed as the managerial key to effective leadership in the 1990s.

PROBLEM SOLVING AND IMPLEMENTING

Problem solving and implementing are integral parts of the managerial process and provide a contrast to the pathfinder's driving sense of mission. The Modern American Business School is held accountable for the recent devotion to analysis, the dominant skill anchoring the problem-solving style. The problem-solving style emphasizes the search for rational, quantitative solutions to organizational problems, ignoring the action requirements or emotional prerequisites surrounding change. As a consequence, problem solving provides a comfort zone for most MBAs, and is the most widely preferred solution used by American management.

Implementing proponents of managerial implementation believe that human emotionality is the spark driving all change. They rely on persuasion, inspiration, negotiation, and other emotional "tools" to make things happen through people. This action focus is about doing, influencing, directing, and changing. This should not be confused with a problem solver's focus on analysis.

CRITICAL STYLE LINKAGES

Over time, executives develop combinations of managerial thinking styles that seem to help them satisfy job and organizational demands. Short-term organizational reward systems and prerequisites further reinforce the CEOs' faith in their existing thinking styles, and the linkages between them. The most familiar linkage—that of problem solving and implementing—has been reinforced by consultants, executives, and academics as the most rational method for turning plans into actions. Alfred P. Sloan's concept of decentralization, management by objectives (MBO), and the development of matrix-structured organizations are strong historical referents to this process.

Leavitt develops a forceful argument that executives' linkages with the pathfinding style have traditionally been the weakest, yet these will become the most important leadership requirements in the competitive, uncertain environments of the future. The pathfinding/problem-solving connection is described as a search for a rational imagination *and* imaginative rationality in leadership. Entrepreneurs and inventor-founders are profiled as leaders struggling to balance pathfinding's start-up excitement with problem-solving stability and control requirements. This represents their major leadership challenge.

The pathfinding-implementing connection is seen as an application of individualism in an increasingly group-oriented, participative work environment. A considerable paradox exists when this linkage advocates strong, assertive, charismatic leadership to forge an atmosphere of participation and cooperation for meeting corporate goals.

PATHFINDING: DEFINING THE RIGHT STUFF

The concept of pathfinding focuses on a style of thinking that stresses divergent, proactive, intuitive, and imaginative approaches to managerial action. Pathfinders exhibit three important and distinguishing attributes: vision, strong and clear value systems, and a determination to convert their visions into realities.

Vision describes a leader's reasonably clear image of a desirable future state for his or her organization. It is built by using imagination and creativity tempered by the wisdom acquired from encounters with the objective realities of the past. Professional socialization and rigid educational experiences often penalize creativity and imagination early in a manager's development. Persuasive evidence suggests that such shaping and censuring activities are very effective, but these need to be counteracted in order for a sense of vision to return to today's managers.

Values are also central to the makeup of pathfinders. Strong, clear beliefs mark the boundaries between what is important and what is trivial. As personal guidelines, values provide the internal control system to distinguish right from wrong in the strategic solutions that a pathfinder may develop. Effective personal leadership depends on clearly communicated values to guide organizational activities on a daily basis.

Determination is the attribute that pathfinders rely on most to convert their own visions into corporate realities. This commitment to follow through must always culminate in action toward problem solutions. Thinking and discourse are not enough for true pathfinders. Blind tenacity has its costs, of course, and consequently fanatical commitment is not enough. It must be tempered with the social awareness that effective managers depend on the efforts of others to accomplish their missions.

Pathfinding leadership is built on the complex interaction of all three attributes. Each attribute, when either deficient or present in excess, cripples the manager's overall ability to lead. Thus, pathfinding depends on self-regulation and self-control.

DEVELOPING PATHFINDERS

Behavioral science research evidence and Leavitt's own personal experiences suggest that pathfinding can be taught and developed in ourselves and in others. The approach depends more on the development of awareness and enabling skills than on the more traditional information-transfer methods. If pathfinding is in large part a manifestation of thought, how can these cognitions become a part of a leader's normal thought-action repertoire? Answers to this question are not carved in stone, but they do depend on a manager's openness to change and a willingness to experiment. His developmental propositions are directed toward uncovering and supporting pathfinding capabilities in individuals holding leadership roles.

Development in Others

While the natural pathfinding talents of Henry Ford, Thomas Watson, Ed Land, and Lee Iacocca are widely recognized, Leavitt argues that *pathfinding talents can be cultivated in most individuals.* Key strategies are offered to encourage vision, clarify values, and foster determination in others.

Efforts at developing pathfinding vision focus on increasing creativity and imaginativeness. One proposition suggests that in order to start thinking creatively one must stop thinking analytically. While admittedly easier said than done, what steps can be taken? First, managers are encouraged to reward, support, and encourage creative behavior wherever it occurs. (However, excessive reliance on extrinsic, monetary rewards has been found to actually discourage creativity.) Second, periods of "planned playfulness" can be used by executives to encourage others to relax their analytical barriers and past training and, by contrast, to support creative thinking. Dropping the corporate dress code on certain days, engaging in simple childhood activities, or providing an unplanned day off are a few of the suggestions for doing so.

Developing pathfinding thinking through value clarification efforts is a more complex task. Value creation and value changes are a function of social learning. Diverse group socialization experiences generate a multitude of values that influence executive leadership and its actions. Value change is difficult, but managers can clarify organizational values daily by their actions and reactions. It is this awareness that executive *consistency* in thought and action can do more to communicate and establish clear values than all the creative rationalizations presented after the fact. Organizations are encouraged to single out a few inviolable values from all the rest and enforce them ceaselessly.

Fostering determination in others is the third developmental challenge facing managers interested in nurturing pathfinding. Providing support for venturesome champions, encouraging personal risk-taking behavior at work, and building managerial self-confidence levels are all offered as options for the executive interested in promoting pathfinding.

Entrepreneurial pathfinding depends on the mix of vision, values, and determination. Thus, combinations of these recommendations, consistently applied and rewarded, have the maximum likelihood of developing the corporate pathfinders of tomorrow. In particular, *daily* purposeful leader-follower interactions are more likely to create significant pathfinding behavior than all of the problem-solving-based training and seminar solutions.

Self-Development

Self-taught pathfinding depends on strong personal investments by the manager before natural leadership behavior will be affected. The emphasis here is on self-help beyond career enhancement strategies. Executives are urged to broaden their perspectives by breaking out of the analytical modes currently prevalent in business. Creative problem *finding* and creative problem *making* are two useful recommendations for broadening executive vision.

Getting in touch with inner-directed values is critical to pathfinding. It is important for pathfinders to identify their value priorities early. Managers might review a personal "bug" list, write their own obituaries, and apply other techniques to identify critical core values and differentiate them from the less desirable tradition-directed and other-directed value sets. These inner-directed core values provide the equilibrium and guidance so necessary to guide organizations effectively into the uncertain future.

Building personal determination can have immediate payoffs for all managers, but especially for pathfinders. Enhancing self-confidence and "leveraged commitment" are two strategies tied to higher determination levels in today's manager. For self-confidence building, Leavitt recommends that managers: (1) make sure they are believers of a new idea before they become preachers; (2) be very selective with support for new ideas; and (3) hold on to key beliefs as heuristics for improving self-confidence. His second strategy depends on an escalation of commitment whereby initial commitment and risk, when satisfied, generate still greater determination.

Developing pathfinders is not an easy task, especially when few formal reward systems support these efforts. Given that vision, values, and determination are the cornerstones of pathfinding, the major responsibility for change remains at the individual level. It is the individual manager who must translate his or her style cognitions into leadership action and behavior.

Imagining, innovating, and implementing pathfinding at the organizational level presents the most complex challenge yet to management. Leavitt forcefully argues that pathfinding organization types are our only preparation for the future. In fact, their creation becomes our strongest offense against an uncertain and unknown business environment. Building this offense requires clarification on several points. First, large organizations must not isolate pathfinding as the sole province of those at the top. There has to be room for pathfinders throughout the organization. Second, Leavitt recommends that the supervision of these interspersed pathfinders depends on an ability to "manage only at the absolutely critical points, letting intrinsic motivation, peer pressure, and personal integrity take care of most of the rest." He warns that formalizing, controlling, and nitpicking efforts are often the quickest ways to destroy pathfinding progress. Last, using this offense to change organizational reality requires "parallel and plural pathfinding." Here the mission is to integrate pathfinding with participative implementation throughout the organization. Development of a culture that puts high positive value on both pathfinding individualism and cooperative implementation is the key.

Developing Pathfinding Cultures

Young, small companies naturally seem to possess the pathfinding culture's spirit and energy. Most are unspecialized, nonhierarchical, improvisational, informal, "groupy," fun, and almost always led by intensely dedicated leaders. While these attributes appear natural in small organizational systems, large organizations must fight to gain, retain, and support such a culture.

Leavitt provides several suggestions to guide these transformations in large problem-solving-dominated organizations. He recommends: the stimulation of innovation through rewards and incentive systems; increasing time-spans-of-discretion, as well as time to explore and experiment; setting up innovation departments; hiring dedicated pathfinder types at all levels; using job rotation to broaden vision; and designing physical spaces in firms to support routine interaction and collaboration. Clearly, long-term culture development requires the management of "meanings" that organizational members can share.

Leadership's Role

The single most powerful internal force shaping an organization's culture is its leadership. Second-generation managers are up against tremendous inertial forces if they wish to reshape an old culture. Typically they are only effective at producing incremental changes. However, major efforts to reshape old traditional cultures have been found effective under three specific conditions. First, an organizational crisis (e.g., recession, merger, or bankruptcy threat) can make it easier for leaders to stimulate radical organizational change and to create a new pathfinding culture. Second, a new leader, by sheer force of personal style and power, can occasionally succeed in producing a radically new organizational culture. Last, radical personnel surgery can change an old culture. This involves replacement of critical personnel with "new culture" members.

Surprisingly, pathfinding leaders do not always build pathfinding cultures. These executives seem to have too great a need to control the whole show to permit such a culture to develop. The pathfinding-implementing leadership combination is championed as the critical match necessary to build and maintain a pathfinding culture. Here the mission-definition capability from the pathfinding style is mated with the action-oriented implementing perspective. To perpetuate a pathfinding culture, the CEO needs to exhibit daily *faith* in pathfinding, yet still be dedicated to producing results.

MANAGERIAL TRINITY

In striving to capture the essence of effective leadership for these turbulent times, Leavitt presents a three-part model of the managing process. He compares the struggle between the Pathfinder, Problem Solver, and Implementer to a long-term horse race, where the lead has changed every twenty years. At present, Pathfinding and Implementing have outdistanced Problem Solving, but the full participation of all three parts of the managerial process are necessary to speed up the pace of the race.

Business conditions have now created the era of the pathfinder. Corporate executives, middle managers, and management educators are urged to develop and nurture this critical leadership dimension. Vision, values, and determination have been reestablished as potent leadership tools for the future.

Competitive Advantage: Creating and Sustaining Superior Performance

Michael E. Porter

Summary by Sara A. Morris

Sara A. Morris received her Ph.D. in business policy and strategy from the University of Texas at Austin. Now an Assistant Professor of Management at Florida International University, she teaches capstone courses in strategic management and graduate seminars in competitive strategy. Her current research is in business ethics and social responsibility and concerns CEO misconduct and the use of unethical techniques for obtaining competitor information.

How can a firm obtain and maintain an advantage over its competitors? The answer lies in an understanding of industries, the five forces that drive competition in an industry, and three generic strategies that a firm can use to protect itself against these forces. An industry is a group of firms producing essentially the same products and/or services for the same customers. The profit potential of an industry is determined by the cumulative strength of five forces that affect competition in an industry.

1. jockeying for position on the part of current competitors in the industry,
2. potential for new competitors to enter the industry,
3. the threat of substitutes for the industry's products or services,
4. the economic power of suppliers of raw materials to the industry,
5. the bargaining power of the industry's customers.

Michael E. Porter, *Competitive Advantage: Creating and Sustaining Superior Performance*, New York: Free Press, 1985.

Three strategies that a firm can use to neutralize the power of these five forces are low costs, differentiation, and focus. Several specific action steps are required to execute each of these three generic strategies.

PRINCIPLES OF COMPETITIVE ADVANTAGE

A firm creates a competitive advantage for itself by providing more value for customers than competitors provide. Customers value either (1) equivalent benefits at a lower price than competitors charge, or (2) greater benefits which more than compensate for a higher price than competitors charge. Thus, there are two possible competitive advantages, one based on costs and one based on differentiation (benefits). Each of these tactics will be discussed in detail, following an examination of the value chain.

THE VALUE CHAIN

The *value chain,* consisting of value-producing activities and margin, is a basic tool for analyzing the large number of discrete activities within a firm that are potential sources of competitive advantage. The inclusion of margin in the value chain is a reminder that, in order for a firm to profit from its competitive advantage, the value to customers must exceed the costs of generating it. Value-producing activities fall into nine categories—five categories of primary activities and four categories of support activities. Primary activities include inbound logistics, operations, outbound logistics, marketing/sales, and service. Support activities include procurement (of all of the inputs used everywhere in the value chain), technology development (for all of the myriad of technologies that are used in every primary and support activity), human resource management (of all types of personnel throughout the organization), and the firm infrastructure (general management, planning, finance, accounting, legal and government affairs, quality management, etc.).

Firms perform hundreds or thousands of discrete steps in transforming raw materials into finished products. The value chain decomposes the nine value-producing activities into numerous subactivities because each separate subactivity can contribute to the firm's relative cost position and create a basis for differentiation. In most subactivities, the firm is not significantly different from its rivals. The strategically relevant subactivities are those that currently or potentially distinguish the firm from competitors.

Value chain activities are not independent from one another but interrelated. The cost or performance of one activity is linked to many other activities. For example, the amount of after-sale service needed depends on the quality of the raw materials procured, the degree of quality control in operations, the amount of training given to the sales force regarding matching customer sophistication and model attributes, and other factors. Competitive advantage can be created by linkages among activities as well as by individual activities. Two ways that firms can derive competitive advantage from linkages are through optimization of linkages and coordination of linkages.

The configuration and economics of the value chain are determined by the firm's *competitive scope.* By affecting the value chain, scope also affects competitive advantage. Four dimensions of scope are:

1. Segment scope—varieties of products made and buyers served
2. Vertical scope—the extent of activities performed internally rather than purchased from outside
3. Geographic scope—the range of locations served
4. Industry scope—the number of industries in which the firm competes.

Broad-scope firms operate multiple value chains and attempt to exploit interrelationships among activities across the chains to gain competitive advantages. Narrow-scope firms use focus strategies to pursue competitive advantages; by concentrating on single value chains, they attempt to perfect the linkages within the value chain.

COMPETITIVE ADVANTAGE THROUGH LOW COST

The starting point for achieving a cost advantage is a thorough analysis of costs in the value chain. The analyst must be able to assign operating costs and assets (fixed and working capital) to each separate value chain activity. There are ten major factors which are generally under the firm's control and which drive costs:

1. Economies (or diseconomies) of scale
2. Learning, which the firm can control by managing with the learning curve and keeping learning proprietary
3. Capacity utilization, which the firm can control by levelling throughput and/or reducing the penalty for throughput fluctuations
4. Linkages within the value chain, which the firm can control by recognizing and exploiting
5. Interrelationships between business units (in multi-industry firms), which the firm can control by sharing appropriate activities and/or transferring management know-how
6. The extent of vertical integration
7. Timing, which the firm can control by exploiting first-mover or late-mover advantages, and/or timing purchases over the business cycle
8. Discretionary policies (regarding products made, buyers served, human resources used, etc.)
9. Location
10. Institutional factors imposed by government and unions, which the firm can influence if not control outright.

Moreover, costs are dynamic; they will change over time due to changes in industry growth rate, differential scale sensitivity, differential learning rates, changes in technology, aging, and the like. Each individual value chain activity must be analyzed separately for its cost drivers and cost dynamics.

By definition, the firm has a cost-based competitive advantage if the total costs of all its value chain activities are lower than any competitor's. A firm's cost position relative to competitors depends on the composition of its value chain compared to competitors' chains, and the firm's position relative to its competitors vis-a-vis the cost drivers of each value chain activity. Two ways that a firm can achieve a cost advantage, therefore, are: (1) by controlling cost drivers, and (2) by reconfiguring the value chain through means such as changing the production process, the distribution channel, or the raw materials. A cost-based competitive advantage will be sustainable only if competitors cannot imitate it. The cost drivers which tend to be harder to imitate are economies of scale, interrelationships, linkages, proprietary learning, and new technologies that are brought about through discretionary policies.

COMPETITIVE ADVANTAGE THROUGH DIFFERENTIATION

Successful *differentiation* occurs when a firm creates something unique that is valuable to buyers and for which buyers are willing to pay a price premium in excess of the extra costs incurred by the producer. This statement begs two questions: (1) what makes something valuable to buyers, and (2) why does the producer incur extra costs? With regard to the first question, a firm can create value for buyers by raising buyer performance, or by lowering buyer costs (in ways besides selling the product at a lower price). With regard to the second question, differentiation is usually inherently costly because uniqueness requires the producer to perform value chain activities better than competitors.

In order to achieve a differentiation advantage, strategists must be thoroughly familiar with the many discrete activities in their own value chain(s) and in the buyer's value chain, and must have a passing knowledge of the value chains of competitors. Each discrete activity in the firm's value chain represents an opportunity for differentiating. The firm's impact on the buyer's value chain determines the value the firm can create through raising buyer performance or lowering buyer costs. Since competitive advantages are by definition relative, a firm's value chain must be compared to those of its competitors.

For each separate activity in the firm's value chain, there are *uniqueness drivers* analogous to the cost drivers described previously. The most important uniqueness driver is probably the set of policy choices managers make (regarding product features, services provided, technologies employed, quality of the raw materials, and so forth). Other uniqueness drivers, in approximate order of importance, are linkages within the value chain and with suppliers and distribution channels, timing, location, interrelationships, learning, vertical integration, scale, and institutional factors.

Buyers use two types of purchasing criteria: (1) *use criteria,* which reflect real value, and (2) *signaling criteria,* which reflect perceived value in advance of purchase and verification. Use criteria include product characteristics, delivery time, ready availability, and other factors which affect buyer value through raising buyer performance or lowering buyer costs. Signaling criteria include the producing firm's reputation and advertising, the product's packaging and advertising, and other factors through which the buyer can infer the probable value of the product before the real value can be known. Differentiators must identify buyer purchasing criteria; the buyer's value chain is the place to start.

Armed with an understanding of multiple value chains, uniqueness drivers, and buyer purchasing criteria, managers can pursue differentiation. There are four basic routes to a differentiation-based competitive advantage. One route is to enhance the sources of uniqueness, by proliferating the sources of differentiation in the value chain, for example. A second route is to make the cost of differentiation an advantage by exploiting sources of differentiation that are not costly, minimizing differentiation costs by controlling cost drivers, and/ or reducing costs in activities that do not affect buyer value. Another route is to change the rules to create uniqueness, such as discovering unrecognized purchase criteria. The fourth route is to reconfigure the value chain to be unique in entirely new ways.

A differentiation-based competitive advantage will be sustainable only if buyers' needs and perceptions remain stable and competitors cannot imitate the uniqueness. The firm can strongly influence the buyer's perceptions by continuing to improve on use criteria and by reinforcing them with appropriate signals. The firm is, nevertheless, at risk that buyers' needs will shift, eliminating the value of a particular form of differentiation. The sustainability of differentiation against imitation by competitors depends on its sources, the drivers of uniqueness. The competitive advantage will be more sustainable if the uniqueness drivers involve barriers such as proprietary learning, linkages, interrelationships, and first-mover advantages; if the firm has low costs in differentiating; if there are multiple sources of differentiation; and/or if the firm can create switching costs for customers.

TECHNOLOGY AND COMPETITIVE ADVANTAGE

One of the most significant drivers of competition is technological change. Because technologies are embedded in every activity in the value chain as well as in the linkages among value chain activities, a firm can achieve and/or maintain low costs or differentiation through technology. The first step in using technology wisely is to identify the multitude of technologies in the value chain. Then, the astute manager must become aware of relevant technological improvements coming from competitors, other industries, and scientific breakthroughs.

A firm's technology strategy involves choices among new technologies, and choices about timing and licensing. Rather than pursuing technological improvements involving all value chain activities and linkages indiscriminately, managers should restrict their attention to technological changes that make a difference. New technologies are important if they can affect (1) the firm's particular competitive advantage, either directly or through its drivers, or (2) any of the five forces that drive competition in the industry. A firm's timing matters in technological changes because the technology leader will experience first-mover advantages (e.g., reputation as a pioneer, opportunity to define industry standards) as well as disadvantages (e.g., costs of educating buyers, demand uncertainty). Thus, the choice of whether to be a technology leader or follower should be made according to the sustainability of the technological lead. When a firm's competitive advantage rests on technology, licensing the technology to other firms is risky. Although there are conditions under which licensing may be warranted (to tap an otherwise inaccessible market, for example), often the firm inadvertently creates strong rivals and/or gives away a competitive advantage for a small royalty fee.

COMPETITOR SELECTION

A firm must be ever vigilant in pursuing and protecting its competitive advantage; however, there are dangers in relentlessly attacking all rivals. It is prudent to distinguish desirable competitors from undesirable ones. Desirable competitors may enable a firm to increase its competitive advantage (e.g., by absorbing demand fluctuations, or by providing a standard against which buyers compare costs or differentiation), or may improve industry structure (i.e., may weaken one or more of the five forces that collectively determine the intensity of competition in an industry). Characteristics of desirable competitors include realistic assumptions; clear, self-perceived weaknesses; enough credibility to be acceptable to customers; enough viability to deter new entrants; and enough strength to motivate the firm to continue to improve its competitive advantage. A smart industry leader will encourage some competitors and discourage others through tactics such as technology licensing and selective retaliation.

SCOPE AND COMPETITIVE ADVANTAGE

An industry consists of heterogeneous parts, or segments, due to differences in buyer behavior and differences in the economics of producing different products or services for these buyers. Therefore, the intensity of competition (i.e., the collective strength of the five competitive forces) varies among segments of the same industry. Moreover, because segments of the same industry have different value chains, the requirements for competitive advantage differ widely among industry segments. The existence of multiple industry segments forces a firm to decide on competitive scope, or where in the industry to compete. The attractiveness of any particular industry segment depends on the collective strength of the five competitive forces, the segment's size and growth rate, and the fit between a firm's abilities and the segment's needs. The firm may broadly target many segments or may use the generic strategy of focus to serve one or a few segments.

The competitive scope decision requires the manager to analyze all the current and potential industry segments. To identify product segments, all the product varieties in an industry must be examined for differences they can create in the five competitive forces and the value chain. The industry's products may differ in terms of features, technology or design, packaging, performance, services, and in many other ways. To identify buyer segments, all the different types of buyers in an industry must be examined for differences they can create in the five competitive forces and the value chain. Buyers can differ by type (e.g., several types of industrial buyers, several types of consumer buyers), by distribution channel, and by geographic location (according to weather zone, country stage of development, etc.).

When the value chains of different segments in the same industry are related at multiple points, a firm can share value-producing activities among segments. Such segment interrelationships encourage firms to use a broad-target strategy, unless the costs of coordination, compromise, and inflexibility in jointly accomplishing value-producing activities outweigh the benefits of sharing. Broad-target strategies often involve too many segments, thereby pushing coordination, compromise, and inflexibility costs too high and making the broadly-targeted firm vulnerable to firms with good focus strategies.

Whereas broad-target strategies are based on similarities in the value chains among segments, focus strategies are based on differences between segments' value chains. A focuser can optimize the value chain for one or a few segments and achieve lower costs or better differentiation than broad-target firms because the focuser can avoid the costs of coordination, compromise, and inflexibility required for serving multiple segments. The sustainability of a focus strategy is determined by its sustainability against (1) broad-target competitors, (2) imitators, and (3) substitutes, the next topic of interest.

Both the industry's product or service and its substitutes perform the same generic function for the buyer (i.e., fill the same role in the buyer's value chain). The threat of substitution depends on (1) the relative value/price of the substitute compared to the industry's product, (2) the cost of switching to the substitute, and (3) the buyer's propensity to switch. The relative value/price compares the substitute to the industry's product in terms of usage rate, delivery and installation, direct and indirect costs of use, buyer performance, complementary products, uncertainty, etc. Switching costs include redesign costs, retraining costs, and risk of failure. Buyer propensity to substitute depends on resources available, risk profile, technological orientation, and the like. The threat of substitution often changes over time because of changes in relative price, relative value, switching costs, or propensity to substitute. To defend against substitutes, the focuser can reduce costs, improve the product, raise switching costs, improve complementary goods, etc.

CORPORATE STRATEGY AND COMPETITIVE ADVANTAGE

Whereas business-level strategy is concerned with the firm's course of actions within an individual industry, corporate-level strategy is generally concerned with the multi-industry firm's course of actions across industries. By exploiting interrelationships among its business units in distinct but related industries, the multi-industry corporation can increase its competitive advantage within one or more of those industries. Porter uses the term *horizontal strategy* to refer to a corporation's coordinated set of goals and policies that apply across its business units, and argues that horizontal strategy may be the most critical issue facing diversified firms today. It is through its horizontal strategy that a corporation achieves synergy.

There are three types of interrelationships among a multi-industry corporation's business units: tangible, intangible, and competitor-induced. *Tangible interrelationships* occur when different business units have common elements in their value chains, such as the same buyers, technologies, or purchased inputs. These common elements create opportunities to share value chain activities among related business units. Sharing activities may lower costs or increase differentiation, thereby adding to competitive advantage. However, the benefits of sharing do not always exceed the costs of sharing. One cost of sharing is the need for more coordination in the shared value chain activities. Another cost is the need for compromise in the way shared value chain activities are performed; the compromise must be acceptable to both business units, but may be optimal for neither. A third cost of sharing is greater inflexibility in responding to changing environmental conditions.

A second type of interrelationship, *intangible interrelationships,* occurs when different business units can transfer general management know-how even though they have no common elements in their value chains. It is possible, though less likely, for intangible interrelationships to lead to competitive advantage. A third type of interrelationship, *competitor-induced interrelationships,* occurs when two diversified corporations compete against each other in more than one business unit. Such multipoint competition between two corporations means that any action in one line of business can affect the entire range of jointly contested industries. Therefore, for multipoint competitors, a competitive advantage in one line of business will have implications for all the linked industries.

Any diversified corporation will face impediments to exploiting interrelationships: the managers of business units that receive fewer benefits than they contribute will resist sharing; managers of all business units will tend to protect their turf; incentive systems may not appropriately measure and reward a business unit's contributions to other units; and so forth. Therefore, corporate-level executives must articulate an explicit horizontal strategy and organize to facilitate horizontal relations. Examples of organizational practices and mechanisms that are particularly helpful are horizontal structures (e.g., groupings of business units, inter-unit task forces), horizontal systems (e.g., inter-unit strategic planning systems and capital budgeting systems), horizontal human resource practices (e.g., cross-business job rotation and management forums), and horizontal conflict resolution processes.

A special case of interrelationships occurs when the industry's product is used or purchased with complementary products. Because the sale of one promotes the sale of the other, complementary products have the opposite effect of substitutes. Three types of decisions that a corporation must make regarding complementary products concern whether to control these products internally (as opposed to letting other firms supply them), whether to bundle them (i.e., sell complementary products together as a package), and whether to cross-subsidize them (i.e., price complementary products based on their interrelationships instead of their individual costs). All three types of decisions have repercussions for competitive advantage.

IMPLICATIONS FOR OFFENSIVE AND DEFENSIVE COMPETITIVE STRATEGY

The *industry scenario* is a planning tool which may be used to guide the formulation of competitive strategy in the face of major uncertainties about the future. Constructing industry scenarios involves identifying uncertainties that may affect the industry, determining the causal factors, making a range of plausible assumptions about each important causal factor, combining assumptions into internally consistent scenarios, analyzing the industry structure that would prevail under each scenario, identifying competitive advantages under each scenario, and predicting the behavior of competitors under each scenario. Managers may then design competitive strategies based on the most probable scenario, the most attractive scenario, hedging (protecting the firm against the worst-case scenario), or preserving flexibility.

Defensive strategy is intended to lower the probability of attack from a new entrant into the industry or an existing competitor seeking to reposition itself. The preferred defensive strategy is deterrence. The old saying about "the best offense is a good defense" holds here; a firm with a competitive advantage that continues to lower its costs or improve its differentiation is very difficult to beat. Nevertheless, when deterrence fails, the firm must respond to an attack underway. When a firm's position is being challenged, defensive tactics include raising structural barriers (e.g., blocking distribution channels, raising buyer switching costs) and increasing expected retaliation.

Sometimes attacking an industry leader makes sense. The most important rule in offensive strategy is never to attack a leader head-on with an imitation strategy. In order to attack an industry leader successfully, the challenger must have a sustainable competitive advantage, must be close to the leader in costs and differentiation, and must have some means to thwart leader retaliation. There are three primary avenues to attack a leader: (1) change the way individual value-producing activities are performed, or reconfigure the entire value chain; (2) redefine the competitive scope compared to the leader; (3) pure spending on the part of the challenger. The leader is particularly vulnerable when the industry is undergoing significant changes, such as technological improvements, changes in the buyer's value chain, or the emergence of new distribution channels.

PART
FIVE

Motivation

There are a number of readings contained in the third edition of *The Manager's Bookshelf* that attempt to focus the manager's attention on the social-psychological side of the organization. Authors, concepts, and suggestions for proactive management call our attention to the importance of recognizing that all organizations have a natural (human) resource that, when appropriately managed, can lead to dramatic performance effects.

This set of readings is initiated with the classic *The Human Side of Enterprise*, published by Douglas McGregor in 1960. Because of the book's popularity, its timeless theme, and genuine relevance for organizations as they prepare to enter the 21st century, there has been a 25th Anniversary printing of McGregor's seminal work.

McGregor presents us with two sets of assumptions that managers might hold and which drive two very different approaches to the management of organizations and their employees. Through the presentation of Theory X and Theory Y, McGregor attempts to get us to see employees as capable of innovation, creativity, commitment, high levels of sustained effort, and the exercise of self-direction and self-control.

Kenneth Blanchard and Spencer Johnson, in (the widely read book) *The One Minute Manager*, build their prescriptions for effective human resource management on two basic principles. First, they suggest that *quality time* with the subordinate is of utmost importance. Second, they adopt Douglas McGregor's notion that employees are basically capable of *self-management.* These two principles provide the basis for their prescriptions on goal setting, praising, and reprimanding as the cornerstones of effective management.

Understanding and motivating employee behavior through the effective use of rewards is the theme of Michael LeBoeuf's book *The Greatest Management Principle in the World.* LeBoeuf identifies the strategies and four action plans for the effective motivation of employee behavior, all of which build upon the idea of the appropriate reinforcement of employee behaviors.

There are, as the title of this section suggests, two major themes presented here. First, managers can (and must) learn much about employees, peers, and opponents by observing them in a variety of contexts. Second, managers can induce and sustain much employee behavior by using the simple tools of cues (through goals) and reinforcement (through praise, listening, and other rewards).

Reading 1

The Human Side of Enterprise

Douglas McGregor

Summary prepared by Gayle Porter

Gayle Porter is a Doctoral Candidate at The Ohio State University in Organizational Behavior and Human Resource Management. Articles and ongoing research interests include the effects of dispositional differences in the workplace, group perceptions of efficacy and esteem, and the comparison of influence on employees through reward systems, leadership, and employee development efforts. Her prior experience includes positions as Director of Curriculum Development for a human resource management degree program; consultant on training programs, financial operations, and computer applications; financial manager for an oil and gas production company; and financial specialist for NCR Corporation.

The Human Side of Enterprise was written during an ongoing comparative study of management development programs in several large companies. In McGregor's view, the making of managers has less to do with formal efforts in development than with how the task of management is understood within that organization. This fundamental understanding determines the policies and procedures within which the managers operate, and guides the selection of people identified as having the potential for management positions. During the late 1950s McGregor believed that major industrial advances of the next half century would occur on the human side of enterprise and he was intrigued by the inconsistent assumptions about what makes managers behave as they do. His criticism of the conventional assumptions, which he labels Theory X, is that they limit options. Theory Y provides an alternative set of assumptions that are much needed due to the extent of unrealized human potential in most organizations.

THE THEORETICAL ASSUMPTIONS OF MANAGEMENT

Regardless of the economic success of a firm, few managers are satisfied with their ability to predict and control the behavior of members of the organization. Effective prediction and control are central to the task of management, and there can be no prediction without some underlying theory. Therefore, all managerial decisions and actions rest on a personally held theory, a set of assumptions about behavior. The assumptions management holds about controlling its human resources determine the whole character of the enterprise.

In application, problems occur related to these assumptions. First, managers may not realize that they hold and apply conflicting ideas and that one may cancel out the other. For example, a manager may delegate based on the assumption that employees should have responsibility, but then nullify that action by close monitoring, which indicates the belief that employees can't handle the responsibility. Another problem is failure to view control as selective adaptation, when dealing with human behavior. People adjust to certain natural laws in other fields; e.g., engineers don't dig channels and expect water to run uphill! With humans, however, there is a tendency to try to control in direct violation of human nature. Then, when they fail to achieve the desired results, they look for every other possible cause rather than examine the inappropriate choice of a method to control behavior.

Any influence is based on dependence, so the nature and degree of dependence are critical factors in determining what methods of control will be effective. Conventional organization theory is based on authority as a key premise. It is the central and indispensable means of managerial control and recognizes only upward dependence. In recent decades, workers have become less dependent on a single employer, and society has provided certain safeguards related to unemployment. This limits the upward dependence and, correspondingly, the ability to control by authority alone. In addition, employees have the ability to engage in countermeasures such as slowdowns, lowered standards of performance, or even sabotage to defeat authority they resent.

Organizations are more accurately represented as systems of *inter*dependence. Subordinates depend on managers to help them meet their needs, but the managers also depend on subordinates to achieve their own and the organization's goals. While there is nothing inherently bad or wrong in the use of authority to control, in certain circumstances it fails to bring the desired results. Circumstances change even from hour to hour, and the role of the manager is to select the appropriate means of influence based on the situation at a given point in time. If employees exhibit lazy, indifferent behavior, the causes lie in management methods of organization and control.

Theory X is a term used to represent a set of assumptions. Principles found in traditional management literature could only have derived from assumptions such as the following, which have had a major impact on managerial strategy in organizations:

1. *The average human being has an inherent dislike of work and will avoid it if possible.*
2. *Because of this human characteristic of dislike of work, most people must be coerced, controlled, directed, and threatened with punishment to get them to put forth adequate effort toward the achievement of organizational objectives.*
3. *The average human being prefers to be directed, wishes to avoid re-*

sponsibility, has relatively little ambition, and wants security above all.

These assumptions are not without basis, or they would never have persisted as they have. They do explain some observed human behavior, but other observations are not consistent with this view. Theory X assumptions also encourage us to categorize certain behaviors as human nature, when they may actually be symptoms of a condition in which workers have been deprived of an opportunity to satisfy higher-order needs (social and egoistic needs).

A strong tradition exists of viewing employment as an employee's agreement to accept control by others in exchange for rewards that are only of value outside the workplace. For example, wages (except for status differences), vacation, medical benefits, stock purchase plans, and profit sharing are of little value during the actual time on the job. Work is the necessary evil to endure for rewards away from the job. In this conception of human resources we can never discover, let alone utilize, the potentialities of the average human being.

Many efforts to provide more equitable and generous treatment to employees and to provide a safe and pleasant work environment have been designed without any real change in strategy. Very often what is proposed as a new management strategy is nothing more than a different tactic within the old Theory X assumptions. Organizations have progressively made available the means to satisfy lower-order needs for subsistence and safety. As the nature of the dependency relationship changes, management has gradually deprived itself of the opportunity to use control based solely on assumptions of Theory X. A new strategy is needed.

Theory Y assumptions are dynamic, indicate the possibility of human growth and development, and stress the necessity for selective adaptation:

1. *The expenditure of physical and mental effort in work is as natural as play or rest.*
2. *External control and the threat of punishment are not the only means for bringing about effort toward organizational objectives. People will exercise self-direction and self-control in the service of objectives to which they are committed.*
3. *Commitment to objectives is a function of the rewards associated with their achievement* (satisfaction of ego and self-actualization needs can be products of effort directed toward organizational objectives).
4. *The average human being learns, under proper conditions, not only to accept but to seek responsibility.*
5. *The capacity to exercise a relatively high degree of imagination, ingenuity, and creativity in the solution of organizational problems is widely, not narrowly, distributed in the population.*
6. *Under the conditions of modern industrial life, the intellectual potentialities of the average human being are only partially utilized.*

The Theory Y assumptions challenge a number of deeply ingrained managerial habits of thought and action; they lead to a management philosophy of integration and self-control. Theory X assumes that the organization's requirements take precedence over the needs of the individual members, and that the worker must always adjust to needs of the organization as management perceives them. In contrast, principle of *integration* proposes that conditions can be created such that individuals can best achieve their own goals by directing their efforts toward the success of the enterprise. Based on the premise that the assumptions of Theory Y are valid, the next logical question is whether, and to what extent, such conditions can be created. How will employees be convinced that applying their skills, knowledge, and ingenuity in support of the organization is a more attractive alternative than other ways to utilize their capacities?

THEORY Y IN PRACTICE

The essence of applying Theory Y assumptions is guiding the subordinates to develop themselves rather than developing the subordinate by telling them what they need to do. An important consideration is that the subordinates' acceptance of responsibility for self-developing (i.e., self-direction and self-control) has been shown to relate to their commitment to objectives. But the overall aim is to further growth of the individual, and it must be approached as a managerial strategy rather than simply as a personnel technique. Forms and procedures are of little value. Once the concept is provided, managers who welcome the assumptions of Theory Y will create their own processes for implementation; managers with underlying Theory X assumptions cannot create the conditions for integration and self-control no matter what tools are provided.

The development process becomes one of role clarification and mutual agreement regarding the subordinate's job responsibilities. This requires the manager's willingness to accept some risk and allow mistakes as part of the growth process. It also is time-consuming in terms of discussions and allowing opportunity for self-discovery. However, it is not a new set of duties on top of the manager's existing load. It is a different way of fulfilling the existing responsibilities.

One procedure that violates Theory Y assumptions is the typical utilization of performance appraisals. Theory X leads quite naturally into this means of directing individual efforts toward organizational objectives. Through the performance appraisal process, management tells people what to do, monitors their activities, judges how well they have done, and rewards or punishes them accordingly. Since the appraisals are used for administrative purposes (e.g., pay, promotion, retention decisions), this is a demonstration of management's overall control strategy. Any consideration of personal goals is covered by the expectation that rewards of salary and position are enough. If the advancement available through this system is not a desired reward, the individuals are placed in a position of acting against their own objectives and advancing for the benefit of the organization only. The alternative (for example, turning down a promotion) may bring negative outcomes such as lack of future options or being identified as employees with no potential.

The principle of integration requires active and responsible participation of employees in decisions affecting them. One plan that demonstrates Theory Y assumptions is *The Scanlon Plan*. A central feature in this plan is the cost-reduction sharing that provides a meaningful cause-and-effect connection between employee behavior and the reward received. The reward is directly related to the success of the organization and it is distributed frequently. This provides a more effective learning reinforcement than the traditional performance appraisal methods. The second central feature of the Scanlon Plan is effective participation, a formal method through which members contribute brains and ingenuity as well as their physical efforts on the job. This provides a means for social and ego satisfaction, so employees have a stake in the success of the firm beyond the economic rewards. Implementation of the Scanlon Plan is not a program or set of procedures; it must be accepted as a way of life and can vary depending on the circumstances of the particular company. It is entirely consistent with Theory Y assumptions.

Theory X leads to emphasis on tactics of control, whereas Theory Y is more concerned with the nature of the relationship. Eliciting the desired response in a Theory Y context is a matter of creating an environment or set of conditions to enable self-direction. The day-to-day behavior of an immediate supervisor or manager is perhaps the most critical factor in such an environment. Through sometimes subtle behaviors superiors demonstrate their attitudes and create what is referred to as the psychological "climate" of the relationship.

Management style does not seem to be important. Within many different styles, subordinates may or may not develop confidence in the manager's deeper integrity, based on other behavioral cues. Lack of confidence in the relationship causes anxiety and undesirable reactions from the employees. No ready formula is available to relay integrity. Insincere attempts to apply a technique or style—such as using participation only to manipulate subordinates into believing they have some input to decisions—are usually recognized as a gimmick and soon destroy confidence.

In addition to manager-subordinate relationships, problems connected to Theory X assumptions can be observed in other organizational associations such as staff-line relationships. Upper management may create working roles for staff groups to "police" line managers' activities, giving them an influence that equates psychologically to direct line authority. Top management with Theory X assumptions can delegate and still retain control. The staff function provides an opportunity to monitor indirectly, to set policy for limiting decisions and actions, and to obtain information on everything happening before a problem can occur.

Staff personnel often come from a very specialized education with little preparation for what their role should be in an organization. With full confidence in their objective methods and training to find "the best answer," they often are unprepared for the resistance of line managers who don't share this confidence and don't trust the derived solutions. The staff may conclude that line managers are stupid, unconcerned with the general welfare of the organization, and care only about their own authority and independence. They essentially adopt the Theory X assumptions and readily accept the opportunity to create a system of measurements for control of the line operations.

To utilize staff groups within the context of Theory Y, managers must emphasize the principle of self-control. As a resource to all parts and levels of the organization, staff reports and data should be supplied to all members who can use such information to control their own job—not subordinates' jobs. If summary data indicate something wrong within the manager's unit of responsibility, the manager would turn to subordinates, not to the staff, for more information. If the subordinates are practicing similar self-control using staff-provided information, they have most likely discovered the same problem and taken action before this inquiry occurs. There is no solution to the problem of staff-line relationships in authoritative terms that can address organizational objectives adequately. However, a manager operating by Theory Y assumptions will apply them similarly to all relationships—upward, downward, and peer level—including the staff-line associations.

THE DEVELOPMENT OF MANAGERIAL TALENT

Leadership is a relationship with four major variables: the characteristics of the leader; the attitudes, needs and other personal characteristics of the followers; the characteristics of the organization, such as its purpose, structure, and the nature of its task; and the social, economic and political environment in which the organization operates. Specifying which leader characteristics will result in effective performance depends on the other factors, so it is a complex relationship. Even if researchers were able to determine the universal characteristics of a good relationship between the leader and the other situational factors, there are still many ways to achieve the same thing. For example, mutual confidence seems important in the relationship, but there are a number of ways that confidence can be developed and maintained. Different personal characteristics could achieve the same desired relationship.

Also, because it is so difficult to predict the situational conditions an organization will face, future management needs are unpredictable. The major task, then, is to provide a heterogeneous supply of human resources from which individuals can be selected as appropriate at a future time. This requires attracting recruits from a variety of sources and with a variety of backgrounds, which complicates setting criteria for selection. Also, the management development programs in an organization should involve many people rather than a few with similar qualities and abilities. Finally, management's goal must be to develop the unique capacities of each individual, rather than common objectives for all participants. We must place high value on people in general—seek to enable them to develop to their fullest potential in whatever role they best can fill. Not everyone must pursue the top jobs; outstanding leadership is needed at every level.

Individuals must develop themselves and will do so optimally only in terms of what each of them sees as meaningful and valuable. What might be called a "manufacturing approach" to management development involves designing programs to build managers; this end product becomes a supply of managerial talent to be used as needed. A preferred alternative approach is to "grow talent" under the assumption that people will grow into what they are capable of becoming, if they are provided the right conditions for that growth. There is little relationship (possibly even a negative one) between the formal structure for management development and actual achievement of the organization, because programs and procedures do not *cause* management development.

Learning is fairly straightforward when the individual desires new knowledge or skill. Unfortunately, many development offerings soon become a scheduled assignment for entire categories of people. Learning is limited in these conditions, because the motivation is low. Further, negative attitudes develop toward training in general, which interferes with creating an overall climate conducive to growth. In many cases, managers may have a purpose in sending subordinates to training that is not shared with or understood by that individual. This creates anxiety or confusion, which also interferes with learning. It is best if attendance in training and development programs are the result of joint target-setting, wherein the individual expresses a need and it can be determined that a particular program will benefit both the individual and the organization.

Classroom learning can be valuable to satisfying needs of both parties. However, it can only be effective when there is an organizational climate conducive to growth. Learning is always an active process, whether related to motor skills or acquisition of knowledge; it cannot be injected into the learner, so motivation is critical. Practice and feedback are essential when behavior changes are involved. Classroom methods such as case analysis and role playing provide an opportunity to experiment with decisions and behaviors in a safe environment, to receive immediate feedback, and to go back and try other alternatives. Some applications of classroom learning may be observed directly on the job. In other cases, the application may be more subtle, in the form of increased understanding or challenging one's own preconceptions. Care must be taken so that pressures to evaluate the benefits of classroom learning don't result in application of inappropriate criteria for success while the true value of the experience is overlooked.

Separate attention is given to management groups or teams at various levels. Within Theory X assumptions, direction and control are jeopardized by effective group functioning. On the other hand, a manager who recognizes interdependencies in the organization—one who is less interested in personal power than in creating conditions so human resources will voluntarily achieve organization objectives—will seek to build strong management groups. Creating a managerial team requires unity of purpose among those individuals. If the group is nothing more than several individuals competing for power and recognition, it is not a team. Again, the climate of the relationships and the fundamental understanding of the role of managers in the organization will be critical. One day the hierarchical structure of reporting relationships will disappear from organizational charts and give way to a series of linked groups. This shift in patterns of relationships will be a slow transition, but will signify recognition of employee capacity to collaborate in joint efforts. Then we may begin to discover how seriously management has underestimated the true potential of the organization's human resources.

SUMMARY COMMENTS

Theory X is not an evil set of assumptions, but rather a limiting one. Use of authority to influence has it place, even within the Theory Y assumptions, but it does not work in all circumstances. A number of societal changes suggest why Theory X increasingly may cause problems for organizations needing more innovation and flexibility in their operating philosophy. It is critically important for managers honestly to examine the assumptions that underlie their own behavior toward subordinates. To do so requires first accepting the two possibilities, Theory X and Theory Y, and then examining one's own actions in the context of that comparison. Fully understanding the implications on each side will help identify whether the observed choices of how to influence people are likely to bring about the desired results.

Reading 2

The One Minute Manager

Kenneth Blanchard and
Spencer Johnson

Summary prepared by Charles C. Manz

Charles C. Manz is an Associate Professor of Strategic Management and Organization in the College of Business at Arizona State University. He holds a Ph.D. in Organizational Behavior from Pennsylvania State University. His professional publications and presentations concern topics such as self-leadership, vicarious learning, self-managed work groups, leadership, power and control, and group processes. He is currently working on a book and an extensive research project focusing on self-leadership and leading others to be self-leaders. He is the author of the book *The Art of Self-Leadership*.

The most distinguishing characteristic of *The One Minute Manager* by Kenneth Blanchard and Spencer Johnson is its major philosophical theme: Good management does not take a lot of time. This dominant theme seems to be based on two underlying premises: (1) *Quality* of time spent with subordinates (as with one's children) is more important than quantity; and, (2) in the end, people (subordinates) should really be managing themselves.

The book is built around a story that provides an occasion for learning about effective management. The story centers on the quest of "a young man" to find an effective manager. In his search he finds all kinds of managers, but very few that he considers effective. According to the story, the young man finds primarily two kinds of managers. One type is a hard-nosed manager who is concerned with the bottom line (profit) and tends to be directive in style. With this type of manager, the young man believes, the organization tends to win at the expense of the subordinates. The other type of manager is one who is concerned more about the employees than about performance. This "nice" kind of manager seems to allow the employees to win at the expense of the

Kenneth Blanchard and Spencer Johnson, *The One Minute Manager*. La Jolla, CA: Blanchard-Johnson Publishers, 1981.

organization. In contrast to these two types of managers, the book suggests, an effective manager (as seen through the eyes of the young man) is one who manages so that both the organization and the people involved benefit (win).

The dilemma that the young man faces is that the few managers who do seem to be effective will not share their secrets. That is only true until he meets the "One Minute Manager." It turns out that this almost legendary manager is not only willing to share the secrets of his effectiveness, but is so available that he is able to meet almost any time the young man wants to meet, except at the time of his weekly two-hour meeting with his subordinates. After an initial meeting with the One Minute Manager, the young man is sent off to talk to his subordinates to learn, directly from those affected, the secrets of One Minute Management. Thus the story begins, and in the remaining pages, the wisdom, experience, and management strategies of the One Minute Manager are revealed as the authors communicate, through him and his subordinates, their view on effective management practice.

In addition to general philosophical management advice (e.g., managers can reap good results from their subordinates without expending much time), the book suggests that effective management means that both the organization and its employees win, and that people will do better work when they feel good about themselves; it also offers some specific prescriptions. These prescriptions center around three primary management techniques that have been addressed in the management literature for years: goal setting, positive reinforcement in the form of praise, and verbal reprimand. The authors suggest that applications of each of the techniques can be accomplished in very little time, in fact in as little as one minute (hence the strategies are labeled "one minute goals," "one minute praisings," and "one minute reprimands"). The suggestions made in the book for effective use of each of these strategies will be summarized below.

ONE MINUTE GOALS

"One minute goals" are said to clarify responsibilities and the nature of performance standards. Without them, the authors suggest, employees will not know what is expected of them, being left instead to grope in the dark for what they ought to be doing. A great deal of research and writing has been done on the importance of goals in reaching a level of performance (c.f., Locke, Shaw, Saari, and Latham, 1981). The advice offered in *The One Minute Manager* regarding effective use of performance goals is quite consistent with the findings of this previous work. Specifically, the authors point out through one of the One Minute Manager's subordinates that effective use of One Minute Goals includes:

- agreement between the manager and subordinate regarding what needs to be done;
- recording of each goal on a single page in no more than 250 words that can be read by almost anyone in less than a minute;
- communication of clear performance standards regarding what is expected of subordinates regarding each goal;

- continuous review of each goal, current performance, and the difference between the two.

These components are presented with a heavy emphasis on having employees use them to manage themselves. This point is driven home as the employee who shares this part of One Minute Management recalls how the One Minute Manager taught him about One Minute Goals. In the recounted story, the One Minute Manager refuses to take credit for having solved a problem of the subordinate, and is in fact irritated by the very idea of getting credit for it. He insists that the subordinate solved his own problem and orders him to go out and start solving his own future problems without taking up the One Minute Manager's time.

ONE MINUTE PRAISING

The next employee encountered by the young man shares with him the secrets of "one minute praising." Again, the ideas presented regarding this technique pretty well parallel research findings on the use of positive reinforcement (c.f., Luthans and Kreitner, 1986). One basic suggestion for this technique is that managers should spend their time trying to catch subordinates doing something *right* rather than doing something wrong. In order to facilitate this, the One Minute Manager monitors new employees closely at first and has them keep detailed records of their progress (which he reviews). When the manager is able to discover something that the employee is doing right, the occasion is set for One Minute Praising (positive reinforcement). The specific components suggested for applying this technique include:

- letting others know that you are going to let them know how they are doing;
- praising positive performance as soon as possible after it has occurred, letting employees know specifically what they did right and how good you feel about it;
- allowing the message that you really feel good about their performance to sink in for a moment, and encouraging them to do the same;
- using a handshake or other form of touch when it is appropriate (more on this later).

Again, these steps are described with a significant self-management flavor. The employee points out that after working for a manager like this for a while you start catching yourself doing things right and using self-praise.

ONE MINUTE REPRIMANDS

The final employee that the young man visits tells him about "One Minute Reprimands." This potentially more somber subject is presented in a quite positive tone. In fact, the employee beings by pointing out that she often praises herself and sometimes asks the One Minute Manager for a praising when she has done something well. But she goes on to explain that when she has done something wrong, the One Minute Manager is quick to respond, letting her know exactly what she has done wrong and how he feels about it. After the reprimand is over, he proceeds to tell her how competent he thinks she really is, essentially praising her as a *person* despite rejecting the undesired *behavior*. Specifically, the book points out that One Minute Reprimands should include:

- letting people know that you will, in a frank manner, communicate to them how they are doing;
- reprimand poor performance as soon as possible, telling people exactly what they did wrong and how you feel about it (followed by a pause allowing the message to sink in);
- reaffirm how valuable you feel the employees are, using touch if appropriate, while making it clear that it is their *performance* that is unacceptable in this situation;
- make sure that when the reprimand episode is over it is over.

OTHER ISSUES AND RELATED MANAGEMENT TECHNIQUES

These three One Minute Management techniques form the primary applied content of the book. Good management does not take a lot of time; it just takes wise application of proven management strategies—One Minute Goals, Praisings, and Reprimands. Beyond this, the book deals with some other issues relevant to these strategies, such as "under what conditions is physical touch appropriate?" The book suggests that the use of appropriate touch can be helpful when you know the person well and wish to help that person succeed. It should be done so that you are giving something to the person such as encouragement or support, not taking something away.

The authors also address the issue of manipulation, suggesting that employees should be informed about, and agree to, the manager's use of One Minute Management. They indicate that the key is to be honest and open in the use of this approach. They also deal briefly with several other issues. For example, the book suggests that it is important to move a subordinate gradually to perform a new desired behavior by reinforcing approximations to the behavior until it is finally successfully performed. The technical term for this is "shaping." A person's behavior is shaped by continuously praising improvements rather than waiting until a person completely performs correctly. If a manager waits until a new employee completely performs correctly, the authors suggest, the employee may well give up long before successful performance is achieved because of the absence of reinforcement along the way.

The authors also suggest substituting the strategies for one another when appropriate. With new employees, for instance, they suggest that dealing with low performance should focus on goal setting and then trying to catch them doing something right rather than using reprimand. Since a new employee's lack of experience likely produces an insufficient confidence level, this makes reprimand inappropriate, while goal setting and praise can be quite effective (so the logic goes). The authors also suggest that if a manager is going to be tough on a person, the manager is better off being tough first and then being supportive, rather than the other way around. Issues such as these are briefly addressed through the primary story and the examples described by its primary characters, as supplemental material to the management philosophy and specific management techniques that have been summarized here.

Eventually, at the end of the story, the young man is hired by the One Minute Manager and over time becomes a seasoned One Minute Manager himself. As he looks back over his experiences, the authors are provided with the occasion to summarize some of the benefits of the management approach they advocate—more results in less time, time to think and plan, less stress and better health, similar benefits experienced by subordinates, and reduced absenteeism and turnover.

THE ONE MINUTE MANAGER IN SUMMARY

Perhaps one bottom-line message of the book is that effective management requires that you care sincerely about people but have definite expectations that are expressed openly about their behavior. Also, one thing that is even more valuable than learning to be a One Minute Manager is having one for a boss, which in the end means you really work for yourself. And finally, as the authors illustrate through the giving attitude of the young man who has now become a One Minute Manager, these management techniques are not a competitive advantage to be hoarded but a gift to be shared with others. This is true because, in the end, the one who shares the gift will be at least as richly rewarded as the one who receives it.

REFERENCES

Locke, E., K. Shaw, L. Saari, and G. Latham. "Goal Setting and Task Performance: 1969–1980." *Psychological Bulletin* 90(1981), 125–152.

Luthans, F. and T. Davis. "Behavioral Self-management (BSM): The Missing Link in Managerial Effectiveness." *Organizational Dynamics* 8(1979), 42–60.

Luthans, F. and R. Kreitner. *Organizational Behavior Modification and Beyond.* Glenview, IL.: Scott, Foresman and Co., 1986.

Manz, C.C. *The Art of Self-leadership: Strategies for Personal Effectiveness in Your Life and Work.* Englewood Cliffs, NJ: Prentice-Hall, 1983.

Manz, C.C. "Self-leadership: Toward an Expanded Theory of Self-influence Processes in Organizations." *Academy of Management Review* 11(1986), 585–600.

Manz, C.C. and H.P. Sims, Jr. "Self-management as a Substitute for Leadership: A Social Learning Theory Perspective." *Academy of Management Review* 5(1980), 361–367.

Reading 3

The Greatest Management Principle in the World

Michael LeBoeuf

Summary prepared by Mark Martinko and Sherry Moss

Mark J. Martinko is an Associate Professor of Management at Florida State University and teaches in the areas of organizational behavior, theory, and change. He has conducted research in a variety of areas but is most well known for his work on reinforcement theory, learned helplessness, and high-performing managers. He is a coauthor of *The Practice of Supervision and Management* and *The Power of Positive Reinforcement*. He has published numerous research as well as practitioner-oriented articles, and has served as a reviewer for the *Academy of Management Review, Management Science,* and *Journal of Management Studies.*

Sherry Moss earned her bachelor's degree in Management from Florida State University. She completed her Ph.D. in Organizational Behavior and Theory at Florida State University, and is now on the faculty at Florida International University.

INTRODUCTION

Michael LeBoeuf's book is short (123 pages), easy to read, humorous, practical, and revolves around the basic concepts and principles of reinforcement theory. The book begins with a short self-test composed of a list of questions regarding employees, bosses, and the reader. This inventory points out that all too often organizations, managers, and individuals engage in counterproductive behaviors. Examples of these include emphasizing commitment and loyalty while laying off employees, giving raises to employees threatening to leave, rewarding activity instead of productivity, reinforcing those who complain the most, and reinforcing conformity rather than creativity.

Michael LeBoeuf, *The Greatest Management Principle in the World.* New York: Berkley Publishing, 1987.

PART I: THE BASICS

In the first section the author describes his search for the *basic principles of human behavior and motivation.* Along the way, he notes many manifestations of serious problems in both the private and public sectors such as poor quality, slow growth rate, the lack of a balanced budget, and employees who are idle for large percentages of time.

"The Greatest Management Principle" is introduced through a parable about a snake and a fisherman. In this parable, a fisherman sees a snake with a frog, feels sorry for the frog, and takes it away from the snake. Then, since he also feels sorry for the hungry snake, he gives it a shot of bourbon. In a brief time, the perplexed fisherman is greeted by the same snake—with *two* frogs! The basic moral of the story and the central theme of the book is that *"you get what you reward."* Thus, according to LeBoeuf, the greatest management principle in the world is "The Things That Get Rewarded Get Done!"

A second lesson, which LeBoeuf titles "The Magic Question," focuses on diagnosing organizational problems. According to LeBoeuf, one can get to the root cause of most organizational and motivational problems by asking the simple question, "What is being rewarded?" LeBoeuf provides a variety of work-related examples illustrating how many managements reward the wrong behaviors such as coming to work rather than producing, generating paper and activity rather than producing, and generating short-term profits rather than risking the development of long-term strategic policies.

PART II: THE STRATEGIES

A number of strategies for the achievement of effective human behavior and motivation are identifiable. In the second part of the book ten strategies are presented, each of which emphasizes a positive productive behavior that should be rewarded and an inappropriate behavior that is counterproductive and should not be rewarded.

Strategy 1. "Reward Solid Solutions Instead of Quick Fixes"

There are major liabilities associated with organizations that reward short-term solutions and profits as opposed to long-term solutions that will enhance the overall value and long-term profitability of the organization. Examples of short-term fixes include emphasizing short-term goals, using outdated equipment to save money, cutting costs excessively, and taking short-term advantage of customers to generate immediate profit. The respective long-term and more effective counterparts of these strategies involve establishing long-term goals, investing in efficient tools and equipment, providing ongoing reinforcement for efficiency, and providing effective service to generate long-term repeat customers.

Strategy 2. "Reward Risk Taking Instead of Risk Avoiding"

Many organizations reward conservative, non-risk-oriented behavior and punish more creative employees. This is illustrated with an example of a bank that reinforces people who "don't do anything wrong," but fails to reward more productive risk-oriented behavior. A number of suggestions could establish a more productive risk-taking climate; bosses might reward efforts whether it leads to success or talking honestly about their own failures, emphasizing that failure is part of the price of success, and encouraging calculated as opposed to reckless risks.

Strategy 3. "Reward Applied Creativity Instead of Mindless Conformity"

Some creative achievements that were initially discouraged include the telephone, the manuscript for *Gone with the Wind,* and the Apple computer. By contrast, several examples and guidelines from corporations for establishing a creative climate are proposed. These guidelines include creating a supportive environment that is relaxed and informal, encouraging competitiveness, supporting people who have strong beliefs about a product or job, tolerating errors, creative goal-setting, providing monetary rewards for innovation, and encouraging creativity through specialized training.

Strategy 4. "Reward Decisive Action Instead of Paralysis by Analysis"

"If Moses had been a committee, the Israelites would still be in Egypt." In other words, groups are seldom decisive, but individuals can (and should) be. The story of Zig and Zag, two aspiring young executives, illustrates this. Zig is a no-nonsense guy who gets things done quickly and efficiently. Zag, on the other hand, creates files, establishes committees, coordinates conferences, and otherwise studies the life out of a problem that Zig would have solved weeks ago. Yet the organization, like many organizations, rewards Zag, who is viewed as an excellent company man because of his thorough painstaking analyses.

Organizations that reward Zags have forgotten that "The Purpose of Any Organization is to Get Results." To get results, LeBoeuf suggests that managers "Decide On What You're Going To Do and Do It Now." People who have the strength of conviction and guts to act usually succeed, because others are so indecisive. A variety of suggestions are provided to encourage decisiveness in organizations and to help individuals who want to be more decisive. The suggestions include setting limits on obtaining information, rewarding people who make decisions, setting deadlines for arriving at decisions, and refusing to take the responsibility of making decision for others.

Strategy 5. "Reward Smart Work Instead of Busywork"

There is often a vast difference between effective goal achievement and mere activity. Several examples of organizations that reward activity instead of productivity are provided. Efficiency studies, for example, generally indicate that people could be as much as fifty percent more productive. In order to emphasize goal accomplishment as opposed to unchanneled activity, several suggestions are provided. These suggestions center around ideas such as encouraging reflective planning time, selecting effective employees, reinforcing the efforts of those who need it, eliminating bureaucratic procedures, clarifying organizational roles, and simplifying the work.

Strategy 6. "Reward Simplification Instead of Needless Complication"

"Good management is the art of making difficult things simple, not simple things difficult." The notion of work simplification is illustrated by the story of Sir Simon Marks, chairman of the board of Marks & Spencer of Britain. Sir Simon began repeatedly questioning the work of individual employees within his stores, found numerous bureaucratic and seemingly meaningless tasks, and led a campaign to simplify work procedures and reduce the volumes of bureaucratic forms. At the conclusion of this major reorganization it was estimated that more than twenty-two million forms weighing more than 100 tons were eliminated. He had effectively made difficult tasks somewhat simple.

The essence of the work simplification process is summarized in three words: "Eliminate the Unnecessary." This simple message is supplemented with a variety of practical suggestions for work simplification, such as the notions of simplifying organizational structure, requiring all employees to justify their jobs in writing, providing reinforcement for employees who simplify their jobs, and developing systems to simplify procedures, controls, and communications.

Strategy 7. "Reward Quietly Effective Behavior Instead of Squeaking Joints"

Many organizations spend their time paying attention to and rewarding employees who have difficulties and complain, while they fail to reinforce the effective performers who *seemingly* need little attention. LeBoeuf tells the powerful story of a manager who obtained considerable productivity gains when he stopped spending eighty percent of his time with the low producers, and began investing the same amount of time in the high producers.

A variety of suggestions are provided for encouraging the quiet, efficient performers. These include identifying and reinforcing the effective performers, ignoring the squeaky wheels, targeting rewards for positive behaviors, and criticizing work constructively.

Strategy 8. "Reward Quality Work Instead of Fast Work"

Overemphasis on doing work faster and cheaper often inadvertently becomes costly because of problems with quality. Several of the payoffs for improving quality include lower costs, increased productivity, worker pride, and loyalty of customers.

LeBoeuf believes that if people know how to do the job correctly and are properly motivated, they can achieve almost perfect levels of quality. For example, the quality problems of parachute packers during World War II were "solved" by requiring all packers to make intermittent parachute jumps. The problem is that quality problems in business persist because high-quality work is not rewarded.

Several suggestions are also provided for developing overall organizational commitment to quality. These include sensitizing personnel to the actual behaviors associated with quality, capitalizing on the expertise of the people doing the job, interacting with customers in a way that generates lifetime partnerships, and training people throughout the organization on basic statistical quality control procedures.

Strategy 9. "Reward Loyalty Instead of Turnover"

"You get loyalty and commitment from people by giving it to them." Although many organizations say they want loyalty and commitment, they often punish loyal employees by giving the highest salaries to the most recently hired employees, giving raises to people who threaten to leave, and failing to promote people from within.

An atmosphere of loyalty can be created if the organization provides employees with job security, supports employee education and development, provides equitable benefits, and keeps clear lines of communications with the employees. The author concludes. "in short, treat people the way you would like to be treated."

Strategy 10. "Reward Working Together Instead of Working Against"

Comprehensive teamwork is required for organizational success. Organizational problems such as backbiting, bickering, personal rivalries, and refusal to help others occur most often in organizations with reward systems that produce a predominance of losers and only a few winners. Although competition and conflict may play an important role in successful organizations, practical team play is most important. Several suggestions for team building are provided. One key notion is that of self-managed work teams, which are assigned significant interdependent pieces of work, and are managed in such a way that each member learns and participates in all aspects of the job, including performance appraisal for each worker. Other suggestions include limiting present and future competition, and emphasizing the group effort throughout all aspects of the work. LeBoeuf concludes that the "single most important word is 'we'."

PART III: FOUR ACTION PLANS

The third part of the book is action-oriented. The author specifies "how to" and "who to" reward. This part includes specific sections on techniques and rewards for good work, managing your boss, and managing yourself.

Action Plan 1. "The Ten Best Ways to Reward Good Work"

There are ten major ways to reward effective behavior. These rewards include recognition, time off, money, part-ownership, fun, personal growth, freedom, advancement, and prizes. The two most important rewards, according to LeBoeuf, are money and social recognition. A major problem with money is that, as frequently administered, it is not contingent on performance, and therefore has little effect in effectively managing or rewarding employee behavior.

By contrast, there are a variety of methods for recognizing productive employee behaviors including job titles, employee-of-the-month awards, bonuses, status symbols, club privileges, and publicity. Employee ownership can also be a potent reward for employee behavior. Each of the ten different kinds of rewards mentioned here can be used to reward the ten different kinds of rewards mentioned here can be used to reward the ten different kinds of productive behavior described earlier.

Action Plan 2. "How To Be A 10/10 Manager"

There are practical guidelines for applying the principles described throughout the book to the management process. As a starting point, managers may note that people get excited about hobbies, sports, careers, *and their jobs* when they have goals, a method of scorekeeping, control over their performance, and rewards for goal accomplishment. In fact, work can be as exciting as play if it is structured correctly.

Five key steps are described for managing employee behavior. In the first, the manager identifies the key results desired. This is done through a participative goal-setting process emphasizing simple *measureable* goals. Second, the manager identifies the behaviors needed to achieve the results. Third, proper rewards to reinforce the desired behaviors and results are selected. The fourth step is the use of positive feedback to praise appropriate behaviors. Finally, when the goal is achieved, rewards are dispensed, success is enjoyed, and the process begins again when new goals are established.

Action Plan 3. "Managing Your Boss with GMP"

The same basic principles used to manage subordinates can be used to manage your boss. Each employee owns half of the relationship with his or her boss, and the employee's behavior is an important reward for the boss's behavior. In order to develop an effective strategy for managing the boss, a four-step process is suggested in which the employee inventories the boss's strengths and weaknesses, builds on both his or her own and the boss's strengths while accommodating weaknesses, decides on how to change the boss's behavior, and rewards positive behavior by the boss.

Action Plan 4. "Be Your Own Best Timesaver"

In this final section, LeBoeuf describes techniques for managing your time and yourself. The first step in this procedure is the development of a time inventory in which individual managers record their daily activities. New habits designed to overcome time wasters are suggested. This section includes a list of twelve techniques to overcome time wasters like cluttered desks, the telephone, meetings, and procrastination. Managers are advised to adopt only one technique at a time and then practice the technique at least three weeks before adopting another. The final steps include choosing self-rewards and applying these rewards.

In the epilogue of the book, LeBoeuf summarizes his basic thesis: "Everybody works smarter when there's something in it for them." Effective use of rewards—the greatest management principle in the world—can induce and sustain this smarter work.

PART
SIX

Empowerment and Participation

For several decades there has been a small number of highly visible advocates of participative approaches to the practice of management. During the early 1960s, University of California-Berkeley Management Professor Raymond Miles, for example, built upon the earlier work of many behavioral management theorists as he advanced the human resource model. This model argues that through employee involvement organizational performance will increase. Increases in performance (accomplishments) are satisfying to employees, and this satisfaction breeds the motivation and commitment for deeper involvement.

In spite of such claims, different participative management approaches (e.g., Management by Objectives, job enlargement, and job enrichment) are not widely practiced in American organizations. The classical (hierarchical, Theory X, top-down) approach continues to dominate the practice of management. The Japanese challenge, continued decline of American productivity and product quality, and other forces are causing many U. S. organizations to reexamine, adopt, and integrate participation into their management philosophies and practices.

In this section of the book themes related to employee involvement and participation will be addressed. The first two books look at the *empowerment* of the employee.

Through a modern-day fable, William C. Byham focuses on ways to improve productivity, quality, and employee satisfaction in his book *Zapp! The Lightning of Empowerment*. The author argues that for organizations to be competitive during this, the latter part of the 20th century, it is essential that the organization's human resources be energized such that they focus their energies on ways of making improvements in the organization's quality, output, sales, and customer satisfaction.

Through the empowerment of people the organization's work force will take on responsibility, experience a sense of ownership, gain satisfaction from accomplishment, and acquire power over the ways things are done. Through this process they will come to know that they are important to the organization, and the organization will have strong, enthusiastic, dedicated employees working toward improved quality and productivity.

Dr. William C. Byham is President and Founder of Development Dimensions International, a human resource training and development company.

Charles C. Manz and Henry P. Sims, Jr., present a unique model of the leader of the future in their book *SuperLeadership: Leading Others to Lead Themselves*. They suggest that excellent leaders must not only be able to engage in self-leadership and self-control, but they must also be able to inspire their followers to do the same. The superleader must create an organizational environment that facilitates the development and the exercise of self-leadership in others, and this process represents a unique form of participative management.

Professors Manz and Sims are Professors of Management at Arizona State University and the University of Maryland respectively. Both have consulted, researched, and written extensively about organizations.

Participation through high-involvement approaches to the management of organizations is the focus of the next book summarized here. University of Southern California Professor of Organizational Behavior Edward E. Lawler III, in his book *High-Involvement Management,* summarizes the nature of several different involvement approaches to management.

High-Involvement Management reviews the promises of participative management, and examines the nature and effectiveness of several popular participative management programs. Specifically, Lawler reviews quality circles, employee survey feedback, job enrichment, work teams, union-management quality-of-work-life programs, gainsharing, and new-design plants. Lawler, based upon nearly three decades of organizational behavior research, provides his insights into the critical design features of an effective participative management program.

Interested readers may wish to examine another book by Lawler. *The Ultimate Advantage* argues that high-involvement management is an economic necessity for firms, and that it builds on the American values of personal responsibility, entrepreneurship, democracy, and teamwork.

Reading 1

Zapp! The Lightning of Empowerment

William C. Byham
with Jeff Cox

Summary prepared by Constance Campbell

Constance Campbell is an Assistant Professor of Management at Georgia Southern University and teaches in the areas of Management and Organizational Behavior. Her research interests include learned helplessness, attribution theory, creativity, and intrinsic motivation. Her research has been published in *Psychological Reports,* the *Journal of Social Behavior and Personality,* and the *Proceedings of the Decision Sciences Institute.* Dr. Campbell received her Ph.D. from Florida State University. She is active in the Academy of Management, the Southern Management Association, and the Decision Sciences Institute.

Zapp! The Lightning of Empowerment is aimed at improving quality, productivity, and employee satisfaction. It is a story about *empowerment* (employee feelings of ownership and personal interest in their jobs) written in the form of a fable containing dragons, trolls, Ralpholators, Sapps, Zapps, and (most importantly) Joe Mode's notebook.

Empowerment involves helping employees take ownership of their jobs. When this happens, they are more likely to take personal interest in improving the organization's performance. The book describes realistic and practical ways to empower people and uses the format of a fable to present its message.

The first part of the book "Situation Normal," describes a typical organizational setting in which the workers are apathetic, the managers are antagonistic toward the workers, and productivity is marginal at best. However, one of the supervisors, Joe Mode, decides to try to improve the situation, with the help of one of the employees. "The Zapping of Dept. N" describes how Joe Mode empowers the people in his department. In Part Three, "Super-Charged Zapp," Joe Mode learns about the collective energy that is generated when groups are empowered to work together. Finally, in Part Four, "The Zapped

Company," Joe Mode and his friends spread their empowerment ideas to the rest of the company. Contrary to the scenario in many fables, however, the characters in this fable do not ride off into the sunset and live happily ever after. Instead, it becomes clear that empowerment is never a finished process. Throughout all of the sections, key ideas regarding empowerment are highlighted in part of Joe Mode's notebook. Each of these sections, including Joe Mode's discoveries, is described in more detail below.

PART ONE: SITUATION NORMAL

In Part One, several characters are introduced who work in the Normal Company, a manufacturer of normalators, in Normalburg, USA. For example, Ralph Rosco, an employee in Normal Company, has been working on developing a revolutionary product, a Ralpholator. Ralph is trying to present his idea to his supervisor, Joe Mode, only to be rebuffed with three reasons that the Ralpholator is not a good idea:

1. It is not what Joe is supposed to be working on.
2. It is not the Normal way to do things.
3. If it really were a good idea, R & D would have already developed it.

Actually, Joe did not have time to worry about Ralph's invention, because Joe had enough problems of his own. With too much to do and not enough time to do it, Joe had been berated by his boss, Mary Ellen Krabofski, for not getting enough work done. Mary Ellen instructs Joe, in no uncertain terms, that he needs to crack the whip harder over his people to get more work out of them.

At the end of this trying day, Joe Mode goes back to his office to contemplate the events of the day and to record his thoughts in his notebook, as is his habit. This day he made entries about the problems he encountered in his job, ending with the lament that his employees rarely do more than the bare minimum. They never get excited about their work, and the results of his motivational efforts are short-lived. Joe could see no viable solution to his problems.

This is the state of life in Normal Company early in the fable: workers who are discouraged and supervisors who want to give up. But soon, things begin to change—due, in large part, to the fact that Ralph decides not to give up on his new idea. He continues working on it during all of his spare time and even some of his work time. Finally, Ralph's machine, the Ralpholator, is complete. With no one around to observe, Ralph decides to test his machine, sits down in the chair, flips a few switches, . . . and disappears. Later that same day, Joe Mode goes back to Ralph's work area and stumbles, literally, onto the Ralpholator, accidentally zapping himself to the same place that Ralph had gone, the twelfth dimension.

The 12th dimension is a place with fog and lightning, dragons and trolls, and fire and ice. As it turns out, as Ralph explains it to Joe, in the twelfth dimension one can see things "that we can't see in the normal world . . . like how people feel, what's going on in their minds, what it's like for them on the inside." With these kinds of visual abilities, Ralph and Joe discover that the people in their department, Dept. N, look pretty dark and dismal.

Joe begins to feel pretty dismal, himself, about the whole picture, until Ralph takes Joe to visit Dept. Z, where the people are glowing and happy. Ralph and Joe watch in amazement as one woman in the department grabs lightning bolts and ZAPPS the people in the department with them. When they are ZAPPed, Joe and Ralph are surprised to see that the Zapp not only doesn't hurt, but it actually increases the light in the people in the Department. It seems to give them added energy.

Naturally, Ralph and Joe are curious about this lightning, but before they have a chance to figure it out, Mary Ellen Krabofski, who is wandering around looking for Joe in Dept. N, manages to trip over the Ralpholator's extension cord and disconnect it from its power source. To their chagrin, this causes Ralph and Joe to become visible again, and they materialize right in the midst of Dept. Z. Standing there in the department, being very visible now, they are greeted by the woman who was Zapping people with lightning in the twelfth dimension, who asks if she can help them. After some fancy footwork (a.k.a. lying) by Joe, the woman, who is Lucy Storm, supervisor of the department, takes them on a tour of the department. During the tour they note that the workers in Dept. Z are productive and content, even though they are in jobs that do not appear to be very challenging at all.

Before Ralph and Joe can solve this puzzle, the tour of Dept. Z ends, and Ralph and Joe go back to their own department, where they find a stark contrast in attitudes from the place they had just seen. Mary Ellen Krabofski is still there, angry about her stumbling encounter with the Ralpholator, and just waiting to take it out on Joe and Ralph. As it happens, she mainly takes it out on Ralph, giving him a three-day suspension from work. Meanwhile, Joe goes back to his office to pick up his notebook once again. In trying to discern what the Zapp of lightning is that he saw flowing into people in the twelfth dimension, he decides to give the lightning a name, calling it *Zapp*, and describes it as "**a force that energizes people**" (p. 38).

Joe's next step is to try to find out how to Zapp people in his department. Of course, asking Lucy Storm for help might have been the easiest way to do it, but Joe had a rule against asking people for help, so Joe tried all sorts of things to Zapp people: Mr. Nice Guy, Mr. Mean Guy, and even Quality Circles. None of them worked. In fact, in looking over the long list of things that had been tried in his department and others, Joe found that they always worked in Lucy Storm's department, but there wasn't much consistency anywhere else. Joe concludes that Zapp is essential for the success of new ideas and programs, for they work with Zapp and they fail without it.

After his suspension time is over, Ralph comes back to work—not too happy to be there—until Joe convinces him to reassemble the Ralpholator so they can both learn about the Zapps. After reassembling the machine, Ralph disappears into the twelfth dimension. What he notices this time is not a Zapp, but a *Sapp*—a force that drains energy instead of giving it. From the twelfth dimension, Ralph watches Joe Sapp his people when he did not listen to them, when he took their problems away from them to solve them himself, and when he made decisions for them.

After further exploration, Ralph learns that Joe is not the only one Sapping people; others are doing it as well. Ralph tries to explain Sapps to Joe, but Joe does not believe it until he sees it himself. After his own trip into the twelfth dimension to observe Sapps, Joe identifies a list of **what Sapps people**:

- lack of trust
- not being listened to
- not enough feedback to judge one's success/failure
- overly-simplified jobs

When Joe and Ralph really think about this list, they realize that Zapp and Sapp are opposite sides of the same coin; that Zapp! gives power and Sapp!; takes it away. In contrasting Zapp and Sapp, Joe writes in his notebook items that people include: teams, recognition for ideas, support (approval, coaching, feedback, encouragement), and flexible controls. Joe decides to try to make his department more Zapped than Sapped.

PART TWO: THE ZAPPING OF DEPT. N

Joe's first real effort at Zapping is to gather everyone and tell them that they are henceforth in control of their own jobs, will be making their own decisions, and should act like they own their jobs. Unfortunately, no one really understands what he means. However, they try it, with some deciding to take a break for the day. The abysmal failure of this approach causes Joe to conclude in his notebook that **"It is easy to Sapp. It is hard to Zapp"** (p. 66).

Ralph comes to Joe's rescue again, though, when he calls in constant reports from his newly-invented Ralphone in the twelfth dimension, and tells Joe that maintaining people's self-esteem is important. Joe decides to try it. Just like everything else he tries, Joe's first efforts at building self-esteem are clumsy at best, but he learns fairly quickly with practice and with help from Ralph that comments designed to built self-esteem must be sincere. It was an important discovery, learning the importance of people's self-esteem, so Joe wrote it in large letters in his notebook:

First Step of Zapp: Maintain Self-Esteem (p. 70).

But there were still other important ideas to learn. The next day, Ralph called on the Ralphone to report that he had discovered that Lucy Storm could Zapp people just by listening to them and then repeating back to the person a short summary of what had been said. Joe decided to try it in Dept. N. As usual, his first effort at listening was not a rousing success, but at least he did keep trying. With practice, he improved.

However, as Ralph and Joe were working on a problem one day, they discovered that merely listening was not enough. In addition to listening, it was important to respond with empathy, showing that the feeling behind the words was noted as well as the message. With that, Joe had discovered the second step of Zapp, which he wrote in large letters in his notebook:

Second Step of Zapp: Listen and Respond with Empathy (p. 78).

At this point, things were going well for Joe and Dept. N. Ralph could observe many more Zapps in the department during his times in the twelfth dimension. But then, one day, a huge dragon appeared. It was wiping out computer data, it was breaking important machines, and it was starting small fires all around the department. People in the department picked up a hose to extinguish the blazes started by the dragon, but, before they knew what happened, Joe Mode appeared on the scene, grabbed the fire hose himself, and took over the fight. Meanwhile, the employees, who no longer were in on the fight, went back to their routine or simply watched Joe practicing his heroics. Needless to say, the fires weren't extinguished effectively.

At the end of the day, a very tired and frustrated Joe approaches Ralph for some twelfth dimension help on how to deal with this situation. In answer, Ralph takes Joe to the twelfth dimension, where the dragon is wreaking havoc all around the company . . . until they arrive in Dept. Z, Lucy Storm's department. As you might have guessed, things were different there. Instead of fighting all of the fires herself, Lucy Storm was asking her people to pitch in and fight the fires together. This led Joe to a new realization, which he wrote in his notebook:

Third Step of Zapp: Ask for Help in Solving Problems (Seek ideas, suggestions, and information) (p. 89).

And so, of course, Joe tried it, although he got it only partly right. He enlisted people's help in coming up with some great solutions, but he took the projects away when it came to implementing the solutions. After thinking about it for a while, Joe realized that he had been taking away from people the responsibility for carrying out the plans. With some practice, he began to learn, and in his thinking process he was able to make a key discovery and record it in his notebook:

The Soul of Zapp! Offer Help Without Taking Responsibility (p. 97).

With everyone in Dept. N now getting Zapped on a regular basis, things were going rather smoothly. Except for one thing: Joe Mode was unhappy. He was worried about what people would do now that they were making the decisions. He knew that he would catch the heat from Mary Ellen Krabofski if something went wrong in the department. He began to realize that there still needed to be some control . . . but how? After several crises erupt in the department, Joe realizes that there is an appropriate amount of control to use, involving the proper balance between delegation and checking on how people are doing. He decides to tailor the amount of control to the situation.

Even then, all of the problems in Dept. N are not conquered. Another problem appears. People are enthusiastic in the department, they are Zapped, and they are working on projects. Unfortunately, though, they are working on the *wrong* projects. People are charged, but are not necessarily moving in the right direction. After thinking about it, Joe realizes that his department has no clear goals; people have been given no direction. So Joe decides to work on it. The goals that he developed had three parts:

1. "Key Result Area—The direction we want to go";
2. "Measurement—A way to know we're moving in the right direction";
3. "Goal—Something to tell us if we're there yet."

Once he got started, Joe had each person develop personal goals, which led to the accomplishment of departmental goals, which led to the accomplishment of company goals. This allowed everyone to see where they fit into the big picture. Soon Joe had initiated the use of feedback charts that kept track of progress toward goals. He even had people keeping track of their own feedback charts.

All was not perfect in Normalburg yet. Joe still had a problem with one of his employees, Mrs. Estello, who went on making mistake after mistake day after day, oblivious to the need to improve the quality of her work. When Joe's pleas for improvement fell on deaf ears, he finally realized that he should be more like a coach with her and less like a boss. He would go through the process of explaining why the job was important and how to do it, demonstrating how to do it, and then watching as Mrs. Estello did it to give her feedback on her performance. Finally, he would express confidence in her ability and agree on follow-up actions. After he took these steps, Mrs. Estello began to improve. All the while, Joe was making sure to notice when she did something right.

By this time, people were getting Zapped right and left in Joe Mode's department, and Joe realized one day that the nature of his job had changed dramatically. Instead of telling people what they should do, his role had become more of a facilitator. He discovered that he provided four things to his department: Direction, as in goals; Knowledge, as in training; Resources, as in facilities; and Support, as in encouragement. After reflecting on this, Joe realized that he was more of a Group Leader than a Supervisor. It was time to move on, time to move to Part Three.

PART THREE: SUPER-CHARGED ZAPP!

It was time for Joe to go back to the Ralpholator and see what things looked like now in the twelfth dimension. When he arrived at Ralph's work station, he discovered that Ralph was already in the twelfth, so Joe took off, too, looking for Ralph. He found Ralph, with Lucy Storm, standing outside of the company observing how the company looked from the twelfth dimension. The company looked like a large imposing tower, but their own departments were fluid shapes that were in a process of continual transformation.

After a bit of discussion about this new finding, the three parted and went back to their areas, and time passed. Then one day Joe and Ralph discovered a new business area in Dept. Z, so they went to check on it. Instead of bolts of lightning, they were surprised to see wheels of lightning. The wheels did not just go from the supervisor to the employee, but they were generated by the group and went around the work group. After discussions with Lucy Storm, Joe discovered that the key to generating these wheels of lightning was having people work in *semiautonomous teams*, where small groups of employees managed their own work affairs.

Joe decided to try it in his area. He used some of the same group leader skills with the teams that he had used to Zapp individuals. He provided direction, knowledge, resources, and support. Part of the knowledge he found that he needed to give people was in the form of training in "people skills," such as how to solve conflicts in the group, since they were working in teams instead of alone. Joe also found that he needed to train people in technology at the appropriate time but just before they needed it, not a long time before they needed it. After some initial rough spots, the groups became effective for the department, enZapping each other in the process of their work. Some of the functions the groups served were to deal with absenteeism and performance issues, schedule vacations, and improve quality and productivity.

With these groups working together and being supercharged in Dept. N, the next move was to focus on the total organization.

PART FOUR: THE ZAPPED COMPANY

Things were going quite well in Depts. N and Z. In fact, from outside of the company in the twelfth dimension, their towers in the company castle looked more like starships prepared to fly away on some lofty errand. But, alas, they were being held to the ground by their attachment to the weighty gray castle that was the rest of the Normal Company.

A look inside the company showed a dismal situation. There were managers running around taking responsibility away from workers, Sapping them right and left. Mary Ellen Krabofski was especially busy driving around in the executive fire truck, taking away firehoses from people and putting out fires herself all around the company. A look at the customer service area indicated that the people there didn't seem to know how to service customers, and, furthermore, didn't seem to care.

After observing these scenes and other interactions around the company, Joe Mode, with the help of Ralph, made an interesting discovery. They discovered that the person's direct boss has the most influence over how Zapped an individual is. The next greatest amount of influence is held by the other people who affect the person's job, followed by top management, and then by the organization and its systems. Joe and Lucy had worked on number one, the direct boss part, but there was not much that they could do in their positions about other people, top management, and the organization. Except . . . talk to Mary Ellen Krabofski.

Now, by this time, everyone in Normal Company had noticed the improvements in Depts. Z and N. So it didn't take long to convince Mary Ellen to let them present their views. Joe and Lucy asked the Zapp teams to prepare a presentation. Their presentations were given with such enthusiasm that Mary

Ellen, being a rather intelligent person after all, decided to begin using the first three steps of Zapp herself:

1. Maintain self-esteem.
2. Listen and respond with empathy.
3. Ask for help in solving problems.

After some success with these three steps, she went straight to the soul of Zapp—offer help without taking responsibility. Since Mary Ellen was near the top of the company, she also realized that she needed to develop an environment where all people in the company could practice Zapp. Like Joe, she had to try and fail a few times, but she eventually became much better at Zapping.

As part of enZapping people, she encouraged under-utilized workers to form teams trying to develop new products for the business. She encouraged work teams to select their own members with guidance and assistance from Personnel, rather than having Personnel do the job completely. The customer service department even received training in how to Zapp the customers. Even old Ralph got to develop his Ralpholator for new product markets! In short, the whole place became Zapped, with lightning flowing everywhere.

Time goes by. A few years later, a rookie manager, Dave, shows up at Joe's office and wants to find out from Joe how to Zapp people. Dave reports that he has heard that Zapp is a source of energy that enables employees to seek and obtain continuous improvement in their jobs. In the process of showing Dave around, Joe let Dave know that this is not a "happily ever after" fable, because Zapp is not a destination (i.e., not a finished process) but a continuous journey. Joe suggests to Dave that he can start using Zapp by reading the notebook containing all of the main ideas, by seeking training in how to Zapp people, and by seeking continually to learn, grow, and improve.

Reading 2

SuperLeadership: Leading Others to Lead Themselves

Charles C. Manz and Henry P. Sims, Jr.

Summary prepared by Charles C. Manz and Henry P. Sims, Jr.

Charles C. Manz is an Associate Professor of Strategic Management and Organization in the College of Business at Arizona State University. He holds a Ph.D. in organizational behavior from Pennsylvania State University. His professional publications and presentations concern topics such as self-leadership, vicarious learning, self-managing work groups, leadership, and group processes. He is the author of *The Art of Self-Leadership*, and *SuperLeadership*.

Henry P. Sims, Jr. is a Professor of Organizational Behavior at the University of Maryland. He has published in a variety of organization and management journals, and has been an active member of the Academy of Management. Professor Sims is the coauthor of *The Thinking Organization* (with Dennis Gioia) and *SuperLeadership* (with Charles C. Manz).

This review has two unique features. First, the authors are summarizing their own book, and there are some advantages to this unusual approach. Since the reviews in *The Manager's Bookshelf* are intended to provide an informative summary of contemporary management literature rather than a critical evaluation, the authors may be most qualified to do this. Nevertheless, "caveat emptor"—the reader is advised to look elsewhere for critical analyses.

A second notable feature is that the topic of the book—superleadership —is on the cutting edge of the most current thinking about modern organiza-

Charles C. Manz and Henry P. Sims, Jr., *SuperLeadership: Leading Others to Lead Themselves*. New York: Prentice-Hall Press, 1989.

tions. At all levels of organizations and societies, leadership has become a critical issue.

PRIMARY LEADERSHIP PHILOSOPHY AND THEMES OF THE BOOK

When most of us think of leadership, we think of one person doing something to another person. This is "influence," and a leader is one who has the capability to influence another. A classic leader is sometimes described as "charismatic" or "heroic." The word "leader" itself conjures up visions of a striking figure on a rearing white horse, crying, "Follow me!" The leader is the one who has either power or authority to command others.

Many historical figures fit this mold: Alexander, Caesar, Napoleon, George Washington, and Churchill. Even today, Lee Iacocca's turnaround of Chrysler Corporation might be thought of as an act of heroic leadership. It is not difficult to think of Iacocca astride his white horse, and he is frequently thought of as "charismatic."

But is this heroic figure of the leader the most appropriate image of the organizational leader of today? Is there another model? We believe there is. We believe that in many modern situations, *the most appropriate leader is one who can lead others to lead themselves.*

Our viewpoint represents a departure from the dominant and, we think, incomplete view of leadership. Our position is that true leadership comes mainly from within a person, not from outside. At its best, external leadership provides a spark and supports the flame of the true inner leadership that dwells within each person. At its worst, it disrupts this internal process, causing damage to the person and the constituencies served by the leader.

Our focus is on a new form of leadership—one designed to facilitate the self-leadership energy within each person. This perspective suggests a new measure of a leader's strength—the ability to maximize the contributions of others through recognition of their right to guide their own destiny, rather than the ability to bend the will of others to one's own. Leading others to lead themselves means bringing out the best, but mainly in others, not just in oneself. This form of leadership brings out the best that lies within those that surround the leader.

Many organizations do not seem to understand how to go about bringing out the wealth of talent that each employee possesses. Many are still operating under a quasi-military model that encourages conformity and adherence, rather than emphasizing how leaders can lead others to lead themselves.

SuperLeadership presents a wide range of behavioral and cognitive strategies designed to lead others to lead themselves to excellence. Some representative themes of the process include the following:

- An important way to measure your own success is through the success of others.

- What makes you successful at one level can be counterproductive at a higher level.
- "This transition is even more difficult for me than other people—I started to realize that I better let some other people do some things and I better start looking at the big picture a little more."—Joseph Vincent Paterno
- The strength of a leader is measured by the ability to facilitate the self-leadership of others—not the ability to bend the will of others to one's own.
- If you want to lead somebody, first lead yourself.
- The best of all leaders is the one who helps people so that, eventually, they don't need him or her.
- Give people a fish, and they will be fed for a day; teach them to fish, and they will be fed for a lifetime.

A PRIMER ON SELF-LEADERSHIP

The primary focus of *SuperLeadership* is on facilitating the self-leadership of others. That is, the vehicle for exercising effective leadership is the facilitation of the inner leadership potential of followers. A primary premise is that everyone is a self-leader but not everyone is currently effective at the process. To achieve optimal success—to become a SuperLeader—the self-leadership of every person needs to be harnessed and enhanced.

Self-leadership can be defined as the influence we exert upon ourselves to achieve the self-motivation and the self-direction we need to perform. The self-leadership process consists of an array of behavioral and cognitive strategies for enhancing our own personal effectiveness. The SuperLeadership process in turn consists of a set of strategies for assisting followers in the development and practice of their own personal self-leadership skills.

Behavioral focused self-leadership strategies are specially designed to help individuals behave more effectively. Specifically, they include self-observation, self-goal setting, the management of cues, self-reward, self-punishment, and rehearsal. Each of these strategies, when practiced consistently and effectively, has been found to be related significantly to higher performance—except self-punishment. While self-punishment (e.g., guilt and self-criticism) can at times serve a useful purpose (we all need to have a conscience), it tends to have a demoralizing and destructive impact when overused. On the other hand, strategies such as setting challenging but achievable performance goals and rewarding ourselves (e.g., with self-praise) when we reach them tend to have a favorable impact on our performance. Also, observing and collecting useful information about our important behaviors and rehearsing (practicing) our planned performances before doing them "for keeps" can contribute to our effectiveness.

Nevertheless, even if we do achieve more effective behavior we cannot become optimally effective without establishing effective patterns of thinking.

BEHAVIORAL FOCUSED STRATEGIES

Self-observation—observing and gathering information about specific behaviors that you have targeted for change

Self-set Goals—setting goals for your own work efforts

Management of Cues—arranging and altering cues in the work environment to facilitate your desired personal behaviors

Rehearsal—physical or mental practice of work activities before you actually perform them

Self-reward—providing yourself with personally valued rewards for completing desirable behaviors

Self-punishment—administering punishments to oneself for behaving in undesirable ways

COGNITIVE FOCUSED STRATEGIES

Building Natural Rewards into Tasks—self-redesign of where and how you do your work to increase the level of natural rewards in your job. Natural rewards that are part of rather than separate from the work (i.e., the work, like a hobby, becomes the reward): result from activities that cause you to feel:

- a sense of competence

- a sense of self-control

- a sense of purpose

Focusing Thinking on Natural Rewards—purposely focusing your thinking on the naturally rewarding features of your work

Establishment of Effective Thought Patterns—establishing constructive and effective habits or patterns in your thinking (e.g., a tendency to search for opportunities rather than obstacles embedded in challenges) by managing your:

- beliefs and assumptions

- mental imagery

- internal self-talk

Figure 1. Self-leadership Strategies

Consequently, self-leadership strategies also include methods for creating orientations toward work that facilitate a natural motivation to perform. That is, self-leaders can both physically and mentally redesign their own tasks to make them more naturally motivating. Other cognitive strategies are designed to assist us in analyzing and managing the assumptions we make about work-related issues. They also address approaches for harnessing the power of imagery and self-talk.

Part of the SuperLeadership approach is designed to assist and guide followers in the development of constructive patterns of thinking by helping them to master these *cognitive focused strategies.* Too often individuals can develop the habit of negative thinking, for example, that causes them to shrink in the face of potential obstacles because of inaccurate assumptions and dysfunctional self-talk and imaging that exaggerates potential risks and problems. Through the development of cognitive self-leadership skills we can learn to keep risks in better perspective and to experience more naturally motivating and positive work situations. A summary of the primary self-leadership strategies addressed in the book is provided in Figure 1.

STRATEGIES OF SUPERLEADERSHIP

A major focus of this book is on tapping the potential of subordinates. From a SuperLeadership point of view every subordinate is viewed as a valuable resource and as a potentially effective self-leader. However, effective self-leadership consists of an extensive array of self-influence skills and strategies. While the perspective of the book is that everyone is already a self-leader—we all make choices that have an impact on our own behavior and effectiveness by the personal standards we set, the way we evaluate and react to our own performance, and so forth—not everyone is by nature an *effective* self-leader. On the contrary, most individuals have significant shortcomings in the way they influence themselves. And this is precisely why SuperLeadership (leading others to lead themselves effectively) is so important.

SuperLeadership consists of a practical set of strategies designed to bring out and develop the self-leadership potential of subordinates. The first strategy is to set a positive self-leadership *model* or example for subordinates. This means that the first step toward becoming a SuperLeader is to become an effective self-leader and then to display one's own effective self-leadership as a learning example for others. The effectiveness of this modeling process is enhanced to the extent that people can establish themselves as credible persons worthy of emulation. Also, the specific self-leadership skills should be displayed in a vivid and detailed manner.

A focus on *goals* is also an important part of the process. Subordinates need to develop skills in setting their own performance goals that are realistic and achievable. These goal-setting skills can be applied to developing self-leadership effectiveness. That is, goals to increase and improve self-leadership activity, in addition to personal performance goals, can be set. A subordinate in sales, for example, might set a goal to develop a self-leadership plan for increasing the motivation to prospect for new clients. The plan itself might consist of a monthly goal for the number of sales calls made, and the establishment of a reward (e.g., eating at a favorite restaurant) to be self-administered each time the goal is reached.

SuperLeadership also involves providing *encouragement* and *guidance* for subordinate self-leadership effectiveness. Through verbal encouragement and support for subordinate initiative and use of self-leadership strategies, the leader can generally stimulate subordinate self-leadership practice. In addition, the SuperLeader is an important source of guidance as these skills are developed. In part, the SuperLeader can accomplish this by practical explanation and instruction on self-leadership strategies. More often, however, this process is less direct. For example, a particularly effective technique is the use of questions that stimulate the follower to think about self-leadership. "What goal are you shooting for?" "How well do you feel you are doing?" "Wow, you sure did a great job on this assignment, are you going to celebrate?" or "How are you going to reward yourself?" and "Have you thought about how you might make your job more naturally motivating by changing the way you do your work?" are all examples of questions that will tend to stimulate thinking about self-leadership. Questions such as these can help indirectly guide subordinates' self-leadership thinking and development and also help them to design a customized approach to their own self-leadership.

Then, when subordinates display self-leadership, the SuperLeader will *reinforce* this desired behavior through praise or other available rewards. The key point here is that the focus of the reward process shifts to a particular focus on self-leadership behavior rather than just on higher performance. The reprimand process for undesired behavior, on the other hand, is left primarily to the subordinate. That is, a shift toward employee self-leadership requires a large degree of tolerance on the part of the leader to allow for subordinate mistakes and small failures that are an inevitable part of the development process. And when criticism does occur it should primarily come from the subordinate, though this too should not be excessive. Clearly, the available evidence indicates that the most effective behavior management approach is to reward successes and attempts to improve, rather than reprimand failures.

Finally, the SuperLeadership process involves the development of *self-leadership cultures* and *sociotechnical systems* that support subordinate growth and initiative. Much of this transition will occur naturally as the leader models, encourages, facilitates goals, guides, and reinforces subordinate self-leadership. Eventually, self-leadership is recognized by subordinates as something that is not only accepted but is expected within the work unit. And subordinates can come to serve as important sources of support for one another. In advanced self-leadership systems, for example, subordinates are often organized into teams that possess significant autonomy for managing themselves on a day-to-day basis. As the supporting values, beliefs, and system components that support self-leadership become more established, the SuperLeadership process is greatly supported. The SuperLeader in turn is then especially able to enjoy the benefits of having dynamic, innovative self-leading subordinates.

EXAMPLES OF SUPERLEADERSHIP IN PRACTICE: SOME CASES

Another feature of the book is the provision of real life cases—"Profiles in SuperLeadership"—that illustrate how SuperLeadership behaviors have been used by real leaders. Further, the text is enriched by the inclusion of many mini-cases and examples. Here is a sampling from three of the profiles: Joseph Paterno, William McKnight, and Dwight Eisenhower.

Joseph Vincent Paterno

Joe Paterno is one of the winningest college football coaches in history. With a winning percentage of over eighty percent, his accomplishments as a football coach are strikingly impressive. He was honored as Coach of the Year after his team won college football's national championship in 1983, and Sportsman of the Year after the 1987 national championship. But Paterno is equally respected for his philosophy and opinions. Sometimes he seems more proud of the graduation rate of his players than he does of his own winning percentage.

In many ways Paterno's leadership style has demonstrated in real life the philosophy of SuperLeadership. In talking with Paterno we learned several things about the man that helped us better to understand his approach. First, Paterno's thoughts on coaching:

> A coach must be able to develop three things in an athlete; pride, poise, and confidence in himself. . . . The coach has to aim high, think big, and then make sure that the players aspire to the highest goals they can achieve. A coach has to be able to get people to reach up. As Browning wrote, "A man's reach should exceed his grasp, or what's a heaven for?"

Later, Paterno talked about allowing his assistants room for failure: "You can't grow (if you don't make mistakes). . . . I've got to give them a chance to do some things (on their own)." Paterno went on to reflect on some of the opportunities he was allowed to have to fail in his early coaching days, and how important they were. But then he also pointed out that there are limits to this strategy, depending on the severity of the consequences: "Ordinarily, a guy comes in and wants to try something. . . . you let him do it . . . but, [in] a big game, if he wants to try something you know won't work . . . I can't afford that kind of luxury."

Perhaps the most interesting aspect of Paterno's views on leadership is his natural inclination to *want* to control every aspect of the coaching process. Intellectually, however, he recognizes that this approach simply will not work, and so he discussed some internal struggles he has had in the past, and his evolution toward a more participatory style: "I can't tell you when it happened, but I started to realize that I better let some other people do some things and I better start looking at the big picture a little more. I've done it, and I've done more and more of it." As Paterno talked, it was apparent that this transition had been difficult. Those highly capable executives who (like Paterno) have been able to succeed in the past largely on their own abilities can easily find letting go of some control a difficult process. Yet, this transition is necessary, especially at higher levels of the organization. Paterno reflected that making this change in his style was probably more difficult for him than for others, but he nevertheless recognized that it needed to take place. The style that he has subsequently evolved in many ways is a model of SuperLeadership in action.

William L. McKnight

3M Company is generally viewed as a model organization. It has been named to popular lists—"Excellent companies," "Best companies to work for," "Best-managed companies." Much of its success can be attributed to its style of management, which emphasizes autonomy and entrepreneurship in creating new ideas and developing them into useful, high-quality, and profitable products. A logical question that follows is, "How did this organization come to operate the way that it does?" The answer appears to lie largely in its history of leadership. And many say that it all began with William L. McKnight, one of 3M's earliest leaders.

3M employees point out that it all started with McKnight's faith in people; he gave his subordinates freedom early in their careers—a practice that is still followed. Among other things, today that translates into a chance for young entrepreneurs to make mistakes on the way to tomorrow's great discoveries. Indeed, McKnight's exemplary leadership style seems to stand for achieving excellence through the unleashing of the vast capabilities of employees. To understand better his leadership views, some of McKnight's comments over the years are particularly instructive. McKnight on delegation and initiative:

> As our business grows it becomes increasingly necessary to delegate responsibility and to encourage men and women to exercise their initiative. . . . Those men and women to whom we delegate authority and responsibility, if they are good people, are going to want to do their jobs in their own way. These are characteristics we want and should be encouraged. . . . Management that is destructively critical when mistakes are made kills initiative and it's essential that we have many people with initiative if we're to continue to grow.[1]

From a study of William McKnight's leadership style and philosophies, it is apparent that he had an underlying belief in the value and worth of every individual. He seemed to view each person as a valuable resource, and throughout his career he sought the input of employees, customers, and suppliers. In his early days in sales and eventually as national sales manager, for example, he advocated going beyond the front office and onto the shop floor. He reasoned that the workers that actually used 3M's products would be the most capable of providing information about their needs. This overarching philosophy carried over into his dealings with his employees as he moved through management to the helm of 3M.

Perhaps this overall belief in the integrity and potential in people is what caused him to place such a high value on initiative and self-reliance. In reflecting back regarding his career at 3M, McKnight would eventually comment, "We lose something valuable if we uproot all notion of personal self-reliance and the dignity of work. . . . To continue our progress and service to America and the world, we need a healthy appreciation of those who exercise the free man's option for excellence. . . ."[2] With these words and with his overall attitude and approach to dealing with people, McKnight epitomized a leader who believed in leading others to lead themselves to excellence.

Dwight D. Eisenhower

Dwight Eisenhower, hero of World War II, is considered by many historians as one of the greatest military leaders in history. His style, unlike that of the prototypical military leader who takes complete charge and commands and manipulates military units as though they were pieces on a chess board, was again powerfully indirect. He based his success on consistently encouraging, developing, and benefiting from the effectiveness of others. He gave much of the credit for his learned approach to leadership to leaders he served under early in his career. In particular, he singled out General George C. Marshall as an especially influential model. As as an example, when Eisenhower proposed a Philippine strategy, Marshall praised his initiative. "Eisenhower, the department is filled with able men who analyze their problems well but feel compelled always to bring them to me for final solution. I must have assistants who will solve their own problems and tell me later what they have done."[3]

Throughout his career Eisenhower demonstrated this same familiar effective theme of believing in people, providing them with significant freedom, and helping them to develop and exercise their abilities. In 1967 he wrote,

> In our Army, it was thought that every private had at least a Second Lieutenant's gold bars somewhere in him and he was helped and encouraged to earn them. . . . I am inclined by nature to be optimistic about the capacity of a person to rise higher than he or she has thought possible once interest and ambition are aroused.[4]

With these words Eisenhower perhaps captured best the spirit of SuperLeadership.

SUMMARY AND CONCLUSIONS

SuperLeadership provides a framework, a process, and a set of specific strategies to achieve people excellence in organizations. It is believed to be the most practical and effective means for reaching this objective within modern organizations. In a nutshell, it says that those managers and executives who want to become SuperLeaders can choose no better strategy than to facilitate and unleash the self-leadership potential of their subordinates. The authors believe that it is time to transcend the notion of leaders as heroes and instead *focus on leaders as hero-makers.* Leaders need first to learn to lead themselves and then to help others to do the same. In the process they will create an environment in which subordinates can achieve excellence and can themselves become SuperLeaders.

NOTES

1. Minnesota Mining and Manufacturing Company, *Our Story so Far: Notes from the First 75 Years of 3M Company.* St. Paul, MN: Minnesota Mining and Manufacturing Company, 1977, p. 12.
2. Ibid., p. 130.
3. Stephen E. Ambrose, *The Supreme Commander: The War Years of General Dwight D. Eisenhower.* New York: Doubleday & Co., Inc., 1970, p. 134.
4. Dwight D. Eisenhower, *At Ease: Stories I Tell to Friends.* New York: Doubleday & Co., Inc., 1967, pp. 141–142.

Reading 3

High-Involvement Management

Edward E. Lawler III

Summary prepared by Sally Riggs Fuller

Sally Riggs Fuller is a doctoral student in management at the University of Wisconsin, Madison. Her research interests include organization culture, symbolism, and the fit between individuals and organizations. She has enjoyed several interesting occupations, including artist and horse trainer, and has extensive work experience in the areas of personnel and management information systems.

THE PROMISE OF PARTICIPATIVE MANAGEMENT

Changing Management

The 1980s saw a decline of productivity, profits, and employee satisfaction in American companies. Many attributed these problems to traditional management styles. In an attempt to improve organizational performance and the quality of work life, organizations began adopting participative management approaches. These allow information, knowledge, rewards, and power to be moved to lower levels in the organization.

Why the Participative Approach

There is no one correct approach to organizing and managing. To be effective, the style must fit the existing conditions at a given time. These conditions include societal values, the nature of the work force, the type of product, and the business environment. These factors are very different today than they were when traditional management approaches originated and prospered. The question becomes, what management style currently will work the best? Some form of participative management is now appropriate because it is consistent with the changing environment. It not only suits the work force, societal values, and technology, but can also impact organizational effectiveness favorably.

Edward E. Lawler III, *High Involvement Management.* San Francisco: Jossey-Bass, 1986.

Organizational Effectiveness and Participation

There are four important elements of a participation program: power, information, rewards, and knowledge. Ideally, all four elements are moved downward in the organization to lower levels of employees. Preferably, a large proportion of the organization will be affected by the approach. Programs with a narrow scope, only affecting a fraction of the organization, have not shown a high degree of success because there is often strong pressure to conform to the rest of the organization.

Five major determinants of organizational effectiveness are motivation, satisfaction, acceptance of change, problem solving, and communication. Participation programs can affect all of these, thus indirectly impacting organizational effectiveness. Participation can improve motivation when employees participate in decisions concerning target goals, have influence over how work is to be accomplished, and understand and influence how financial rewards are tied to performance. Higher levels of satisfaction can result from participation when employees desire (and experience) control, participation, self-fulfillment, and self-esteem. High absenteeism and turnover could result from not providing participative opportunities to these individuals.

Participation also has a probable impact on resistance to change. Changes will be accepted more readily when people are given a role in designing those changes. Employee participation in problem solving can lead to more effective solutions to problems involving the employee's work situation. The final method by which participation can impact organizational effectiveness is enhanced communication and coordination between work groups. Participation in decision making increases employees' overall knowledge about the organization, which results in better communication and coordination.

For effective implementation of participative approaches, attention must be paid to all parts of the organization. A participative program's effectiveness can be assessed by determining the extent to which it moves power, information, rewards, and knowledge downward in the organization.

PARTICIPATIVE PROGRAMS

Quality Circles

Quality circles have enjoyed widespread adoption in the United States; however, their effectiveness is still in doubt. As with all participative programs, they can be examined in terms of how they affect information, power, knowledge, and rewards in the organization. Quality circles facilitate the upward, but not downward, flow of information. Although quality circle members do not have direct power over organizational decisions, a subtle change may occur. Lower-level participants may acquire added power from the knowledge and information gained through this approach. The increase of knowledge resulting from quality circles stems from training in problem solving and interpersonal skills.

Quality circles have little or no impact on reward systems in organizations. Overall, due to their limited effects on information, power, knowledge, and rewards, quality circles cannot be expected to have a major impact on organizational effectiveness. Their main advantage appears to be as a starting point for an organization's overall move toward increased participation, rather than as a permanent, sufficient approach alone.

Employee Survey Feedback

Attitude surveys are considered a participative approach when feedback from them is used to encourage, structure, and measure the effectiveness of employee involvement. Although the total effect of survey feedback programs on power is limited, there are two ways that they may have an impact on lower participants. These employees acquire temporary power simply by suggesting improvements to management. In addition, if organizations use the survey information to evaluate and control managers, employees have the potential to affect managers' careers. The survey feedback process substantially increases the upward flow of information, and, when well done, offers improvements in the downward movement. The effect on knowledge is minimal, and limited primarily to management employees. The survey feedback program has no direct impact on organizations' reward systems.

This type of program can be viewed as temporary, doing little to institute a long-term participative approach. It has been shown to have positive, but limited, effects on employee satisfaction and organizational effectiveness.

Job Enrichment

Job enrichment involves creating jobs in which individuals can be responsible for an entire product or service. Expansion occurs both horizontally and vertically. Correctly implemented, this participative program increases knowledge, information, and power in lower levels of organizations. Employees gain knowledge and power because of their broader responsibility and authority. They are also likely to have increased information because better feedback accompanies the design of enriched jobs. Job enrichment often is implemented in only a small subset of organizational systems; therefore, to have a continuing positive effect, it must be accompanied by other organization changes.

Work Teams

Participative work teams are groups of employees who are given considerable responsibility to decide how their groups will operate. The team acquires functions normally performed by management. Work teams are extremely effective in moving power to lower levels in the organization, often to the lowest levels. This participative program also has an important impact on employee knowledge. Expansion of knowledge occurs both horizontally and vertically. Because the team takes responsibility for vertical skills, it also acquires additional information. Due to the installation of skill-base pay with work teams, rewards systems are also sometimes changed. Overall, because of these significant effects, work teams may have a meaningful positive impact on organizational effectiveness. This occurs because a satisfying, rewarding work environment affects individual behavior in a way that increases productivity and reduces costs. A problem occurs with this program, however. Because of its significant downward movement of power, information, knowledge, and rewards, traditional managers often do not accept it. Work teams are valuable, but that value arises primarily when other organizational systems are also designed to encourage participation.

Union-Management Programs

Traditional relationships between unions and management were adversarial. However, changes have been occurring since the early 1970s, and today, participative union-management quality-of-work-life (QWL) programs are widespread. Power is not directly shifted to lower participants, but a subtle effect can result from the QWL committee structure that makes recommendations for changes. Sharing information is often the most important impact of QWL programs. Communication channels open, and individuals gain new insight concerning business operations. Extrinsic rewards are not affected by these programs, primarily because contractual issues are explicitly excluded from the scope of QWL committees. Increased knowledge and skill also result from QWL programs, especially for the employees who serve on the committees.

Because the QWL programs cannot impact collective bargaining issues such as job structure and reward systems, they should not be viewed as a complete, consistent participative approach. Although QWL programs seem to lead to improved employee well-being and job satisfaction, there is no evidence that they provide long-term increases in productivity or organizational effectiveness. They appear to represent a valid first step in a transition to a participative union-management relationship.

Gainsharing

Gainsharing—basing employee bonuses on organizational performance—creates a direct link between participative management and financial rewards. Participation is an integral part of gainsharing programs; their success relies heavily on employee acceptance, input, and cooperation.

The effect of gainsharing on participation is significantly different from that of the five previous programs. Lower participants receive financial rewards based on organizational performance; this serves as an effective motivator. Because rewards are linked to an organization's financial results, substantial information is made available to employees. Although little powersharing occurs, there is some increase because of the additional information that moves downward. Often, groups obtain added power if they are given the responsibility for a budget and implementation of solutions. The primary effect on knowledge is through the increase in employee knowledge about the organization's financial matters.

One of the most important strengths of gainsharing is the fact that the program affects all members of an organization. Gainsharing represents a significant first step toward high-involvement management in the total organization. Because participation occurs at the lowest levels, and because the programs reward organizational performance, such programs can lead to more significant changes.

New-Design Plants

New-design plants have been created to facilitate an organization-wide approach to participative management. Common practices in new-design plants include employee selection by group members, physical layout that facilitates work group tasks, a team approach to job design, egalitarian pay systems, lack of hierarchical organization structure, heavy emphasis on training and development, and a clear management philosophy.

Because of their design, these programs are very effective approaches to increased participation, especially in the areas of knowledge, information, and power. The system moves knowledge to lower levels through economic education, cross-training, and group-skills training. Although new-design plants do not explicitly move information downward, they often make additional information available to employees through reports and open information systems. Lower levels acquire power through decentralized decision-making throughout the organization. The primary weakness of new-design plants lies in the area of rewards. Many new-design systems do not implement a gainsharing-type system along with the design, and therefore, lower-level employees do not participate in financial rewards.

New-design plants involve changes to such a broad range of organizational systems that they are much like whole new organizations. Although there are very few studies of new-design plants, initial reports of organizational effectiveness have been positive. Organizations have reported improvements in productivity and quality of work life. The approach does, however, involve problems. Organizations are challenged to take advantage of its benefits by incorporating appropriate features into a complete model of a participative system.

HIGH-INVOLVEMENT MANAGEMENT

How It Works

After examining the seven participative management approaches, it becomes possible to determine how the various features fit together into a high-involvement organization. This must be accomplished in a way that provides maximum participation for all employees, and maximum organizational effectiveness. As a goal, critical organization features must be designed to be congruent with high employee involvement.

The first component of a high-involvement organization must be a management philosophy which reflects employee involvement and responsibility for decision-making as core values. Organization structure serves as a key feature of a high-involvement organization; it must exhibit few levels of management and little staffing. Having fewer managers helps ensure that decisions get delegated to lower levels. The fundamental organizational grouping should be individual units that are responsible for a particular product or service.

Job design is another critical component of a high-involvement organization. Whether the job enrichment takes the form of individual jobs or teams depends on the technology. Information systems are especially crucial to high-involvement organizations because of the lack of hierarchy and staff support. Systems must provide employees with the capability for self-regulation, and must provide needed information to all organizational members. Physical layout must also be examined. The work environment should be safe, pleasant, and egalitarian. This reinforces the organization's classless structure and de-emphasizes hierarchy.

The reward system in a high-involvement organization must also reflect different values. Skill-based pay helps develop employee knowledge. In addition, gainsharing, profit-sharing, and stock ownership plans create links between organizational success and employee rewards. Personnel policies should be developed in a participative manner to increase commitment to them, and should be designed to allow choices among options.

The career system is another very important feature of a high-involvement organization. For cross-training and skill-based pay to be effective, employees must be made aware of career options and necessary skills. The career system must recognize individuality and stress learning and growth. Because high-involvement organizations are quite different from traditional ones, employee selection becomes critical. Employees must be oriented toward learning, growth, and individual development, and possess a desire to be responsible for their own behavior. Because employee learning, growth, and development are essential, training takes on a new emphasis, and is often tied directly to the skill-based pay system.

Leadership style in high-involvement organizations is quite different from that in traditional organizations. High-involvement management encourages self-motivating and self-regulating employees. Managers use leadership skills to build trust and openness, provide and communicate a vision, move decision making to the appropriate level, and empower employees.

The role of unions in high-involvement organizations emerges as very different from the traditional role. The new relationship must be that of a partnership. It should be flexible, with the contract always open for change on an as-needed basis. Unions can help the movement of power, rewards, information, and knowledge to all levels in the organization.

The keys to a successful high-involvement organization are congruence and consistency. The combination of the features described above creates an organization in which the practices fit together to impact the entire organization, and deal consistently with all employees. Rewards, knowledge, information, and power are all affected. The reward system encourages development of skills, the training and selection systems provide knowledge, the information system creates the foundation necessary for skill utilization, and work design gives employees the power and tasks to use their skills. These combine to form an effective high-involvement organization.

Managing the Change

The question now becomes, how are high-involvement organizations created? There is no one best way to implement this type of change; there are, however, some general guidelines. There are many possible reasons to begin a change effort, but only one characterizes the most successful changes: change because the organization's survival depends on it. According to Lawler this does not necessarily mean that the organization must be desperate, but just that there must be a compelling reason for a corporate-wide change effort.

In changes specifically designed to move from traditional to participative management, the process should begin with something that employees are concerned about. Efforts can begin at the top of the organization, or at the bottom and work up. Because it may be dangerous to begin at the lower levels if there is no complementary strategy at the top, the best method is to begin at the top of the organization. However, the remainder of the organization still must be receptive to the change.

The best participative program to begin the move to high-involvement management depends on how far away the organization currently is from high-involvement management. If little has been done to move rewards, power, information, and knowledge to lower levels in the organization, the program should begin with a basic approach, such as quality circles and survey feedback. In successful change projects, a shared vision of the goals of the program exists. Change programs can also be energized by appealing to employees' values and beliefs. Moves toward high-involvement management are based on openness, personal growth, and participative decision making. Perhaps the most critical aspect of implementing a change to a high-involvement organization is the focus on the long term. Although some participative programs can result in relatively fast improvements, organization-wide change can take decades. It should be approached with commitment, with a vision of an effective, competitive organization, and with a highly involved work force.

PART
SEVEN

Leadership

This is the "decade of the leader." Nationally we seem to be looking for the hero who can turn us around, establish a new direction, and pull us through. Organizations are searching for visionary leaders—people who by the strength of their personalities can bring about a major organizational transformation. We hear calls for charismatic, transformational, and transactional leadership. A myriad of individuals charge that the problems with the American economy, declining organizational productivity, and lost ground in worldwide competitive markets are largely a function of poor management and the lack of good organizational leadership.

John Gardner, former U.S. Secretary of Health, Education, and Welfare, and currently the Miriam and Peter Haas Centennial Professor at Stanford Business School, is the author of *On Leadership.* In his book Gardner suggests that one of the biggest problems and challenges facing America today is one of leadership and the "issues behind the issues" of leadership (e.g., shared values, institutional renewal, and motivation). Gardner argues that the large-scale and complex organizations that dominate society tend to stifle those who enact roles within these social systems. Not only does Gardner highlight many of the grave problems challenging us, but he also provides insight into how we can make these organizations flexible and adaptive systems—much of which can be achieved through leadership.

Warren Bennis is a Professor of Business Administration at the University of Southern California. He has been a part of a small group of individuals who for several decades have attempted to focus attention on the critical role of leaders within organizations. In his book *Why Leaders Can't Lead: The Unconscious Conspiracy Continues*, Bennis argues that today's organizations are overmanaged and underled.

In *The Managerial Mystique*, Abraham Zaleznik charges that American business suffers from widespread managerial mediocrity and desperately needs new leadership to return to competitive worldwide economic status. Zaleznik, a Harvard Business School Professor, suggests that American managers are preoccupied with methods, structure, process, and control—the managerial mystique—as the means to guide their organizations in pursuit of their goals. The cure to the problem is not more structure, not more control, but leadership!

Jay A. Conger is an Associate Professor of Organizational Behavior at the Faculty of Management, McGill University. His book *The Charismatic Leader: Behind the Mystique of Exceptional Leadership* provides illustrations of individuals like Steve Jobs, Lee Iacocca, Mary Kay, John DeLorean, and Ross Perot to define the characteristics of the charismatic leader. Vision, articulation skills, empowerment, unconventionality, and risk-taking are a set of attributes that Conger suggests set apart the charismatic from the noncharismatic leader. He details how the charismatic leader motivates others to act in a self-assured manner and to be willing to take risks.

A wide array of other books on leadership have appeared. Alternative perspectives can be found in Tichy and Devanna's *The Transformational Leader*, Covey's *The Seven Habits of Highly Effective People* and his follow-up book, *Principle-Centered Leadership*, Koestenbaum's *Leadership: The Inner Side of Greatness*, and Conger's *Learning to Lead: The Art of Transforming Managers into Leaders*.

Reading 1

On Leadership

John W. Gardner

Summary prepared by James R. Meindl

James R. Meindl is an Associate Professor of Organization at the State University of New York at Buffalo, where he teaches and conducts research on organizational behavior, leadership, power, and justice. He received his M.A. and Ph.D. in social psychology from the University of Waterloo. He has served on the editorial boards of *Administrative Science Quarterly, Academy of Management Journal,* and *Academy of Management Review.*

On Leadership is the result of an intensive five-year field study of organizations and interviews with hundreds of contemporary leaders. Gardner attempts to illuminate aspects of leadership that may be useful as society faces many tough social, ecological, and economic problems. More frightening than the problems themselves are the questions they raise concerning our capacity to meet them. The institutions which have served us so well in the past have lost much of their capacity to focus our energies and to sustain our commitments to resolve tough problems. The fragmentation and divisiveness in American life have made it difficult for people to channel their efforts to any worthy common purpose. When motivation and confidence in our institutions slip too far, the efforts of leaders are gravely diminished. *The great challenge of leadership in America today*—in corporations, labor unions, schools, government agencies, and so forth—*is to renew and reinvigorate our human institutions,* with matters of motivation, values, social cohesion, and reawakening a sense of community as the real "issues behind the issues."

The book contains three major themes. The first few chapters describe and analyze what leadership is and is not. The middle chapters present ideas about the tasks, attributes, and morality of leadership within difficult social and institutional contexts. The last few chapters focus on leadership development.

THE NATURE AND TASKS OF LEADERSHIP

The concept of leadership too often carries near-mystical connotations. Thinking clearly about the topic requires a demystification of it. *Leadership* is a process by which an individual (or leadership team) induces a group to pursue objectives held by the leader or shared by the leader and his or her followers. Leadership ought not be confused with status, power, and official authority. High-ranking bureaucrats are not necessarily selected for their leadership skills; dictators can coerce their subjects; and officials have subordinates who often are not their followers.

Leaders vs. Managers

The commonly used distinction between leaders and managers is misleading. First-class managers are often likely to possess a good measure of leadership as well. These leader/managers distinguish themselves from run-of-the-mill managers in that the former think in the longer term, they grasp how their unit fits within a larger system, they are able to influence others beyond their jurisdictions and thus can integrate fragmented constituencies, they emphasize intangibles such as vision, values, and intuition, they have good political skills in coping with conflict, and they think in terms of renewal, seeking to revise and improve the status quo. Such qualities, however, do not lead to a single profile or image of an idealized leader. There are many kinds of leaders with unique constellations of personal strengths and attributes, and their effectiveness often represents the matching of strengths with historical contexts and the particular contemporary settings in which they act.

Leadership functions

There are at least ten significant functions of leadership, and leaders differ strikingly in terms of how well they perform them. The ten functions are: envisioning goals, affirming and regenerating important group values, motivating others toward collective goals, managing the processes through which collective goals can be reached, achieving unity of effort within a context of pluralism and diversity, creating an atmosphere of mutual trust, explaining and teaching, serving as a symbol of the group's identity, representing the group's interests to outside parties, and renewing and adapting the organization to a changing world.

The various tasks of leadership are intermingled in the complex interplay between leaders and their followers. In this relationship, leaders are never as much in command and followers never as submissive as one might imagine. Leaders and followers must shape each other. In such a process, two-way communication is extremely important, as is mutual trust. It is also true that failures of leadership are often also failures of followership; qualities such as apathy, passivity, and cynicism invite the abuse of power by the leader. The purposes of the group are best served when the leader enables followers to build their own initiative.

THE CONTEXTS AND ATTRIBUTES OF LEADERSHIP

The interaction between leaders and followers does not take place in a vacuum, but it is located in a historic and cultural context, within some institutional setting. These contexts affect the nature of the interaction and the leadership attributes that are effective. Great leaders emerge because their attributes match the contexts in which they operate. In a contemporary world, the context is increasingly one of interdependence.

Leadership Attributes

Despite the interplay between contexts and personal attributes, there are some attributes which seem to be linked with higher probabilities that a leader in one situation could also lead in another. These include:

1. Physical vitality and stamina
2. Intelligence and action-oriented judgment
3. Eagerness to accept responsibility
4. Task competence
5. Understanding of followers and their needs
6. Skill in dealing with people
7. Need for achievement
8. Capacity to motivate people
9. Courage and resolution
10. Trustworthiness
11. Decisiveness
12. Self-confidence
13. Assertiveness
14. Adaptability/flexibility.

Leadership and power

Effective leaders must be willing to use the power available to them. Much leadership talent is lost because so many young people abhor the image of power as exemplified by leadership roles. If we are to attract more young people to leadership roles, we must show them more positive aspects of the leader's task. Power is, after all, ethically neutral.

Leaders and their exercise of power are ultimately judged within a moral framework of values. In the contemporary U.S., morally acceptable leaders can be defined in terms of their objectives with respect to the group and the individuals who comprise it. These include the release of human energy and talent, balancing individual interests and communal needs, adherence to a moral order, and active involvement of followers in the pursuit of group goals.

An important characteristic of contemporary leadership is the necessity for the leader to work with and through extremely complex organizations and institutions. The sheer size of organizations can create problems for a leader interested in creativity and change. Getting rid of turf fights, overcoming communication barriers, appropriate decentralization schemes with the proper allocation of functions, and maintaining high levels of motivation and initiative are a few of the problems that need to be resolved. Leaders need to take advantage of their strategic centrality, their agenda-setting powers, and their capacity to mobilize lower-level leaders to overcome the problems of large-scale organizational systems.

COMMONWEAL INTERESTS AND RENEWAL

We live in a fragmented, rather than a tightly knit society. A central problem in a fragmented society is the war which takes place between narrow, parochial interests, and those of the common good. Pluralism places a special burden on leadership. The task for leaders is not just to work across boundaries to achieve the goals of their own groups, but to act in a way which supports commonweal interests. Networking, conflict resolution, coalition building, and political compromises are important to commonweal concerns.

Community-building skills

Failures of leadership today are often traceable to a breakdown of community: a disintegration of coherence, continuity, and allegiance in American life. Skill in building and rebuilding a community is one of the highest and most essential skills a contemporary leader can command. Such skills must be aimed at creating the conditions which foster the development of community. These include:

1. Wholeness which incorporates diversity
2. Shared norms and values
3. Good internal communication among community groups
4. Attitudes of caring, trust, and teamwork
5. Institutionalized provisions for governance
6. Sharing of leadership tasks
7. Development of young people
8. Permeable boundaries to the outside world.

The effective contemporary leader lives with the idea of renewal, and overcomes the "trance of nonrenewal." Measures must be taken to enhance the possibility of renewal: enabling young leaders to move into positions where they can do the most good; periodically reassigning talented leaders; surrounding oneself with people who can motivate; creating a climate of experimentation and risk-taking; freeing-up communication; renewing self; and paying attention to the culture. Above all else, leaders must see their primary renewal task as the release of human energy and talent.

How can we define the role of leaders in a way that most effectively releases the creative energies of followers in the pursuit of shared purposes? The answer is that *leadership must be shared.* This begins with the notion of leadership teams, a circle of close advisors, but ought to extend down through all levels of an organization and to the farthest reaches of the system. It is important, though, even when leadership is distributed throughout a system, that power be held accountable. *The task is to design more empowering systems, but in a way that ensures accountability.*

DEVELOPING LEADERS AND RELEASING THE HUMAN POTENTIAL

Where have all the great leaders gone? The Jeffersons and Lincolns of today *are* among us. There are many unawakened leaders who have neither felt an overpowering call to lead nor are yet aware of their own potential. These individuals require leadership development. Leadership can be taught and it can be learned. But most human talent along these lines remains undeveloped. As a result, our society faces a severely diminished supply of leaders today. Common obstacles include:

1. Slowly developing crises as opposed to explosive ones which seem to call forth leadership talents
2. The suppressive effects of large and complex organizations and communities
3. The prestige of specialist, professional training
4. An educational system which places too much emphasis on individual performance and
5. Negative publicity often associated with public office.

The leaders of today must nurture the development of tomorrow's potential leaders. Leadership development is a lifelong process. Traditional selection and recruiting are often incapable of identifying leadership potential. Organizational cultures also have invisible selection processes which may select out those with deep commitments to the group in favor of opportunistic careerists. Schools and colleges in particular need to take a more active role. Higher education typically removes most young people from the mainstream of the American experience, at a time when they should be brought closer to it. More opportunities are needed to develop and test skills, as well as more role models and mentors to observe and from whom to learn.

In order to develop others, leaders must be motivators. Motivation by coercion is inherently imperfect because it offers too many ways for group members to frustrate group purposes, and it stunts growth. It's not enough that leaders are committed; they must also develop commitment in others. The task is to help people see how both personal and group needs can be met by shared action. The chances of doing that are enhanced by recognizing the needs of followers, building a system of shared values, regenerating a sound moral order, getting others to see interdependencies between group and individual interests, and committing people to visions of a better future and for things which extend beyond themselves. Leadership entails the obligations and duties without which freedom and liberty cannot be sustained.

The development of human potential is often held in check by negative attitudes toward the future, by over-aversion to risk taking, and undue discouragement in the face of hardships. In order to develop others, leaders must themselves maintain their morale and optimism. There must be a sense of confidence in others and in the future, expectations of success and a breaking away from attitudes of defeat and discouragement, and a commitment to human nature and its potential for greatness. The will to act cannot be maintained without the conviction that, however negative the outward appearances, everyone has the leadership potential to help build civilizations. It simply must be released, developed, and appropriately used.

Reading 2

Why Leaders Can't Lead

Warren Bennis

A moment of truth came to me toward the end of my first ten months as president of the University of Cincinnati. The clock was moving toward four in the morning, and I was still in my office, still mired in the incredible mass of paper stacked on my desk. I was bone-weary and soul-weary, and I found myself muttering, "Either I can't manage this place, or it's unmanageable." I reached for my calendar and ran my eyes down each hour, half-hour, quarter-hour, to see where my time had gone that day, the day before, the month before.

Nobel laureate James Franck has said he always recognizes a moment of discovery by "the feeling of terror that seizes me." I felt a trace of it that morning. My discovery was this: I had become the victim of a vast, amorphous, unwitting, unconscious conspiracy to prevent me from doing anything whatever to change the university's status quo.

Even those of my associates who fully shared my hopes to set new goals and new directions and to work toward creative change were unconsciously often doing the most to make sure that I would never find the time to begin. I found myself thinking of a friend and former colleague who had taken over one of our top universities with goals and plans that fired up all those around him and who said when he left a few years later, "I never could get around to doing the things I wanted to do."

BENNIS'S FIRST LAW

This discovery, or rediscovery, has led me to formulate what might be called Bennis's First Law of Academic Pseudodynamics: Routine work drives out nonroutine work and smothers to death all creative planning, all fundamental change in the university—or any institution.

These were the institutions facing me: To start, there were 150 letters in the day's mail that required a response. About fifty of them concerned our young dean of the School of Education, Hendrik Gideonse. His job was to bring

Reprinted from the *Training and Development Journal*, April 1989, pp. 35–39.

about change in the teaching of teachers, in our university's relationship to the public schools, and to students in the deprived and deteriorating neighborhood around us. Out of these urban schools would come the bulk of our students of the future—as good or as bad as the school had shaped them.

But the letters were not about education. They were about a baby, the dean's ten-week-old son. Gideonse felt very strongly about certain basic values. He felt especially so about sex roles, about equality for his wife, about making sure she had the time and freedom to develop her own potentials fully. So he was carrying the baby into his office two days a week in a little bassinet, which he kept on his desk while he did his work.

The daily *Cincinnati Enquirer* heard about it, took a picture of Hendrik, baby, and bassinet, and played it on page one. TV splashed it across the nation. And my "in" basket began to overflow with letters that urged his arrest for child abuse or at least his immediate dismissal. My only public comment was that we were a tax-supported institution, and if Hendrik could engage in that form of applied humanism and still accomplish the things we both wanted done in education, then, like Lincoln with Grant's whiskey, I'd gladly send him several new babies for adoption.

Hendrik was, of course, simply a man a bit ahead of his time. Today, his actions would be applauded—maybe even with the Father of the Year award. Then, however, Hendrik and his baby ate up quite a bit of my time.

Also on my desk was a note from a professor, complaining that his classroom temperature was down to sixty-five degrees. Perhaps he expected me to grab a wrench and fix it. A student complained that we wouldn't give him course credit for acting as assistant to a city council member. Another was unable to get into the student health center. The teacher at my child's day school, who attended the university, was dissatisfied with her grades. A parent complained about four-letter words in a Philip Roth book being used in an English class. The track coach wanted me to come over to see for myself how bad the track was. An alumnus couldn't get the football seats he wanted. Another wanted a coach fired. A teacher had called to tell me the squash court was closed at 7:00 P.M. when he wanted to use it.

Perhaps twenty percent of my time that year had been taken up by a problem at the general hospital, which was city-owned but was administered by the university and served as the teaching hospital of the university medical school. Some terminal-cancer patients, with their consent, had been subjected to whole-body radiation as possibly beneficial therapy. Since the Pentagon saw this as a convenient way to gather data that might help protect civilian populations in nuclear warfare, it provided a series of subsidies for the work.

When this story broke and was pursued in such a way as to call up comparisons with the Nazis' experiments on human guinea pigs, it became almost impossible for me or anybody else to separate the essential facts from the fantasized distortions. The problem eventually subsided, after a blue-ribbon task force recommended significant changes in the experiment's design. But I invested endless time in a matter only vaguely related to the prime purposes of the university—and wound up being accused by some of interfering with academic freedom.

The radiation experiment and Hendrik's baby illustrate how the media, particularly TV, make the academic cloister a goldfish bowl. By focusing on the lurid or the superficial, they can disrupt a president's proper activities while contributing nothing to the advancement of knowledge. This leads me to Bennis's Second Law of Academic Pseudodynamics: Make whatever grand plans you will; you may be sure the unexpected or the trivial will disturb and disrupt them.

In my moment of truth, that weary 4:00 A.M. in my trivia-cluttered office, I began trying to straighten out in my own mind what university presidents should be doing and not doing, what their true priorities should be, how they must lead.

THE OLD ARMY GAME

Lead, not *manage,* there is an important difference. Many an institution is very well managed and very poorly led. It may excel in the ability to handle each day all the routine inputs, yet may never ask whether the routine should be done at all.

All of us find ourselves acting on routine problems because they are the easiest things to handle. We hesitate to get involved too early in the bigger ones—we collude, as it were, in the unconscious conspiracy to immerse us in routine.

My entrapment in routine made me realize another thing: People were following the old army game. They did not want to take the responsibility for or bear the consequences of decisions they properly should make. The motto was, "Let's push up the tough ones." The consequence was that everybody and anybody was dumping his "wet babies" (as the old State Department hands call them) on my desk, when I had neither the diapers nor the information to take care of them.

So I decided that the president's first priority—the sine qua non of effective leadership—was to create an "executive constellation" to run the office of the president. It could be a mixed bag, some vice-presidents, some presidential assistants. The group would have to be compatible in the sense that its members could work together, but neither uniform nor conformist—a group of people who knew more than the president about everything within their areas of competency and could attend to daily matters without dropping their wet babies on the president's desk.

What should the president him- or herself do? The president should be a conceptualist. That's something more than being just an "idea man." It means being a leader with entrepreneurial vision and the time to spend thinking about the forces that will affect the destiny of the institution. The president must educate board members so that they not only understand the necessity of distinguishing between leadership and management but also can protect the chief executive from getting enmeshed in routine machinery.

Leaders must create for their institutions clear-cut and measurable goals based on advice from all elements of the community. They must be allowed to proceed toward those goals without being crippled by bureaucratic machinery that saps their strength, energy, and initiative. They must be allowed to take risks, to embrace error, to use their creativity to the hilt, and to encourage those who work with them to use theirs.

These insights gave me the strength to survive my acid test: whether I, as a "leading theorist" of the principles of creative leadership, actually could prove myself a leader. However, the sum total of my experiences as president of the University of Cincinnati convinced me that most of the academic theory on leadership was useless.

LEADERS ARE DIVERSE

After leaving the university, I spent nearly five years researching a book on leadership. I traveled around the country spending time with ninety of the most effective, successful leaders in the nation, sixty from corporations and thirty from the public sector. My goal was to find these leaders' common traits, a task that required much more probing than I had expected.

For a while, I sensed much more diversity than commonality among them. The group included both left-brain and right-brain thinkers, some who dressed for success and some who didn't, well-spoken, articulate leaders and laconic, inarticulate ones; some John Wayne types and some who were definitely the opposite.

I was finally able to come to some conclusions, of which perhaps the most important is the distinction between leaders and managers: Leaders are people who do the right thing; managers are people who do things right. Both roles are crucial, but they differ profoundly. I often observe people in top positions doing the wrong things well.

This study also reinforced my earlier insight—that American organizations (and probably those in much of the rest of the industrialized world) are underled and overmanaged. They do not pay enough attention to doing the right thing, while they pay too much attention to doing things right. Part of the fault lies with our schools of management; we teach people how to be good technicians and good staff people, but we don't train people for leadership.

The group of sixty corporate leaders was not especially different from any profile of top leadership in America. The median age was fifty-six. Most were white males, with six black men and six women in the group. The only surprising finding was that all the CEOs not only were still married to their first spouses but also seemed enthusiastic about the institution of marriage. Among the CEOs were Bill Kieschnick, then chair and CEO of Arco, and the late Ray Kroc, of McDonald's.

Public-sector leaders included Harold Williams, who then chaired the Securities and Exchange Commission (SEC); Neil Armstrong, a genuine all-American hero who happened to be at the University of Cincinnati, three elected officials; two orchestra conductors; and two winning athletics coaches. I wanted conductors and coaches because I mistakenly believed that they were the last leaders with complete control over their constituents.

WHAT MAKES A LEADER

After several years of observation and conversation, I defined four competencies evident to some extent in every member of the group: management of attention; management of meaning; management of trust, and management of self.

Management of Attention

The first trait apparent in these leaders is their ability to draw others to them, not just because they have a vision but because they communicate an extraordinary focus of commitment. Leaders manage attention through a compelling vision that brings others to a place they have not been before.

One of the people I most wanted to interview was one of the few I could not seem to reach—Leon Fleisher, a well-known child prodigy who grew up to become a prominent pianist, conductor, and musicologist. I happened to be in Aspen, Colorado, one summer while Fleisher was conducting the Aspen Music Festival, and I tried again to reach him, even leaving a note on his dressing-room door. Driving back through downtown Aspen, I saw two perspiring young cellists carrying their instruments, and I offered them a ride to the music tent. They hopped in the back of my Jeep, and as we rode I questioned them about Fleisher. "I'll tell you why he's so great," said one. "He doesn't waste our time."

Fleisher finally agreed not only to be interviewed but to let me watch him rehearse and conduct music classes. I linked the way I saw him work with that simple sentence, "He doesn't waste our time." Every moment Fleisher was before the orchestra, he knew exactly what sound he wanted. He didn't waste time, because his intentions were always evident. What united him with the other musicians was their concern with intention and outcome.

When I reflected on my own experience, it struck me that when I was most effective, it was because I knew what I wanted. When I was ineffective, it was because I was unclear about it.

So the first leadership competency is the management of attention through a set of intentions or a vision, not in a mystical or religious sense but in the sense of outcome, goal, or direction.

Management of Meaning

The second leadership competency is management of meaning. To make dreams apparent to others and to align people with them, leaders must communicate their vision. Communication and alignment work together.

Consider, for example, the contrasting styles of Presidents Reagan and Carter. Ronald Reagan is called "the Great Communicator"; one of his speech writers said that Reagan can read the phone book and make it interesting. The reason is that Reagan uses metaphors with which people can identify. In his first budget message, for example, Reagan described a trillion dollars by comparing it to piling up dollar bills beside the Empire State Building. Reagan, to use one of Alexander Haig's coinages, "tangibilitated" the idea.

Leaders make ideas tangible and real to others, so they can support them. For no matter how marvelous the vision, the effective leader must use a metaphor, a work or a model to make that vision clear to others.

In contrast, President Carter was boring. Carter was one of our best-informed presidents; he had more facts at his fingertips than almost any other president. But he never made the meaning come through the facts. I interviewed an assistant secretary of commerce appointed by Carter, who told me that after four years in his administration, she still did not know what Jimmy Carter stood for. She said that working for him was like looking through the wrong side of a tapestry; the scene was blurry and indistinct.

The leader's goal is not mere explanation or clarification but the creation of meaning. My favorite baseball joke is exemplary: In the ninth inning of a key playoff game, with a three-and-two count on the batter, the umpire hesitates a split second in calling the pitch. The batter whirls around angrily and says, "Well, what was it?" The umpire snarls back, "It ain't nothing until I call it!"

Management of Trust

The third competency is management of trust. Trust is essential to all organizations. The main determinant of trust is reliability, what I call constancy. When I talked to the board members or staffs of these leaders, I heard certain phrases again and again: "She is all of a piece." "Whether you like it or not, you always know where he is coming from, what he stands for."

When John Paul II visited this country, he gave a press conference. One reporter asked how the pope could account for allocating funds to build a swimming pool at the papal summer palace. He responded quickly, "I like to swim. Next question." He did not rationalize about medical reasons or claim that he got the money from a special source. A recent study showed that people would much rather follow individuals they can count on, even when they disagree with their viewpoints, than people they agree with but who shift positions frequently.

I cannot emphasize enough the significance of constancy and focus. Margaret Thatcher's re-election in Great Britain is another excellent example. When she won office in 1979, observers predicted that she quickly would revert to defunct Labor Party policies. She did not. She was not turned; she had been constant, focused, and all of a piece.

Management of Self

The fourth leadership competency is management of self, knowing one's skills and deploying them effectively. Management of self is critical; without it, leaders and managers can do more harm than good. Like incompetent doctors, incompetent managers can make life worse, make people sicker and less vital. There is a term, "iatrogenic," for illnesses caused by doctors and hospitals. There should be one for illnesses caused by leaders, too. Some give themselves heart attacks and nervous breakdowns; still worse, many are "carriers," causing their employees to be ill.

Leaders know themselves; they know their strengths and nurture them. They also have a faculty I think of as the Wallenda Factor. The Flying Wallendas are perhaps the world's greatest family of aerialists and tightrope walkers. I was fascinated when, in the early 1970s, seventy-one-year-old Karl Wallenda said that for him living was walking the tightrope, and everything else was waiting. I was struck with his capacity for concentration on the intention, the task, the decision.

I was even more intrigued when, several months later, Wallenda fell to his death while walking a tightrope without a safety net between two high-rise buildings in San Juan, Puerto Rico. Wallenda fell still clutching the balancing pole he had warned his family never to drop lest it hurt somebody below. Later, Wallenda's wife said that before her husband had fallen, for the first time since she had known him he had been concentrating on falling, instead of on walking the tightrope. He had personally supervised the attachment of the guide wires, which he had never done before.

Like Wallenda before his fall, the leaders in my group seemed unacquainted with the concept of failure. What you or I might call a failure, they referred to as a mistake. I began collecting synonyms for the word "failure" mentioned in the interviews, and I found more than twenty: "mistake," "error," "false start," "bloop," "flop," "loss," "miss," "four-up," "stumble," "botch," "bungle" . . . but not "failure."

One CEO told me that if she had a knack for leadership, it was the capacity to make as many mistakes as she could as soon as possible, and thus get them out of the way. Another said that a mistake is simply "another way of doing things." These leaders learn from and use something that doesn't go well; it is not a failure but simply the next step.

EMPOWERING EMPLOYEES

Leadership can be felt throughout an organization. It gives pace and energy to the work and empowers the work force. Empowerment is the collective effect of leadership. In organizations with effective leaders, empowerment is most evident in four themes:

- **People feel significant.** Everyone feels that he or she makes a difference to the success of the organization. The difference may be small—prompt delivery of potato chips to a mom-and-pop grocery store or developing a tiny but essential part for an airplane. But where they are empowered, people feel that what they do has meaning and significance.
- **Learning and competence matter.** Leaders value learning and mastery, and so do people who work for leaders. Leaders make it clear that there is no failure, only mistakes that give us feedback and tell us what to do next.
- **People are part of a community.** Where there is leadership, there is a team, a family, a unity. Even people who do not especially like each other feel the sense of community. When Neil Armstrong talks about

the Apollo explorations, he describes how a team carried out an almost unimaginably complex set of interdependent tasks. Until there were women astronauts, the men referred to this feeling as "brotherhood." I suggest they rename it "family."

- **Work is exciting.** Where there are leaders, work is stimulating, challenging, fascinating, and fun. An essential ingredient in organizational leadership is pulling rather than pushing people toward a goal. A "pull" style of influence attracts and energizes people to enroll in an exciting vision of the future. It motivates through identification, rather than through rewards and punishments. Leaders articulate and embody the ideals toward which the organization strives.

People cannot be expected to enroll in just any exciting vision. Some visions and concepts have more staying power and are rooted more deeply in our human needs than others. I believe the lack of two such concepts in modern organizational life is largely responsible for the alienation and lack of meaning so many experience in their work.

One of these is the concept of quality. Modern industrial society has been oriented to quantity, providing more goods and services for everyone. Quality often is not measured at all but is appreciated intuitively. Our response to quality is a feeling. Feelings of quality are connected intimately with our experience of meaning, beauty, and value in our lives.

Closely linked to the concept of quality is that of dedication to, even love of, our work. This dedication is evoked by quality and is the force that energizes high-performing systems. When we love our work, we need not be managed by hopes of reward or fears of punishment. We can create systems that facilitate our work, rather than being preoccupied with checks and controls of people who want to beat or exploit the system.

Ultimately, in great leaders and the organizations surrounding them, there is a fusion of work and play to the point where, as Robert Frost says, "Love and need are one." How do we get from here to there? I think we must start by studying change.

Reading 3

The Managerial Mystique

Abraham Zaleznik

Summary prepared by Philip Anderson

Philip Anderson is a University Professor of Management at the University of St. Thomas, where he teaches strategic planning and organization behavior. He received his Ph.D. from the University of Minnesota and is an active member in several professional associations, including the Academy of Management and the Association for Business Simulation and Experiential Learning.

"Business in America has lost its way, adrift in a sea of managerial mediocrity, desperately needing leadership to face worldwide economic competition," states Abraham Zaleznik (p. 11) as the underlying premise of his book, *The Managerial Mystique.* The decline of American business has occurred in market share, productivity, and real income. It results from an overemphasis on profits and stock prices, and a neglect of innovation and long-term goals.

The underlying cause of this loss of momentum and lack of direction is American business' belief in the *managerial mystique.* This mystique is founded on the belief that "solid methods produce good results." Structure and process are relied on to control behavior and yield progress toward desired organizational goals. Personal influence cannot be depended upon to guide the organization. The process, not the individual, is held accountable for the success or failure of a decision. The managerial mystique has grown out of an emphasis on management, rather than on the leadership of an organization.

The book contains five parts. In Part I (The Argument) Zaleznik presents evidence that a gap exists between the leading and the managing of organizations. Part II (The Analysis) historically outlines how and why this gap occurred and the managerial mystique developed. The consequences of relying on this mystique are detailed in Part III. Zaleznik presents his solution to the problem in Part IV (The Cure: Leadership). The conclusion, Part V, focuses on ways to restore leadership in business.

Abraham Zaleznik, *The Managerial Mystique: Restoring Leadership in Business.* New York: Harper & Row, 1989.

THE ARGUMENT

The Leadership Gap

Zaleznik argues that American business executives have the mistaken belief that management and leadership are synonymous—that is, that managing and leading an organization are the same. Failure to recognize the fundamental differences between these two dimensions has resulted in reliance on structure and process to guide the organization in the absence of true leadership. Managers have created a mystique that systems and control are more important to an organization's success than the personal influence and commitment exercised by leaders.

What are the differences between management and leadership? Leadership is based on a "compact" between leader and follower that binds them together—morally, intellectually, and emotionally—to pursue mutual goals. Leaders focus on stimulating innovative ideas and using personal charisma to handle conflicts that may arise. They relate to people on the basis of feelings and ideas.

To contrast leadership with the practice of management, management is based on a "contract" rooted in the pursuit of self-interest rather than mutual goals. This eliminates the need to convince followers that the organization's goals are worth pursuing. It is only necessary that the pursuit of their self-interest lead to attainment of the manager's goals. Because managerial rewards are generally based on the attainment of these goals, this pursuit of self-interest by followers allows the manager to prosper independent of the success of the organization. As a consequence, managers focus on process and procedure to achieve order and control and ensure the attainment of their own goals. Managers use compromise and rules to handle conflict. They relate to people according to their own role and position in the organization.

Management and Leadership

As the gap between management and leadership widens, structure and process receive increasing emphasis. This is because of the mistaken belief that good results will naturally follow from these efforts to control human behavior. Managers strive to eliminate disorder and unpredictability from their environment. By contrast, leaders use this chaos to foster innovation. This instability can result in inconsistent performance by a leader, while a manager's order and structure yield more predictable behavior and results.

As order and consistency became more valued, the autocratic, and often erratic, leader faded from the American business scene. The inconsistent leader was replaced by the predictable manager and the mystique that structure and process would yield successful results. Commitment, creativity, and experimentation were replaced with principles of bargaining, emotional control, and quantitative analysis.

THE ANALYSIS

As order and predictability became more important to the business enterprise, a manager's ability to be objective, analytical, and evaluative increased in value. Inherent in this approach was the ability to minimize emotional influences that create uncertainty and unpredictability in the environment.

Managers need to be able to predict behavior in order to plan effectively for the future. For managers, the fewer surprises, the better. Good managers demonstrate the ability to manage change according to a predetermined plan. Expectations must match realizations. Control of behavior comes about by rewarding desired behavior. Managers expect that everyone will act in their own self-interest and pursue their rewards. This allows predictability and yields cooperation, but fails to produce commitment to the organization or to the manager. People are only expected to play their designated role in the organization. As a result, many employees become detached from the organization. This makes the manager's ability to control dependent upon the ability to reward.

Importance of Rationality and Efficiency

Frederick Taylor's (the father of scientific management) application of scientific approaches to management was the historical beginning of the managerial mystique. In an effort to escape the problems associated with autocratic leadership, Taylor developed a program for increasing productivity based on *rationality* and *efficiency*. Scientific management combined the application of physical sciences with a logical approach to finding a better way to coordinate the flow of work from start to finish. Inherent in Taylor's approach was the inquisitive pursuit of improved performance, and communication between worker and manager on how to achieve the desired improvements. Implicit in this approach was management's knowledge of the nature of the work performed. Without this knowledge, opportunities for improvement are limited. Unfortunately, managers grasped the tools of scientific management, but not its philosophy. The focus was on increased performance, but without the increased communication. As a consequence, the conflict between worker and manager that Taylor sought to eliminate continued.

Importance of Cooperation

Taylor's pursuit of rationality was followed by Elton Mayo's promotion of the importance of cooperation. *Cooperation* between worker and manager would facilitate accomplishment of organizational goals. Mayo argued for a humanistic approach to managing, involving participation, to achieve cooperation. Distrust in the objectivity and fairness in the application of principles of scientific management precluded the cooperation necessary to achieve success.

Rise of Analytical Control Systems

Cooperation depends on continuity and commitment. The control systems and statistical-quantitative techniques developed during World War II emphasized decision making based on numerical analysis rather than continuity, and the emphasis on cooperation faded. With these control tools, managers derived power from the selective use of "objective" analysis, not from cooperative support between managers and workers. Managers used financial and managerial accounting tools in the design of control systems to exercise power and distribute rewards throughout the organization. Control systems were built on the assumption that individuals would act in their own self-interest. Consequently, managers used control systems to direct the behavior of people, as well as to measure performance and evaluate information. Predictable control of performance became the trade-off for loyalty, responsibility, and creativity.

Professionalism

The use of control systems culminated in the development of professionalism. Professionalism eliminated emotion from the management of the organization through individual self-control. The code of a professional delineated acceptable behavior and placed a premium on self-control to restrict behavior to this code. This allowed work to proceed with a minimum of wasted energy. For the professional, time spent on personal issues diminished efficiency. The code also fostered the suppression of feelings and resulted in diminished communication. Energy was spent on doing things right, rather than doing the right things.

The increased emphasis on the M.B.A. degree epitomizes the development of professionalism and, as a consequence, the managerial mystique. The number of students receiving an M.B.A. degree grew from 5,000 in 1965 to 67,000 in 1986. The M.B.A. degree became a credentialing tool, signaling an individual's intention to become a professional manager. However, M.B.A. graduates are trained in the tools of managing, but not leading. Even organizational behavior courses do not study the behavior of people at work, but instead focus on events that are part of the process in organizations, such as budgeting, performance evaluation, and compensation. Issues regarding individual variations are assumed away by using statistical averaging. Such business education fabricates technically oriented managers, but fails to educate leaders.

CONSEQUENCES

Organizational Politics

As one consequence of moving from leaders to managers and professionalism, organizational politics increase. Professionalism operates based on a utilitarian view of organizations, with the value of an individual determined analytically and objectively. Individual loyalty is not a factor in this assessment, for it is emotionally based, and emotions diminish predictability and control. Individual value is established by "trading off" contributions for rewards. Calculation and exchange form the basis for this analytical assessment. While this focus on objective utility over loyalty enhances control, it reduces commitment.

People protect themselves in this environment by applying three principles of power economics. They are dependency reversal, power enhancement, and manipulation of the relationship between personal investment and organizational rewards. *Dependency reversal* seeks to make the boss dependent on the employee, typically by the employee becoming reliable. This predictability allows the boss to focus his or her energies in other places and increases the employee's value.

Power enhancement involves forming alliances with others who are less powerful. Typically, the alliances are formed based on access to knowledge. The combined effect provides members of the alliance with the ability to negotiate trade-offs. Power alliances are most prevalent in heterogeneous companies where individuals in positions of authority often know little about the businesses for which they are responsible. As a consequence, individuals with knowledge are able to trade off this knowledge for increased value and power in the relationship.

The third approach to organizational politics is to *adjust the level of personal investment* in the organization to achieve a balance with the rewards received. A reduction in investment enables the individual to become more emotionally distanced from the organization and its goals. This results in less commitment, ego involvement, and innovation.

Corruption of Power

As politics become the organizational norm, the potential for the corruption of power increases. The destructive use of power results from a person's psychological dysfunctions rooted in childhood experiences. Flaws in character convert constructive power into a destructive force. The absence of strong moral and ethical standards allows an immature powerholder to apply power destructively. In this situation, organizational constraints are needed to prevent the use of power to overcome felt inadequacies and unconscious fears. The organization needs to establish moral standards to protect against individuals who lack them personally. Instead, organizations concern themselves with technical efficiency and in the process become amoral. This allows the misapplication of power to occur. Several vignettes are employed by the author to support this contention.

Diffusion of Identity

Zaleznik attacks the excessive flexibility and adaptability found in organizations. As with the corruption of power, he argues, it has its roots in childhood and can be best understood and identified through psychotherapy.

Organizations prize the ability to be adaptable, flexible, and play multiple roles. The adaptive professional succeeds in an open organization, while it responds to external and internal pressures. Flexibility allows the individual to change with the organization. However, this adaptability is dysfunctional when carried too far. It results in a diffusion of the individual's identity. Individuals may be successful, but are not happy, and feel alienated from themselves. This degree of flexibility and adaptability can harm the organization in the long run, because it undermines the creativity and leadership that an organization needs.

Stress and Power

Stress does not stem from the decisions that have to be made when a person is in a position of power. Rather, stress comes from the fear of *losing* power once it has been obtained. Power gives one the feeling of control over one's actions. Loss of power produces a loss of control. By contrast, the power to make decisions can be therapeutic. It is the *lack* of power that creates stress and its associated illnesses. Experiences of the Canadian Broadcasting Corporation in the 1970s are employed to support this argument.

Fear of the loss of power leads managers to be defensive and conservative. Managers implement structure and control systems to buffer themselves from reality and to protect their position in the organization. If decisions result in failure, the process that produces them gets blamed. Managers are simultaneously in control (by virtue of their position in the process) and free from accountability (because of the power vested in the process). Managers trade off being in touch with the organization for their personal security and freedom from stress.

THE CURE: LEADERSHIP

American business must return leadership to a place of prominence in order to overcome the problems inherent in its preoccupation with structure and control. But what is true leadership?

The Substance of Leadership

Zaleznik believes that corporate leadership consists of three elements:

1. It is *substantive*, involving ideas about what to do rather than how to do it;
2. It is *having a vision* that projects a company's future;
3. It is the *staying power* to see the vision to its conclusion.

Imagination lies at the heart of leadership; it represents the ability to turn issues or problems into opportunities, and to translate visions into goals to pursue. This process consists of more than simply motivating others to find the answers. Leaders must be able to create opportunities and develop solutions to problems. Imagination consists of the ability to visualize what might be. Opportunism gives this vision a practical shape. The leader must be optimistic, since it is the leader who must give vision the form and substance necessary for others to embrace it.

Imagination in business exists in many forms, including marketing, manufacturing, and financial imagination. In all cases, imagination relies on conceptualization of the problem. It focuses on the "what" rather than the "how," the shift from the particular to the conceptual, and flexibility in approaching the problem. Imagination in business is basically imitative and applied. It consists of the application of experience toward finding solutions to problems. Imagination and creativity are not the same, for creativity represents a movement into new territory.

Zaleznik views marketing imagination as the "premier imagination in business leadership." Empathy distinguishes marketing imagination from the other forms of business imagination. It puts the focus on the customer, the user of the outputs of business. This external focus frees the leader to think beyond the current products or services being offered. Imagination goes beyond the current boundaries to explore new territory. This inquisitive, exploratory attitude is an inherent quality of leadership.

Personal Influence

The managerial mystique denies the importance of personal influence, and assumes that the organization is driven by structure and process. People are only incidental to the process. Accountability, which resides with a person, does not exist.

Leadership cannot exist without personal influence. This influence comes in many forms. One form of personal influence is *identification.* This occurs when one person incorporates the beliefs and values of another. Identification creates a subtle influence over individual behavior.

A more direct influence is shown in the formation of *alliances,* which are based on obligation. Zaleznik describes *amicitia,* an alliance in which members agree to protect each other's interests. Implicit in the conditions of this alliance is the acceptance of obligations only to the extent that they do not neglect self-interest. Amicitia combines a calculated assessment of the contributions to be made by the alliance members and the personal relationships of the members. The durability of these alliances depends on strong leaders. Without the leader's ability to engender commitment to mutual goals, the alliance will break down into competing factions.

Charisma is another form of personal influence that can be distinguished from influence based on authority or expertise. It elicits strong positive emotions based on the personal characteristics of an individual. The potential for abuse by that individual and the dependence on the uniqueness of that individual weakens the organization's control. The need for control has led organizations to favor managing, using roles or positions instead of charismatic leaders. (The influence exercised by Carnegie, Rockefeller, and Ford is cited to dramatize the positive and negative consequences of charismatic leadership.)

For leaders to exercise their influence over others, they must go through a personal transformation as the result of being severely tested. This personal crisis forces introspection and a clearer understanding of self. Such a transformation allows leaders to communicate their values and beliefs with conviction, which serves as a guide for the quality of human relationships in the business. Leaders use their personal experience to influence others. By contrast, managers rely on process and procedure as guidelines for behavior.

Listening is also a form of influence, as it allows for an understanding of the desires and values of others. Listening helps prevent the leader from forcing conflict by unwittingly asking others to do something that contradicts their beliefs.

Personal influence can also be exercised through the use of mutual respect, clear expectations, meaningful participation, and the delivery on promises made.

Moral Dimension

While personal influence can stimulate commitment and performance, it opens the possibility for manipulation. As a consequence, it becomes important to control the moral dimensions of individual behavior as well.

The tenets of professionalism provide organizations with the objectivity to overcome biases and promote an "open system" that allows many people to influence a decision. This lessens the chance of an individual exercising immoral behavior. Unfortunately, professionalism takes effect slowly and does not overcome the incentives that exist to behave unethically and illegally. Zaleznik describes a number of examples from Watergate, ITT, and GE's price fixing to illustrate the inability of process and professionalism to prevent immoral behavior. The depersonalization created by professionalism provides fertile soil for the growth of unethical conduct. The process (rather than an individual) is condemned as the cause of the behavior. Accountability and responsibility of managers at the top of the hierarchy are avoided. The system, not the individual, sets the model for behavior.

CONCLUSION—RESTORING LEADERSHIP IN BUSINESS

Managers believe that without structure and process to establish and maintain control, organizational chaos will occur. Control can be dangerous, because its predictability leads to boredom and the loss of innovation and imagination. As managers accepted the managerial mystique of structure and process they lost sight of the importance of the substance of the work itself. Leadership must be restored to a position of prominence for American business to recapture its vitality and innovative spirit.

The Charismatic Leader

Jay A. Conger

Summary prepared by Jim Laumeyer

Jim Laumeyer has an MBA from the University of Minnesota, Duluth. He is the Director of Administration for the Minnesota Department of Transportation. He also serves as an instructor at the University of Minnesota, Duluth, and is a member of the Society for Human Resource Management's National Employee and Labor Relations Committee.

IDENTIFYING THE CHARISMATIC LEADER

Archie J. McGill (AT & T), Dee Hock (Visa), Lee Iacocca (Chrysler), and Steve Jobs (Apple) are four examples of individuals who are frequently identified as charismatic leaders. All of these individuals found themselves in organizations that were poised at a crossroad leading either to crisis or to regeneration dependent upon the organization's next move. Their organizations elected to take a risk and commission a new type of leader. Each firm needed an individual who would embark on a mission designed to bring about a major organization change. Unfortunately, the organizations were not always eager and totally willing to embrace either the leader or the change sought by the leader.

This demonstrates that although charismatic leaders sometimes do wonderful things, they are not always appreciated or cherished by all the other individuals in their organization. Not only do they typically impact others negatively on a personal basis, but their accomplishments sometimes also result in them becoming ostracized by forces within the organization.

Perception plays a powerful role in the definition of the charismatic leader. Comparisons of various charismatic leaders, such as Adolf Hitler and Franklin D. Roosevelt, often reveal very different personalities. If there were a single and simple charismatic personality, America would have perceived Hitler as charismatic, just as many Germans did. Instead, the charismatic phenomenon is quite complex in nature.

The basic dilemma lies in the apparent ambiguity of the term. It has commonly been used to describe a number of leaders with very different personalities operating under a variety of conditions. There is, however, a valid criterion for discerning and defining the charismatic leader—a behavior model for organizational transformation that accents the charismatic person's ability to induce quantum change in organizations. A *charismatic leader* builds one's trust in self and senses unexplained opportunities, formulates and communicates an idealized vision and support for the vision, and provides the means for achieving it.

There are stages in the development of charismatic leadership:

Stage One: Sensing Opportunity and Formulating a Vision

Research suggests that charismatic leaders possess two skills that often set them apart from other leaders. The first is a sensitivity to their constituents' needs (both employees and customers). The second quality is an unusual ability to see the deficiencies of the existing situation as well as the untapped opportunities. Once this is done, an idealized vision (a challenging and desirable future state) must be formulated.

Stage Two: Articulating the Vision

Charismatic leaders tend to be different from others because of their goals and the way in which they communicate these goals. Charismatic leaders usually have a profound sense of strategic vision and a remarkable capacity to convey the essence and viability of that to a broad group of people.

Stage Three: Building Trust in the Vision

For the leader to be effective, it is often important that subordinates must desire and support the goals the leader proposes. Commitment by coercion or edict is not likely to provide sufficient motivational energy for long-term success. Thus the leader must build exceptional trust among subordinates—trust in the leader and trust in the viability of the goals to be sought. The charismatic leader does this through personal risk taking, unconventional expertise, and self-sacrifice.

Stage Four: Achieving the Vision

In the final stage, charismatic leaders generally differ from others because of their extensive use of personal example and role modeling, their reliance on unconventional tactics, and their use of empowerment practices to demonstrate how their vision can be achieved.

SEEING BEYOND CURRENT REALITIES

A very critical impetus for the desired transformation of an organization, which is the mission of every charismatic leader, is the leader's vision. The vision is essential not only for the leader, but also for the individuals that the leader must enlist and/or influence in order to be successful. The *vision* is a mental image or a dream of a highly desirable future state for the organization. The leader and others must find the vision desirable enough so that they will commit substantial energy to make this vision a reality. In essence, the vision must become the "Piped Piper's" tune, launching the leader and the followers on their mission.

These dreams or visions must be perceived as exciting, but yet they must be realistic, reasonable, and attainable. In essence, the vision must become the common cause for the leader and supporters if it is to become the basis for the desired organizational transformation.

To this end, visions must be both strategic and compatible with the organization's purpose. While compatible, the vision must create broader parameters so that all individuals perceive more authority, develop a broader mindset, and perceive more value in their personal contributions. Accordingly, a paradox for visions is that they must fit the organization's purpose and mission, while providing an impetus for a significant cultural shift relative to how the organization will serve that purpose. The charismatic leader not only seeks to keep the organization's purpose constant, but tries to change dramatically the way the organization operates to serve its mission. Visions, therefore, enlist commitment and mobilize the group to achieve the organization's purpose.

Visions may be categorized along two dimensions—focus (broad or narrow) and orientation (internal v. external). These differences create four major types of visions:

1. Produce/service innovation (narrow and external)
2. Contribution to society (broad and external)
3. Organizational transformation (narrow and internal)
4. Contribution to the work force (broad and internal).

BUILDING IMPRESSIONS OF TRUSTWORTHINESS AND EXPERTISE

Even with the best vision, the charismatic leader would accomplish nothing without involving others. The mission of charismatic leaders is to bring about organizational transformations. For this to occur, followers must place trust in the leader and believe that the mission will be successful. Accordingly, they must perceive the charismatic leader as unique, extraordinary, and almost bigger than life.

In order to determine whether leaders who may have charisma are real and trustworthy, their expertise and commitment must be assessed. Leaders must demonstrate that they know what they are talking about, since this is a critical factor in the development of employee perceptions that they can accomplish this mission successfully.

Similarly, the mission to transform an organization requires risk and commitment from each individual. Followers are not inclined to make that commitment unless they believe that the leader is totally committed.

EMPOWERING OTHERS TO ACHIEVE THE DREAM

After establishing the appropriate trust level, charismatic leaders must motivate their subordinates to accomplish the improbable. Not only must they motivate their subordinates to great heights, but they must also be able to sustain that level of motivation for the often prolonged and difficult period of time necessary to bring about the organizational change. Successful charismatic leaders use any number of techniques for empowering others. Charismatic leaders generate power through their accomplishments, verbal persuasion, emotional arousal, and vicarious experience.

A TRIP TO THE DARK SIDE

There is, however, a somewhat negative element to the charismatic leadership phenomenon. While sometimes helping organizations achieve near-miracles, charismatic leaders can also be seen as agents of destruction. These disastrous outcomes may stem from the self-righteous mission of the leader or from other problems such as a faulty vision, assumption of excessive risk, inaccurate perceptions of market environment, failure to recognize or be informed about flaws, and disintegration of managerial functions.

DEVELOPING EXCEPTIONAL LEADERSHIP

Increasingly, organizations are discovering that they need to initiate major transformations. To achieve this magnitude of change, they will likely need charismatic leaders. Several actions can help bring this about. First, they need to recruit and develop men and women who show potential for charismatic leadership. Second, organizations must widely champion examples of effective behavior demonstrated by its core of charismatic leaders. Finally, organizations must realize that this new commitment to leadership will require a significant culture change and shift in attitudes and processes in order for it to succeed. For example, decentralization, more tolerant supervisory styles, and more (charismatic) leadership skill training will be necessary. In addition, organizations need to recognize that the management of a charismatic leader requires a more flexible approach than previously used. Charismatic leaders—especially if they are infused at all levels of the organization—will require more freedom to operate in unique ways. They will also likely be more comfortable with, and challenged by, environments featured by ambiguity, risk, and even crises.

There is a sense of urgency for American business to embrace and develop charismatic leadership. Organizations and their members need to be prepared to respond productively to such leadership when it appears. The key lies in eliciting appropriate leader and follower behaviors in the same organization at the same time.

PART
EIGHT

Managing Diversity

A wide range of biases (e.g., racism, sexism) still find themselves strongly entrenched in our society and organizations. Universities are being hit by lawsuits regarding discrimination against their female faculty; the U. S. military during Desert Storm still did not allow women to command battleships, fly fighters, or go into combat; and corporate America finds itself with a limited number of female upper-level managers, presidents, and board chairs. Contemporary business publications regularly feature stories about the plight of women in management, "the mommy trap," and other issues. This discriminatory track does not find itself limited just to women. There are a number of different groups within our society who find themselves singled out and subjected to discriminatory treatment.

We are regularly reminded that diversity in the workplace will become increasingly common as we move through the remainder of the 1990s and into the twenty-first century. As a consequence we have chosen to include this section, focusing on diversity and the management of diversity in the workplace.

Several interesting books and reports have been written on the changing nature of demographics in America, and the implications for work organizations. In this section of _The Manager's Bookshelf_, we highlight two of these books.

Ann M. Morrison, Randall P. White, Ellen Van Velsor, and the Center for Creative Leadership note in their book, _Breaking the Glass Ceiling_, that women have made significant gains in the corporate world. Despite this encouraging observation, the authors raise the question as to whether or not women reasonably can expect to make it to the top. Morrison and her colleagues explore the successes and failures of women in reaching the inner sanctum of top-level management, and they shed light on some of the roadblocks that remain to be dealt with as women attempt to grab the organizational brass ring. Morrison has also written _The New Leaders: Guidelines on Leadership Diversity in America_.

Marilyn Loden (author of _Feminine Leadership_) and Judy B. Rosener have a new book entitled _Workforce America! Managing Employee Diversity as a Vital Resource_, in which they explore the rapidly changing demographic nature of the American work force. They remind us that by the twenty-first century, less than forty percent of the total American workforce will be characterized by the white male, as women and people of color will fill seventy-five percent of the new jobs created in the United States. Loden and Rosener focus on three themes. First, they define diversity and focus on its institutional impact. Second, they examine the problems and challenges to be encountered when organizations employ diverse populations. Finally, the authors articulate a specific set of strategies that can be implemented to change organizational culture so that it comes to value diversity.

Breaking the Glass Ceiling: Can Women Reach the Top of America's Largest Corporations?

Ann M. Morrison, Randall P. White, Ellen Van Velsor, and the Center for Creative Leadership

Summary prepared by Stephen Rubenfeld

Stephen Rubenfeld is Professor of Human Resource Management in the School of Business and Economics at the University of Minnesota, Duluth. He received his Ph.D. from the University of Wisconsin, Madison, and was previously on the faculty of Texas Tech University. His professional publications and presentations have covered a variety of personnel and labor relations topics, including job search behaviors, discrimination in employment, employee selection and staffing, concessionary bargaining, and social desirability bias. He is a member of the Industrial Relations Research Association, the Academy of Management, and the Southern Management Association.

Women have gained a significant toehold in the corporate world, but can they reasonably expect to make it to the top? One view holds that as the pipeline fills with women, the most outstanding may be catapulted into the executive suite. Despite significant inroads by women into management, there is also a less optimistic scenario. Invisible organizational barriers may exist that will prevent women from reaching the top jobs. *Breaking the Glass Ceiling* explores the successes and failures of women in reaching the inner sanctum of top-level management. It sheds light on the hidden roadblocks that may be derailing women in their quest for the organizational brass ring. There is no doubt that women have come a long way in gaining access to formerly male-

Ann M. Morrison, et al., *Breaking the Glass Ceiling.* Reading, MA: Addison-Wesley, 1987.

dominated corporate positions, for women now occupy nearly one-third of corporate middle management positions. The primary question is whether the glass ceiling will prove to be an unbreakable hurdle to these women on the way up.

The authors, all associated with the Center for Creative Leadership, conducted a three-year study of top female executives in twenty-five Fortune 100-sized firms to better understand why so few women make it to the executive suite. Extensive interviews were conducted with seventy-six women in or just below the general management level. A companion study of twenty-two senior-level managers, mostly male, was also undertaken. These "savvy insiders" were included primarily because they have responsibility for identifying and selecting executives for their firms. The Executive Women Project sought answers to a number of questions critical to the upward mobility of women: What factors propel women into the executive suite or derail them en route? Are these factors the same for women and men? Do women managers need the same opportunities for development as men?

The recent influx of women into management positions has brought with it dozens of books that provide guidance on how to succeed in the male world of management. Typically upbeat and sometimes inspirational, these guides have for the most part focused on *behaviors* that will increase the likelihood of success. Some offer advice on how to make it through the organizational maze despite being female *(The Right Moves: Succeeding in a Man's World Without a Harvard MBA),* while others contend that it is neither necessary nor desirable for women to emulate the characteristics of male managers *(Feminine Leadership: Or How to Succeed in Business Without Being One of the Boys). Breaking the Glass Ceiling* differs from much of the how-to-do-it literature in that it does not start from an unrealistically rosy premise that anything is possible if you just play the game correctly. By exploring the unseen and often unspoken impediments to the advancement of women managers, the challenges faced by upwardly mobile female managers are identified. More importantly, a series of behaviors and career choices that may increase the likelihood of breaking the glass ceiling are presented.

SUCCESS FACTORS

According to the sampled senior executives ("savvy insiders"), women who had "made it" shared six prominent characteristics or attributes:

1. *Help.* Each of the successful women had help from above. Sponsors or mentors were sources of tutelage, advice, inspiration, and influence in the organization.
2. *Achievement.* A proven track record is a key to continued advancement. Successful women have shown their knowledge, professionalism,

and leadership, and have repeatedly proven they could deliver the goods.

3. *Desire.* Most of the successful executives were characterized by a passion to succeed. Through hard work, long hours, and personal sacrifice, they demonstrated their willingness to do what it takes to get the job done.

4. *Management.* A demonstrated competence in managing subordinates characterized most of the successful women. The ability to get people to perform while maintaining their respect and trust was seen as particularly important.

5. *Risk taking.* Career moves—even though they often required relocation and travel, and carried with them the risk of failure—were seen as essential in broadening business experience.

6. *Tough, decisive, and demanding.* Successful women had demonstrated their ability to be aggressive, make hard decisions, and say what was on their minds. They were not afraid to fight for what they believed was right.

A number of characteristics were shared by women whose career advancement had been halted. Some of these derailed executives had quit or been fired, and others had plateaued in their careers because of:

1. *Inability to adapt.* Not being willing or able to adapt to the expectations of others, to organizational culture, or to environmental pressures is often associated with failure.

2. *Wanting too much.* Asking for too much, too soon, can send the signal that a woman is not a team player. Making too much of "women's issues" can likewise raise concerns among other managers.

3. *Performance problems.* Not meeting performance expectations can quickly derail future advancement.

WOMEN ARE NOT MEN

All executives have to meet rigorous and demanding performance expectations, but the woman executive also must confront a variety of gender expectations. A male manager is seen as a *manager,* while a female manager is seen as a *female manager.* She not only has to perform, but do so without violating norms of acceptable behaviors for women. There is an "attitude" that expects selective retention of feminine characteristics, such as flexibility and charm, while stereotypic "soft" traits that reflect weakness, indecisiveness, or emotionalism must be suppressed. The key to success is for the executive woman to demonstrate that she can pick and choose from sex stereotypic behavior patterns to adopt male behaviors (without being too macho) and retain female behaviors (without being too feminine).

Women executives were found to be very much like executive men in terms of management abilities, goals and motivation, and personality, as well as behaviors. There were differences, however. For example, executive men were more likely than executive women to be comfortable in their work environment, to see things as their peers do, and to feel equal to work life and home life demands. Women executives, on the other hand, were more likely than men to behave as individuals and to move in new directions.

More significant than these differences are the vast areas of behavior and personality where, contrary to stereotypes, women and men did *not* score differently. In comparison with executive men, executive women are:

- *not* more impulsive
- *not* more humanitarian
- *not* more touchy
- *not* more suspicious
- *not* more concerned with self-presentation

Relative to their male counterparts in management, women are also:

- *not* less self-disciplined
- *not* less able to cope with stress
- *not* less self-confident
- *not* less dominant in leadership situations
- *not* less even-tempered

These findings, drawn from published research as well as the personality test scores of thousands of managers and professionals who participated in programs at the Center for Creative Leadership, show that, as individuals, "executive women may be virtually identical to executive men psychologically, intellectually, and emotionally" (p. 54). Put another way, women are more like their male counterparts than they are different from them. For this reason, the continued use of assumptions about the differences between men and women to make executive staffing decisions is not justified.

LESSONS FOR SUCCESS

The experiences of the seventy-six women interviewed for this project form the basis of a number of recommended strategies for success. These "lessons for success" are, in the words of the authors, ". . . requirements for success—what female executives must do to succeed in a large corporation" (p. 74). Each lesson is individually important, but together they represent a package deal. The aspiring executive woman must address *each* of these issues.

Lesson 1: Learn the Ropes

Listen to what people tell you, learn by observing others, and actively solicit feedback. Doing a good job may not in itself be enough to assure continued advancement. Women executives must also understand the rules to survive.

Since rules, expectations, and opportunities are often communicated informally by word of mouth, it is essential to find a way into the network.

Lesson 2: Take Control of Your Career

When it comes right down to it, your career is *your* responsibility: "You can't always rely on the natural processes of the system. You can't rely on a mentor. No one is going to take care of you" (p. 85). Upwardly mobile women must seek out the "right" jobs, be assertive (ask for what they think best serves their interests), and be careful to avoid mistakes that can derail a career.

Lesson 3: Build Confidence

Having self-confidence is often a forerunner of earning the confidence of others. Self-confidence may also permit executive women to accept negative feedback, admit mistakes, and take some risks that may ultimately be critical to success. Ways in which the women in this sample built their confidence included taking on risky assignments (and succeeding), becoming successful at outside activities, and realizing that they compared favorably to their management peers.

Lesson 4: Rely on Others

The successful executive woman has made effective use of a broad network of supporters. No one person can be expected (or relied on) to provide the broad range of support and guidance that is critical to career advancement. It is best to ally oneself with *and be receptive* to a variety of sponsors, mentors, and role models. This list must also include subordinates, as no one can do it alone.

Lesson 5: Go for the Bottom Line

It is a fact of organizational life that executives are held accountable for their job responsibilities and ultimately for the "bottom line." To move forward, the woman manager must do the right thing and get results. Performance is not the only requirement for success, but it is essential.

Lesson 6: Integrate Life and Work

Many women resent having to carry a disproportionate share of home and family responsibilities (relative to their male counterparts), yet be expected to perform equally on the job. As one woman put it, "Most men here are married. They seem to think food magically appears in a refrigerator. They can't comprehend chores" (p. 113). Career-oriented females need to set priorities, sacrifice, and recognize that the price of success may be high. With few exceptions, the sampled executive women had made the decision to put their careers first and fit in the rest of their lives in whatever time remained.

STEPPING OFF THE FAST TRACK

Beyond the pressures of the job itself, the female executive carries with her the sometimes burdensome responsibility of being a role model for other women on the way up. Her successes may open doors for other women, but her failures may likewise limit opportunities. The demands of life outside of work add to the multiple hurdles faced by women managers. The realities of a changing society have contributed to a gradual evolution in sex-defined roles of maintaining a household and raising children, but many women still carry most of the load in this life domain.

Whether because of the roadblocks of stereotype and tradition or the other pressures of being a woman in management, many highly qualified women have failed to penetrate the glass ceiling. Others have beaten the odds and made it to the general management level only to find a new set of barriers standing between them and senior management. They may find that they are unable to escape the stigma of being "staff," or that the support system that stood by them as their careers blossomed has suddenly vanished.

Executive women at this level may also continue to be pushed or pulled by the multiple and sometimes conflicting expectations they have had to shoulder throughout their careers. Finally, along with these ongoing pressures, exhaustion may take its toll. The constant stress, competition, and fatigue lead some to step off the fast track. This may either result in an acceptance of the status quo or an effort to find a new and different work environment. For many, the odds are too long and the costs too high to stay in the rat race.

THE FUTURE

Getting into organizations is a far smaller problem for women than is advancing once they are through the door. Much progress already has been made, but attitudes and organizational culture change slowly. *Breaking the Glass Ceiling* paints a realistic picture of the challenges that are faced by the upwardly mobile woman. Despite the finding that there are indeed *very high hurdles* that must be cleared in this race to the top, there is still reason for optimism. Things are changing. There is progress. Organizations are attempting to remove the bars that have confined the careers of talented and successful women.

But perhaps most encouraging is the finding that women themselves *can* affect the likelihood of breaking the glass ceiling. Women who are beginning their career climb might benefit by following five "commandments":

1. *Be able.* Work hard and be knowledgeable. Competence is the basic building block of career success.
2. *Be seen as able.* Choose jobs and assignments with care, and make sure your competence is *visible* to others.
3. *Prepare to be lucky.* Hard work often *creates* lucky breaks. Be ready to take advantage of opportunities when they arise.

4. *Know what you want.* Define what success means *to you* and be prepared to act to achieve it.
5. *Help others to help you.* Let people know what you want, recognize that networks are built on relationships, and show appreciation for the help you receive.

ADDITIONAL READING

Gary N. Powell, *Women and Men in Management,* Newbury Park, CA: SAGE Publications, Inc., 1988.

Felice N. Schwartz, "Management Women and the New Facts of Life," *Harvard Business Review,* January–February 1989, pp. 65–76.

Marilyn Loden, *Feminine Leadership: Or How to Succeed in Business Without Being One of the Boys,* New York: New York Times Books, 1985.

Charlene Mitchell and Thomas Burdick, *The Right Moves: Succeeding in a Man's World Without a Harvard MBA,* New York: Macmillan. 1985.

WORK FORCE AMERICA!
Managing Employee Diversity as a Vital Resource

Marilyn Loden and Judy B. Rosener

Summary prepared by Linda E. Parry

Linda E. Parry is an Assistant Professor of Organizational Studies in the Management Studies Department at the University of Minnesota, Duluth, where she teaches strategic management. She received her Ph.D. from the State University of New York at Albany. Her research interests are in the areas of macro-organizational theory, organizational responsiveness, and organization culture.

The face of the American work force is rapidly changing. The traditional picture of the white, middle-aged male worker is being replaced by a medley of different faces representing a variety of ages, ethnic groups, and races. By the twenty-first century, white men will account for less than forty percent of the total American work force. At the same time, women and people of color will fill seventy-five percent of the new jobs created in the United States. This dramatic shift in demographics provides the foundation for Marilyn Loden and Judy B. Rosener's book *Work force America! Managing Employee Diversity as a Vital Resource.*

Based on observations both from their research and professional experience, Loden and Rosener contend that diversity can be an asset to organizations. *Work force America!* is divided into three parts. Part One, "Raising Awareness," defines diversity and focuses on its impact on institutions. Part Two, "Managing Key Issues," examines the problems and challenges often encountered when employing diverse populations. Part Three, "Diversity and Organization Change," gives specific strategies that can be implemented to change organizational culture so that it values employee diversity.

PART ONE: RAISING AWARENESS

Everyone is made up of several dimensions. *Primary dimensions* are those characteristics that are inborn or immutable. They comprise such factors as age, ethnicity, gender, race, physical characteristics, and sexual/affectional orientation. *Secondary dimensions* are acquired and encompass such characteristics as educational background, geographic location, income, and marital status. Although each dimension can be examined separately, the interconnectedness of these dimensions really shapes identities, values, and perceptions. For example, a young black male lawyer would in all likelihood have different priorities and perceptions than an elderly black boxer, although both people are the same race and gender.

Diversity is the result of these dimensions and the multiple ways in which they can be combined. In the past, organizations ignored the impact that diversity had on the attitudes and behaviors of employees. After all, most Americans lived in homogeneous communities where they worked and associated with others of similar backgrounds. Diversity simply was not an issue. However, twenty-five years of political, social, and legal change brought new groups of employees into the workplace. These others were different from the dominant group along several dimensions of age, ethnicity, gender, race, sexual orientation, and so on. At first, organizations attempted to handle these others through assimilation. People were expected to "fit in." Equal treatment in the workplace meant the same treatment for each employee. Ignoring individual differences became the norm. As a result, assimilation often resulted in pressure to conform, exclusion and isolation, and reinforcement of the dominant group values. This problem became compounded as the number of diverse groups within organizations increased and the number of white men, who traditionally made up the work force, declined. The stage was set for a change in the ways in which American corporations handled diversity.

PART TWO: MANAGING KEY ISSUES

The American worker has often been portrayed as a rugged individual (e.g., the "Marlboro Man" or Lee Iacocca). These are plain-talking, risk-taking adventurers. They are also white, Protestant, male, heterosexual, and in excellent health. When others enter the work force who do not fit this image, people attempt to place them into categories. Often these classifications are based on stereotypes which reinforce underlying prejudices about others.

Prejudices foster ageism, racism, heterosexism, sexism, and so on. Moreover, when combined with institutional power, prejudices can be systematically used to disadvantage others. Ignoring prejudices is not the solution. Those institutions that chose to do "business as usual" have been plagued with a high turnover among non-traditional employees, low morale within the organization, underutilization of employee skills, numerous intergroup conflicts, low productivity, and an inability to attract new workers.

Prejudices should not only be recognized but also managed. A five step process includes

1. Accepting responsibility for the problem;
2. Identifying problem behaviors;
3. Assessing the impact of problem behavior on others;
4. Modifying negative behavior;
5. Obtaining feedback from others.

For example, in the past some male managers pretended not to notice the small number of qualified women employees who were being promoted into senior management positions. They hoped that as the number of women increased, the problem would simply go away. Unfortunately, this did not happen. Although the number of women in the work force has increased, the U.S. Department of Labor reports that there are still barriers to senior management for women. Consequently, corporations that want to retain women and benefit from their contributions have initiated programs to identify, mentor, and place women employees in responsible positions.

In order to be successful in managing diversity, three key issues must be confronted. These are issues of communication, group dynamics, and cultural class. If people are going to interact proactively with others, communication needs to be straightforward and clear. Often people are unaware of how the nuances and innuendos of the words they use can lead to garbled communication. For example, the term *minority* is often used to describe people of color. This term is numerically incorrect since there are far more people of color than there are white people in the world. Also, the term is inappropriate because it implies less power as in "majority versus minority." The term *handicapped* is also frequently used. However, it is a term which focuses on a problem rather than on the total person. A less ambiguous term is *differently abled* which focuses on abilities while acknowledging physical and/or developmental differences. Unfortunately, there is no complete lexicon of words that can be used in communicating inoffensively with others. Nevertheless, some terms are currently considered appropriate when communicating with such diverse groups as older adults, Native Americans, women, and black people.

Communication

The preferred emphasis is not to focus on rules but rather to improve the quality of communication. Four key variables should be recognized when evaluating the impact of one's style on others. These variables include identifying one's own communication style, continually testing one's own assumptions, acknowledging one's style when communicating with others, and being aware of differences in cultural context. For instance, most Americans are accustomed to giving explicit messages in which the actual words carry most of the meaning. In Asian cultures, by contrast, words carry only a small part of the message. The rest is implicit in the context of the communication. Consequently, communicating with Asians can be frustrating for Americans who place a great weight on words and miss the contextual message. By understanding cultural differences in communication, the risk of garbled communication can be reduced.

Group Dynamics

Group dynamics is another key issue. Since *group dynamics* by definition refers to the pattern of interaction that occurs within groups, they can help or hinder the accomplishment of tasks. When groups are formed in an atmosphere of cooperation and respect, disputes are aired and open communication encouraged. When groups are formed along primary and secondary dimensions of diversity, they can consciously or unconsciously reinforce stereotypic attitudes, behaviors, and norms. Cliques develop and soon subgroups find themselves competing for a limited supply of resources. Clique members seldom go against the group norms since doing so risks alienation and ostracism.

In research of major corporations, four factors are particularly important for the effective functioning of groups:

- There needs to be open membership in which all individuals feel accepted without restriction.
- There needs to be an atmosphere of shared influence in which all the group members feel that they have an opportunity to have input in decisions that affect goal-setting and the establishment of group priorities.
- There needs to be mutual respect among the group members so that core differences are realized and viewed as having value to the group.
- There needs to be candor within the group so that members feel free to raise issues, challenge others, and disclose personal opinions and feelings.

Culture Clash

Cultural clash is also a key issue when discussing diversity in the workplace. *Culture clash* is conflict over basic values that occurs between groups of different core identities. It usually occurs when the values, attitudes, and behaviors of the dominant group are questioned by others. Culture clash can be threatening, confusing, or enhancing. In the first two conditions, it can be an impediment to an organization. Consider the case of the Los Angeles City Fire Department, where the mayor attempted to institute a policy of desegregation in 1953. The initial reaction by the department included avoidance, defensiveness, denial, and hostility. Although there were 1,700 fire fighters in the department, only fifty-five were black. These black fire fighters were all assigned to two stations in predominantly black neighborhoods. Although eighty percent of the men requested transfers, the Chief routinely turned them down to avoid potential culture clash between black and white employees.

When culture clash is enhanced, it can improve the effectiveness of an organization. Another example from the Los Angeles Fire Department illustrates the point. This time it was 1982 and the commissioner mandated that the department institute a program to prepare women to enter the service. A gym, an outreach program, and several informational programs resulted in seventy-seven women fire fighters and paramedics. Such an approach added diversity to the department without compromising the professionalism or downgrading standards.

The differences between the positive and negative effects of culture clash appear to be in perceptions of the dominant group. If the dominant group perceives that the inclusion of others has little value to them or the organization, the likelihood of negativism is high. In instances where the dominant group recognizes the "value added" that the group brings to the task, the likelihood of developing creative solutions is high. The rewards for diversity in work groups are clear. According to the Los Angeles Fire Chief, Donald Manning, "There is strength in heterogeneity. When there is inbreeding or homogeneity in an organization, it loses its ability to be objective—to meet the needs of a diverse community" (p. 131).

PART THREE: DIVERSITY AND ORGANIZATION CHANGE

Today, many organizations are involved in efforts to manage employee diversity. The most successful of these organizations share some common characteristics. First, there is a commitment by senior management to the value of diversity. For instance, at Levi Strauss & Company, senior managers not only attend classes on "valuing diversity," but they also participate in team building sessions designed to encourage open communication with employees. Second, the operating philosophy endorses "different but equal." Managers recognize the critical difference between equal treatment and the same treatment. They respect the varied perspectives and communication styles of employees. Third, there is an effort to reward people on their ability to contribute to the organization's goals and not just on their ability to maintain the status quo.

Organizations that value diversity also have pluralistic, rather than participative, leadership. *Participative leadership* assumes that something can be learned from employees. It emphasizes empowerment and increased employee input in decision making. *Pluralistic leadership* not only emphasizes empowerment and increased employee input, but goes further and assumes that organizational culture must change for diversity to happen. Such culture change mandates that everyone in the organization be consulted. A pluralistic leader proactively provides the vision, inspires ethical commitment to fairness, is aware of the primary and secondary dimensions of diversity, and provides a model for organizational change.

Leading-edge organizations have adopted several practices that have helped them institutionalize the value of diversity. One practice links the concept of diversity to the organization's strategic vision. For example, Stanford University, after being criticized for its lack of diversity, entirely revamped its curriculum to reflect the teachings of diverse cultures and is "now committed to building an interactive, pluralistic community of students, faculty, and staff" (p. 167).

Since managers are ultimately responsible for coaching and developing employees, another practice is to involve managers in all efforts to change the culture. To insure that managers can perform these tasks, successful organizations train managers as facilitators of change and reward appropriate performance.

However, training and appropriate reward systems are not just for managers. Successful companies make sure that everyone within the organization has the opportunity to learn about the importance and value of diversity. For instance, within US West, employees at all levels are included in diversity training. Currently, the program offers two programs to its more than 70,000 employees. A one-day workshop addresses the problem of stereotyping. A three-day seminar explains the relationship between effective leadership and employee diversity. Rewards are then distributed to employees on the basis of performance results and not just on style.

For those organizations that truly value diversity, certain assumptions begin to emerge among employees. One assumption is that employee diversity is a competitive advantage and valuable in the marketplace. The principle behind this belief is straightforward. Basically, the company that values diversity can attract a larger and better pool of applicants than companies which limit themselves to a traditional work force. Another assumption is that the process of accepting diversity has made the organization and its members more flexible. This ability to adapt is critical in a rapidly changing world. The third assumption is that organization culture can change (not just people). Unlike traditional times when people were forced into fitting into the mainstream, managers recognize the need to accommodate the culture to fit the people. Although this may require additional effort, it forces managers to look for core reasons for problems rather than just blaming individuals.

The blueprint for creating an organization that values diversity is a three-phase approach. In Phase One, the organization acknowledges that there is a difference between equal employment opportunity and valuing diversity, and it articulates a vision for pluralism. In Phase Two, the organization implements an educational and change agenda. Awareness training is supplied, support is solicited from everyone within the organization, structures are created to support change, and reward systems are put into place that reflect diverse employee priorities. Phase Three involves monitoring the recruitment, hiring, development, and training operations within the organization so that valuing diversity in the workplace becomes an ongoing activity and not just a quick fix for temporary problems.

Clearly, the American work place is at a crossroads. Organizations can continue to follow their traditional path of hiring or they can follow a new path which values diversity in the workplace. Recent shifts in demographics indicate that following traditional paths may lead to high turnover, low morale, and lagging productivity where as the advantages for embracing diversity include full utilization of human resources, enhanced working relationships, greater innovation, and improved productivity. If the American workplace is to be competitive for the year 2000, organizational cultures must be changed to value diversity.

NINE

Preparing for the Twenty-First Century

*E*ach of the three books summarized in this section focuses attention in a unique, interesting, and thought-provoking way on the Twenty-first century environment.

Twenty-first century capitalism is likely to be characterized by organizations operating as a loosely configured network seeking to operate across national borders as though they were part and reflections of a global economy. Robert B. Reich, in his book *The Work of Nations: Preparing Ourselves for Twenty-First Century Capitalism,* observing money, technology, and ideas flowing across borders, argues that jobs will ultimately go wherever they can be performed most efficiently. As corporations lose their national identities, the early and big winners will be those who become the generators and brokers of ideas—those who identify and solve problems, and create the necessary connections to bring products and services to areas of need.

Robert B. Reich, who is a member of the faculty of the John F. Kennedy School of Government at Harvard University, provides us with insight into what nations must do if their citizens are to prosper during the next century. Along with his discussion of the forces giving rise to globalization, Reich identifies issues that need to be addressed at the national level, if as a nation we hope to have organizations that will be capable of actively participating in this new arena. Without major shifts in national, organizational, and labor policy, a significant portion of our society will fall farther and farther behind those who are becoming part of the global web.

Alvin Toffler has clearly emerged as one of today's most highly visible social thinkers, having authored several books that have received worldwide attention (e.g., *Future Shock, The Third Wave,* and *The Adaptive Corporation*). Toffler has served as a Visiting Professor at Cornell University, a Washington correspondent, and a Visiting Scholar at the Russell Sage Foundation. In his most recent work *Powershift: Knowledge, Wealth, and Violence at the Edge of the Twenty-First Century,* Toffler argues that "knowledge" will be the factor (and source of power) around which wealth creation will occur.

Peter Vaill, in his book *Managing as a Performing Art,* attempts to challenge and revise some of the traditional thinking about management strategies. Addressing issues of leadership, organizational excellence, communication, teamwork, change, and ethics, Vaill argues that there is a need for dynamism, fluidity, complexity, and individuality in one's approach to management. The management of organizations should be seen and approached as a performing art.

The constants for managers and their organizations are change and the chaos that accompanies the uncertainty produced by change. Instead of presenting a set of "principles" for the practice of management, Vaill provides the reader with a number of ideas and concepts that need application as though management were a performing art.

Reading 1

The Work of Nations

Robert B. Reich

Summary prepared by Robert E. Heller

Robert E. Heller is the Director of the Small Business Development Center and
Small Business Institute, and a Lecturer in the School of Business and
Economics at the University of Minnesota, Duluth. Prior to assuming this
position, Mr. Heller practiced law, specializing in the areas of business,
employment, and intellectual property law. He also served as general counsel
of Jeno's, Inc., and general counsel and president of Paulucci Enterprises. Mr.
Heller received his B.A. degree from DePauw University and his J.D. degree
from the University of Michigan Law School.

"A nation's economic role is to improve its citizens' standard of living by enhancing the value of what they contribute to the world economy" (p. 301). This
is the basic premise of Robert B. Reich's book, *"The Work of Nations,"* which
is based on several years of research, interviews, and discussions. Our national
economic leaders are caught up in viewing and planning the economy on the
basis of "vestigial" (historic and outdated) understandings of the goals of economic achievement. A new picture of the world economy is needed in which
future economic policies should be aimed at developing our nation into one
composed of *symbolic analysts.* These are the people who will control and
contribute to wealth in the twenty-first century economy.

Most nations' leaders direct their efforts toward the development of a
national economy. These leaders assume that there *is* a national economy, and
that the public interest is served by national economic growth. Economic independence is believed to provide the means to face the threat of foreign competition. However, this picture of a national economy is outdated.

These policies were once correct for a variety of reasons, but this is no
longer true. First, corporations are no longer as profitable as they once were.
Second, organized labor continues to contract. Third, many corporations are
now owned by foreigners. At the same time, Americans' investment in foreign
corporations has increased more rapidly than their investment in domestic
corporations. Finally, the difference between executive and workers' compen-

sation has grown. For example, in 1960, the typical chief executive officer earned about forty times as much as the average factory worker. By 1989, the average chief executive officer earned ninety-three times the compensation of the average factory worker.

A new economic picture needs to be described in more detail, and recommendations for policies to prepare for twenty-first century capitalism need to be offered. The challenge is to prepare *symbolic analysts* who are capable of adding value to the global economy. The symbolic analysts will be paid the most compensation and thereby be able to achieve higher standards of living. Historically, national economic policy has frequently reduced the taxes of the wealthy in order to promote their investment in the national economy. As the global economy has gained in stature and dominance, the wealthy increasingly invest in the global economy. As a result, a nation's gross national product, national economic growth, and competitiveness are no longer important.

What *is* important is the economic welfare of a nation's people, as distinguished from the national economy per se. The challenge is whether high-income Americans, a minority, can sacrifice to help the majority participate in the new global economy. Does a nation's people still have concern for a national society and its economic well being, or has the idea of a "nation" become passé? These questions are addressed next, ending with some recommendations for dealing with the twenty-first century world economy.

THE ECONOMIC NATION

"Economic Nationalism" during the last century meant producing what you need at home and exporting manufactured items. This typically resulted in accumulating wealth in the home economy. The goal was to improve the overall well-being of the nation's population. Patriotism was defined in terms of working for the good of the country, and therefore the good of its population. In turn, the nation, as a whole, supported the development of its industries. The historical rationale revolved around the beliefs that (1) a strong manufacturing base increased the nation's revenue and wealth, (2) opportunities for employment grew, (3) immigration was stimulated, (4) foreign capital was attracted, and (5) the nation became more independent and secure. Countries implemented protectionist policies, such as import tariffs and subsidies, which were thought to protect their businesses. In addition, countries spent money on internal improvements such as roads, bridges, and harbor construction.

Large-Volume Producers

In the nineteenth century, inventions transformed production into large-volume or mass production. Transportation and communications improvements escalated the efficiencies of economic achievement. This resulted in production outstripping demand and drove nations to seek new markets. At the same time, nations increased tariff rates to protect their domestic markets. High-volume manufacturing caused a shift in population from rural areas to cities. By the start of the twentieth century, economic nationalism had taken root. It was nation against nation.

Merger Era

In the next stage, production became consolidated in large national-based corporations. Citizens' well-being was linked to success of the national economy, which revolved around the success of giant corporations. The United States moved slowly in this direction. People remained somewhat skeptical, however, as corporations continued to buy up their competition and to consolidate vertically to avoid protected prices. Mergers proliferated. Consolidation, it was argued, was a necessary result of foreign competition.

Growing Middle Class

At the same time, government agencies were created to police the large corporations, and national planning evolved. By the late 1950s free enterprise became the watchword, along with mass production and mass consumption. Large corporations led the economy and set industrial norms, prices, wages, and methods of high-volume production. Growth of the large corporations resulted in growth of a large middle class of skilled and semiskilled workers. Wealth was not based on rank or ownership. The corporate bureaucracy became military-like. National leaders came from the corporate world. Decisions made by these corporate leaders affected the nation as a whole. Even organized labor acquired the same type of bureaucratic structure.

As the 1960s dawned, less and less regulation of corporations emerged. Government developed policies that stimulated mass consumption: for example, offering low interest home loans and manipulating the money supply. Second, government fostered preparing children for gainful employment; therefore, even education became mass-produced. Third, national defense became an economic policy. All of these decisions and trends benefitted the large corporations. These policies resulted in the rise of a large middle class which would work for the general welfare. The prosperity of the middle class was premised on high-volume, standardized production of goods.

By the late sixties, foreign competition existed in mass-produced goods. The reaction of economic policy makers was once again based upon older views of a national economy. First, these policy makers sought to keep foreign goods out of the market through tariffs. This protectionist strategy provided only temporary relief. It actually resulted in the diminution of foreign markets and increased costs at home. Second, the policy was to cut costs at home to meet the foreign competition. If foreigners could produce goods cheaply, so could Americans. However, profits of these corporations continued to plummet no matter how much cost cutting went on. Third, economic policy makers further encouraged conglomerate mergers in order to promote efficiencies. This policy didn't work either. Profits still continued to decline.

The picture that these economists were using to set their policies was incorrect. There is no longer a national economy; U.S. industry is now part of a *global web*. The standard of living of a nation's people no longer depends on the success of large corporations, but on the worldwide demand for skills and insights.

THE GLOBAL WEB

The evolution of a nation's economy into *global webs* has several features. Corporations are no longer high-volume producers, they are no longer American, and they are becoming high-value producers serving the unique needs of particular customers. This specialization leads to higher profits and results in less competition from high-volume producers. Corporate policies now focus on worldwide searches to achieve their goals. In order to be successful within these global webs, three skills are required. First, skills at solving problems are required in order to put things together in unique ways. Second, problem identification skills are required to develop new ways to use products and to persuade others of the correctness of these ways. Finally, strategic brokering skills are required to link the problem solvers with the problem identifiers. Every high-value enterprise can be described as being in the business of providing these skills. These skills include "the specialized research, engineering and design services necessary to solve problems; the specialized sales, marketing, and consulting services necessary to identify problems; and the specialized strategic, financial and management services for brokering the first two" (p. 85). The worldwide economy has evolved into one where the demand for these skills and insights is the basis for the picture of our global economy now and in the twenty-first century.

Enterprise Webs

The old pyramidal structure of an organization is no longer appropriate in today's global economy. Problem solvers, problem identifiers, and strategic brokers work together to create a profit without the traditional bureaucratic structure. The new picture looks like a "spider's web." The strategic broker is at the center with all sorts of connections to problem solvers and problem identifiers. In these *enterprise webs,* stress is placed on rapid problem identification and problem solving.

Enterprise webs acquire a variety of shapes. First, there is the *independent profit center,* where middle-level managers are eliminated and product development is the goal. Second, in the *spin-off partnership,* strategic brokers form groups of problem solvers and problem identifiers to nurture ideas. These ideas are then sold off with part ownership retained. Third is the *spin-in partnership.* In this enterprise web, strategic brokers purchase ideas from groups of problem solvers and problem identifiers. An example is the computer software house. A fourth enterprise web is the *licensing web.* Brand names are licensed, with strategic brokers given the responsibility of putting together the licensing network and ensuring compliance. The final web is *pure brokering*, in which the strategic broker contracts out with problem solvers and problem identifiers, and for the production of components. All items produced and coming from elsewhere are then sold, with the proceeds going to the broker.

High-Value Assets

The ownership and control of a corporation is no longer as clear as it once was. The assets of a high-value corporation are the skills of the individuals involved in linking solutions to particular needs. The real power depends on the capacity of individuals to add value to the enterprise web. The result is that those persons who are the strategic brokers, problem solvers, and problem identifiers are the ones who are richly rewarded. Receiving less are the production workers and owners. In the high-value enterprise, the ability to identify problems, solve problems, and broker become the key assets, and through experience these assets take on greater value.

Global Webs

Enterprise webs are reaching across the globe. Corporations are no longer national corporations. Groups of problem solvers, problem identifiers, and strategic brokers are formed around the world. These *global webs* combine to create something of value for customers. They are bound together through threads such as computers, fax machines, and satellites. Many contemporary politicians, however, still try to inhibit this flow because of their vestigial view of a national economy. Old products have distinct nationalities, new products are individualistic, and nationality no longer matters. Even though nations create restrictions, global webs, through their problem solvers, problem identifiers, and strategic brokers, figure out ways or find loopholes to beat down the barriers. What nations' leaders have to ask is whose workers gain in the enterprise webs and what effect the restrictions have on nations' workers.

Corporations sell products created through global webs. Nationality of a firm has little to do with where a firm or its owners invest and with whom it contracts. Monies are spent around the world, so that the problem solver, problem identifiers, and strategic brokers may become part of the web. American and foreign corporations look more and more alike. Standardized production, no matter what nationality a corporation holds, occurs in the low-wage countries. Corporations look for high-value problem solving, problem identifying, and strategic brokering wherever they can be found. The high-value global enterprise evolves into an international partnership for combining the insights of skilled people. The enterprise then contracts with unskilled workers from around the world to produce standardized products in high volume.

Implications of Global Webs

What are the implications of global webs? First, national savings will be invested wherever products can be produced the cheapest. Second, a nation's competitiveness is based on what its citizens can do. Third, United States trade imbalances are not due to foreign predators but to U.S.-owned firms making things abroad. As corporate executives are pushed to make a profit they will inevitably look to global webs for solving these problems. Cross-national ownership will continue to increase as electronic training networks link different areas of the world. Brokers will scour the globe to find good investments. Therefore, the total return to U.S. investors doesn't depend solely on the success of U.S. firms, but on the global network of enterprise webs.

The concern about foreign ownership should be forgotten. Foreigners invest in the United States to make use of United States assets and workers in order to make a profit. By investing in the United States they believe they can make better use of these assets and be more competitive. American investments in foreign companies are based on the same premise that they can make better use of the foreign assets and be more competitive. The key lies in having American problem solvers, problem identifiers, and brokers residing in the United States. The people in the web with the most valuable skills and insights will receive the largest rewards.

The perils of vestigial thought remain. Policy makers still want to restrict foreign ownership. This policy creates a barrier to the improvement of problem-solving, problem-identifying, and strategic brokering skills at home. As a result, Americans are losing out on the remuneration that might be paid for these services. National policy should encourage the development of these skills in the United States even through foreign investment. Policy makers continue to miss the picture that *the critical assets are embedded in the capabilities of Americans to be problem solvers, problem identifiers, and strategic brokers.* Once the policy makers realize that corporations are global webs rather than national entities, they will change their thinking from the profitability of U.S. corporations to encouraging improvement in skills that will add value to the world economy.

THE RISE OF THE SYMBOLIC ANALYST

Classifications of twenty-first century workers are important for understanding that it is not the nationality of a company nor of its owners but the identification of the most valuable employees that is most important. Who are they? What skills do they possess?

Classification of Workers

Three broad categories of workers exist in the world economy. The first group of workers are the *routine producers.* These people perform routine jobs which are done over and over. They represent about twenty-five percent of the work force and might be compared to the old line workers. These types of people do repetitive jobs. An example might be a stuffer of computer circuit boards. Because companies seek to pay as little as possible for these workers, the number of them in United States has been declining over the past decade. For competitive reasons, companies increasingly have been locating routine production in other areas of the world.

The second category of worker is the *in-person server*. This group also performs tasks which are simple and repetitive; however, they perform services which are provided person-to-person. These services are not sold worldwide. In-person servers have direct contact with the ultimate beneficiaries of their work. In-person servers include waiters, waitresses, janitors, and taxi drivers. Thirty percent of the work force in 1991 was composed of in-person servers in the United States.

The third category of worker is the *symbolic analyst*. Symbolic analysts include the problem solvers, problem identifiers, and strategic brokers. Their work can be traded worldwide. They are the research scientists, engineers, lawyers, and some creative accountants. These people use analytic tools, are well-educated, and represent twenty percent of the U.S. job force. The other twenty-five percent of the work force are farmers, miners, or government employees, who are somewhat sheltered from global competition.

The Problem Described

Since the mid-seventies, the trend has been toward a growing disparity of income between the twenty percent who are classified as symbolic analysts and the rest of the workers, primarily the in-person servers and routine production workers. No longer is the middle class growing. Several reasons account for this trend. Taxes on the rich have decreased and taxes on the poor have increased as a percentage of income. The rich spend their money, not nationally, but globally. The social policies of the Reagan era caused a decrease in the amount of welfare, thereby making it harder for the less fortunate to move out of the routine producer or in-person server class into the strategic analyst class. The growth of the single-parent family has resulted in less opportunity to move from one type of worker classification to another. Also, the baby boomers have arrived in the job market. Based on the functions performed by workers within global webs, this disparity continues to increase. Symbolic analysts continue to receive more money because they can market their specialized skills worldwide. In the twenty-first century, they will be compensated most highly for their services, while routine producers and in-person servers will remain at a relatively low level of compensation.

Skills of the Symbolic Analyst

Four basic skills are required for the symbolic analyst. The first skill, *abstraction*, is that of discovering patterns and meanings. The symbolic analyst is able to interpret and reinterpret information so that it can be understood and manipulated to the benefit of those for whom the symbolic analyst is working. Second, the symbolic analyst is capable of *system thinking*, which is the capacity to see the whole, and to understand how the processes are linked together. A strategic analyst looks at how the problem arises and connects it to other problems to look for different solutions. A third skill of the symbolic analyst is *experimentation.* Utilizing information, the symbolic analyst, through trial and error, develops the capacity to explore different paths emanating from the same set of data, to test the outcomes, and to draw conclusions from the tests. Through this process, symbolic analysts continue to learn and become more valuable. *Collaboration* is the fourth skill. Symbolic analysts do not work in isolation but rather work in teams or groups of teams. They must communicate in order to achieve an outcome.

Because of the nature of this work, *symbolic analytic zones* are created. These zones are areas in which symbolic analysts live, work, and learn with each other. An example of such a zone is Silicon Valley in California for computers, or Minneapolis for medical devices. As symbolic analysts gather together in zones, the disparity between them and other workers grows. The question emerges: "What can be done to stop this growing disparity?"

THE MEANING OF NATION

Policies are needed that will promote the advancement and expansion of the symbolic analyst. The ultimate economic success of a country depends upon how well its citizens are able to live and whether their standards can be sustained and improved. The challenge to the symbolic analyst in America is to improve the living standards of the majority who are now routine producers and in-person servers. The critical factor is whether the symbolic analyst has the will to be a part of, and implement, solutions.

The Question Restated

The question is whether the symbolic analyst is willing to make the sacrifices necessary to achieve the solutions. The wealthy must limit spending on themselves and must spend more for the benefit of the routine producers and in-person servers, so that they might be promoted to symbolic analysts.

Possible Solutions

There are three possible solutions. First, tax loopholes should be closed, and a truly progressive income tax should be implemented. Second, any reasonably talented child should be able to be educated to become a symbolic analyst. Third, symbolic analysts need to play a role in increasing opportunities for routine producers and in-person servers to gain experience at symbolic analysis and thereby have a chance to become symbolic analysts. Three components of these solutions are (1) education and training, (2) nutrition, and (3) health care at all levels. Job training efforts, free day care, and remedial courses in reading, writing, math, and preschool programs are necessary. Methods of education must be improved, and the political infrastructure must have the will to implement these types of proposals.

Without appropriate infrastructure, the nation is doomed to becoming one of routine producers and in-person servers. To avoid this, governments must be willing to spend money on training symbolic analysts and providing for their development. They must reverse the trend of laissez-faire. They must stop forcing states and cities to spend for education and welfare. The current policy of doing so only fosters the development of symbolic analytic zones. Those communities that can afford to spend on education and training will continue to spend on education and training whereas those who can't will not be able to.

Positive economic nationalism is needed. This would encourage public spending to enhance the capacities of citizens to lead full and productive lives. Policy makers should limit competition with other areas of the world so that these areas can also develop. Enhancing global welfare is the ultimate goal. Subsidies to high-value-added production companies should be encouraged. Also needed is a common fund for worldwide retraining when overcapacity exists. Finally, international policies should promote the upgrading of workers in third world countries to symbolic analysts.

Results

If the policy makers, the rich, and symbolic analysts make the investment in developing a work force that is knowledgeable and skilled in dealing with complex issues, wealth will be spread to that work force. Global webs of enterprises will be developed and, in turn, will generate more jobs for symbolic analysts. As the skills of these symbolic analysts increase, the demand for them becomes greater, and more workers will enjoy better circumstances.

Powershift: Knowledge, Wealth, and Violence at the Edge of the Twenty-First Century

Alvin Toffler

Summary prepared by Thomas A. Kolenko

Thomas A. Kolenko is an Associate Professor of Management at Kennesaw State College, where he teaches organizational behavior and human resource management. He received his Ph.D. from the University of Wisconsin, Madison, after several management positions within General Motors Corporation. His research and consulting interests have been focused in the areas of person-job matching, strategic human resource planning, and executive self-management.

As the last installment of a trilogy of change-centered books, Alvin Toffler leaps beyond *Future Shock*'s probe of the **process** of change and beyond *The Third Wave*'s focus on **directions** of change to target the critical questions surrounding the **control** of change in *Powershift.* Beginning in the 1950s and running into the year 2025, Toffler's three texts identify patterns beyond the headlines and point to issues and agendas only the future can confirm. *Powershift* zeros in on the dynamic power struggles confronting leaders, organizations, and nations in an effort to understand who will shape the twenty-first century and, more importantly, how. Managers capable of understanding these patterns and forces can position their organizations strategically to take advantage of these power transformations.

"Powershift" refers to more than just the restructuring of power relationships or new power transfers and focuses on the very nature of power itself. While brute force, wealth, and knowledge have been acknowledged as historically preferred levers of power, it is the dynamic interaction of these power tools that will direct people's actions. Knowledge has become the ultimate substitute for force and money as a power tool in the years ahead. Toffler argues that of the three power sources, knowledge offers the most bang for the buck.

It represents a high-quality, efficient, and versatile power source capable of multiplying the effects of the other two bases of the power triad.

Knowledge is the key to the powershift that will close this century. Battles for the control of knowledge and its dissemination channels will expand in the years ahead. Since knowledge is infinitely expandable and doesn't get used up when exerted, the rules governing applications of force and wealth are inadequate for the knowledge power game of the future. Knowledge control will drive future global struggles for power.

SUPER-SYMBOLIC ECONOMY

An entirely new system of wealth creation has arrived which is entirely dependent on the generation, interpretation, and dissemination of information, ideas, and symbols. Business commandos and electronic pirates will seize power by capturing data. Knowledge becomes the key weapon in the construction of the super-symbolic economy.

While violence as a tool of power has been transmuted in today's world, money provides a much more versatile tool of power. Paper money and the issuance of stock were but early transformations of wealth whereby capital becomes symbolic. While symbolic replacements for real wealth accelerate, currencies of the future threaten to make national and central banking structures obsolete. These future credit cards or "smart cards" combine real-time electronic record-keeping systems with a central bank of information on each transaction. This knowledge base will shake all existing economic systems to their core as it spans borders in real transaction time. Time lag in financial transactions has been eliminated forever through technology. Toffler argues that knowledge has become the central resource of the advanced economy.

THE INFORMATION WARS

Battles over the control of knowledge will be fought everywhere in the years ahead. Understanding powershifts will ultimately determine survival and prosperity. Toffler illustrates this best by tracing the traumatic impact that the introduction of bar codes and optical scanning systems have had on power relationships for retailers, especially supermarkets.

From 1950 to 1980, supermarket retailers relied on the market research of the largest mass advertisers and manufacturers to attract customers into their stores. Economic power was held by those manufacturers who controlled information to customers and who held data about their customers. Today, bar-code-generated retail data has shifted that power relationship 180 degrees. For it is now the retailers who possess the richest, most vital information on customer purchasing behavior, and thus, power in the marketplace. Toffler warns that similar powershifts will accelerate the battle for information and ultimately the power of knowledge.

Profit margins will depend on who holds the richest consumer data. Networked relationships between credit card purchases, the assortment of purchases, and instantaneous real-time record keeping will create this strategic weapon of the future. These neural pathways of the super-symbolic economy will grow increasingly complex as VANs (Value Added Networks), EDIs (Electronic Data Interchanges), and MAPs (Manufacturing Automation Protocols) all establish an ever-escalating web of information exchanges. Controlling the global standards for information exchange and transmission, whether it be HDTV (High Definition Television), cellular telephone codes, or computer operating systems, will intensify the info-war.

Thus, it is easy to see that *knowledge about knowledge* will be the real key to power generation in the next century. Competitive intelligence, holistic espionage, and directed "commercial covert action" could be used to fine-tune corporations into total info-war fighting machines.

POWER IN THE FLEX-FIRM

While revolts against bureaucracy have been venerated in recent years as the "must do" on every businessperson's agenda, Toffler argues that the very organization of knowledge must be attacked in organizational restructuring efforts. Bureaucracies have locked information in cubbyholes. They use managers primarily to control transmission channels. Some knowledge is perishable and has been known to die in this infinity of cubbyholes and choked channels. But free-flow knowledge systems are the strategic weapons needed to execute the super-symbolic economy's agenda.

The new flex-firm supports and nurtures an information system that attempts to exploit the innovative energies of corporate "colonies" that had been previously governed by bureaucracy. American managers typically think of organizations as machines whose components need adjustments, tune-ups, and lubrication. Japanese managers, however, conceptualize corporations as living creatures built as a network of self-adjusting information flows. These pulsating organizations bypass the tribal chiefs and corporate commissars of old and allocate natural authority based on knowledge to those workers instrumental to the challenges at hand.

What of the inhabitants of this new flex-firm? Autonomous, self-managing employees will be needed to support this antibureaucratic structural revolution. With their knowledge load and decision load being redistributed, continuous learning cycles for all employees must be supported. Having workers function as active rule makers and knowledge generators requires sharing the past power bank controlled by bosses. Information clusters will form naturally. The knowledge network will be egalitarian. Organizations will have to be redesigned and restructured continuously by their members to get the job done.

A totally different power relationship has to be forged between employer and employee in the flex-firm. Intelligent failures have to be tolerated if the innovation and speed imperatives of the future are to be accomplished. Toffler warns that fear to change is the primary "idea-assassin." Power relationships of the past must change to nurture workers demanding increased access to information necessary to perform their jobs.

First-level supervisors have traditionally resisted this fundamental shift in power relationships. However, if workers are required to demonstrate initiative, participate fully, and share responsibility for organizational success, then managers must adopt a new power contract for these relationships.

"Power mosaics" will be defined by these new economic and industrial relationships. Instead of hierarchical concentrations of power shared by a few giant firms, multidimensional information infrastructures will evolve, restructuring organizations in the super-symbolic economy into collections of small operating units. Velcro-type attachments will be formed among inside and outside units and data bases. These power mosaics will support the speed and innovation priorities of organizational survival in the twenty-first century. The recent IBM-Apple joint venture represents just such a relationship. It is the rapid exchange of data, information, and knowledge functioning in the super-symbolic economy that will create wealth locally and globally.

POWERSHIFT POLITICS

Congruence between wealth creation and political governance systems is necessary or one system will eventually destroy the other. As the wealth creation system uncouples to form new power alliances, so must the political monoliths of old. Toffler believes that radical shifts in power will generate four distinct political groupings: localists, regionalists, nationalists, and globalists. Political agendas will follow and challenge past economic agendas. Ethnic diversity will explode. Mass democracies will give way to "mosaic democracies" with a multiplicity of new ideologies.

The historical changes in the Soviet Union have left a hodgepodge of political groupings to fend for themselves. As economic restructuring occurs, so must political restructuring. Policies calling for privatization of government-owned operations whenever possible mirror the restructuring divestiture efforts of business. This return to strategic priorities in both economic and political arenas after restructuring will transform all traditional power bases.

INFO-TACTICS

Political "info-tactics" will be used in power plays and ploys where strategic information manipulation will precede any media leaks or coverage. Knowing how and when to use these tactics will be the responsibility of each info-warrior in the years ahead. Secrecy, guided information leaks, masked sources, and the "need-to-know"/"need-not-to-know" techniques are readily used by power players in government arenas. Power tactic options abound. Omissions, strategic timing tactics, informational dribble releases, informational tidal waves designed to drown receivers in data, vapor and smoke screen tactics, and blow-back ploys will escalate the "info-wars" for years to come. The 1990 U.S. presidential election campaigns provided rich illustrations of many of these "info-tactics."

Thus, it is knowledge *about* knowledge that will provide power to those capable of executing these new "info-tactics." Power will shift to those who can master knowledge transformations in the years ahead. Second-tier knowledge warfare methods will even emerge and prosper.

Meta-tactics will dominate certain information arenas. They represent strategies used in higher-level power struggles which manipulate event outcomes directly. Computerized ballot box manipulations are a good example of these outcome-targeted tactics. The real experts in meta-tactics know that impacting data base construction or creation decisions is far more effective than trying later to control user access. Battles over information system standards will be brutal as public- and private-sector knowledge systems expand to global levels.

International economic intelligence systems have grown with the dissolution of the Cold War, the increased globalization of industries, and the creation of huge electronic data bases. Few debate that the Japanese are leaders in organizing systems of economic intelligence. However, privatization of spying will become increasingly attractive as nations disband those huge military-budget line items. Satellite spy systems will provide customized economic intelligence for the highest bidder. Battles over public access and "right to know" issues will intensify as info-politics evolve in the super-symbolic economy. The growing reliance of power on knowledge will buttress the importance of info-politics in our future.

Global media barons such as Ted Turner, Rupert Murdoch, and others recognize that power lies in the interplay of different information technologies (e.g., print, television, radio, cable, cellular, etc.). These new multi-media systems are creating a "powershift accelerator." Continuous feedback and monitoring systems tied to overseas suppliers from developing countries will set new world speed-response standards. With each unit of time saved more valuable than the last, competitive advantages are leveraged at blinding speeds. Many LDCs or "less developed countries" will be driven from the international marketplace if they cannot meet these speed standards. This is a fact not lost on the existing power holders in this world.

PLANETARY POWERSHIFT

As Japan and Europe emerge as rivals of the United States in the 21st century, global power struggles will focus on the "K-Factor." This knowledge component will transform applications of economic violence and wealth into a complex economic neural network capable of vanquishing all opponents. National boundaries will give way to informational boundaries and knowledge consortia.

In the super-symbolic economies, the entire wealth-creation cycle will be globally monitored in "real time." With instantaneous and continual feedback, knowledge systems will be used to shrink time intervals in all transactions. The repercussions of this "acceleration effect" will be devastating on LDCs and the have-not nations of the world. LDCs which have historically leveraged their strategic military locations or their cheap labor supplies will be outliers in the new economic order.

Informational logistics will determine military capabilities and also reduce the labor component in industrial production. The gap between nations will first be informational and speed-driven. With information and knowledge used as the raw materials of twenty-first century growth, economic competition will intensify differences between LDCs and the economic superpowers. Consequently, global powershift is about the key relationships between the power triad components (i.e., knowledge, violence, and wealth) which determine national economic stature and survival.

Of the global power players, Toffler identifies the United States as a wounded giant. With the Soviet threat to Western Europe dissipating and China and the Philippines confronting civil war, the United States' grand strategy needs revision at the top. Yet U.S. power over the long run really resides in its knowledge systems.

Given that these knowledge systems will dictate national power beyond that afforded by arms or wealth, it is imperative that the U.S. build on this competitive edge. The English language itself is the whole world's language in scientific and technological fields today. This language also blankets the globe with American culture and media. Thus, when one evaluates the recent economic triad of Tokyo, West Berlin, and Washington, the U.S. still holds the most balanced power portfolio and leads from its edge in knowledge power.

SUMMARY

With power at the center of the social phenomena universe, the transformation of the nature of power warrants everyone's attention. However, this powershift is not likely to be orderly or without its abuses. Overcontrol of citizens and economic systems will destroy the development of knowledge, the basis for the highest-quality power of all. While nations will not give up the awesome power of the sword or wealth, they must adjust to the new power relationships redefined by knowledge in the twenty-first century.

Managing as a Performing Art

Peter B. Vaill

Summary prepared by Richard S. Blackburn

Richard S. Blackburn is an Associate Professor at the Kenan-Flagler Business School at the University of North Carolina at Chapel Hill. He earned his MBA and Ph.D. at the University of Wisconsin, Madison. He teaches in the undergraduate, MBA, doctoral, and executive programs at UNC. His research interests include creativity and innovation, causes and consequences of service quality in professional organizations, and the impact of corporate design and identity on corporate performance. His research work has been published in both professional and academic journals, and he has served on several editorial review boards. He is co-author of *Managing Organizational Behavior*.

Managing as a Performing Art provides managers with ideas for coping in chaotic environments. These ideas are organized around the twin themes of chaotic change and organizational action. Appropriate actions are seen as dynamic, fluid, extraordinarily complex, and fundamentally personal organizational action. His performing arts metaphor generates a fresh perspective on the managerial world.

PERMANENT WHITE WATER

What metaphors do managers hold about their work environments? *Permanent white water* is one, and Chinese baseball (Siu, 1980) is a second. A manager rarely finds calm water, but lurches instead from one change to another as a raft through rough waters. Chinese baseball reflects this continuously changing context. The game is played like American baseball, but whenever the ball is in the air, the team in the field can move the bases anywhere they wish. Consider the strategies employed to play this game successfully. Would the most runs scored still be the best measure of success?

To operate in chaotic environments, managers must "work smarter." Historically, this meant managers worked *harder* by working longer hours, worked *more intelligently* by learning to be better managers, or worked *more shrewdly* by playing politics to be more effective. Working smarter in these ways helped when management was about planning, organizing, and controlling in stable environments. Those days are over. One-time management principles are now myths: a single all-powerful manager/leader, managing a single, freestanding organization; a pyramidal chain of command; producing a product via the establishment of official goals and rational analysis without concern for people or culture.

New managerial jobs have emerged that replace these "myths" with the following characteristics:

1. More accountability
2. More need for leadership
3. More emphasis on teamwork
4. More intense involvement with people
5. Greater ambiguity of authority
6. Greater emphasis on one's individuality
7. More involvement of the whole person
8. More stress
9. A new mix of an intellectual and an action orientation

Today's managers must work smarter in new ways. They must work smarter *collectively* (developing supportive attachments to others), *reflectively* (reframing perspectives on organizational problems), and *spiritually* (attuning themselves to timeless truths).

THE THEORY OF MANAGING IN THE MANAGERIAL COMPETENCY MOVEMENT

How do managers improve in times of continuing and complex changes? One school asserts that mastering certain competencies improves job performance. Researchers and educators subscribing to this competency perspective ask not "What do managers do?" but "What are the main factors in the manager's job?" By analyzing lists of factors gathered from experts and managers, a series of job functions is identified. Unfortunately, managers do not experience their jobs as a list, but in a variety of other ways. The competency movement (CM) makes a number of other equally dubious assumptions about management and the managerial environment:

CM Assumptions	Counter-Arguments
Competencies are distinct and independent.	Competencies exist in clusters.
Managers produce identifiable outputs from the exercise of various competencies.	Not all managers produce identifiable, physical outputs related to competencies.
Increased organizational effectiveness is greatly influenced by competencies.	Organizational effectiveness is affected by many more important factors than managerial competencies.
Managers create and/or restore order.	Managers must be innovators and creators of disorder.
Possessing a competency implies knowing when, where, and how to use it.	Perceptions distort judgments about when, where, and how to use competencies.
Competencies can be used regardless of the party who is the target of this use.	Interaction with others influences the the effectiveness of competency usage.
No untoward effects of correct competency use on the system will occur. If they do, competencies to deal with these can be learned.	Even the correct use of competency can create systemic problems.

The increasingly precise definitions of managerial competencies may lead to undesirable specialization in management. Managers need to cling to their own definitions of being a whole person with unique purposes in a situation, while also recognizing that others will have their own objectives.

WINNING IS ONLY THE THING YOU THINK WINNING IS

In organizations, managers can no longer view goals as etched in stone. Winning, success, or effectiveness must be defined as actions proceed, and differences about such definitions create a myriad of disagreements. Managers are quick to define what they see as "truth" while forgetting that others may define "truth" differently.

To minimize these problems, management engages in *purposing,* which is continuous leadership action to induce clarity, consensus, and commitment regarding the organization's basic purposes. This process demands ongoing efforts at *values clarification,* which is a highly critical task for managers, but one whose significance is often underestimated.

Values clarification requires a framework suggesting where value-related issues will arise in the future. The following categories of values reflect key stakeholder concerns in any definition of "winning" that the organization chooses to propose. These categories include:

1. Economic Values—reflecting what the firm's bottom line will be
2. Technological Values—reflecting how the firm will do what it chooses to do
3. Communal Values—reflecting the kind of "home" the firm will be for its employees
4. Sociopolitical Values—reflecting the kind of neighbor the firm will be to external constituencies
5. Transcendental Values—reflecting what the firm means at a deeper level to those same constituencies

These five categories are not independent, and choices made in one category will have multiple effects in the other categories. What any firm must develop via this values clarification process is a value *system* to identify the purpose for the organization and those associated with it.

THE PEAK PERFORMANCE CULT

Organizational excellence and peak performance have attained a certain cultishness, arising because (1) excellence and peak performance are too "American" to be questioned; (2) the urgency for organizational revitalization prohibits these ideas of seemingly practical worth from being tinkered with; (3) the commercial value of peak performance packaging crystallizes ideas, thus discouraging changes in the packaging; and (4) excellence requires commitment in its presentation to others, reinforcing cultishness.

There are a variety of unsolved problems arising from this "process of excellence." We know little about how excellent organizations attain the clarity of purpose so often attributed to them. Does "burnout" sap the strength of those asked to provide peak performance over long periods of time? Can groupthink arise when high-performing firms are unwilling to accept different perspectives on certain issues? Since high-performing firms are attuned to their own uniqueness, how are boundary-spanning activities conducted? Can excellence and peak performance be sustained over long periods of time? If excellent organizations are unable adequately to explain how they got that way, is it even possible to design processes by which other organizations can achieve excellence? Finally, does the belief in the ultimate rightness of an excellent organization's strategy close its value system to examination and comment by external stakeholders?

These unanswered questions may lead the managers of excellent organizations to confront a basic paradox:

In order to become excellent, it (the organization) needs to conduct among its members and stakeholders a creative process of values clarification in all five of these (previously discussed values) categories, including their inter-relationships; but the more excellent it becomes by its own values, the more it will feel that the need for continued discussion is not necessary, while its stakeholders will feel that the organization's growing potency (excellence) makes the need for such discussion more necessary than ever (p. 76).

THE GRAND PARADOX OF MANAGEMENT

The education of managers tries to provide both an understanding of what is going on in the organization (comprehension) and ways in which these events can be controlled (control). Despite fifty years of education in schools and organizations, the grand paradox of management remains: organizations are simultaneously "mysterious, recalcitrant, intractable, unpredictable, paradoxical, absurd, and funny" (p. 77).

There are two other paradoxes management confronts. First, the more we develop comprehensive management models, the more likely we are to identify factors excluded by the models that nevertheless influence organizations. Second, the impact of a manager's actions on an organization can never be completely determined because the manager is part of the system.

Traditional management training views paradoxes as problems to solve. But paradoxes represent conflicts between apparent truths, waiting to be resolved. Contemplation of and reflection on paradoxes rather than attempts at their resolution frequently yield better comprehension and control. Firms are urged to develop corporate cultures that are friendly to paradox. To do so requires: (a) the realization that paradoxes abound in organizations; (b) more holistic thought about situations; (c) more dynamic views of the world; (d) a willingness to drop cherished truths; and (e) that rather than thinking of the present as the means and the future as the end, managers begin to think of the future as the means and the present as the end.

REFLECTION AND THE TECHNOHOLIC

Technoholics solve problems with cookbook techniques. They despise the contingencies and reverse causal loops typifying organizational life. They live for the *technique,* believing that dogged adherence to the plan will yield desired solutions regardless of changes in the situational context. Technoholics suffer from "domino theory thinking," "reification," and a preference for "how-to-do-it" over "why-to-do-it."

The *domino theory* asserts that as long as some predetermined plan is followed, the steps of the plan will yield desired results despite changes in reality that made previous steps invalid. *Reification* involves "making a thing out of what is not a thing" (p. 90). So a plan becomes a thing, and the technoholic ignores or reinterprets events that do not fit into the plan. The "how" question is the technoholics' turf. They never ask, *"Why* are we doing this?"

Antidotes to technoholism arise by analyzing the assumptions that must hold for technology to work as intended. Assumptional grounds can be found in: (1) the amount, quality, and timing of the technology's inputs; (2) the impact of technology's operation and outputs on its human users; (3) the side effects of the technology; and (4) the fit between technology and existing norms and mores. Consideration of such assumptions forces the humanization of technology.

SATCHMO'S PARADOX

Earlier, the concept of "purposing" was discussed. But how does a top manager communicate this purpose to key constituents when permanent white water forces changes in purpose or confusion about current purposes? Managers must overcome *Satchmo's Paradox*—a lament reflecting the late jazz man's helplessness at being unable to explain jazz to the lay person. (Satchmo once said, "If you have to ask what jazz is, you'll never know.")

At issue is communicating information to the uninitiated about some managerial gestalt or "big picture" for the organization. Certain ideas only have meaning within these gestalts, but managers acquire these gestalts in unknown ways; the gestalt prevents these same managers from seeing their worlds in other ways, and the ideas are nearly impossible to communicate to others. For years, communicating this gestalt/vision was done by persistence, force, and/or coercion. But coercion can have deleterious side effects on commitment, creativity, and innovation levels of the coerced. What are some noncoercive alternatives for such communication?

This communication must occur in felicitous circumstances, suggesting an off-site location with a format less like a military briefing and more conversational and open-ended. Participants need not leave with specific deliverables nor with concrete plans. Discussions should involve key stakeholders and be open to examining the values underlying the communications. Practice at "gestalt passing" is useful as is use of a variety of media in communicating the gestalt.

MANAGING AS A PERFORMING ART

The "list-of-functions" approach to management currently dominates management education. But *knowing* that managers perform discrete functions (planning, organizing, controlling, etc.) and actually *doing* these functions are not the same thing. The former perspective ignores what the latter perspective appreciates; doing requires a "whole person in a whole environment in relation to other whole persons, embedded in time, with all actions viewed as concrete processes, and the entire process thoroughly suffused with turbulence and change" (p. 115). "Management as a performing art" is a metaphor well-suited to this holistic perspective on management and leadership.

This metaphor provides the manager with several unique managerial insights. First, the performing arts do not confuse competency in function with the whole performance. The dancer's technical skills are subsumed within the entire display. Second, performing arts' functions are related to a particular performance and are not generalizable across performances. Third, successful performances result from functions done correctly, with the necessary resources, and sufficient rehearsal until the performance is ready. Fourth, critics to the contrary, the definition of a quality performance is established by the performer. And the process of performance is the major concern, not merely reaching some objective. Fifth, performers take pleasure in performing. Sixth, every performance is unique. Seventh, a performer brings a variety of human skills to a performance, and performers develop "an organic unity of *feeling* . . . (to) bring a coherence and flow to what would otherwise be only a loosely related collection of parts" (p. 121). Finally, success in the performing arts depends on the context of the performance. A strong supporting cast and ample resources can yield heroic performances from otherwise mediocre talent. Successful productions view cast and crew not as interchangeable pieces to be transferred between roles at the whim of a director, but as highly interdependent contributors extremely sensitive to disruptive changes in context.

The performing arts also offer insights into the role of creativity in organized endeavors. Spontaneity is valued, but only within the framework of a script or musical score. Performing artists are able to generate creative efforts within the confines of a highly interdependent system. Similarly, the arts allow and encourage the spontaneous generation of new and innovative ideas. All of this occurs within a culture of quality and creativity. Ideally, managers and corporate cultures would accomplish the same things.

IT'S ALL PEOPLE

Management and leadership revolve around people. Why, then, is our thinking about people in organizations so superficial? The behavioral sciences have been trying to understand the behavior and attitudes of people for years, but the theories that have evolved all seem to be about someone called "Superficial Man (SM)."

Until recently, SM was a white, male, middle-class adult, engaging in observable and classifiable behavior. He was unlikely to undertake any novel actions, so his behavioral tendencies were predictable. Everything about SM could be labeled and explained. This is the image of individuals and individual behavior that is frequently communicated to managers and students of management. And the list-of-functions approach is how we study SM in his managerial role.

Such theories of SM are inadequate, however, because they are evaluated in terms of their utility and parsimony. What would our theories of human behavior look like if they were judged on levels of *stewardship* or ethical foundations? In other words, to what extent does a theory *value* the individual it aspires to explain? Toward a more "robust" stewardship, theories should meet the following criteria:

1. The theory realizes it is a theory (and not untestable dogma).
2. The theory takes a "process" view of human beings and not a static view.
3. The theorist believes the theory applies to him- or herself.
4. The theory will be accepted by those whom it is to explain.
5. The theory avoids "scientism" and a preoccupation with methodology.
6. The theory appreciates the inherent tensions between conformity and freedom.
7. The theory makes it easier to appreciate and love those to whom it applies.

Theories that meet these criteria will exhibit a concern for the inherent value of the individuals who are their focus. We have few of these theories now. We need new ones.

THE END OF CULTURE AND THE DIALEXIC SOCIETY

Culture has been a popular topic recently for a variety of reasons. Discussions of culture are "juicy." We can talk of things we know well and feel strongly about. These discussions are not psychologically threatening. They provide a means to talk about attitudes, values, and actions of those in the culture, allowing managers to move from discussions about culture to discussions about using culture as a management tool.

Culture is oversold and unreliable. By definition,

> Culture is a *system* of attitudes, actions, and artifacts that *endures over time* and that operates to produce among its members a relatively *unique common psychology (UCP)* (p. 147).

To change an organization's culture requires changing the UCP. This requires a much more intense change effort than current culture change programs can provide. But culture is dying. Ours has become a "dialexic" society—one with a compulsion to speak dialectically and to assume that the world is not as it seems. Events, actions, or individuals that might become parts of our culture are undercut by expert analysis, by parody (simplification, standardization, and commercialization), and by ennui (the inability to take events of culture seriously).

Dialexic discussions do not benefit organizations. They merely give reasons for noninvolvement in what is happening in the organization. Unfortunately, technoholism and dialexia have become major elements of the UCP and they are mutually reinforcing. Given this, it becomes easier to understand the difficulty in actually changing an organization's culture.

WHAT SHOULD THE TOP TEAM BE TALKING ABOUT?

Strategic management is *what* the top team should be talking about. However, it is easier to talk about strategic management than to do it. The issue of *how* to implement the results of the strategic management decision is the *most* important topic for top team discussion.

To achieve a position on a top management team, team members develop strong action orientations, are competitive, have an understanding of organizational politics, and have learned to suppress their feelings. This last quality prevents team members from truly understanding what is happening on the top team. An inability to express feelings leads to the almost ritualistic discussions that characterize dialexia. Top management teams need ways to unblock feelings. Options for unblocking include team development offered by a trained OD consultant, immediate intervention, or "going back to school together."

Immediate intervention might take the form of the top team considering the problem of blocked feelings within the larger organization. Consideration of how to unblock the rest of the organization may create a spill-over effect where the same issue is discussed within the context of the team. An alternative is to find or develop an educational program for the entire team designed to consider such issues as strategic leadership, organizations and their environments, anticipating the future, and personal assessment and development.

Successful top teams contain members willing to contribute *time* (long hours), *focus* (a thorough knowledge of relevant activities), and *feeling* (respect for, and devotion to, both the work system and the people in it). Time and focus are in ample supply on top teams. But time and focus without feeling yield competent, yet shallow, teams. Feeling and time without focus yield spirit without content. Feeling and focus without time yield wisdom but lethargy. The top team *should* be talking about ensuring that its members are competent, wise, and spirited.

TAOIST MANAGEMENT

The concept of "wu-wei" or "nonaction" is central to Taoism. *Wu-wei* refers to the idea of not forcing something, or going with the grain. There is much that Western managers, in their desire to take action, can learn from Taoism and nonaction.

In sports, being "in the zone" is frequently cited as key to peak performance. A oneness of mental, physical, and spiritual energies often surfaces in descriptions of peak performance. This may be the closest Western thought comes to the concept of wu-wei. But the Taoist would not use words like "peak" and "performance." Language differences create some of the problems in translating the subtleties of wu-wei for Western managers. Western language and imagery extol victory and triumph. Terms like "cutting our competition off at the knees" reflect this toughness in managerial image and language. Wu-wei views such terminology as "forcing" in nature.

Myth	Wu-Wei Interpretation
1. A single person called the manager	Managing occurs throughout the organization
2. A single free-standing organization	Organization is a temporary abstraction from the totality
3. Control via chain of command	A more democratic leveling of power differences
4. Organization as pure instrument	Organization as a field within which many purposes and processes play out
5. The irrelevance of culture	An understanding of synergies available from many unique common psychologies
6. Primary output is a product	Awareness of all the organization is and does to produce its outputs
7. Rational analysis for understanding	Rational analysis in the service of philosophy of life

Westerners tend to split the present from the future, thought from action, and the manager from the system managed. Wu-wei maintains the unity of time, of thought and action, and of self and environment. A wu-wei interpretation of the seven management myths discussed earlier reflects this desire for reduced fragmentation.

MANAGEMENT AS SNAKE HANDLING

How much of a manager's work is done with as strong a faith as that held by those who handle snakes as part of a religious ritual? The five categories of values discussed earlier contain the bases for determining an organization's definition of effectiveness. Good judgment is needed in that process, but also faith in oneself and one's organization. What is crucial is the basis for one's faith. To this end, the author shares a fanciful conversation between himself and five deceased spokesmen, one for each of the five value categories. Adam Smith speaks for Economic Values, Frederick W. Taylor for Technological Values, Elton Mayo for Communal Values, John L. Lewis for Sociopolitical Values, and Ralph Waldo Emerson for Transcendental Values.

One powerful question is addressed to each participant: "How much faith is involved in the acceptance of the premises and major assertions of your respective fields?" The outcome of each conversation suggests that our modern managers do have faith in theories and ideas, but too many of them have not stopped to think what that really means. *Managers are insensitive to the underlying assumptions of these theories.* It has been faith in the general correctness of what managers are trying to do that protects them when particular snakes bare their fangs.

THE REQUISITES OF VISIONARY LEADERSHIP

Just as a becalmed sailor retains his faith in the wind, a manager needs faith in his/her personal and organizational excellence even if it has yet to appear. To continue one's pursuit of managerial breezes, one must work spiritually smarter. *Spirituality* is seen as the pervasive yet elusive force that energizes individuals. While difficult to define, everyone has experienced the spirit associated with an all-engaging project. But the permanent white water in which managers operate can drain the spirit. As a river floods its banks, so spirit can flow out as quickly as it flows in.

How can managers renew their faith and spirituality in the work place? How can they make work more inspiring? The workaholic, technoholic, or powerholic approaches to working smarter are not the answer. Ignoring Satchmo's Paradox and practicing dialexia are not the answer. Where might the answers reside?

Spiritual leadership can come from any level in the organization. Vision alone is not enough, for it is the spirit within the vision that energizes the visionary. We need new metaphors and symbols to complement the rather sterile psychological terms we use in today's organizations. *Role model, facilitator,* even *CEO* have little in the way of spirit attending them. What about *voyager, knight, quarterback,* or *servant* as alternatives?

True leadership is spiritual leadership in the sense that it brings out the best in others. Accomplishing this becomes a quest; it is seeking a goal without a map, and the spirit can be discovered as the search progresses. Living in this way at home or in the office will force new and different relationships. Old ones may fall by the wayside, but new ones will be stronger. This quest is an intensely personal one. It cannot bring spiritual answers to others. But such a quest will insure that work and relationships will be more spirited in the future.

TEN

Innovation and Organizational Change

*E*xperts frequently advise American managers to invest in research and development (R&D). Many charge that *one* of the reasons for the decline in the competitiveness of U. S. industry revolves around its failure to innovate at sufficient levels.

Peter F. Drucker, who has held professional positions at Bennington College, New York University, and the Claremont Graduate School, is probably the foremost philosopher on management in the United States. His recent book, *Innovation and Entrepreneurship,* provides insight into the thinking that has made Drucker the "Dr. Spock of American business."

Innovation and Entrepreneurship accents the increasing trend among today's organizations to provide employees with a greater degree of autonomy than they have traditionally received. Two underlying assumptions frequently provide the rationale for doing so:

1. Many employees have untapped potential for making greater contributions to their organization than have previously been obtained from them.
2. Employees are more likely to release those resources when given a greater sense of ownership and control over what they do.

Readers will find Drucker's presentation of "creative imitation" and "entrepreneurial judo" insightful, and his numerous corporate illustrations cogent, relevant, and stimulating. Of particular interest is his identification of the reasons for the downfall of established organizations: arrogance, creaming the market, false quality, premium price, and maximizing versus optimizing.

James Belasco, Professor of Management at San Diego State University, wrote the book *Teaching the Elephant to Dance.* In his book Belasco focuses attention on issues related to overcoming organizational resistance to change. The author offers some insightful ideas on how to devise and implement an organizational vision.

A philosopher once noted that a person never steps foot in the same river twice. Contemporary organizations have their own "river"—a turbulent environment around them. Consequently, managers of today's organizations are being called upon to integrate their organizations with a changing external environment. To do this, they must often adapt their organization's internal structure, processes, and strategies to meet these environmental challenges. The ability to manage change is far different from the ability to manage and cope with the ongoing and routine side of the organization.

Rosabeth Moss Kanter, in her book *When Giants Learn to Dance,* discusses challenges and management strategies that will be necessary for the 1990s. Among her themes are: invest in the future without losing sight of your short-term goals, support entrepreneurial risk taking, streamline your operations, and yet make your organization a great place to work!

If organizations are going to survive in the turbulent environment presented by the decade of the 1990s, they need to undergo a major restructuring: learning how to do more with less, learning how to cope with disorder and distraction, learning how to develop strategic alliances in their external environment, and learning how to develop a supportive internal climate in the midst of change and uncertainty. Kanter, with coauthors Barry A. Stein and Todd Jick, have also written *The Challenge of Organizational Change: How Companies Experience It and Leaders Guide It.*

Tom Peters, in his book *Thriving on Chaos,* provides a comprehensive description of corporate practices at a wide range of firms. Peters passionately advocates total responsiveness to customers, the need for fast-paced innovation, the benefits of empowering people, and the need to instill flexibility and a love for change in employees. These characteristics should allow an organization to prosper in a world that is both chaotic and increasingly characterized by international competition. Peter's newest book is *Liberation Management: Necessary Disorganization for the Nanosecond Nineties.*

Reading 1

Innovation and Entrepreneurship

Peter F. Drucker

We only began quite recently to talk of "strategies" in connection with a business.[1] Of late, of course, strategy has become the "in" word with any number of books written on it.[2] However, I have not come across any discussion of entrepreneurial strategies. Yet they are important, they are distinct, and they are different.

"FUSTEST WITH THE MOSTEST"

Being "Fustest with the Mostest" was how a Confederate Cavalry general in America's Civil War explained his consistently winning his battles. When applying this strategy to the contemporary business, the entrepreneur aims at leadership, if not dominance, in a new market or new industry. Being "Fustest with the Mostest" does not necessarily imply creating a big business right away—though often this is indeed the aim. However, it does from the start aim at achieving a permanent leadership position.

Being "Fustest with the Mostest" is the approach which many people consider the entrepreneurial strategy *par excellence.* Indeed, if one were to go by the popular books on entrepreneurship[3] one would conclude that "Fustest with the Mostest" is the *only* entrepreneurial strategy. A good many entrepreneurs, especially the high-tech ones, seem to be of the same opinion.

They are wrong, however. To be sure, a good many entrepreneurs have indeed chosen this strategy. Yet "Fustest with the Mostest" is not even the dominant entrepreneurial strategy, let alone the one with the lowest risk or the highest success ratio. On the contrary, of all entrepreneurial strategies, it is the greatest gamble. And it is unforgiving, making no allowances for mistakes and allowing no second chance.

But, if successful, being "Fustest with the Mostest" is highly rewarding.

Following are some examples which show what this strategy consists of and what it requires.

- Hofmann-LaRoche of Basel has for many years been the world's largest and, in all probability, its most profitable pharmaceutical company. But its origins were quite humble. Until the mid-1920s, Hofmann-LaRoche was a small and struggling manufacturing chemist which made a few textile dyes and was totally overshadowed by the huge German dye-stuff makers and three much bigger chemical firms in its own Switzerland. Then it gambled on the newly-discovered vitamins—at a time when the scientific world still could not quite get itself to accept that such substances, could exist. It acquired the vitamin patents—which nobody else wanted. It hired the discoverers away from Zürich University at several times the salary they could ever hope to get as professors—salaries that even industry had never before paid. It invested all the money it had and could borrow in manufacturing and marketing these new substances. Sixty years later—long after all vitamin patents have expired— it still controls nearly half the world's vitamin market, which amounts to billions of dollars a year. Hofmann-LaRoche followed the same strategy twice more: in the 1930s, it went into the new sulfa drugs—even though most scientists of the time "knew" that systemic drugs could not be effective against infections; and then, twenty years later, it went into the muscle-relaxing tranquilizers Librium and Valium—which at that time were equally "heretical" and incompatible with what "every scientist knew."
- Du Pont followed the same strategy when developing Nylon. In the mid-1920s, it was already the leading American chemical company (though still confined almost completely to explosives). Du Pont hired a chemist named Wallace H. Carothers and provided him with funds and facilities to do research in polymer chemistry—something which most chemists had either discounted or given up on. For a dozen years, Carothers produced no results. But when he finally came up with the first truly synthetic fiber, Nylon, Du Pont at once mounted massive efforts. It built huge plants, went into mass advertising (Du Pont had never before had consumer products to advertise), and created the industry we now call "plastics."

These are "big-company" stories, it will be said. But when it started in vitamins, Hofmann-LaRoche was but an ailing dwarf. Following are some more recent examples of companies that started from nothing with a strategy of "Getting There Fustest with the Mostest."

- The "Word Processor" is not much of a "scientific" invention. It does not do much more than hook up three existing instruments: a typewriter, a display screen, and a fairly elementary computer. But this combination resulted in a genuine innovation which has radically changed office work. Dr. An Wang was a lone entrepreneur when he conceived of this combination some time in the mid-1950s. He had no track record as an entrepreneur and had a minimum of financial backing. Yet from the beginning he clearly aimed at creating a new industry that would revolutionize office work—and Wang Laboratories has, of course, become a very big company.

- Similarly, the two young engineers who started the Apple computer—in the proverbial garage and without financial backers or previous business experience—aimed from the beginning at creating an industry and dominating it.

Not every "Fustest with the Mostest" strategy needs to aim at creating a big business—though it must always aim at creating a business that dominates its market. The 3M Company in St. Paul, Minnesota, does not—as a matter of deliberate policy, it seems—attempt an innovation that might result in a big business by itself. Nor does Johnson & Johnson, the health care and hygiene producer. Both companies are among the most fertile and most successful innovators. Both look for innovations that will lead to medium-sized rather than to giant enterprises which are, however, dominant in their markets.

Being "Fustest with the Mostest" is not confined to businesses. It is also available to public-service institutions.

- When Wilhelm von Humboldt founded the University of Berlin in 1809, he clearly aimed at being "Fustest with the Mostest." Prussia had just been defeated by Napoleon and had barely escaped total dismemberment. It was bankrupt—politically, militarily, and above all financially. It looked very much the way Germany looked after Hitler's defeat in 1945. Yet Humboldt set out to build the largest university the Western world had ever seen or heard of—three to four times as large as anything then in existence. He set out to hire the leading scholars in every single discipline, beginning with the foremost philosopher of the time, Georg W. F. Hegel. He paid his professors up to ten times as much as professors had ever been paid before at a time when first-class scholars were going begging (the Napoleonic Wars had forced many old and famous universities to disband).

- A hundred years later, in the early years of this century, two surgeons in Rochester (an obscure Minnesota town far from population centers or medical schools) decided to establish a medical center based on totally new—and totally heretical—concepts of medical practice. They focused on building teams in which outstanding specialists would work together under a coordinating team leader. Frederick William Taylor, the father of "Scientific Management," had never met the Mayo Brothers. But in his well-known testimony before the Congress in 1911, he called the Mayo Clinic the "only complete and successful scientific management" he knew. These unknown provincial surgeons aimed from the beginning at dominance of the field, at attracting outstanding practitioners in every branch of medicine, and at attracting patients able and willing to pay what were then outrageous fees.

- Twenty-five years later, the strategy of being "Fustest with the Mostest" was used by the "March of Dimes" to organize research on infantile paralysis (polio). Instead of gathering new knowledge step by step—as all earlier medical research had done—the "March of Dimes" aimed from the beginning at total victory over a completely mysterious disease. No one before had ever organized a "research lab without walls" in which a large number of scientists in a multitude of research institutions were commissioned to work on specific stages of a planned and managed research program. The "March of Dimes" established the pattern on which the United States, a little later, organized the first great research projects of World War II: the atom bomb, the Radar Lab, the Proximity Fuse, and then another fifteen years later, "Putting a Man on the Moon"—all innovative efforts using the "Fustest with the Mostest" strategy.

These cases show first that being "Fustest with the Mostest" requires an ambitious aim; it is bound to fail otherwise. It always aims at creating a new industry or a new market. At the least, as at the Mayo Clinic or the March of Dimes, being "Fustest with the Mostest" aims at creating a new and quite different—and highly unconventional—process. The Du Ponts surely did not say to themselves in the mid-1920s, when they brought in Carothers: "We will establish the plastics industry" (indeed, the term was not in wide use until the 1950s). But enough of the internal Du Pont documents of the time have been published to show that the top management people did aim at creating a new industry. They were far from convinced that Carothers and his research would succeed. But they knew that they would have founded something big and brand-new in the event of success, and something that would go far beyond a single product or even beyond a single major product line. Dr. Wang did not coin the term "the Office of the Future," as far as I know. But in his first advertisements, he announced a new office environment and new concepts of office work. From the beginning, both the Du Ponts and Wang clearly aimed at dominating the industry they hoped they could succeed in creating.

Because being "Fustest with the Mostest" must aim at creating something truly new and different, non-experts and outsiders seem to do as well as "experts," in fact, often better. Hofmann-LaRoche, for instance, did not owe its strategy to chemists, but to a musician who had married the granddaughter of the company's founder and needed more money to support his orchestra than the company then provided through its meager dividends. To this day the company has never been managed by chemists, but always by financial men. Wilhelm von Humboldt was a diplomat with no earlier ties to academia or experience in it. Du Pont's top management people were businessmen rather than chemists and researchers. And while the Brothers Mayo were well-trained surgeons, they were totally outside the medical establishment of the time and were isolated from it.

Of course, there are also the true "insiders": a Dr. Wang, or the people at 3M, or the young computer engineers who designed the Apple computer. But when it comes to being "Fustest with the Mostest" the outsider may have an advantage. He does not know what everybody within the field knows, and therefore does not know what cannot be done.

Continued Efforts

Being "Fustest with the Mostest" has to hit the bull's eye or it misses the target altogether. Or, to vary the metaphor, being "Fustest with the Mostest" is very much like a moon shot; a deviation of a fraction of a minute of the arc and the missile disappears into outer space. Once launched, the "Fustest with the Mostest" strategy is difficult to adjust or to correct.

For this strategy to succeed requires thought and careful analysis of the opportunities for innovation. Even then, it requires extreme concentration of effort. There has to be *one* goal and all efforts have to be focused on it. And when this effort begins to produce results, the innovator has to be ready to mobilize resources massively. As soon as Du Pont had a usable synthetic fiber—long before the market had begun to respond to it—Du Pont built large factories and bombarded both textile manufacturers and the general public with advertisements, trial presentations, speeches, and so on.

After the innovation has become a successful business, the work really begins. Then the strategy of "Fustest with the Mostest" demands substantial and continuing efforts to retain leadership position. Otherwise, all one has done is to create a market for a competitor. The innovator has to run even harder than ever once he has the position of leadership. He has to continue innovative efforts, and on a very large scale. The research budget has to be higher *after* the innovation has successfully been accomplished. New uses have to be found and new customers have to be supplied, identified, and persuaded to try the new product. Above all, the entrepreneur who has succeeded in being "Fustest with the Mostest" has to be able to make his product or process obsolete before a competitor can. Work on the successor to the successful product or process has to start immediately, with the same concentration of effort and the same investment of resources that led to the initial success.

The Du Pont Company went much further. It systematically sought out and helped bring competitors into the Nylon business by granting them a license. This way it kept control of the market to a large extent. By doing this they put people into business who then, on their own part, found new markets, new uses, and new customers. This helped expand and develop the market much faster than Du Pont, despite patent protection, could possibly have hoped to do alone as the sole supplier.

Finally, the entrepreneur who has attained leadership by being "Fustest with the Mostest" has to be the one who systematically cuts the price of the product or process. To keep prices high simply encourages potential competitors.

The longest-lived private monopoly in economic history is the Dynamite Cartel founded by Alfred Nobel after his invention of dynamite. The Dynamite Cartel maintained a worldwide monopoly until World War I and even beyond—long after the Nobel patents had expired. It did this by cutting prices every time demand rose by ten to twenty percent. By that time, the companies in the Cartel had fully depreciated the investment they had had to make to get the additional production. This made it unattractive for any potential competitor to build new dynamite factories, while the Cartel itself maintained its profitability. It is no accident that Du Pont has consistently followed this same policy in the United States; the Du Pont Company was the American member of the Dynamite Cartel. Wang has done the same with respect to the word processor, Apple with its computers, and 3M with all of its products.

The Risk of Failure

These are all success stories. They do not show how risky the strategy of being "Fustest with the Mostest" actually is. The failures disappeared. Yet we know that for every one who succeeds with this strategy, many more fail. There is only one chance with the "Fustest with the Mostest" strategy. If it does not work right away, it is total failure.

Everyone knows the old Swiss story of Wilhelm Tell the archer, whom the tyrant promised to pardon if he succeeded in shooting an apple off his son's head on the first try. If he failed, he would either kill the child or be killed himself. This is exactly the situation of the entrepreneur in the "Fustest with the Mostest" strategy. There is no "almost success" and no "near-miss." There is only success or failure.

Even the success stories may be successes only by hindsight. At least we know that in several of the examples, failure was very close; only luck and chance saved them.

Du Pont only succeeded in Nylon because of a fluke. Carothers' final result was a fiber. But there was no market for a Nylon fiber. It was far too expensive to compete with cotton and rayon, the cheap fibers of the time. It was actually even more expensive than silk, the luxury fiber which the Japanese, in the severe depression of the late 1930s, had to sell for whatever price they could get. What saved Du Pont was the outbreak of World War II, which stopped Japanese silk exports. By the time the Japanese could start up their silk industry again (around 1950), Nylon was firmly entrenched, with its cost and price down to a fraction of what both had been in the late 1930s.

The strategy of being "Fustest with the Mostest" is risky because it is based on the assumption that it will fail far more often than it can possibly succeed. It will fail because the will is lacking. It will fail because efforts are inadequate. It will fail because, despite successful innovation, not enough resources are deployed, are available, or are being put to work to exploit success. While "Fustest with the Mostest" is indeed highly rewarding if successful, it is much too risky and much too difficult to be used for anything but major innovations. It requires profound analysis and a genuine understanding of the sources of innovation and of their dynamics. It requires extreme concentration of efforts and substantial resources. In most cases there are alternative strategies that are available and preferable—not because they carry less risk, but because for most innovations the opportunity is not great enough to justify the costs, the efforts, and the investment of resources required for the "Fustest with the Mostest" strategy.

"HIT THEM WHERE THEY AIN'T"

Two completely different entrepreneurial strategies can be derived from a saying of another battle-winning Confederate general, "Hit Them Where They Ain't." They are called "Creative Imitation" and "Entrepreneurial Judo."

Creative Imitation

Creative imitation is a contradiction in terms. What is "creative" must surely be "original." If there is one thing imitation is not, it is being "original." Yet the term fits. It describes a strategy which is "imitation" in its substance. Here, the entrepreneur does something somebody else has already done. It is "creative" because the entrepreneur who applies this strategy understands what the innovation *represents* better than the people who made the innovation.

The foremost practitioner of this strategy, and the most brilliant one, is IBM. It is also the strategy which Proctor & Gamble has been using to obtain and maintain leadership in the soap, detergent, and toiletries markets. The Hattori Company in Japan, whose Seiko watches have become the world's leader, also owes its domination of the market to "creative imitation."

- IBM built a high-speed calculating machine in the early 1930s to do calculations for the astronomers at New York's Columbia University. A few years later, it built a machine that was designed as a computer—again, to do astronomical calculations (this time at Harvard). By the end of World War II, IBM had built a real computer—the first one that had the features of the true computer: a "memory" and the capacity to be "programmed." And yet there are good reasons why the history books pay scant attention to IBM as a computer innovator. For as soon as it had finished its advanced 1945 computer—the first computer to be shown to lay public—IBM abandoned its own design and switched to the design of its rival, the "ENIAC" developed at the University of Pennsylvania. The ENIAC was far better suited to business applications such as payroll—however, its designers did not see this. IBM then restructured the ENIAC so that it could be manufactured and serviced and could do mundane "numbers crunching." When IBM's version of the ENIAC came out in 1953, it immediately set the standard for commercial, multipurpose mainframe computers.

This is "creative imitation." It waits until somebody else has introduced the new, but only in a limited way. Then it goes to work—and within a short time it comes out with what the new really should be to be useful, to satisfy the customer, to do the work customers want and pay for. Then, the "creative imitation" sets the standard and takes over the market.

- IBM practiced "creative imitation" again with the personal computer. The original idea was Apple's. Everybody at IBM "knew" that a small, freestanding computer was a mistake—uneconomical, far from optimal, and expensive. Yet the personal computer was a success. IBM immediately went to work to design a machine that would become the standard in the personal computer field and dominate, or at least lead, the entire field. The result was the PC—and within two years it had taken the leadership position away from Apple, became the fastest-selling brand, and became the standard in the field.

- When semi-conductors became available, everyone in the watch industry knew that they could be used to power a watch much more accurately, much more reliably and much more cheaply than traditional watch movements. The Swiss were the first to introduce a quartz-powered digital watch. But they had so much invested in traditional watch-making that they decided on a gradual introduction of quartz-powered digital watches over a long period of time, during which these new timepieces would remain expensive luxuries. The Hattori Company in Japan had long been making conventional watches for the Japanese market. It saw the opportunity and went in for "creative imitation." It developed and marketed the quartz-powered digital watch as a *standard* timepiece. By the time the Swiss had woken up, it was too late. Seiko watches had become the world's best sellers, with the Swiss almost pushed out of the market.

Like being "Fustest with the Mostest," creative imitation is a strategy aimed at market or industry leadership, if not at market or industry dominance. It is less risky than being "Fustest with the Mostest." By the time the creative imitator moves, the market has been established and the new has been accepted. Indeed there is usually more demand for it than the original innovator can easily supply. The market segmentations are known or at least knowable. Most of the uncertainties that abound when the first innovator appears have been dispelled or at least analyzed and studied. No one has to explain anymore what a "personal computer" or a "digital watch" are and what they do.

Of course, there is the risk that the original innovator may do it right the first time, thus closing the door to "creative imitator"—as Hofmann-LaRoche did with vitamins, Du Pont did with Nylon, and Wang did with the word processor. But the number of entrepreneurs engaging in "creative imitation"—and their substantial success—indicates that perhaps the risk of the first innovator's preempting the market by doing it right is not an overwhelming one.

Another example of creative innovation is Tylenol, "the non-aspirin aspirin." This case shows more clearly than any other I know what "creative imitation" consists of, what its requirements are, and how it works.

- Acetaminophen (the substance in Tylenol) had been used for many years as a painkiller. Until relatively recently, it was available in the U.S. only by prescription. Also until not too long ago, aspirin, the much older painkiller, was considered perfectly safe and had the pain-relief market to itself. Acetaminophen is a less potent drug than aspirin. It is effective as a painkiller but has no anti-inflammatory effect and also no effect on blood coagulation. Because of this, it is free from the side effects (especially gastric upset and stomach bleeding) which aspirin can cause, especially if used in large doses and over long periods of time (e.g., for arthritis).

- When acetaminophen became available without prescription, the first brand on the market was presented and promoted as a drug for those who suffered side-effects from aspirin. It was eminently successful, indeed, far more successful than its makers had anticipated. But it was this very success that created the opportunity for "creative imitation." Johnson & Johnson realized that there was a market for a drug that *replaced* aspirin as the painkiller of choice, with aspirin confined to the fairly small market where anti-inflammatory and blood coagulation effects were needed. From the start, Tylenol was promoted as the safe, *universal* painkiller. Within a year or two, it had taken over the market.

Creative imitation, these cases show, does not exploit the failure of the pioneers as "failure" is commonly understood. On the contrary, the pioneer must be successful. The Apple computer was a great success story, and so was the acetaminophen brand which Tylenol ultimately pushed out of market leadership. But the original innovators failed to understand their success. The makers of the Apple were product-focused rather than user-focused, and therefore offered additional hardware where the user needed programs and software. In the Tylenol case, the original innovators failed to realize what their own success meant.

The creative innovator exploits the *success* of others. Creative imitation is not "innovation" in the sense in which the term is most commonly understood. The creative imitator does not invent a product or service, he perfects and positions it. The way it has been introduced it lacks something. It may lack additional product features. It may lack segmentation so that slightly different versions fit slightly different markets. It may lack proper positioning of the product in the market.

The creative imitator looks at products or services from the point of view of the customer. IBM's personal computer is practically indistinguishable from the Apple in its technical features. But from the beginning, IBM offered the customer programs and software. Apple maintained traditional computer distribution through specialty stores. IBM developed—in a radical break with its own traditions—all kinds of distribution channels, specialty stores, major retailers like Sears Roebuck, its own retail stores, and so on. It made it easy for the consumer to buy and it made it easy for the consumer to use the product. These, rather than hardware features, were the "innovations" which gave IBM the personal computer market.

Altogether, "creative imitation" starts out with markets rather than with products, with customers rather than with producers. It is market-focused and market-driven.

Creative imitation requires a rapidly growing market. Creative imitators do not succeed by taking away customers from the pioneers, rather they serve markets the pioneers have created but do not adequately service. Creative imitation does not create demand, rather it satisfies demand that already exists.

Creative imitation has its own risks—and they are considerable. Creative imitators are easily tempted to splinter their efforts in the attempt to hedge their bets. Another danger is to misread the trend and imitate creatively what then turns out not to be the winning development in the marketplace.

IBM—the world's foremost and, in many ways, its most successful creative imitator—exemplifies these dangers in its approaches to office automation. It successfully imitated every major development. As a result it has the leading product in every single area. But its products are so diverse and so incompatible with one another that it is all but impossible to build an integrated, automated office out of IBM building blocks. Being designed to imitate creatively the developments of half a dozen different pioneers, the IBM products outdo them, but they do not, by themselves, constitute a unified approach—each having different architecture, different logic, and different software. It is thus still doubtful that IBM can assume leadership in the automated office and provide it with the integrated system that will be the main market of the future. The *risk of being too clever* is inherent in the creative-imitation strategy.

Creative imitation is likely to work most effectively in "high tech" areas for one simple reason: "high tech" innovators are least likely to be market-focused, and most likely to be technology- and product-focused. The innovators therefore tend to misunderstand their own success and to fail to exploit and supply the demand they have created. However, they are by no means the only ones to do so.

Because creative imitation aims at market dominance, it is best suited to a major product, process, or service. By the time "creative imitators" go to work, the market has already been identified and the demand has already been created. But what it lacks in risk, creative imitation makes up for in its requirements for alertness, flexibility, and willingness to accept the verdict of the market. Above all, it requires hard work and massive efforts.

Entrepreneurial Judo

- In 1947, Bell Laboratories invented the transistor. It was at once realized that the transistor was going to replace the vacuum tube, especially in consumer electronics such as the radio and the then-brand-new television set. Everybody knew this, but nobody did anything about it. The leading manufacturers—at that time they were all Americans—began to "study" the transistor and to make plans for conversion to the transistor "sometime around 1970." Till then, they proclaimed, the transistor "would not be ready." In Japan, Sony read about the transistor in the newspapers. At that time, Sony was practically unknown outside of Japan and was not even in consumer electronics. But Akio Morita, Sony's president, went to the United States and bought from Bell Labs a license for the new transistor for a ridiculous sum (all of $25,000). Two years later, Sony brought out the first portable transistor radio, which weighed less than one-fifth of comparable vacuum-tube radios on the market and cost less than one-third. Three years later, Sony had the market for cheap radios in the United States. Five years later, the Japanese had the radio market all over the world.

Sony's success is not the real story. What explains the fact that the Japanese repeated this same strategy again and again and again? And always with success, always surprising the Americans? They repeated it with television sets and digital watches and hand-held calculators. And they repeated it with copiers when they moved in and took a large share of the market away from the original inventor, the Xerox Company. The Japanese, in other words, have been successful again and again in practicing "entrepreneurial judo" against the Americans.

Americans have also been successful in practicing this strategy. MCI and Sprint used the Bell Telephone System's (AT&T) own pricing to take away from the Bell System a very large part of the long-distance business. ROLM was also successful when it used Bell System's policies against it to take a large part of the private branch exchange (PBX) market. Similarly, Citibank met with success when it started a consumer bank in Germany, the *Familienbank* ("Family bank"), which within a few short years came to dominate German consumer finance.

- The German banks knew that consumers had obtained purchasing power and had become a desirable bank customer. They went through the motions of offering banking services to consumers, but they really did not want them. Consumers, they felt, were beneath the dignity of a major bank with its business customers and its rich investment clients. If consumers needed an account at all, they should have it with the postal savings bank. Whatever their advertisements said to the contrary, the banks made it abundantly clear that when consumers came into the august offices of the local branch, the bank had little use for them. This was the opening Citibank exploited when it founded its *Familienbank* and catered to no one but consumers, designed the services consumers needed, and made it easy for consumers to do business with a bank. Despite the tremendous strength of the German banks and their pervasive presence in a country where there is a branch of a major bank on every downtown street corner, Citibank's *Familienbank* attained dominance in the German consumer banking business within five years.

All these newcomers—the Japanese, MCI, ROLM, Citibank—practiced "entrepreneurial judo." Of all entrepreneurial strategies, especially the strategies aiming at obtaining leadership and dominance in an industry or a market, "entrepreneurial judo" is by all odds the least risky and the most likely to succeed.

Every policeman knows that a habitual criminal will always commit his crime the same way. He will, for instance, crack a safe the same way or enter a building he wants to loot the same way. He leaves behind a "signature" which is as individual and as distinct as a fingerprint. And he will not change his "signature" even though it leads to his being caught again and again.

It is not only the criminal who is set in his habits. All of us are. And so are businesses and industries. The habit will be persisted in even though it leads again and again to loss of leadership and loss of market. American manufacturers persisted in habits that enabled the Japanese to take over their market again and again.

If the criminal is caught, he rarely accepts that his habit has betrayed him. On the contrary, he will find all kinds of excuses—and will continue the habit that led to his being captured. Similarly, businesses that are being betrayed by their habits will not admit it and will find all kinds of excuses. The American electronic manufacturers, for instance, blame the Japanese successes on "low labor costs" in Japan. Yet the few American manufacturers that have faced up to reality (e.g., RCA and Magnavox in television sets) are able to turn out products in the United States that are competitive in both price and quality with those of the Japanese—all this despite their paying American wages and union benefits. The German banks uniformly explain the success of Citibank's *Familienbank* with its taking risks they themselves would not touch. But *Familienbank* has lower credit losses with consumer loans than the German banks, and its lending requirements are as strict as those of the Germans. The German banks know this, of course, yet they keep on explaining away their failure and *Familienbank*'s success. This is typical and is the reason why the same strategy—the same "entrepreneurial judo"—can be used over and over again.

There are five fairly common bad habits which enable newcomers to use "entrepreneurial judo" and catapult themselves into a leadership position against established companies.

- The first bad habit is what American slang calls *"NIH"* ("Not Invented Here"), the arrogance that leads a company or an industry to believe that something new cannot be any good unless they themselves thought of it. Thus, the new invention is spurned, as was the transistor by the American electronics manufacturers.
- The second bad habit is the tendency to *"cream"* a market, that is, to get the high-profit part of it.
- This is basically what Xerox did and what made it an easy target for the Japanese imitators of its copying machines. Xerox focused its strategy on the big users, the buyers of large numbers of machines or of expensive high-performance machines. It did not reject the others; but it did not go after them. In particular, it did not see fit to give them service. In the end it was dissatisfaction with the service—or rather with the non-service—which Xerox provided for its smaller customers which made them receptive to competitors' machines.
- "Creaming" is a violation of elementary managerial and economic precepts. It is always punished by loss of market.
- Xerox was resting on its laurels. They were indeed substantial and well-earned, but no business ever gets paid for what it did in the past. "Creaming" is an attempt to try to get paid for past contributions. Once a business gets into that habit, it is likely to continue in it and thus continue to be vulnerable to "entrepreneurial judo."
- Even more debilitating is the third bad habit: the belief in *"quality."* "Quality" in a product or service is not what the supplier puts in. It is

what the customer gets out and is willing to pay for. Contrary to what most manufacturers believe, a product is not "quality" because it is hard to make and costs a lot of money. That is incompetence. Customers pay only for what is of use to them and gives them value. Nothing else is "quality."

- The American electronics manufacturers in the 1950s believed that their products with all those wonderful vacuum tubes were "quality" because they had put thirty years of effort making radio sets bigger, more complicated, and more expensive. They considered the product to be "quality" because it needed a great deal of skill to turn out, whereas a transistor radio was simple and could be made by unskilled labor on an assembly line. But in consumer terms, the transistor radio was clearly of far superior "quality." It weighed much less so that it could be easily taken to the beach, on a trip, or to a picnic. It rarely had something go wrong; there were no tubes to replace. It cost a great deal less. In range and fidelity it very soon surpassed even the most magnificent Super Heterodyne with sixteen vacuum tubes (one of which always burned out when needed).

- Closely related to both "creaming" and "quality" is the fourth bad habit, the delusion of the *"premium"* price. A "premium" price is always an invitation to the competitor.

- Since the days of J.B. Say in France and David Ricardo in England in the early years of the nineteenth century, economists have known that the only way to get a higher profit margin, except through a monopoly, is through lower costs. The attempt to achieve a higher profit margin through a higher price is always self-defeating. It holds an umbrella over the competitor. What looks like higher profits for the established leader is in effect a subsidy to the newcomer who, in a very few years, will unseat the leader and claim the throne for himself. "Premium prices" should always be considered a threat and a dangerous vulnerability.

- Yet the delusion of higher profits to be achieved through "premium prices" is almost universal, even though it always opens the door to "entrepreneurial judo."

- Finally, there is a fifth bad habit which is typical of established businesses and leads to their downfall. Again, Xerox is a good example. They *maximize rather than optimize.* As the market grows and develops, they try to satisfy every single user through the same product or service.

- As a hypothetical example, let's say a new analytical instrument to test chemical reaction is being introduced. At first its market is quite limited, let's say to industrial laboratories. Then, university laboratories, research institute, and hospitals all begin to buy the instrument. But each wants something slightly different. And so, the manufacturer puts in one feature to satisfy this customer, another one to satisfy that customer, and so on, until what started out as a simple instrument has become complicated. The manufacturer has maximized what the instrument can do. As a result, the instrument no longer satisfies anyone; for by trying to satisfy everybody, one always ends up satisfying nobody. The instrument has also become expensive. It has also become hard to use and hard to maintain. However, the manufacturer is proud of the instrument—his full-page advertisement lists sixty-four different things the instrument can do. This manufacturer will almost certainly become the victim of "entrepreneurial judo." What he thinks is his very strength will be turned against him. The newcomer will come in with an instrument designed to satisfy one of the markets, the hospital, for instance. It will not contain a single feature the hospital people do not need, but it will have a higher performance capacity than the multi-purpose instrument can possibly offer. The same manufacturer will then bring out a model for the research laboratory, for the government laboratory, for industry. In no time at all, the newcomer will have taken away the markets with instruments that are designed for the users, instruments that optimize rather than maximize.

- Similarly, when the Japanese came in with their copiers in competition with Xerox, they designed machines that fitted specific groups of users—the small office, for instance, whether that of the dentist, the doctor, or the school principal. They did not try to match the features of which the Xerox people themselves were the proudest—e.g., the speed of the machine or the clarity of the copy. They gave the small office what the small office needed the most, a simple machine at a low cost. Once they had established themselves in that market, they then moved in on the other markets, with products designed to optimally serve a specific market segment.

- Similarly, Sony first moved into the low end of the market, the market for cheap portables with limited range. Once it had established itself there, it moved in on the other market segments.

"Entrepreneurial judo" first aims at securing a beachhead, one which the established leaders either do not defend at all or defend only halfheartedly (as was the case when the Germans did not counterattack when Citibank established *Familienbank*). Once that beachhead has been secured, that is, once the newcomers have an adequate market and adequate revenue, they then move in on the rest of the territory. In each case, they repeat the strategy. They design a product or a service which is specific to a given market segment and optimal for it. Almost never do the established leaders beat them to this game. Almost never do the established leaders change their own behavior before the newcomers have taken over the leadership and have acquired dominance.

There are three situations in which the "entrepreneurial judo" strategy is likely to be particularly successful.

- The first is the common situation in which the established leaders refuse to act on the unexpected, whether success or failure, and either overlook it altogether or try to brush it aside. This is what Sony exploited.

- The second is the Xerox situation. A new technology emerges and grows fast. But the innovators who introduced the new technology—or the new service—behave like the classical "monopolists": they use their leadership position to "cream" the market and to get "premium prices." They either do not know or refuse to know what has been amply proven: a leadership position, let alone any kind of monopoly, can only be maintained if the leader behaves as a "benevolent monopolist" (a term coined by Joseph Schumpeter). A benevolent monopolist cuts his prices before a competitor can cut them. He makes his product obsolete and introduces a new product before a competitor can do so. There are enough examples of this around to prove the validity of the thesis. It is the way, for instance, in which the Du Pont Company has acted for many years and in which the American Bell Telephone System (AT&T) used to act before it was overcome by the inflationary problems of the 1970s.

• Finally, "entrepreneurial judo" works when market or industry structure undergo rapid change—e.g., the *Familienbank* story. As Germany became prosperous in the 1950s and 1960s, ordinary people became customers for financial services beyond the traditional savings account or the traditional mortgage. The German banks stuck to their old markets at the sacrifice of the new ones.

"Entrepreneurial judo" is always market-focused and market-driven. To use the "entrepreneurial judo" strategy one starts out with an analysis of the industry: the producers and the suppliers, their habits (especially their bad habits), and their policies. Then one looks at the markets and looks for the place where an alternative strategy would meet with the greatest success and the least resistance.

"Entrepreneurial judo" requires some degree of genuine innovation. It is, as a rule, not good enough to simply offer the same product or the same service at lower cost. There has to be something that distinguishes it from what already exists. When the ROLM Company offered a private-branch exchange (a switchboard for business and office users) in competition with AT&T, it built in additional features designed around a small computer. These were not "high tech," let alone new inventions. Indeed, AT&T itself had designed similar features. But AT&T did not push them—and ROLM did. Similarly, when Citibank went into Germany with the *Familienbank* it put in some innovative services which German banks as a rule did not offer to small depositors (e.g., travelers checks and tax advice).

It is not enough, in other words, for the newcomer to do as good a job as the established leader and at a lower cost or with better service. The newcomers have to make themselves distinct.

Like being "Fustest with the Mostest" and "creative imitation," entrepreneurial judo aims at obtaining a leadership position and eventual dominance. But it does not do so by competing with the leaders—or at least does not do it where the leaders are aware of competitive challenge or are worried about it. Entrepreneurial judo "Hits Them Where They Ain't."

NOTES

1. The 1952 edition of the *Oxford Concise Dictionary* still defined "strategy" as: "Generalship; the art of war; management of an army or armies in a campaign." Alfred D. Chandler, Jr., first applied the term in 1962 to the conduct of a business in his pioneering *Strategy and Structure* (Cambridge, MA: MIT Press, 1962) which studied the evolution of management in the big corporation. But when I, shortly thereafter in 1963, wrote the first analysis of business strategy, the publisher and I found that the word could not be used in the title without risk of serious misunderstanding. Booksellers, magazine editors, and senior business executives all assured us that "strategy" for them meant the conduct of military or election campaigns. The book discussed much that is now considered "strategy"—it uses the word in the text. But the title we chose was *Managing for Results* (New York: Harper & Row, 1964).
2. Of the books on the subject of strategy, the one I have found most useful is Michael Porter's *Competitive Strategies* (New York: The Free Press, 1980).
3. Perhaps the most readable recent examples of books on entrepreneurship is George Gilder's *The Spirit of Enterprise* (New York: Simon & Schuster, 1984).

Reading 2

Teaching the Elephant to Dance

James Belasco

Summary prepared by Kim A. Stewart

Kim A. Stewart is an Assistant Professor of Management at the University of Denver. She holds a Ph.D. in management from the University of Houston, and teaches courses in strategic management and organizational behavior. Her research interests focus on the post-acquisition integration of acquired firms, and entrepreneurship.

Today's competitive and environmental conditions demand that organizations change to become more efficient, effective, and competitive. However, although the pressures for change are ongoing and often enormous, many organizations are surprisingly resistant to change. One view suggests that organizations resist change because they are like shackled elephants. Although it has the strength to "pull the stake and move beyond," the organization/elephant stands still, bound by earlier conditioned restraints such as past learning or success, or the standard "We've always done it this way." *Teaching the Elephant to Dance* presents a multi-point strategy for organizations to break free of such conditioned constraints and achieve effective change through a strategy that is driven by a vision for the organization.

GET READY FOR THE CHANGE

Preparing for change requires building an urgency for change by convincing employees of the need to change. This can be done by first obtaining "symptoms" of inadequate performance such as customer complaint letters, field sales reports, or competitors' comparisons and then communicating these symptoms to employees via mechanisms such as newsletters, competitor comparison displays in the plant, employee letters, or meetings. Management must also create the clear path of change on which employees will travel and communicate a simple-to-understand destination (the vision). Behaviors that are vital to change (e.g., active listening, quickly handling customer complaints) should be identified, communicated to employees, and reinforced and rewarded when they occur.

ANTICIPATE OBSTACLES

Five potential problems can beset major change initiatives:

1. *Time* Effective change always takes much more time to achieve than people expect. New behaviors are slowly learned and easily forgotten. As a result, leaders must recognize the substantial time requirements and make sure they're committed to spend the time necessary to realize lasting change. They must also report a continual stream of short-term progress produced by the change effort to employees so people don't lose interest in the change vision.

2. *Exaggerated expectations* Once people are actively on the change bandwagon, most want results—now. Unfortunately, results are rarely immediately forthcoming, and worse, inevitable mistakes occur which leave people questioning the wisdom of continuing the change effort. This obstacle can be combatted by clarifying the relationship between the organization's biggest problems and the change effort/vision, by empowering employees to take responsibility for implementing the vision, and by being honest about the problems in implementing the change.

3. *Carping Skeptics* In every organization, some individuals loudly and persistently point out the negatives in any situation or change effort. They can be ignored (which usually works in the short run). However, a better strategy is to confront the critics and their concerns early and directly. Change leaders should show personal interest in skeptics' concerns, and enlist their aid and support in the change effort. The enthusiasm of other employees and the progress measured to date can also be effectively used to convert skeptics.

4. *Procrastination* Given employees' workload and the intangibles of change efforts that many managers like to avoid (e.g., customer attitudes and employee motivations), it's easy for people to postpone vision-supporting activities. Procrastination can be dealt with by breaking change-supporting actions into small, more doable steps, by keeping up a steady but reasonable pressure for change behaviors, and by emphasizing the successes in an immediate and dramatic way.

5. *Imperfection* Mistakes are made and failures occur in all major change initiatives. However, organizations must strive for continual improvement in

the change effort rather than explicit perfection. Mistakes should be seen positively—as learning experiences and as an opportunity to refocus efforts on the change vision.

BUILD A NEW ORGANIZATIONAL STRATEGY

Major internal changes often require a new internal strategy. Four strategies (*nichemanship, focus, efficiency,* and *customer service*) merit the attention of changing organizations that are striving to build a better product or service. Companies that purse a *nichemanship* strategy fulfill a segment of unmet demand in a larger market. For example, Von's Supermarket moved from fourth place to the top spot among grocery store chains in southern California by identifying and fulfilling specific niches. This included Spanish neighborhoods in Fresno, California, where Von's introduced into its stores a wider selection of Hispanic foods, new lighting and displays, and a black-and-red colored decor. Success at nichemanship requires that companies dominate the niche, stay on top of customer needs, find upscale applications for commodity products, use advertising to enhance the company's niche image, stay flexible, avoid direct competition with major players, and avoid dependence on a small number of suppliers and customers.

The *focus* strategy involves getting back to the basics—focusing on those things that are essential to the company's success, such as customer needs. The *efficiency* strategy focuses on achieving long-term efficiencies often via the use of automated equipment to cut manufacturing/distribution costs. The *customer service* strategy seeks to enhance service via highly selective recruiting and extensive training of employees, measuring service levels continuously, and consistently rewarding top-service performers.

FOCUS RESOURCES ON THE CHANGE EFFORT

Strategy alone does not achieve the change vision; people and funds are essential tools in realizing the "new tomorrow." Effectively addressing the people factor in change involves identifying the "leverage positions"—those jobs which have the most impact on achieving change and realizing the vision (e.g., R&D staff in a new product development strategy). For each leverage job, the skills, knowledge, attitudes, and behaviors needed to do the job well should be identified, and the individual who best matches this "ideal profile" should be hired. Two major tasks concern resources. The first involves reducing spending on the nonessential activities. The second entails lowering the costs of essential activities by such strategies as simplifying operations (reducing steps in manufacturing, eliminating decision-making and layers of management), tapping employee creativity, and improving quality that reduces the costs of product rework, scrap, and warranties.

CREATE A VISION

The vision drives major organizational change. The vision should be:

- "a short, simple statement . . .
- "of some value-adding and marketplace-advantage factors . . .
- "which positively distinguishes the organization in the minds of everyone with whom the organization interacts (customers, employees, suppliers) . . .
- "and provides clear, inspiring criteria for decision making."

Honda Motors' vision, for example, is one that meets these criteria. It accents (1) "Quality in all jobs—learn, think, analyze, evaluate, and prove; (2) reliable products—on time, with excellence and consistency; and (3) better communication—listen, ask, and speak up."

In crafting a vision, the major change initiators should be sure that the vision is practical and is consistent with their personal values. The vision statement should be reviewed with people from all areas and levels of the organization to be sure it is clearly understood (as people can only be empowered by a vision they understand).

EMPOWER PEOPLE TO USE THE VISION

Actions that lead to employee empowerment to use and realize the vision can take many forms. Initially it is essential that the CEO or change initiator identify the behaviors and actions that reflect the vision and then personally demonstrate these behaviors in highly visible situations. For example, CEO J.W. Marriott, Jr., believes that Marriott guests value the little touches that distinguish between average and great service. So he spends much of his time touring Marriott's hotels, personally inspecting those little things and making sure that hotel employees see him doing it.

The CEO must also continually remind people that the vision is working, in part by identifying behaviors that are key to realizing the vision, and keeping a very public charting of those behaviors. For example, in the employee cafeteria at Springfield Remanufacturing Company, a large electronic board flashes the plant's hourly results of activities (e.g., labor usage) that are critical to the company's profitability.

The CEO should use employee meetings to discuss the vision and report change progress. The CEO can utilize group management meetings in efforts to empower managers to accept and use the vision. The CEO should work on getting managers to understand the vision by discussing specific action steps that support the vision, and developing short-term action plans that managers can more easily implement.

DEVELOP EXPECTATIONS AND MEASURES

Once the vision is established, it should be translated into specific quantitative measures by which employee behavior and performance will be evaluated. The measures should be simple and limited to those activities that support the new vision (a long list of measures can be confusing and diffuse employee efforts). Clear, quantitative, and short-term expectations should be clearly communicated to employees. People should receive direct and fast feedback concerning the behaviors needed and desired.

USE THE PERSONNEL SYSTEM TO EMPOWER CHANGE

Concerning the recruitment element of the personnel system, a selection profile should be developed that includes characteristics that support the vision. Interviewers and those who make hiring decisions should be trained to use the profile, looking for the right knowledge, skills, and attitudes. (Indeed, these individuals should reflect the vision.) Orientation programs are an excellent opportunity to communicate the vision. Immediate supervisors can also develop a specific orientation program concerning how the vision is used in the particular department. Training programs can be used to reinforce the vision. For example, at United Parcel Service over eighty percent of the full-time work force attend voluntary workshops held after work that focus on the company's competitive challenges. These workshops support the UPS vision: boosting efficiency and customer service. Some part of every training program can also focus on how a particular tool or information can be applied to support and reinforce the vision.

Behaviors that are essential to the vision should be included in the performance appraisal system. The organization's compensation system should reward vision-related performance. Rewards can be group-based or individual (for example, Genentech Company provides instant bonus "Genenchecks" of $1,000 for employees who develop new research applications). Recognition is also a powerful motivation tool. For example, at Transco Energy in Houston, quarterly "bragging sessions" are held where individuals tell all attending employees about what they've done to boost customer services and cut operational costs. According to CEO George Slocum, these sessions have helped to save over $18 million.

DEVELOP A VISION-BASED CULTURE

If the vision is new, a new culture that supports the vision must be created, and the old vision (and culture supporting it) must be laid to rest. A ritual of passage is essential to mark this transition. In this meeting with all employees, the CEO should recall the best of the organization's past (which can be contrasted with the present which is less positive), and point to a better future. The actual risks and challenges of implementing the new vision should be addressed. Once the organization is on the path to the new vision, this transition-in-the-making should be celebrated.

Beyond this passage ritual which launches the transition to the new vision, the new culture can be further developed by building work activities that support and reflect the vision. For example, Hewlett-Packard's long-held vision of product innovation was for years encultured by the company's tradition of the "next desk." Here, engineers were encouraged to leave their work on their desk so others could look it over and contribute their own ideas to its development.

Shared social activities and special events can also be created to develop the culture. Again at H-P, Friday afternoon beer busts are held which the company believes enhance the values of individual respect and communication. A vision-supporting culture can be developed by crafting phrases that aptly convey the vision and repeating them frequently in company media, and by communicating stories about "heroes" (individuals whose actions exemplify the new vision). AT&T, for example, has a number of heroes that populate its rich history. Among the most aptly remembered heroines was a telephone operator who remained at her station amidst a raging fire so that she could maintain crucial telephone connections.

EMPOWER INDIVIDUAL CHANGE AGENTS

This task involves bringing the vision and the change process down to the gut level for each and every individual in the organization. Doing so involves first developing for each business unit or department *strategic business issues* (SBIs)—those issues which are critical to the unit's performance and success. The vision should be linked to the resolution of the issues. These linkages should be communicated to the unit's employees, to enhance the commitment of employees to the vision. It is also useful to encourage all employees to identify their own contributions to the unit's strategic business issues, to focus efforts on those issues and vision-relevant behaviors.

Another way to empower individual change agents is to identify, within each unit, each individual's suppliers and customers. (For a production control manager at a metal fabrication plant, for example, a supplier is a purchasing agent who provides the materials the manager needs; a customer is the manager of the plant's second shift who uses the first manager's finished parts). Then, employees should regularly meet with their suppliers and customers to establish and update "contracts" which specify how each party helps the other in the performance of their jobs. These contracts should be linked to the department's SBIs and the organizational vision, and the contracts should focus on "specific, quantifiable, short-stroke deliverables."

Reading 3

When Giants Learn to Dance

Rosabeth Moss Kanter

Summary prepared by Robert C. Ford

Robert C. Ford is a Professor in the Department of Management at the University of Alabama at Birmingham. Prior to joining UAB, he was a member of the faculty at the University of North Florida. He holds a Ph.D. in management from Arizona State University. In addition to publishing texts on principles of management and organization theory, he has authored or coauthored articles on applied management practices, human resource management, and social responsibility in both practitioner and academic journals. He is an active member of the Academy of Management, the Southern Management Association, and the Society for Human Resource Management.

Are organizations ready for the Global Olympics? Can corporate giants (organizational elephants) learn to dance with the grace and nimbleness of the practiced ballerina or even, for that matter, the untrained kid at the prom? This is the question that Rosabeth Moss Kanter seeks to answer by reviewing the lessons learned on her multiple-year journey through the organizational experiences of her clients at Goodmeasure and her research investigations as a scholar in the Harvard Business School. Her answer is maybe. But first there must be a sea of change in the corporate culture and managerial style for those organizations who seek to compete successfully in the rapidly changing and highly competitive world arena. Kanter details the strategies that organizations can adopt to meet these changes as well as the reasons why the "old answers" simply don't work any more.

COMPETING IN THE CORPORATE OLYMPICS

Corporations are competing in a worldwide arena in which the rules of the game are not unlike the croquet game in *Alice in Wonderland* where everything is alive, changing, unpredictable, and moving. The whole field of competition is in motion, and the old rules, the expectation of some consistency in the game, and the availability of clearly defined goals to guide strategy and decision-making have become anachronisms. American businesses, once the proud exemplar of modern management, are now trying to adjust to a new world of contradictions. Now they seek to find ways of becoming lean and mean, a great company to work for, competitive in a global marketplace, and able to do more with fewer resources.

These are not only competing demands; they are increasingly important challenges for those firms that wish to compete successfully in the "Corporate Olympics." The solution can be found in the rise of the post-entrepreneurial organization. This relatively new form of organization is somewhere between the classical and too-familiar bureaucratic form of a Kodak, a PacTel, or a General Electric that Kanter terms a "Corpocracy" and the highly individualist, young, highly entrepreneurial form of organization of an Apple Computer that she labels "Cowboy." As the bureaucratic Kodak struggled to become more entrepreneurial and the cowboy Apple struggled to be less individualistic, they both gravitated towards a middle ground by adopting the strategies which characterize the post-entrepreneurial organization.

This form of organization is one that effectively implements three strategies:

1. Restructuring to create synergistic relationship
2. Creating strategic alliances with key stakeholders (e.g. suppliers, customers, and venture partners)
3. Developing specific programs to nurture, encourage, and support entrepreneurial activity within their organizations.

While different organizations may implement these strategies differently, those who are set on winning will find a way of doing so. The next two sections explain how to implement these strategies, and the consequences for the corporation, the employees, and society as a whole.

DOING MORE WITH LESS

Restructuring

Too many efforts to restructure organizations have failed to solve the people and economic problems that such corporate upheavals create. Therefore, they miss achieving the gains expected through synergy. This failure leads to discontinuity, disorder, and distraction. *Discontinuity* is caused by moving from the old to the new (restructured) organization. Whether the restructuring is a result of downsizing, merger, or buy-out, the uncertainty to the participants is the same, as they attempt to bury the old and create something different: new structures, cultures, and interpersonal relationships. *Disorder* arises from the confusion created as the restructured organization builds new channels of information, loses key resources and people, and redefines new corporate values and job expectations. *Distraction* results from management's inevitable shift of focus and energy away from the process of running the business to the more immediate problems created by the restructuring. Restructuring can, therefore, create an enormous vulnerability to problems at precisely the same time that everyone's attention, energy, and focus are distracted. This very point in time the organization desperately needs the recommitment, rededication, and reinvigoration of its employees so that it can gain the expected benefits of its restructuring, yet it is most at risk to lose them all. Since reorganization leads to uncertainty and insecurity, and employee commitment requires certainty and security, the successful post-entrepreneurial organization must strike a balance between these competing forces.

Obtaining Synergy

This balance can be achieved by restructuring in ways that create a new whole that is greater than the sum of its previous parts. This search for *synergy* has two levels. At one level is the search for organizational gains that can be obtained by finding good combinations of parts and avoiding bad combinations. This can be done through a "value-added" test. At the other level are the people gains obtained by restructuring the intellectual content and personal responsibility. This can be done through various strategies of empowerment.

Finding good combinations of organizational parts is a result of thoughtful consideration of what each part contributes to the entire organizational purpose. The idea of "value-added" forces those considering a restructuring to think through whether or not any new organization units will in fact allow them to gain the efficiencies of economies of scale, fill out a product line, access new management or technical expertise, attract better people through better career opportunities, enhance access to competitive information or previously unavailable markets, and reaffirm a shared value structure with a commitment to performance. Using this "value-added" test forces a reassessment of every part of the organization, to see what that part actually contributes and whether or not there might be a better way to obtain that contribution. In short, the post-entrepreneurial organization thinks of itself as a central information and command center for all of its component elements, constantly evaluating each organizational components to decide what it wants to do itself and what it is better off letting someone else do for it. No part of the organization should be immune from this "value-added" test.

Those organizations which actually gain these synergies have three characteristics in common. First, top management leads the way. Senior executives show their commitment to finding the synergies by creating the methods and developing the managers who identify them. Second, the organization shifts its incentives and reward programs to focus everyone's attention on cooperating with each other in pursuit of the corporate well-being instead of competing against each other in pursuit of their individual goals. The third characteristic is the existence of a culture of cooperation, which leads to good interpersonal and interdepartmental relationships and information sharing. These characteristics allow the post-entrepreneurial organization to respond flexibly and effectively to the changing environment.

Creating Strategic Alliances

It is not enough, however, to improve the cooperation and communication only within the organization. The post-entrepreneurial organization recognizes the need to build the same quality of communication and cooperative relationships with those upon whom its effectiveness depends. It recognizes the importance of the extended "economic family" and finds ways to keep these relationships healthy.

There are three basic strategies for accomplishing these ends. They are "(P)ooling," "(A)llying," and "(L)inking." *Pooling* refers to a method by which the organization shares resources with another. *Allying* refers to the formation of temporary corsortia or joint ventures. *Linking* is the process whereby the organization forms a partnership to link together specific parts of itself with another organization. All three strategies have as their goal the creation of organizational "PALs" which replace the traditional adversarial relationship between those inside and those outside the firm with a collaborative and cooperative one: strategic alliance.

These new forms of relationships created by PAL strategies are not only important to improving the post-entrepreneurial organization's ability to respond flexibly and efficiently in the rapidly changing world market place, but they also have significant and important impact inside the organization as well. When management seeks to build cooperative linkages *between* organizations, this causes further disruptions inside the organization itself. PALs, for example, challenge the traditional hierarchical power relationships by shifting managerial authority orientation from control to collaborative. Managers must now learn how to manage a network of collaborative, cooperative relationships rather than merely controlling people. Problems can include overmanagement, undermanagement, conflicts over scope, and hedging on resource allocations by one or all of the partners.

The Six "I's"

There are six ingredients (six "I's") which must be in place for a partnership to be successful. These are:

1. The relationship must be Important to all partners.
2. There is an agreement for a long term Investment which balances the rewards over time.
3. The partners have thought through and defined their Interdependence to balance the power relationships.
4. The partners have built into their organizations points of Integration to ensure smooth communication and cooperation.
5. Each keeps the other Informed about its plans and expectations.
6. The partnership is somehow Institutionalized through both formal

legal documents and informal social ties and shared cultures which can maintain mutual trust.

Newstreams

Besides the use of PALs which permit flexible response to changing market demands by organizations, there are internal strategies as well. These are based on managers being able to develop newstreams of products and services while not neglecting their mainstream. Mainstream products and services are closely associated with the past and present organizational survival and profitability. *Newstream* reflects future products and services, and they present management with an entirely different set of concerns. Newstream differs from mainstream in the type of performance criteria used to measure success, the amount of uncertainty associated with dealing with untested ideas, and in the impact that the newstream may have on the existing structure, people, and power relationships. Since the potential payoffs are so great, the requirements for organizational commitment to newstreams are likewise great.

Newstreams are important to the post-entrepreneurial organization not only because they represent the future products and services necessary to compete in the Corporate Olympics, but also because of what they represent in defining the culture. The message that emphasis on newstream sends throughout the organization is one of commitment to innovation in all aspects of the organization. This emphasis does, however, create some dilemmas. One is that newstream efforts require personnel to be effective change agents. Newstream projects need autonomy but not so much that they lose their linkages to the mainstream organization. Newstream peoples' efforts are driven on by an entrepreneurial energy, but the fruits of these efforts must be captured or shared by the organization. This raises some interesting problems for the post-entrepreneurial organization. How can it allow some elements of its organization to have the thrill, rewards, and energizing experience of discovering newstream products and services without at the same time finding similar rewards and experiences for its mainstream people? If newstream people can be trusted to be creative and entrepreneurial, why can't the mainstream? Management can't allow the organization to separate into "haves" and "have-nots" without compromising its ability to secure commitment and effort from all of its people in the face of continuing uncertainty and change. This raises the question of how it can ensure that all the members are included in the "haves" category.

JOBS, PEOPLE, MONEY

Consequences of the Post-Entrepreneurial Revolution

As the post-entrepreneurial organization comes to grips with the need for PALs and the Newstream ventures also come to grips with their impacts on traditional personnel policies, management must rethink its reward systems. The hierarchy upon which the traditional organization depended as a means for assigning power, status, and money is increasingly challenged in an organization driven by the power of new and creative ideas and people. Increasingly, people expect pay to reflect contribution and not just longevity or position in the chain of command. The pressure on organizations to encourage the needed entrepreneurial activity which leads to newstreams means that they must reshape their traditional pay plans to encourage and reward fairly this type of employee behavior.

New Pay Plans

The response has been to develop gainsharing systems, pay for skills, pay for performance, profit sharing, and merit pay that is meaningful. Managing pay plans in the post-entrepreneurial organization is a delicate balancing act as the organization seeks a reward system which fairly balances recognition of individual contributions (to reward individual effort) with recognition of the group (to maintain the necessary interdependencies of all individuals), the unit accomplishments with overall organizational achievements, and the traditional internal pay structure and external market forces with individual contributions. The post-entrepreneurial organization is likely to discover that the pay scheme it finds most workable is one that incorporates recognition of all these diverse elements.

The post-entrepreneurial organization is not only finding the need to discover new pay schemes, but it is also confronting new types of jobs and the pressures on its employees that go with them. These jobs are rich with challenge and opportunity. They are exciting, and people become committed to them, think about them intensely, and take time away from family and outside activities to pursue them. This leads to information overload and job-related stress. The very nature of entrepreneurial activity creates more time commitments. Time is required to ensure that the necessary communications partnerships and interactions develop. Time is required to handle the inevitable stream of new tasks and activities that change creates. And time is required to respond to the flatter, more fluid, organizations that allow a variety of people to initiate ideas to which someone has to listen and respond.

Post-entrepreneurial organizations have an important and often unrecognized role to play here. Successful organizations do three things to help. First, they delegate the authority to go along with the expanded responsibilities to eliminate the need to spend time checking with the boss. Second, they minimize the number of changes occurring simultaneously by prioritizing the important and less important issues and not trying to implement everything at the same time. Finally, they simplify by constantly rethinking the systems, procedures, rules, and regulations so there is not any unnecessary burden on their people. In addition, managers need to recognize a legitimate role for life outside the firm. Also, for these people, most work is done in cycles of intense effort followed by lulls. The lulls could be used to allow mini-sabbaticals, vacations, and time away from the job, which help people to regroup and get revitalized.

Careers

The last major impact on the individual from the creation of post-entre-preneurial organizations is a redefinition of the individual career. Traditionally, people have thought of a career as something that takes place in one organization where a person progresses up some functional career ladder. Thus, marketing trainees work their way up the corporate ladder, perhaps rising to senior marketing positions, as they enter the twilight of their "corporatic" careers. There is a strong attachment to the organization and weak attachment to the task or work group. The organization rewards loyalty and seniority by gradual promotion up the hierarchy. Room is made for these promotions by expanding growth and narrowing spans of control to allow more senior-level positions to become available.

Two Career Paths

This idyllic scenario will be less and less true in the emerging post-entre-preneurial organization. The hierarchy is getting flatter while organizations are downsizing and eliminating opportunities for career growth in the traditional way. Instead, there will be two new paths for individuals to follow. One is the professional career where people make a career out of seeking excellence in their own areas of functional expertise, moving from one task and organization to another, continuously seeking new opportunities to display that expertise as well as adding to their professional reputation.

The second new path is the entrepreneurial career. Here individuals leave the corpocracy behind and strike out on their own. These people are ready and willing to take the risk of gaining the freedom, independence, and control over their own economic and personal life that owning their own business can bring. Further, they give business and the economy more flexibility by being available to supplement the efforts of the traditional organization on an "as-needed," value-added basis. These career professionals and the entrepreneurs are critical in helping the giant to dance with grace and nimbleness in the global market-place.

CONCLUSION

Corporations that hoped to succeed in the Corporate Olympics need to use the four "Fs":

1. Focused on what they're doing.
2. Fast in redeploying their resources to meet the changing environment.
3. Friendly toward their PALs and own employees.
4. Flexible in responding to the changing environmental circumstances they face.

This means that their leaders will also need to learn seven new skills to gain the value-added synergies available through new alliances and newstreams while maintaining a dynamic, committed, and motivated work force energetically seeking new ideas. First, these new leaders must learn to manage without relying on the traditional authority of the hierarchy. Instead, they need to learn how to exercise personal influence and interpersonal skills to get things done. Second, these leaders must learn how to compete in a way that promotes healthy cooperation to achieve excellence instead of an unhealthy quest for devastating the competition. Third, these leaders must be ethical to retain the trust necessary to make these cooperative relationships work. Fourth, they must be humble enough to listen to other ideas and receptive to learning new ways of doing things. Fifth, they need to develop a respect for the process of how things are done rather than focusing solely on what is done. Sixth, these new leaders need to be flexible enough to seek out and build new relationships within and outside the organization when they can add value, and be able to cut them loose when they don't. Finally, these new business leaders must find satisfaction in performance instead of status and in attaining results instead of promotions. This portrays a new type of manager for a new type of organization managing a new type of employee with new types of relationships to the organization and to the work itself. While the challenge is considerable, the rewards for those giants that do learn to dance are equally great.

Thriving on Chaos

Tom Peters

Summary prepared by Ann Wiggins Noe

Ann Wiggins Noe has her B.A. and M.B.A. in Personnel/Human Resource Management from Michigan State University. She has taught and conducted research in Human Resource Management for several years. In addition, she has done independent consulting work in the training and legal arenas. Currently she is finishing her Ph.D. in Staffing, Training and Development, and Organizational Behavior at the Industrial Relations Center of the University of Minnesota, Minneapolis.

Tom Peters, the coauthor of the best-selling management books *In Search of Excellence* and A *Passion for Excellence,* begins his third book with the provocative assertion that "There are no excellent companies." He believes that it is no longer possible to be classified as being an excellent company based on what you have done. Rather, firms that wish to approach excellence will have to be ready for constant change and actually thrive on chaos. Excellent companies will be those that *are doing* rather than those that *have done.*

The need to thrive on chaos is derived from a rapidly changing business climate. This change is due to a number of factors including the American decline in business as compared to other countries, the increased uncertainty in the arena of corporate structuring that is currently characterized by mergers and buyouts, and the rapidly changing technological environment. In addition, the American emphasis on "bigger is better" and the minimization of labor's organization role have all helped to bring about the chaotic atmosphere in which today's managers must manage.

In *Thriving on Chaos,* Peters takes a more prescriptive stance than in his previous two books. He outlines 45 "Prescriptions for a World Turned Upside Down." He draws upon numerous organizational examples, and details the first steps that managers can take to implement his prescriptions for achieving excellence while thriving on chaos.

Tom Peters. *Thriving on Chaos.* New York: Alfred A. Knopf, 1987.

CREATING TOTAL CUSTOMER RESPONSIVENESS

The emphasis in the first section is on the *Customer,* and it highlights the importance for organizations to identify and attach to their customers. The need to create new markets and customers for the organization's products is also stressed. Of the ten prescriptions presented, the first is the guiding premise advocating "Specialize/Create Niches/Differentiate." This premise suggests that the organization must take a three-pronged approach that includes moving away from a mass-production mentality, while attempting to be more of a specialist. For example, instead of being a community hospital, market the organization as a hospital with the best radiation therapy facilities outside of the Mayo Clinic (as one successful community hospital in Elgin, Illinois did). In addition, work to create new market niches by convincing new customers of the need for your product (e.g., the way Apple Computer created a market for their computers in the educational arena). Finally, make sure to differentiate your product or service from that of other similar competitors by adding on value such as better quality, service, or special features.

The next five prescriptions are value-adding strategies. The first urges managers to "Provide Top Quality, as Perceived by the Customer." Managers must understand the great necessity for quality improvements, while keeping in mind that all the changes in the world are not going to be effective if the customer does not *perceive* any changes in the quality level. While it is important to stress quality, it is equally important to find out what the customer would consider high quality for that particular good or service and then build it into the product.

Next, "Provide Superior Service/Emphasize the Intangibles." Treat every customer as if he or she were your most important one. Follow through on commitments and don't overpromise things that you cannot deliver. The next strategy is to "Achieve Extraordinary Responsiveness." This strategy, for example, highlights the need to have an electronic system connecting the organization with its customer, suppliers, and distributors so as to be fast and efficient in responding to customer needs. Electronic systems should enable an organization to process information immediately and therefore respond to a customer need quickly. Being responsive eliminates taking an hour to search for an inventory item. In addition, suppliers and distributors and other agents in the distribution channel should be viewed as partners, not enemies, all working to serve the customers' needs.

The fourth value-adding strategy is to "Be an Internationalist." Organizations should look to other cultures for success principles that may be cross-cultural in nature, as well as see other countries as possible places in which to manufacture or market their good or service. The fifth value-adding strategy is to "Create Uniqueness." In this highly competitive world it is important for an organization to be seen as different (and better) than its competitors.

In order to execute the five value-adding strategies, Peters discusses three capability building blocks. The first of these is "Becoming Obsessed with Listening." Find out as much as you can from your customers, and don't just hear what you would like to hear; instead, call on—talk to—and listen to your disgruntled customers. Next, act quickly on what you hear and provide feedback to let individuals know that their concerns have been addressed.

The second building block is to "Turn Manufacturing into a Marketing Weapon." Manufacturing is the nerve center of the product and includes the source of quality, innovation, and response time. Have the different functions (e.g., marketing and manufacturing) interact with one another and gain a mutual appreciation. Allow manufacturing to have a say in the decision-making processes of the organization.

As a third building block, "Make Sales and Service Forces into Heroes." If necessary, "overinvest" in these key organizational people in areas like the salaries paid, the amount of training given, the support and time given, and listening time spent. Sales and service forces are the front line in terms of customer interactions. They are vitally important in the organizational image that they portray to potential customers. Furthermore, they are the primary source of information about the needs, preferences, and concerns of the customers.

"Launch a Customer Revolution" suggests that organizations must become customer-obsessed. Create new customers while at the same time keeping current customers happy. Every lost customer is a loss in revenue. Treating customers well will not only help you to keep them, but may also help you take customers away from those competitors who are not customer-obsessed.

PURSUING FAST-PACED INNOVATION

Section Two emphasizes *Innovation,* with a guiding premise to "Invest in Applications-Oriented Small Stars." In this changing and chaotic environment it is nearly impossible to develop "big" innovations effectively, since things change too quickly for a big project ever to get off the ground. Instead, focus on numerous small projects focused on small markets. Maintain a customer focus rather than overdoing a technological focus. Innovation does not have to consist of the development of completely new products and services; instead, innovation can be seen in terms of a continuous updating of current offerings.

The guiding premise of innovation is accompanied by four key strategies to encourage implementation as well as four specific management tactics to encourage innovation. First, "Pursue Team Products/Service Development." This entails using multi-function teams as well as "outsiders" such as customers, suppliers, and distributors in all developmental activities. The second strategy is to "Encourage Pilots of Everything." Instead of talking and writing about potential new projects, actually do a pilot study or develop a prototype. The time it takes to bring an innovation from the idea stage to the implementation stage can be greatly decreased through the use of pilot testing.

The third strategy is to "Practice 'Creative Swiping.'" Learn from the successes and failures of other organizations. Avoid the negative mindset of "not invented here" and utilize the work of others. Add an enhancement to an existing product or service; this is a much faster innovation process than designing an entire system from scratch.

Fourth, "Make Word-of-Mouth Marketing Systematic." Much of the information about new products or services is spread by word of mouth. Attempt to reach the respected and innovative potential users, since these individuals will do a great deal to influence others and therefore should not be ignored in your marketing strategy.

The fourth management tactic to encourage innovation entreats us to "Support Committed Champions." Most new innovations do not succeed, and failure can discourage the search for new innovations. For this reason, it is important to support those in the organization who persistently work on new innovations. People who continue to stand up and be committed to projects even in the face of likely failure have the commitment necessary to bring forth the occasional successful innovation. The second management tactic goes even further by suggesting that not only should innovators be supported, but that managers should "Model Innovation/Practice Purposeful Impatience." Managers must give more than lip service to the importance of innovation; they must practice it in every way, every day. Reward innovations both big and small and allow the time and resources necessary to come up with successful innovations. Closely related, the third tactic is to "Support Fast Failures." While encouraging commitment to innovations, support getting out of projects at the lowest possible cost of failure. Encourage stories about failure, and stress that innovations only come through repeated trial and error. In this way, people in the organization will be encouraged to try new innovations, while feeling free to abandon a new project when signals suggests that it might not be successful as currently developing.

The final management tactic is to "Set Quantitative Innovation Goals." Actually measure your organization's rate of innovation. While it is very difficult to define and quantify innovation, the aim is to foster quicker and increased action in the area of innovation. Only through measurement will people come to understand the importance that the organization places on innovation, as well as being able to see how the organization is progressing on this dimension across time.

The final prescription for innovation is to "Create a Corporate Capacity for Innovation." Everyone in the organization must be involved constantly in innovating, from the R & D people to the finance whiz kids to the middle-line managers. Learning to innovate is difficult and requires a long-term commitment on the part of the organization.

ACHIEVING FLEXIBILITY BY EMPOWERING PEOPLE

The theme in Section Three is *People,* and two guiding premises characterize it. They are "Involve Everybody in Everything" and "Use Self-Managing Teams." In order to execute the prescriptions presented in Sections One and

Two, it is necessary to have the full support and involvement of everyone in the organization. Peters says companies should be guided by the axiom: "There are no limits to the ability to contribute on the part of a properly selected, well-trained, appropriately supported, and, above all, committed person." Create an organizational climate that encourages involvement and innovation by people throughout the company. To get to that level of involvement, Peters suggests a team focus with the self-managing team as the building block of the organization. The development of self-managing teams will lead to the elimination of first-line supervisors who will be replaced with group spanners. These are individuals who work with several groups as facilitators and as information resource people.

The next five prescriptions are intended to encourage high levels of involvement. First, "Listen/Celebrate/Recognize." That is, listen continuously (as previously mentioned) and help to emphasize the sharing of experiences, information, successes, and failures. Celebrate "wins," both big and small. Second, "Spend Time Lavishly on Recruiting." Hire not only technically sharp individuals, but also those who will fit in with the team—individuals who buy into the company's interest in *heavy* involvement and innovation. Managers who will be working with the new hires should actively participate in the recruitment and selection process.

The third aid is to "Train and Retain." The organization's labor pool is very important and should be treated as such. The firm should spend time keeping these people trained so they can work to the best of their ability. In addition to skill training, the organization should actively work in the socialization of people so that they share the organization's values and vision.

Through training, employees may come to realize why innovation is so important and how they might be able to innovate in their own positions. Once employees have been trained to be their best, they should be compensated accordingly. "Provide Incentive Pay for Everyone" by basing pay on important organizational outcomes such as productivity, profits, and quality innovations. When adopting an incentive pay system it is important to give employees the ability to influence the outcome through their involvement. Finally, Peters recommends that management "Provide an Employment Guarantee." Within a range of acceptable performance, employees should feel secure that they have some promise of continuous employment. In a constantly changing environment this is possible only with the use of careful planning and flexibility on the part of all persons in an organization.

In addition to these five supporting prescriptions there are three prescriptions concerning potential inhibitors that must be removed from the work environment in order to ensure the successful achievement of the guiding premises. First, "Simplify/Reduce Structure," since an excessively complex organizational structure only encourages slow response time to changing conditions. Set up an organization structure that is very "wide" with a few layers of management as possible. This paring process can be very difficult for an established firm, but it is vital in order for the firm to be able to survive and thrive in a chaotic environment. Along with this prescription, it will also be necessary to "Reconceive the Middle Manager's Role." The middle manager should become more of a facilitator between groups, the boundary spanner between self-managing teams. Finally, organizations must "Eliminate Bureaucratic Rules and Humiliating Conditions." Reduce the amount of paperwork that needs to be completed—this time can better be spent innovating. Further, don't have special perks and bonuses that are reserved only for a special core of individuals in the organization (typically top management). Company cars, special reserved parking spots, executive dining rooms, big bonuses only serve to create an "us-them" mentality that prevents effective group and organization functioning.

The fourth section concentrates on the prescription associated with *Leadership*. The guiding premise of this section is the "Master Paradox." (A paradox is something that might seem false, but is in fact true.) The Master Paradox is that in order to deal effectively with a chaotic atmosphere, organizations must attempt to create internal stability. The overall vision or mission of the organization must be stable and clear so that all organization members may work toward conquering the changing environment with the same end goals in mind. There are three leadership tools for establishing direction, the first of which is to "Develop an Inspiring Vision." Articulate and live a clear specific vision that leaves enough room for others to innovate. Consistently update your vision to fit with the times, since innovations shape the company direction (and company direction shapes innovations). A related prescription is to "Manage by Example." The actions of the leader will color those of his or her subordinates. Make sure that employees can not only "do as you say" but also "do as you do." Promote those individuals who are successfully following the vision as intended. Finally, the third tool is to "Practice Visible Management," similar to Peters' earlier call to "Manage by Walking Around." It is vital to get out into the work force and find out what people are saying (by listening) and show that you are personally interested and involved.

Four prescriptions will help managers lead by empowering people. For example, the simple admonition "Pay Attention!" stresses that it is imperative to listen. This is true of everyone, particularly leaders. Also, "Defer to the Front Line." Give the doers (the organizational heroes) the opportunity to do what is necessary to be successful. Staff personnel should be recognized to the extent that they support the line personnel. Within this same realm, "Delegate." Organizations cannot be run successfully by one person. They need the combined efforts of many to respond to change as quickly as they need to respond. Finally, "Pursue 'Horizontal' Management by Bashing Bureaucracy." Avoid bureaucratic tendencies, including the desire to check up on subordinates continually. If individuals are to be committed and involved in self-managing teams they must believe that they are trusted to act appropriately.

The final two prescriptions in this section argue that leaders must love change. To this end, they must also "Evaluate Everyone on His or Her Love of Change." Effective change will be achieved when everyone in the organization sees the need for change and participates in the incremental change process every day. It is important to focus on change (what were the total number of innovations piloted last month), not just results. The last prescription in this section is to "Create a Sense of Urgency." Keep people moving, on the go, and looking out for new opportunities. Hustle is important, because those that stay still will be passed by the competition. People must keep active, keep innovating, and neither wait nor slow down out of a fear of failure.

BUILDING SYSTEMS FOR A WORLD TURNED UPSIDE DOWN

The last section of prescriptions looks at *Systems*. Here the guiding premise is to "Measure What's Important." Develop simpler measuring systems that will allow greater participation and better information. Measure those things that are important, such as quality, customer satisfaction, and time needed to launch a new product. "Revamp the Chief Control Tools"—specifically, performance appraisal, objective setting, and job descriptions. Flexibility is much more important than rigid control systems, and therefore the control system itself, like everything else, should be in a state of constant evolution.

In order to be involved and successful, everyone must have access to information and be in on the planning. Therefore, organizations must "Decentralize Information, Authority, and Strategic Planning." Information is a great motivator and helps to build people's commitment to a project and to a company. Getting people involved in the planning stages builds a sense of responsibility and ownership for results.

The final two prescriptions help establish trust through systems. This is done through "Set(ting) Conservative Goals" and the "Demand (for) Total Integrity." Simply put, it is best to set conservative and achievable financial goals in a volatile market filled with much uncertainty. This does not mean to set easy goals; rather, set goals that can be achieved without overpromising and underdelivering. Finally, the organization should demand total integrity from everyone associated with it. An organization that can be counted on to be honest and upright is more likely to survive and even thrive in a changing and chaotic environment.

In summary, Tom Peters outlines a current business climate where organizations must be prepared to thrive on chaos. He outlines forty-five prescriptions that must be followed in order to ensure survival in this ever-changing climate. He makes it clear that it is important to look at these prescriptions as a total package. That is, it is not enough to implement five or six of the prescriptions, but rather all forty-five must be worked toward as quickly as possible. Given the impossibility of implementing everything simultaneously, he recommends beginning with the prescriptions pertaining to customers and innovation, since the rest follow these.

ELEVEN

Organizational Decline and Renewal

In the Greek fable, Icarus flew so high and close to the sun that his waxed wings melted and he plummeted into the sea. Danny Miller, Professor of Business Administration at H. E. C., Montreal, and Visiting Professor at McGill University and the University of Alberta, is the author of *The Icarus Paradox.* In this book Miller discusses how it is that "exceptional" companies often bring about their own downfall. Much in the same fashion as Icarus, who employed his greatest asset—the ability to soar high above the earth—a myriad of organizations allow their strengths to blind them, thereby contributing to their own downfall. From studying hundreds of organizations, Miller identifies and discusses four factors that appear to be associated with the rise and fall of major corporations.

Marshall W. Meyer and Lynne G. Zucker provide an interesting perspective on organizations that find themselves surviving over long periods of time even though their performance is consistently low. Through illustrations of four organizations—Los Angeles Herald Examiner, Rath Meat Packing, Cathedral High School, and the U. S. steel industry—the authors highlight, through their discussion of organizational pluralism, the dynamics that contribute to the *Permanently Failing Organizations.* In addition to providing a discussion of the key factors that lead to persistent failure, Meyer and

Zucker provide insight into how organizations might avoid permanent failure.

Richard Pascale, in *Managing on the Edge*, explores the successes and failures of a diverse set of organizations that sought to turn themselves around. Pascale notes that in highly competitive markets, simply trying harder to do things right (e.g., fine tuning existing efforts, applying someone else's tried-and-true management strategies) is often not enough; instead, organizations need a more dramatic and fundamental type of change. There is often a need for creating and breaking existing management paradigms.

Michael Beer, Russell A. Eisenstat, and Bert Spector (Professor of Business Administration and Assistant Professor of Business Administration at the Harvard Business School, and Associate Professor of Human Resources at Northeastern University, respectively) have focused their recent energies on management of corporate revitalization. In *The Critical Path to Corporate Renewal*, Beer and his colleagues present a comprehensive theory of corporate revitalization. Based upon a study of six large corporations, a set of principles of change management is presented.

The Icarus Paradox

Danny Miller

The fabled Icarus of Greek Mythology is said to have flown so high, so close to the sun, that his artificial wax wings melted and he plunged to his death in the Aegean Sea. The power of Icarus' wings gave rise to the abandon that so doomed him. The paradox, of course, is that his greatest asset led to his demise. And that same paradox applies to many outstanding companies today: their victories and their strengths often seduce them into the excesses that cause their downfall. Success leads to specialization and exaggeration, to confidence and complacency, to dogma and ritual. This general tendency, its causes, and how to control it, are what this book is all about.

It is ironic that many of the most dramatically successful organizations are so prone to failure. The histories of outstanding companies demonstrate this time and time again. In fact, it appears that when taken to excess the very factors that drive success—focused tried-and-true strategies, confident leadership, galvanized corporate cultures, and especially the interplay among all these things—can also cause decline. Robust, superior organizations evolve into flawed purebreds; they move from rich character to exaggerated caricature as all subtlety, all nuance, is gradually lost. That, in a nutshell, is the book's thesis.

Many outstanding organizations have followed such paths of deadly momentum—time-bomb trajectories of attitudes, policies, and events that lead to falling sales, plummeting profits, even bankruptcy. These companies extend and amplify the strategies to which they credit their success. Productive attention to detail, for instance, turns into an obsession with minutia; rewarding innovation escalates into gratuitous invention; and measured growth becomes unbridled expansion. In contrast, activities that were merely deemphasized—that were not viewed as integral to the recipe for success—are virtually extinguished. Modest marketing deteriorates into lackluster promotion and inadequate distribution; tolerable engineering becomes shoddy design. The result: strategies become less balanced. They center more and more upon a single, core strength that is amplified unduly, while other aspects are forgotten almost entirely.

Such changes are not limited to strategy The heroes who shaped the winning formula of a company gain adulation and absolute authority, while others drop to third-class citizenship. An increasingly monolithic culture impels firms to focus on an ever smaller set of considerations and to rally around a narrowing path to victory. Roles, programs, decision-making processes—even target markets—come to reflect the central strategy and nothing else. And avidly embraced ideologies convert company policies into rigid laws and rituals. By then, organizational learning has ceased, tunnel vision rules, and flexibility is lost.

This riches-to-rags scenario seduces some of our most acclaimed corporations: our research on over one hundred such outstanding companies has turned up four variations on the theme, four very common "trajectories" of decline (see Table 1).[1]

- The *focusing* trajectory takes punctilious, quality-driven *Craftsmen*, organizations with masterful engineers and airtight operations, and turns them into rigidly controlled, detail-obsessed *Tinkerers,* firms

Table 1   THE FOUR TRAJECTORIES

	Focusing	
	Craftsman ————————▶	*Tinkerer*
Strategy	Quality leadership	Technical tinkering
Goals	Quality	Perfection
Culture	Engineering	Technocratic
Structure	Orderly	Rigid
	Venturing	
	Builder ————————▶	*Imperialist*
Strategy	Building	Overexpansion
Goals	Growth	Grandeur
Culture	Entrepreneurial	Gamesman
Structure	Divisionalized	Fractured
	Inventing	
	Pioneer ————————▶	*Escapist*
Strategy	Innovation	High-tech escapism
Goals	Science-for-society	Technical utopia
Culture	R&D	Think-tank
Structure	Organic	Chaotic
	Decoupling	
	Salesman ————————▶	*Drifter*
Strategy	Brilliant marketing	Bland proliferation
Goals	Market share	Quarterly numbers
Culture	Organization man	Insipid and political
Structure	Decentralized-bureaucratic	Oppressively bureaucratic

whose insular, technocratic cultures alienate customers with perfect but irrelevant offerings.

- The *venturing* trajectory converts growth-driven, entrepreneurial *Builders,* companies managed by imaginative leaders and creative planning and financial staffs, into impulsive, greedy *Imperialists,* who severely overtax their resources by expanding helter-skelter into businesses they know nothing about.
- The *inventing* trajectory takes *Pioneers* with unexcelled R&D departments, flexible think-tank operations, and state-of-the-art products, and transforms them into utopian *Escapists,* run by cults of chaos-loving scientists who squander resources in the pursuit of hopelessly grandiose and futuristic inventions.
- Finally, the *decoupling* trajectory transforms *Salesmen,* organizations with unparalleled marketing skills, prominent brand names, and broad markets, into aimless, bureaucratic *Drifters,* whose sales fetish obscures design issues, and who produce a stale and disjointed line of "me-too" offerings.

These four trajectories have trapped many firms. The names include IBM, Polaroid, Proctor & Gamble, Texas Instruments, ITT, Chrysler, Dome Petroleum, Apple Computer, A&P, General Motors, Sears, Digital Equipment, Caterpillar Tractor, Montgomery Ward, Eastern Air Lines, Litton Industries, and Walt Disney Productions.

A CASE HISTORY

The glorious and ultimately tragic history of ITT well demonstrates the course of the second, so-called venturing trajectory.

Harold S. Geneen was a manager's manager, a universally acclaimed financial wizard of unsurpassed energy, and the CEO and grand inquisitor of the diversified megaconglomerate ITT. It was Geneen, the entrepreneurial accountant, who took a ragtag set of stale, mostly European telecommunications operations and forged them into a cohesive corporate entity. With his accountant's scalpel, he cut out weak operations, and with his entrepreneur's wand, he revived the most promising ones. He installed state-of-the-art management information systems to monitor the burgeoning businesses. And he built a head-office corps of young turks to help him control his growing empire and identify opportunities for creative diversification.[2]

At first, this diversification paid off handsomely, as it so aptly exploited the financial, organizational, and turnaround talents of Geneen and his crack staff. Many acquisitions were purchased at bargain prices and most beautifully complemented ITT's existing operations. Also, a divisional structure in which managers were responsible for their units' profits provided a good deal of incentive for local initiative. And Geneen's legendary control and information systems—

with frequent appraisal meetings and divisional accountants reporting directly to the head office—ensured that most problems could be detected early and corrected.

Unfortunately, ITT's success at diversification and controlled decentralization led to too much more of the same. Their skills at acquisition and control made Geneen and his staff ever more confident that they could master complexity. So, diversification went from a selective tactic to an engrained strategy to a fanatical religion; decentralization and head-office control were transformed from managerial tools into an all-consuming, lockstep way of life. The corporate culture worshiped growth, and it celebrated, lavishly paid, and quickly promoted only those who could attain it. The venturing trajectory had gotten under way, and the momentum behind it was awesome.

In order to achieve rapid growth, Geneen went after ever more ambitious acquisitions that were further afield from his existing operations. From 1967 to 1970, just six of ITT's larger acquisitions—Sheraton, Levitt, Rayonier, Continental Baking, Grinnell, and Canteen—brought in combined sales of $1.8 billion; and a seventh, Hartford Fire, one of the largest property and casualty insurers in the United States, was about to be added. Loads of debt had to be issued to fund these acquisitions. In less than ten years Geneen the imperialist bought a staggering one hundred companies, a proliferation so vast that it exceeded the complexity of many nation-states; 250 profit centers in all were set up. Geneen, quite simply, had created the biggest conglomerate on earth, encompassing, by 1977, 375,000 employees in eighty countries.

Even Geneen and his sophisticated staff troops, for all their mastery of detail and their status as information-system gurus, could not manage, control, or even understand so vast an empire. But they tried, meddling in the details of their divisions, and pressing home the need to meet abstract, often irrelevant, financial standards. Political games took place in which head-office controllers would try to impress Geneen by making the divisions look bad; and divisional executives would, in turn, try to fool the controllers.

This obsession with acquisitions and financial control detracted from the substance of divisional strategy. The product lines of many units were neglected and became outmoded. Return on capital fell, and by the late 1970s many of the divisions were experiencing major operating problems. A subsequent CEO, Rand Araskog, had to sell off over a hundred units in an attempt to revive the company, in the process shrinking the work force by over sixty percent. The great ITT had become a flabby agglomeration of gangrenous parts.

The general pattern is clear. Over time, ITT's success—or, more specifically, its managers' reactions to that success—caused it to amplify its winning strategy, and to forget about everything else. It moved from sensible, measured expansion to prolific, groundless diversification; from sound accounting and financial control to oppressive dominance by head-office hit men; and from an invigorating use of divisionalization to a destructive factionalism. The substance of basic businesses—their product lines and markets—was lost in a welter of financial abstractions. By concentrating exclusively upon what it did best, ITT pushed its strategies, cultures, and structures to dangerous extremes, while failing to develop in other areas. Greatness had paved the way for excess and decline as ITT the Builder became ITT the Imperialist.

CONFIGURATION AND MOMENTUM

The example of ITT reveals two notions that surfaced again and again when we looked at outstanding companies: we call these configuration and momentum.

Outstanding organizations are a little like beautiful poems or sonatas—their parts or elements fit together harmoniously to express a theme. They are perhaps even more akin to living systems whose organs are intimately linked and tightly coordinated. Although organizations are less unified than organisms, they too constitute *configurations:* complex, evolving systems of mutually supportive elements organized around stable central themes. We found that once a theme emerges—a core mission or a central strategy, for example—a whole slew of routines, policies, tasks, and structures develops to implement and reinforce it. It is like seeding a crystal in a supersaturated solution—once a thematic particle is dropped into solution, the crystal begins to form naturally around it. Themes may drive from leaders' visions, the values and concerns of powerful departments, even from common industry practices.

ITT's configuration, like all others, had a central theme and a "cast of players" (human, ideological, strategic, and structural) that completed the scenario. The theme was "rapid growth through expansion"; the cast included an entrepreneurial, ambitious CEO with his strategy of diversification and acquisi-

Table 2. THE CONFIGURATIONS COMPARED

	CRAFTSMAN	BUILDER	PIONEER	SALESMAN
Strategies:	Quality Leadership	Expansion Diversification Acquisition	Differentiation via Innovation	Marketing Differentiation
Product-market scope:	Focused	Broad	Focused	Broad
Strategic change:	Stable	Dynamic	Dynamic	Stable
Key Goals:	Quality	Growth	Technical Progress	Market Share
Dominant Depts.:	Operations, Production, & Engineering	Planning & Control; Finance	R&D	Marketing
Structure:	Bureaucracy Many Controls	Divisional Profit Centers	Organic Flexible	Divisional Bureaucracy
Trajectory:	*FOCUSING*	*VENTURING*	*INVENTING*	*DECOUPLING*
Destination:	TINKERER	IMPERIALIST	ESCAPIST	DRIFTER

tion, a powerful financial staff who dominated because they could best implement this strategy, elaborate information systems and sophisticated controls, even decentralized profit centers that infused expertise into the far-flung divisions amassed by diversification. All these "players" complemented one another and were essential to the enactment of the play. And as with every configuration, the parts only make sense with reference to the entire constellation.[3]

Our research uncovered four exceptionally common but quite different configurations associated with stellar performance. We termed these Builders, Craftsmen, Pioneers, and Salesmen, and found that each was subject to its own evolutionary trajectory.

Our second finding was that organizations keep extending their themes and configurations until something earthshaking stops them, a process we call *momentum.* Firms perpetuate and amplify one particular motif above all others as they suppress its variants. They choose one set of goals, values, and champions, and focus on these more and more tightly. The powerful get more powerful; others become disenfranchised as firms move first toward consistency, then toward obsession and excess. Organizations turn into their "evil twins"—extreme versions or caricatures of their former selves.

Once ITT began to diversify, for example, it accelerated this policy because it seemed successful, because it was very much in line with the visions of what leaders and their powerful financial staffs wanted, and because it was undergirded by a vast set of policies and programs. Similarly, having implemented its financial control systems, ITT continued to hone and develop them. After all, these systems were demanded by the expanding scope of the firm; they were favored by the growing staff of accountants; and they were the only way top managers could exert control over existing operations and still have time to scout out new acquisitions.

But momentum itself is contagious and leads to a vicious cycle of escalation. At ITT, as diversification increased, so, in order to cope, did the size of the head-office staff and the time spent on divisional meetings. The staff's role was to generate still more attractive candidates for diversification, and that's what they did. Diversification increased still further, requiring even larger legions of accountants and financial staff. And so the spiral continued. In short, momentum, by extending the Builder configuration, led to the dangerous excesses of imperialism.

Such findings led us to expect that *outstanding firms will extend their orientations until they reach dangerous extremes; their momentum will result in common trajectories of decline.* And since successful types differ so much from one another, so will their trajectories.

THE TRAJECTORIES

The four trajectories emerged in a study we conducted of outstanding companies. Our earlier research suggested four very common, wonderfully coherent configurations, with powerful strategic advantages. To study the long-term evolution of these types for this project, we searched for successful companies that conformed to each type and had enough written about them to be analyzed in detail. We then tracked the companies for many years to discover what in fact happened to them. (The types are described and compared in Tables 1 and 2.)

Many of the organizations will be well known to the reader. This was inevitable since we studied legendary performers that had been the subject of numerous articles and books. Also, many of our examples go back some years as we had to observe some rather protracted declines and revivals. Despite the familiarity of some of their subjects, however, our narratives have a rather unusual twist. Instead of looking at how marvelous the good performers were, we will persistently be eliciting the seeds of decline from the flowers—and the fruits—of greatness.

Craftsmen, Builders, Pioneers, and Salesmen were each susceptible to their own unique trajectories. And firms of a given type followed remarkably parallel paths, albeit at differing speeds. For purposes of simple comparison, the four strategies are classified, in Figure 1, along two dimensions: *scope* refers to the range of products and target markets; *change* to the variability of methods and offerings. Excellent businesses are driven toward extremes along both of these dimensions (among others). Take scope. Firms that excel by focusing on one product or on a precisely targeted market come ultimately to rely on too narrow a set of customers, products, and issues. Conversely, firms that thrive by aggressively diversifying often become too complex, fragmented, and thinly spread to be effective. The same tendencies apply to strategic change as dynamic firms become hyperactive while conservative ones inch toward stagnation.

The characteristics of each of our four trajectories are summarized below.

From Craftsmen to Tinkerers: The Focusing Trajectory

Digital Equipment Corporation made the highest quality computers in the world. Founder Ken Olsen and his brilliant team of design engineers invented the minicomputer, a cheaper, more flexible alternative to its mainframe cousins. Olsen and his staff honed their minds until they absolutely could not be beat for quality and durability. Their VAX series gave birth to an industry legend in reliability, and the profits poured in.

But Digital turned into an engineering monoculture. Its engineers became idols; its marketers and accountants were barely tolerated. Component specs and design standards were all that managers understood. In fact, technological fine-tuning became such an all-consuming obsession that customers' needs for smaller machines, more economical products, and more user-friendly systems were ignored. The Digital personal computer, for example, bombed because it was so out of sync with the budgets, preferences, and shopping habits of potential users. Performance began to slip.

Craftsmen are passionate about doing one thing incredibly well. Their leaders insist on producing the best products on the market, their engineers lose sleep over micrometers, and their quality-control staff rule with an iron,

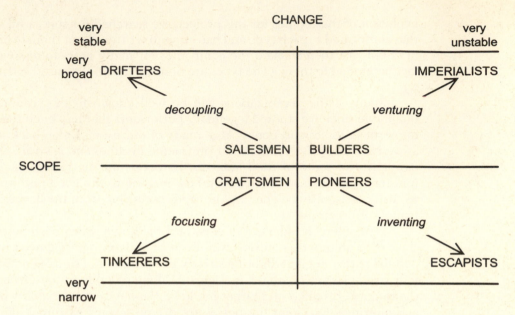

Figure 1 The Configurations and Trajectories Arrayed

unforgiving hand. Details count. And quality is the primary source of corporate pride; it gets rewarded, and is the paramount competitive advantage. Indeed, it is what the whole corporate culture is about. Shoddiness is a capital offense.

But in becoming Tinkerers, many Craftsmen become parodies of themselves. They get so wrapped up in tiny technical details that they forget that the purpose of quality is to attract and satisfy buyers. Products become overengineered but also overpriced; durable but stale. Yesterday's excellent designs turn into today's sacrosanct anachronisms. And an ascendant engineering culture so engrosses itself in the minutia of design and manufacture that it loses sight of the customer. Before long, marketing and R&D become the dull stepchildren, departments to be seen but not heard. And unfortunately, the bureaucratic strictures that grew up to enforce quality end up suppressing initiative and perpetuating the past.

From Builders to Imperialists: The Venturing Trajectory

Charles "Tex" Thornton was a young Texas entrepreneur when he expanded a tiny microwave company into Litton Industries, one of the most successful high-technology conglomerates of the 1960s. By making selective, related acquisitions, Litton achieved an explosive rate of growth. And its excellent track record helped the company to amass the resources needed to accelerate expansion still further. Sales mushroomed from $3 million to $1.8 billion in just twelve years.

But Litton began to stray too far from familiar areas, buying larger and more troubled firms in industries that it barely understood. Control systems were overtaxed, the burden of debt became unwieldy, and a wide range of problems sprang up in the proliferating divisions. The downward spiral at Litton was no less dramatic than its ascent.

Builders are growth-driven entrepreneurial companies, with a zeal for expansion, merger, and acquisition. They are dominated by aggressive managers with ambitious goals, immense energy, and an uncanny knack for spotting lucrative niches of the market. These leaders have the promotional skills to raise capital, the imagination and initiative to exploit magnificent growth opportunities, and the courage to take substantial risks. They are also master controllers who craft acute, sensitive information and incentive systems to rein in their burgeoning operations.

But many Builders develop into Imperialists, addicted to careless expansion and greedy acquisition. In the headlong rush for growth, they assume hair-raising risks, decimate their resources, and incur scads of debt. They bite off more than they can swallow, acquiring sick companies in businesses they don't understand. Structures and control systems become hopelessly overburdened. And a dominant culture of financial, legal, and accounting specialists further rivets managerial attention on expansion and diversification, while stealing time away from the production, marketing, and R&D matters that so desperately need to be addressed.

From Pioneers to Escapists: The Inventing Trajectory

By the mid-1960s, Control Data Corporation of Minneapolis had become the paramount designer of supercomputers. Chief engineer Seymour Cray, the preeminent genius in a field of masters, had several times fulfilled his ambition to build the world's most powerful computer. He secluded himself in his lab in Chippewa Falls, working closely with a small and trusted band of brilliant designers. Cray's state-of-the-art 6600 supercomputer was so advanced that it caused wholesale firing at IBM, whose engineers had been caught completely off guard by their diminutive competitor.

CDC's early successes emboldened it to undertake new computer development projects that were increasingly futuristic, complex, and expensive. These entailed substantial lead times, major investments, and high risks. Indeed, many bugs had to be purged from the systems, long delays in delivery occurred, and costs mushroomed. Science and invention had triumphed over a proper understanding of the competition, the customers, and production and capital requirements.

Pioneers are R&D stars. Their chief goal is to be the first out with new products and new technology. Consistently at the vanguard of their industry, Pioneers are, above all, inventors. Their major strengths lie in the scientific and technological capacities of their brilliant R&D departments. Typically, Pioneers are run by missionary leaders-in-lab-coats; PhDs with a desire to change the world. These executives assemble and empower superb research and design teams, and create for them a fertile, flexible structure that promotes intensive collaboration and the free play of ideas.

Unfortunately, many Pioneers get carried away by their coups of invention and turn into Escapists—firms in hot pursuit of a technological nirvana.

They introduce impractical, futuristic products that are too far ahead of their time, too expensive to develop, and too costly to buy. They also become their own toughest competitors, antiquating prematurely many of their offerings. What is worse, marketing and production come to be viewed as necessary evils; clients as unsophisticated nuisances. Escapists, it seems, become the victims of a utopian culture forged by their domineering R&D wunderkinder. Their goals, which soar to hopelessly lofty heights, are expressed in technological rather than in market or economic terms. And their loose, "organic" structures might suffice to organize a few engineers working in a basement, but make for chaos in complex organizations.

From Salesmen to Drifters: The Decoupling Trajectory

Lynn Townsend ascended to the presidency of Chrysler at the youthful age of forty-two. He was known to be a financial wizard and a master marketer. "Sales just aren't made; sales are pushed," Townsend would say. In his first five years as president, he doubled Chrysler's U.S. market share and tripled its international one. He also conceived the five-year, 50,000-mile warranty. But Townsend made very few radical changes in Chrysler's products. Mostly he just marketed aggressively with forceful selling and promotion, and sporty styling.

Chrysler's success with its image-over-substance strategy resulted in an increasing neglect of engineering and production. Also it prompted a proliferation of new models that could capitalize on the marketing program. But this made operations very complex and uneconomical. It also contributed to remote management-by-numbers, bureaucracy, and turf battles. Soon Chrysler's strategies lost focus and direction and its profits began to plummet.

Salesmen are marketers par excellence. That is their core strength. Using intensive advertising, attractive styling and packaging, and penetrating distribution channels, they create and nurture high-profile brand names that make them major players in their industries. And to place managers in especially close contact with their broad markets, Salesmen often are partitioned into manageable profit centers, each responsible for a major product line.

Unfortunately, Salesmen too are subject to a dangerous momentum that can transform them into unresponsive Drifters. They begin to substitute packaging, advertising, and aggressive distribution for good design and competent manufacture. Managers come to believe that they can sell anything as they concoct a mushrooming proliferation of bland, "me-too" offerings. This growing diversity of product lines and divisions makes it tough for top managers to master the substance of all their businesses. So they rely increasingly on abstract financial controls and an elaborate bureaucracy to replace the hands-on management of products and manufacturing. Gradually Drifters become unwieldy, sluggish behemoths whose turf battles and factionalism impede adaptation. In scenarios that come straight from Kafka, the simplest problems take months, even years to address. Ultimately, the leader is decoupled from his company, the company from its markets, and the product lines and divisions from each other.

These four trajectories show how outstanding companies—firms with character and a terrific strategic edge—can become specialized and even monomaniacal. Strengths are amplified to the point where one goal, one strategic vision, one department, and one skill overwhelms all others. All subtlety is lost. Design-whiz Craftsmen become hyper-focused Tinkerers, entrepreneurial Builders turn into impulsive Imperialists, inventive Pioneers become utopian Escapists, and responsive Salesmen become fragmented Drifters. Nuances vanish; only the bold, exaggerated features, the core obsessions, remain.

FORCES TO WATCH FOR

In reading about these four trajectories, you might want to keep in mind some of the "subtexts"—the hidden causes at work behind the scenes that drive every one of them.

Sources of Momentum

Leadership Traps Failure teaches leaders valuable lessons, but good results only reinforce their preconceptions and tether them more firmly to their "tried-and-true" recipes. Success also makes managers overconfident, more prone to excess and neglect, and more given to shaping strategies to reflect their own preferences rather than those of their customers. Some leaders may even be spoiled by success—taking too much to heart their litany of conquests and the praise of their idolizing subordinates. They become conceited and obstinate, resenting challenges and, ultimately, isolating themselves from reality.

Monolithic Cultures and Skills The culture of the exceptional organization often becomes dominated by a few star departments and their ideologies. For example, because Craftsmen see quality as the source of success, the engineering departments that create it and are its guarantors acquire ever more influence—as do their goals and values. This erodes the status of other departments and concerns, rendering the corporate culture more monolithic, more intolerant, and more avid in its pursuit of a single goal.

To make matters worse, attractive rewards pull talented managers toward rich, dominant departments, and bleed them away from less august units. The organization's skill set soon becomes more spotty and unbalanced, compromising versatility and the capacity for reorientation.

Power and Politics Dominant managers and departments resist redirecting the strategies and policies that have given them so much power. Change, they reason, would erode their status, their resources, and their influence over rival executives and departments. The powerful, then, are more likely to reinforce and amplify prevailing strategies than to change them.

Structural Memories   Organizations, like people, have memories—they implement successful strategies by using systems, routines, and programs. The more established and successful the strategy, the more deeply embedded it will be in such programs, and the more it will be implemented routinely, automatically, and unquestioningly. Managers will rely on ingrained habits and reflex actions rather than deliberating and reflecting on new problems. Indeed, even the premises for decision making—the cues that elicit attention and the standards used to evaluate events and actions—will be controlled by routines. Yesterday's programs will shape today's perceptions and give rise to tomorrow's actions. Again, continuity triumphs.

Configuration and Momentum

The elements of leadership, culture, power, and structural memory are by no means independent. Indeed, they interact and configure to play out a central theme. Over time, organizations become more and more consistent with that theme. So much so that an adaptable, intelligent company can turn into a specialized, monolithic machine.

Take the Pioneer. Successful innovations reward and empower their creators, who will tend to recruit and promote in their own image. The resulting horde of "R&D types" then set up the flexible structures and design projects they find so invigorating. This further encourages innovation and the search for clients who value it. Meanwhile, other departments begin to lose influence and resources, and their skills diminish. So, cultures become monolithic, strategies more narrowly focused, skills more uneven and specialized, and blind spots more common. The firm has embarked on the inventing trajectory.

"Chain reactions" such as this make an organization more focused and cohesive. At first, the firm benefits greatly. But ultimately, concentration turns into obsession. All the prominent features become exaggerated, while everything else—auxiliary skills, supplementary values, essential substrategies, and constructive debate—vanishes.

The Paradox of Icarus

And this brings us to the Icarus paradox that traps so many outstanding firms: over confident, complacent executives extend the very factors that contributed to success to the point where they cause decline. There are really two aspects to the paradox. The first is that *success can lead to failure.* By engendering overconfidence, carelessness, and other bad habits, success can produce excesses in strategies, leadership, culture, and structures. Icarus flew so well that he got cocky and overambitious.

The second aspect of the paradox is that many of the preceding causes of decline—galvanized cultures, efficient routines and programs, and orchestrated configurations—were initially the causes of success. Or, conversely, that *the very causes of success, when extended, may become the causes of failure.* It is simply a case of "too much of a good thing." For example, a focused strategy can produce wonderful competitive advantages as it mobilizes resources so efficiently; but when taken too far it becomes narrow obsession. Favoring certain departments and skills creates distinctive competences and galvanizes effort; but it can also produce intolerant corporate cultures. Similarly, routines promote efficiency and simplify coordination, but they can blind managers and mire the organization in its past. And, above all, cohesive, orchestrated configurations are indispensable for companies to operate effectively, but they can also create myopia. Icarus' wings and his courage were strengths; but when pushed to the limit, they became deadly.

Unfortunately, it is very hard sometimes to distinguish between the focus, harmony, and passionate dedication so necessary for outstanding performance, and the excesses and extremes that lead to decline.

1. Much of the earlier research is reported in Danny Miller and Peter H. Friesen's *Organizations: A Quantum View* (Englewood Cliffs, N.J.: Prentice-Hall, 1984). See also Danny Miller, "Configurations of Strategy and Structure," *Strategic Management Journal* (1986), 6 pp. 233–249, and "Relating Porter's Business Strategies to Environment and Structure," *Academy of Management Journal* (June 1988), 31, pp. 280–308. The present study is described in the Appendix.

2. This vignette of ITT was compiled using the many sources on that company that are referenced in Chapter 3. References for the other case histories in this chapter can be found in Chapters 2 through 5.

3. Configurations are quite enduring. Try to remove or alter one piece, and the remaining parts will kick in to regenerate or restore it. For example, at ITT, any attempt to slow down diversification would have been resisted by the growth plans, the incentive system, and the staff culture. Similarly, any campaign to pay more attention to divisional product lines and operations would have faltered because of the bottom-line values of ITT, the vast amount of time divisional managers had to spend at head-office meetings, and the obsession of top management with new acquisitions.

Reading 2

Permanently Failing Organizations

Marshall W. Meyer & Lynne G. Zucker

Summary prepared by Linn Van Dyne

Linn Van Dyne is a Ph.D. student in the Department of Strategic Management and Organization at the University of Minnesota. She is concentrating in organizational behavior and has research interests in proactive employee behaviors involving initiative, such as affiliative and challenging behaviors that extend beyond role requirements. She is also interested in the dynamic effects of work group composition and peer respect on effectiveness. Linn completed an MBA from the University of Minnesota in General Management and had fifteen years of business experience in a variety of human resources positions.

CAUSES OF PERMANENT FAILURE

Some organizations survive for relatively long periods of time even though their performance is consistently low. Electric interurban railways functioned in the United States at a loss for five or more years, and they are a prime example of permanent failure. The underlying cause of this interesting combination of low performance and continued existence is found in the conflict between owners and "dependent actors" when performance declines. *Dependent actors* are those individuals or other organizations such as employees, customers, suppliers, and community members who would prefer to keep their jobs or continue to do business with the organization. Their relationships are dependent on the continued existence of the firm. If the firm does not survive, they no longer can maintain their roles as employees, customers, suppliers, etc.

Owners, on the other hand, are motivated to obtain the highest return on their investment in the organization. When firm performance is low, owners become more risk-seeking as they attempt to "turnaround" a bad situation. If performance does not improve, they may ultimately withdraw their capital investments and shut down the organization. In contrast, dependent actors become more risk-averse when performance is low and the survival of the organization is threatened. They are motivated to maintain the status quo in order to protect their relationships with the organization. Accordingly, firms with sustained low performance contain conflicting forces. Owners try to make risky strategic changes while dependent actors resist these changes. The result is permanent failure. Although owners have the formal authority and power to determine organizational strategic decisions, their efforts to make significant changes are often resisted both passively and actively by dependent actors.

Permanent failure sets in when there is little expectation that efficient and effective conduct will be restored, yet there is little serious disruption of existing organizational patterns of behavior.

A PLURALISTIC MODEL OF ORGANIZATIONS

Although the label "permanent failure" has a negative connotation, individuals who are dependent on an organization often prefer for that organization to survive so that they can keep their jobs or continue to supply the firm with raw materials or services. In fact, during periods of low performance, dependent actors may be more highly motivated to preserve the organization than the owners. This is because owners often have opportunities to invest their capital in other ventures, while employees may have difficulty finding other jobs and suppliers may not be able to find other outlets for their products. Therefore the model of permanent failure stresses the plurality of interests. Not all who are associated with an organization place highest priority on financial performance. Permanent failure is, therefore, an outcome of divergent preferences.

ORGANIZATIONAL SURVIVAL IS NOT NECESSARILY BASED ON PERFORMANCE

Much of the business literature stresses the importance of organizational efficiency and profitability. Yet this literature recognizes three types of exceptional situations in which survival appears to be unrelated to performance. First is *temporary low performance*—perhaps during start-up or major reorganization. Second is *declining industries,* where low performance may be expected or tolerated. Third is *family-owned firms,* where multiple goals may reduce the emphasis on profitability. The four cases examined earlier are not examples of these unusual exceptions, but instead illustrate the more commonplace occurrence of persistent low performance and continued organizational existence.

Financial performance does not necessarily determine whether or not an organization will survive. Overall, research suggests that the relationship between performance and survival is uncertain. Research provides little evidence that profitability improves over time and, in fact, hints that firm performance often declines with age.

During times of high performance the goals of owners and dependent actors are more likely to be congruent. When the organization is successful, jobs are more secure or may be expanding, promotion opportunities may exist, and business relationships with vendors and customers are likely to be stable or growing. Although the organization is still characterized by pluralistic constituencies, there is less built-in conflict over the organization's strategy and goals.

During times of low performance the goals of owners and dependent actors are more likely to be incongruent and in conflict. Owners attempt to make fundamental changes in order to improve performance, while at the same time dependent actors who place a lower priority on organizational profitability see the changes as a threat and resist them. Employees want to preserve their jobs, wages, and benefits; unions want to protect jobs and receipt of union dues; customers want uninterrupted supply of product; suppliers want outlets for their goods and raw materials; and municipalities want continued payroll, property, and income taxes.

THE IMPORTANCE OF NONRATIONAL FACTORS

Permanent failure has three key attributes: long-run decline, multiple goals, and the hope of improvement in the future. These beliefs, however, can only be sustained if nonrational elements and differences in actor goals and priorities are considered. There are three potential nonrational responses to organizational decline, failure, or low performance:

- *The psychology of commitment* suggests that after repeated failure, actors often increase their public commitment to a cause.
- *Loyalist behavior* suggests that some actors may deliberately choose to remain in a declining firm rather than leave because they still believe that their best efforts will lead to improvement.
- *Goal succession* suggests that organizational goals evolve or change over time. Thus if a goal is achieved, a new goal can be set. Likewise, if the situation changes and a goal appears to become unrealistic, a new goal can be set.

KEY FACTORS LEADING TO PERSISTENT FAILURE

Factors leading to persistent failure can be assessed on two dimensions: whether interests are *divergent* or *convergent,* and whether action is taken *independently* or *jointly.*

Case #1: The Los Angeles *Herald Examiner* newspaper remained in business in spite of declining circulation and advertising revenues.

The *Herald Examiner* case is an example of permanent failure based on divergent interests and independent action in the sense that the owners were indecisive and did nothing.

Case #2: The unprofitable Rath meat packing company was sold to its employees and continued to operate unprofitably until these employees actually went out on strike against their own company.

Rath Packing illustrates divergent interests and joint action taken by employees when they acquired ownership of the firm.

> Case #3: Consolidation of Cathedral High School in Los Angeles was prevented by a coalition of alumni, community groups, and political leaders despite its declining enrollment.

In the Cathedral High School case, interests converged between diverse community members and they took joint action to prevent the school from being closed.

> Case #4: The U.S. steel industry's ability to shut plants and lay off workers was limited by unions, churches, and communities.

Finally, in the case of the U.S. steel industry, interests converged and the action was independent. There was no coordination between the different actors, but forces simply converged to force the industry to change its practices of shutting down plants and laying off workers.

EXTENDING THE MODEL TO NONPROFIT AND GOVERNMENT ORGANIZATIONS

Permanent failure is not restricted to for-profit organizations. Nonprofit organizations and government organizations also contain pluralistic interests that conflict during periods of low performance and can lead to permanently failing organizations. Although nonprofit and government organizations do not typically measure performance by profitability, they do, at some level, have fairly well-defined goals. When low performance confronts policy makers in these organizations, they may try to implement fundamental changes that may threaten the existing patterns of behavior. To the extent that dependent actors have few alternatives, they will be committed to maintaining the status quo in their organizations. In public and nonprofit agencies, values and commitments are more ambiguous and dependent actors may be more likely to exercise power in attempts to prevent major changes.

HOW ACTIONS BY DEPENDENT ACTORS LEAD TO PERSISTENT FAILURE

If dependent actors consistently resist attempts to change practices which are directed at improving performance or if dependent actors passively refrain from implementing new techniques designed to improve performance, a temporary drop in performance can extend into sustained low performance. This can, in turn, generate more drastic change actions which may be more threatening to dependent actors and most likely will increase the likelihood of permanent failure. While changes intended to improve performance may be essentially costless to owners of non-performing firms, these changes may mobilize dependent actors through alignment of interests, coalitions, and collective action in order to block the changes that were intended to improve organizational performance.

AVOIDING PERMANENT FAILURE

There are a number of strategies that can be used to reduce the occurrence of permanent failure. These can be divided into two categories: strategies that increase the flexibility of the organization and strategies that limit the power of dependent actors. Strategies that increase the choices available to owners include growth, innovation in organizational structure, and shifting employment relationships. Growth provides additional jobs and allows addition of new members who are less likely to resist management initiatives. Changing the organizational structure to separate strategic decisions from day-to-day decisions can provide structural justification for retention of critical decision-making at the top of the organization. The final example in this category of increasing the flexibility of organizations is externalization of employment. This refers to the increased freedom with which organizations can hire and terminate temporary workers or short-term contract workers.

Strategies that limit the power of dependent actors include changes in organizational structure, privatization, and externalization of employment. Changes in organizational structure can minimize the influence attempts made by dependent actors regarding critical strategic issues. When strategic decisions are removed from routine operations, alignments of interest, coalitions, and collective action are less likely and less effective. Privatization of the public sector generally involves removing activities from direct administrative control of the government. Work conducted in the public sector is often subject to constraints (e.g., legislative oversight, civil service regulations, prevailing wage clauses, notification requirements, extensive post-auditing, and political patronage) that are not present in the private sector. Privatization removes many of these constraints and accordingly reduces the influence that dependent actors can have on organizations. Similarly, hiring temporary workers reduces the possibility that these workers will get involved and form coalitions in order to resist management initiatives. In addition, temporary employees often have no property rights with which to challenge changes made by owners.

CONCLUSION

Permanently Failing Organizations concludes that maintenance of low-performing organizations is a natural and normal outcome of social processes. Permanent failure is a relatively common occurrence and not an exception. As dependent actors gain power, performance deteriorates and persistence is enhanced. Political activity (alignment of interests, coalitions, and collective action) degrades performance but enhances persistence in organizations.

Reading 3

Managing on the Edge: How the Smartest Companies Use Conflict to Stay Ahead

Richard Pascale

Summary prepared by Stephen Rubenfeld

Stephen Rubenfeld is Professor of Human Resource Management in the School of Business and Economics at the University of Minnesota, Duluth. He received his Ph.D. from the University of Wisconsin, Madison, and was previously on the faculty of Texas Tech University. His professional publications and presentations have covered a variety of personnel and labor relations topics, including job search behaviors, discrimination in employment, employee selection and staffing, concessionary bargaining, and social desirability bias. He is a member of the Industrial Relations Research Association, the Academy of Management, and the Southern Management Association.

With rallying cries of global competitiveness, quality, and customer satisfaction as a backdrop, the business media offer master plans for reviving an endless stream of business organizations. By contrast, there are relatively few reports of successes in correcting organizational ills or even sustaining the competitive achievements of those organizations which are dominant in their respective markets. The pressure to perform is incontrovertible; the corporate "grave-yard" is filled with the historical remnants of organizations that for a variety of reasons were unable to respond quickly enough to the changing realities of the marketplace. Their epitaphs vary, but most include the observation that they tried harder and harder, but in the end it wasn't enough. The inescapable conclusion is that in their quest for competitiveness, organizations of all types must accept the view that meaningful change is a prerequisite for long-term survival. *Managing on the Edge* explores the successes and failures of a diverse set of organizations as they sought to transform themselves. "Trying harder" can lead to incremental improvements, but these changes alone do not yield the quantum leaps that are necessary to move forward in an extremely competitive world. A more dramatic and fundamental type of change is needed.

Drawing on his consulting experience, extensive interviews, survey data, and a diverse literature base, Pascale concludes that failed change efforts tend to be based on the application of tried-and-true management strategies, embellished with a broad sampling of state-of-the-art (faddish) prescriptions for organizational improvement. Regardless of the packaging or glowing descriptions found in press releases, these efforts for the most part have been directed at *incremental* improvement: trying to squeeze a little more from the way things have always been done. Where creative pursuit of more fundamental change has been tried, it often was doomed by applying the "tools of transformation" without a corresponding shift in the underlying management *paradigm*. These paradigms make up the fundamental assumptions or mindset which guide management decision-making.

Assuming that there are practical limits to gains from fine-tuning efforts which eventually necessitate more fundamental changes to assure long term viability, it follows that a critical job of management must be to stimulate the organization to question and even challenge its operating paradigm. There is some irony here in that the traditional management paradigm has both guided the growth and vitality of the organization, but at the same time, may be the single most important reason why the organization is no longer able to grow and remain viable. This paradox only serves to reinforce the conclusion that for transformation to occur, managers must create and break paradigms.

Two messages are important for managers. First, the paradigm which directs organizational decision-making, unless questioned and challenged, will inhibit and limit change efforts. The types of incremental changes that are forthcoming in this business-as-usual scenario are likely to be inadequate in a highly dynamic environment. Second, the organization must be structured and managed in a way that assures that entropy (organizational deterioration growing out of disorder) and closed thinking will not be tolerated. There must be mechanisms along with a culture that will counter the very predictable temptation to seek comfortable answers, and that will resist closed-loop thinking. A conceptual framework for identifying the characteristics of organizations that are poised to move forward is offered, and numerous and detailed organizational examples are used to illustrate these points.

A MINDSET FOR CHANGE

Case studies can be effective tools, but using "excellent" organizations as role models is risky. Even among the firms judged previously to be "excellent," many have found it difficult to sustain their vitality. There also are risks associated with jumping on the bandwagon and following the latest business fads which purport to offer solutions to all that ails an organization. While any of these fads may have value in some circumstances, companies typically have seen them as panaceas and impatiently applied these ideas and strategies in a haphazard fashion. Perhaps more importantly, they have been implemented without consideration of the broader organizational context and mindset.

Studying successful organizations and blindly adopting their approaches does not provide sufficient tools for coping with future challenges. Organizations must create a mindset of change, a new paradigm that is not only receptive to, but also guides transformational change. Four key ideas underlie the quest for this new organization reality:

- Organizations must accept the premise that their current management mindset is self-limiting.
- Organizational attributes and behaviors that lead to stagnation and those that encourage renewal should be identified.
- Conflict, as an ever-present force in organizations, must be harnessed constructively.
- A new definition of management roles must be sought to reconcile the tensions inherent in an organization living on the edge of its own paradigm.

Pursuing a new mindset is important because managers have run from the challenge of guiding their organizations through the maze of an ever-changing world. The nature and magnitude of dynamic environmental change requires managers to defy their natural tendency toward business as usual. Managers need to do the illogical to live out of balance.

ATTRIBUTES FOR CHANGE

The model advanced for studying organizational adaptivity and potential for transformational change has four primary components:

- *Fit*—Internal coherence and consistencies which define the extent to which the pieces fit together and the gears mesh
- *Split*—Physical, organizational, or operational ways of encouraging and sustaining a sense of autonomy within the confines of the larger organization
- *Contend*—Management's role in utilizing constructive conflict and contradictions that are natural outcomes in complex organizations
- *Transcend*—The management of disequilibrium and complexity in the pursuit of organizational renewal

On the surface, there is an inherent contradiction in simultaneously pursuing fit and split strategies. But it is likely that more organizations have been hurt by the excessive reliance on a fit *or* split orientation than by the tensions growing out of the ongoing tug-of-war between these two forces. When viewed independently, "fit" contributes to focus, effective control systems, uniform standards, and complementary values. Similarly, many persuasive arguments can be advanced that "split" can advance flexibility and responsiveness, as well as provide a variety of advantages with respect to human behaviors and attitudes. The simple truth is that there are advantages both to "being big" and "acting small." When carried to excess, either of these strategies can become dysfunctional: Fit risks overadaptation, while split diffuses energy.

The potential for conflict from the pursuit of fit or split provides the *raison d'etre* for contention management. Managers must simultaneously orchestrate tension and harness contending opposites, not sweep them under the rug. The ability to capitalize on contention is a vital element of the lifeblood of the organization. Nevertheless, this is a domain of activity which is foreign to most managers who were weaned on "either-or" decision-making. Approaching problem solving from a perspective that not only doesn't give credence to either-or choices, but also doesn't glorify compromise (splitting the difference) may be a monumental challenge to a manager still grasping the traditional paradigm. This challenge must be met head-on. In dealing with contemporary problems, organizations need solutions that embrace both poles of the continuum—a *dynamic synthesis* of the range of possible positions. With regard to the categories of issues managers must often deal with, the challenge is to deal simultaneously with what often appear to be contending opposites:

- Strategy (Planned ⟷ Opportunistic)
- Structure (Elitist ⟷ Pluralist)
- Systems (Mandatory ⟷ Discretionary)
- Style (Managerial ⟷ Transformational)
- Staff (Collegiality ⟷ Individuality)
- Shared Values (Hard Minds ⟷ Soft Hearts)
- Skills (Maximize ⟷ Meta-mize)

The management of contention can be difficult and frustrating. The most daunting challenge is coping with the reality that problems must be dealt with in the context of a dynamic equilibrium. Not all problems have static solutions. Problems cannot be permanently solved, but only temporarily resolved. This type of outcome requires managers to be involved continually in monitoring, challenging, and examining the balance which has been achieved. Permanent closure is a rare commodity.

Transcendent management occurs when managers not only embrace the operational reality of balancing fit, split, and the value of constructive tensions, but also look to the dynamic synthesis of contending opposites as an opportunity and the basis for ongoing organizational self-renewal. It derives from the belief that the management of disequilibrium is a preferred strategy for adaptation. But for an organization to move forward, it is not sufficient for these attributes, values, and behaviors to be clustered in the executive suite. Transformation requires a critical mass of significant changes throughout the organization.

TRANSFORMATIONAL ORGANIZATIONS

Ford and General Electric, two very different companies, undertook fundamental change efforts. Neither organization began with a detailed master plan for transforming itself. Rather, they were guided by a vision for the future and a confluence of organizational change initiatives in concert with an openness to learn from their experiences, and the willingness to take bold steps to achieve a desired outcome. Ford was in financial crisis and was driven to act by the reality that incremental change would not be sufficient to restore financial solvency, while Jack Welch at General Electric had to create a sense of crisis to convince employees of the urgency of change.

But regardless of the differing leadership challenges involved in mobilizing their organizations, both Ford and General Electric were in the midst of dramatic strategic realignments and both faced the necessity of substantially reducing their costs. In very different ways, both undertook efforts to fine-tune their operations, focus on fundamentals, deal with nonproductive conflict, and otherwise pursue other patterns of activities that loosely followed the formula of fit, split, conflict, and transformation. Although the GE change effort has been somewhat less successful in enlisting the support of the rank-and-file workers, both organizations attempted to capitalize on contention as a strategy for self-renewal. Despite their many differences, both organizations met the following perquisites as they made dramatic strides toward transforming themselves:

- Develop and support a critical mass of change initiatives.
- Respond to the need for strong and situationally appropriate leadership.
- Demonstrate responsiveness, persistence, courage, and openness to learning.

ANATOMY OF REVITALIZATION

The successful adaptive organization must be capable of changing the traditional management paradigm. This is a formidable challenge, for several reasons:

- Usually the prevailing mindset is not explicitly documented and it exists unquestioned.
- Change is difficult. Managers cling to ideas with which they are comfortable.
- New ideas come in fits and starts, and are rarely seen as universal truths.

Nevertheless, this is a challenge which must be met. Managers must rethink how they manage their organizations. Their resistance to change often is based on the illusion that their past successes will somehow reassert themselves. The truth is that their past will *not* carry them forward. They must face reality and revitalize their organizations.

Reading 4

The Critical Path to Corporate Renewal

*Michael Beer, Russell A. Eisenstat, and
Bert Spector*

Summary prepared by Warren Candy

A native of Australia, **Warren Candy** received his B.S. in Production
Engineering from Swinburne College of Technology in Melbourne, Australia.
His career in the United States has been in industrial engineering, and as the
Leader of the Organizational Development Team at Minnesota Power, an
investor-owned utility in northern Minnesota. He currently is the Director of
the Clay Boswell power generation facility with the utility and is active within
several industrial engineering and organizational innovation associations.

In the battle to reclaim competitiveness, a powerful approach that is being used
by an increasing number of American companies is that of organizational revitalization. Leaders in these companies look beyond the need to manage financial assets wisely by recognizing that competitiveness is inexorably linked to the
abilities and effectiveness of their employees.

Six large corporations engaged in a conscious effort to make fundamental
change in their patterns of management were studied. The companies were
selected on a number of criteria: the need for a variety of industries, for representation in the manufacturing and service sectors, for inclusion of both single
and multibusiness firms, and their willingness to provide open research access.
The companies' sales ranged from $4 billion to $10 billion. Five were in the
manufacturing sector, and one was a large international bank. Although the
companies and individuals in the study are real, all names used are fictitious.
They are referred to as Continental Glass and Container, General Products,
Fairweather Corporation, Livingston Electronics, Scranton Steel, and U.S. Financial.

A comprehensive theory of corporate revitalization is presented that will
help managers develop an adaptive organization. In these firms, organizational

members understand all the plans and strategies, know and anticipate one another's roles and responsibilities, and are eager to work together by looking at the success of the business, rather than their own function or job.

THE CHALLENGE OF REVITALIZATION

Revitalization involves enhancing the abilities of, and contributions made by, managers, workers, and the organization as a whole to cope with an increasingly competitive environment. Revitalized corporations reduce their exclusive reliance on the authority of management, on rules and procedures, and on a strict and narrow division of work. Instead, employees at all levels are involved in decision-making; teamwork is encouraged among functions, business units, union and management; information concerning performance and the competitive environment is shared and communicated throughout the corporation; and responsibility and accountability are pushed far down the hierarchy.

The degree to which an organization can achieve cost, quality, and innovation is affected by the extent to which it has the necessary level of coordination through teamwork, commitment through motivation and competence in business knowledge, and analytical and interpersonal skills required to solve problems as a team. These human resource attributes are in turn determined by elements of the organization's design: structure, people, roles/responsibilities/relationships, and systems.

SUCCESSFUL REVITALIZATION: AN OVERVIEW

The results of the six-company research established that, at both the company and the unit level, several key elements were identified that characterize the successful organizations, and were absent in the "lagging" organizations.

Specifically, it was found that:

- Change efforts that begin by creating corporate programs to alter the culture or the management of people in the firm are inherently flawed, even when supported by top management.
- Formal organizational structure and systems are the *last* things an organization should change when seeking renewal—not the first, as many managers assumed.
- Effective changes in the way an organization manages people do *not* occur by changing the organization's human resource policies and systems.
- Starting corporate renewal at the very top is a high-risk revitalization strategy *not* employed by the most successful companies.
- Organizations should start corporate revitalization by targeting small, isolated, peripheral operations, not large, central, core operations.

- It is not essential that top management consistently practice what it preaches in the early stages of renewal, although such action is undoubtedly helpful.

For the task-driven organization to function effectively, far higher levels of coordination and teamwork—across functions, borders, business units, organizational levels, as well as between management and union—will be needed. To achieve that coordination, higher levels of employee commitment and competence will be required at all levels of the organization. Successful unit-level renewal occurs only when units directly align a call for new employee behaviors and skills with an urgent response to the unit's central competitive challenge.

While renewal can be achieved by mandating changes in formal systems and structure, that approach reduces commitment and fails to develop the competence people need to function effectively within the newly-aligned organization. The *Critical Path* identifies a sequence of interventions, which creates task alignment in a way that increases coordination as well as commitment and competence.

THE TASK-DRIVEN ORGANIZATION

The new competitive environment requires a flexible and adaptive organization, as well as a different pattern of work behavior. Managers and workers must be aware of what the customer wants and what competitors are doing. They must translate this knowledge into effective decisions about improvements in product, service, quality, and cost, and they must implement these decisions at all levels. The competitive environment requires using the skills and abilities of a much larger number of employees than ever before.

Managers are becoming aware that it is impossible to respond rapidly to changing customer demands and meet lower cost and higher quality requirements without radically improving coordination and teamwork.

This kind of quick responsiveness and adaptability are possible because the task, rather than the hierarchy, is the basis for assigning roles and responsibilities. Knowledge replaces formal authority as the basis for influence. A firm that uses this approach is called a *task-driven organization.*

In virtually all cases of successful revitalization, management focused on the business' central competitive challenges as the means for motivating change and developing new behaviors and skills. This is called *task alignment,* and it involves a redefinition of work roles, responsibilities, and relationships within a unit in a way that will enhance the coordination required to accomplish the tasks critical to the success of the business.

By changing how people work together around core tasks, without changing the organizational chart, a commonly understood and legitimated ad hoc team organization emerges. Because it focuses on the most important problem facing a business, task alignment occurs within units small enough for a group of individuals to have responsibility for a common goal, not within a large and diverse corporation as a whole.

THE CRITICAL PATH TO RENEWAL

Revitalization efforts in twenty-six plants and business units across the six companies revealed that effective renewal occurred not when managers chose one alternative course of action or the other. Instead, effective revitalization occurred when managers followed a *critical path* that obtains the benefits of top-down as well as bottom-up change efforts, while minimizing their disadvantages.

The critical path is a general manager-led process that implements task alignment at the unit level by following six steps:

1. Mobilizing energy for change among all stakeholders in the organization by involving them in a diagnosis of the problems blocking competitiveness.
2. Developing a task-aligned vision of how to organize and manage for competitiveness. Without a vision, employees do not have an understanding of how the organization will function in the future or a clear rationale for the changes in roles, responsibilities, and relationships they are being asked to make.
3. Fostering consensus that the new vision is "right," developing competence to enact it, and creating cohesion to move the change along.
4. Spreading revitalization to all departments of the unit in a way that avoids the perception that a program is being pushed from the top, but at the same time ensures consistency with the organizational changes already under way.
5. Consolidating changes through formal policies, systems, and structures that institutionalize revitalization to ensure the long-term success of a revitalization effort, particularly given the inevitability that managers will move on to other jobs.
6. Continually monitoring and strategizing in response to predictable problems in the revitalization process.

The experience of revitalization uncovers strengths and weaknesses in an organization. Since organizations are interdependent systems, changes in one part of an organization lead to stresses and strains in other parts. These problems are not signs of failure. Rather, they represent dilemmas to be addressed and managed.

REVITALIZATION LEADERS

Corporate renewal is not an impersonal process unfolding of its own accord. It is possible only when individual managers at the unit and corporate level have sufficient commitment and skill.

The research indicated that leaders at the unit level had to be willing to break traditions of management and labor relations that may have existed for many years. To do this, they raised dissatisfaction with the status quo by articulating with some urgency the core tasks (improving quality, decreasing cost, and/or increasing product innovation) that their organizations had to perform to compete successfully. They then managed a participative change effort that aligned the organization and management process with the business' core task. All this required commitment to renewal as well as conceptual and consensus-building skills.

WHO WERE THE REVITALIZATION LEADERS?

Who were the members of the small group capable of running with the baton of revitalization? Surprising as it may seem, this group of corporate leaders did not necessarily include the very top executive. However, the key leaders were at high levels, including an executive vice president of a major business group, a vice president of manufacturing, and the chief operating officer. They had responsibility for sufficiently large company segments to get revitalization started, and they typically exerted influence over other parts of their companies by their persuasive powers and, often, through their transfer from one segment to another.

For revitalization to succeed at the unit level it was essential that the general manager be actively engaged as its leader. Perhaps because of the smaller size and relative homogeneity, no examples of successful unit-level revitalization were seen that were not led by the general manager. Conversely, many failures occurred where general management leadership was lacking.

Although revitalization leaders functioned at all levels of the organization, it was found that they generally shared a common set of attributes. At the unit level, three attributes were found that distinguished those managers who were most successful in leading revitalization:

1. *A persistent belief that revitalization is key to competitiveness* Effective revitalization leaders shared a common conviction. They believed that fundamental changes in organizing and managing people would have a significant impact on the bottom line of their organizations.

2. *The capacity to articulate this conviction in the form of a credible and compelling vision* Effective revitalization at any level cannot occur without a vision of the future state of the organization, a vision that aligns new patterns of management with the performance of the organization's core task. Effective leaders also had the capacity to present their visions in a way that appealed to their constituents. That appeal allowed employees to commit to change emotionally, not just intellectually.

3. *The ability to implement this vision through a consistent pattern of words and behaviors* Revitalization leaders communicated values and intentions not only through words, but also through actions.

WHERE AND HOW TO START A REVITALIZATION EFFORT

Corporate revitalization rests on the capacity of leaders to develop an organizational context that will influence people—managers, workers, and union leaders alike—to change behavior and attitudes. However, each change leader's capacity to begin and sustain revitalization is also a function of the environment within which he or she operates. The unit manager's ability to manage change is affected by the many policies and practices handed down from headquarters and the support for revitalization provided by top management. Top management's ability to manage and sustain renewal is in turn affected not only by business conditions and capital markets that shape the economic environment of the corporation, but also by the response of its board to external factors.

A manager's efforts to revitalize, while a function of personal conviction and skills, is also a function of a corporate environment that can be influenced, but not controlled. Given this reality, it is easy for a manager to conclude that there is nothing that can be done to start revitalizing the organization. This is far too pessimistic an attitude and is self-defeating.

American corporations will become more competitive only when individuals at every level take the initiative to create a favorable environment for renewal in the domain over which they have some control. A good-faith effort to work cooperatively with the next level up to shape the environment so that it supports revitalization initiatives is also desired.

A PARTNERSHIP OF CHANGE LEADERS

Any one of a number of people can begin the process of revitalization, whether it be the unit general manager, corporate human resource manager, union leader, or top management, so long as that person recognizes the unique role each plays and what each can or cannot do. Thus, simply beginning the process is the most important step.

The transformation of a large corporation requires that change leaders work as a team. Each has a different and valuable perspective. Each commands the respect and loyalty of a different constituency. Each is able to influence some, but not all, of the many conditions for company-wide learning. Each requires help and support from others. Together, they can succeed in creating the task-driven corporate organization that can survive and prosper in the hotly contested global markets of the 1990s and beyond.

TWELVE

Managing Quality in Customer-Driven Organizations

W. Edwards Deming's name has, during the past decade, become synonymous with strategies to infuse "quality" into manufacturing. During the 1950s Deming went to Japan to teach statistical control, where his ideas received a very warm reception. The Japanese built upon Deming's ideas and moved the responsibility for quality from the ranks of middle management down to the shop floor level. Deming's ideas on quality control were extended and have become a common part of Japanese management. Total quality control (TQC) means that responsibility for quality is a part of every employee's job. *Out of the Crisis* calls for long-term organizational transformation through the implementation of a 14-step plan of action focusing on leadership, constant innovation, and removal of barriers to performance.

Many other authors, such as Joe Juran *(Juran on Leadership for Quality)* and Phil Crosby have written about their approaches to quality. Interested readers may also wish to explore follow-up books, such as *Driving Fear Out of the Workplace,* by Kathleen Ryan and Daniel Oestreich.

In 1982 Thomas J. Peters and Robert H. Waterman published their book *In Search of Excellence,* which was followed three years later by *A Passion for Excellence* by Peters and coauthor Nancy Austin. These books served to heighten the level of managers' awareness about a key issue: that the traditional disregard for the customer, in a service-oriented organization and service-oriented society, has great risks. They vividly called attention to the importance of listening and responding to customer needs, to caring about customer satisfaction, and even to making the purchasing experience fun.

Since that time several books have appeared which have focused on the strategic importance of being a highly customer-sensitive organization. In this section five books, each focused on the customer-driven organization, are summarized.

Moments of Truth: New Strategies for Today's Customer-Driven Economy by SAS president Jan Carlzon provides his views on managing service organizations. Carlzon has had a very successful career managing in the fiercely competitive airline industry. He provides his insights into the issues of leadership, strategy, flattening the pyramid, taking risks, communicating, working with boards and unions, measuring performance results, and networking with employees.

Karl Albrecht and Ron Zemke's book *Service America!* calls attention to the fact that Industrial America is now Service America. As a consequence, the style of management also needs to change. Their book focuses on the challenges of managing in the service sector, and the managerial skills that are required.

Karl Albrecht and Ron Zemke are both management consultants. Both have written other books focused on the same topic, such as *At America's Service* (Albrecht), *The Service Edge* (Zemke and Schaff), and *Delivering Knock Your Socks Off Service* (Anderson and Zemke).

Creating value for customers leads to organizational success. This is the theme of William A. Band's recent book *Creating Value for Customers: Designing and Implementing a Total Corporate Strategy.* Band describes techniques for value creation, while providing anecdotes about their successful application in North American and international firms. The result is a compendium of strategic initiatives that managers can employ in order to increase the value delivered to their customers.

Wal-Mart Corporation has achieved spectacular growth and financial success in recent years, rising to a position of prominence among the nation's retailers. Sam Walton, founder of Wal-Mart, (with John Huey) provides an overview of the guiding principles that led to this success in *Sam Walton: Made in America—My Story.* Walton accents providing quality customer service and product value, and achieves this through a corporate culture that emphasizes making his associates feel like they are responsible for (and rewarded for) company success.

Reading 1

Out of the Crisis

W. Edwards Deming

Summary prepared by William B. Gartner and M. James Naughton

William B. Gartner is a Professor at Georgetown University.
M. James Naughton is the owner of Expert-Knowledge Systems, Inc.

Deming provides an ambitious objective for his book when he begins by saying:

> The aim of this book is transformation of the style of American management. Transformation of American style of management is not a job of reconstruction, nor is it revision. It requires a whole new structure, from foundation upward. *Mutation* might be the word, except that *mutation* implies unordered spontaneity. Transformation must take place with directed effort.

Few individuals have had as much positive impact on the world economy as Dr. W. Edwards Deming. With the broadcast of the NBC white paper, "If Japan Can, Why Can't We?" on June 24, 1980, Dr. Deming gained national exposure as the man responsible for the managerial theory that has governed Japan's transformation into a nation of world leaders in the production of high quality goods. This transformation did not happen overnight. Since 1950, when Dr. Deming first spoke to Japan's top managers on the improvement of quality, Japanese organizations have pioneered in the adaptation of Dr. Deming's ideas.

As a result of his seminars, Japan has had an annual national competition for quality improvement (the Deming Prize) since 1951. Japan has numerous journals and books devoted to exploring and furthering the implications of Deming's theory. However, it has only been within the last few years that a number of books have been published in the United States on "the Deming Theory of Management." An overview of the ideas that underlie Deming's theory, which cut across all major topical areas in management, will be provided here.

W. Edwards Deming, *Out of the Crisis.* Cambridge, MA: MIT Press, 1986.

DISEASES AND OBSTACLES

Deming's book is not merely about productivity and quality control; it is a broad vision of the nature of organizations and how organizations should be changed. Deming identifies a set of chronic ailments that can plague any organization and limit its success. These, which he calls "deadly diseases," include an over-emphasis on short-term profits, human resource practices that encourage both managers and employees to be mobile and not organizationally loyal, merit ratings and review systems that are based on fear of one's supervisor, an absence of a single driving purpose, and management that is based on visible figures alone.

The reason that managers are not as effective as they could be is that they are the prisoners of some structural characteristics and personal assumptions that prevent their success. Among the obstacles that Deming discusses are the insulation of top management from the other employees in the organization, lack of adequate technical knowledge, a long history of total reliance on final inspection as a way of assuring a quality product, the managerial belief that all problems originate within the work force, a reliance on meeting specifications, and the failure to synthesize human operators with computer systems for control.

THE CONCEPT OF VARIABILITY

The basis for Deming's theory is the observation that variability exists everywhere in everything. Only through the study and analysis of variability, using statistics, can a phenomenon be understood well enough to manipulate and change it. In many respects, using statistics is not very radical. Statistics are fundamental to nearly all academic research. But Deming asks that the right kind of statistics (analytical) be applied to our everyday lives as well. And that is the rub. To recognize the pervasiveness of variability and to function so that the sources of this variability can be defined and measured is radical. In Deming's world, the use of statistical thinking is not an academic game; it is a way of life.

The concept of variability is to management theory and practice what the concept of the germ theory of disease was to the development of modern medicine. Medicine had been "successfully" practiced without the knowledge of germs. In a pre-germ theory paradigm, some patients got better, some got worse, and some stayed the same; in each case, some rationale could be used to explain the outcome. With the emergence of germ theory, all medical phenomena took on new meanings. Medical procedures thought to be good practice, such as physicians attending women in birth, turned out to be causes of disease because of the septic condition of the physicians' hands. Instead of rendering improved health care, the physicians' germ-laden hands achieved the opposite result. One can imagine the first proponents of the germ theory telling their colleagues who were still ignorant of the theory to wash their hands between patients. The pioneers must have sounded crazy. In the same vein, managers and academics who do not have a thorough understanding of variability will fail to grasp the radical change in thought that Deming envisions. Deming's propositions may seem as simplistic as "wash your hands!" rather than an entirely new paradigm of profound challenges to present-day managerial thinking and behaviors.

An illustration of variability that is widely cited in the books on Deming's theory is the "red bead experiment." Dr. Deming, at his four-day seminar, asks for 10 volunteers from the attendees. Six of the students become workers, two become inspectors of the workers' production, one becomes the inspector of the inspectors' work, and one becomes the recorder. Dr. Deming mixes together 3000 white beads and 750 red beads in a large box. He instructs the workers to scoop out beads from the box with a beveled paddle that scoops out 50 beads at a time. Each scoop of the paddle is treated as a day's production. Only white beads are acceptable. Red beads are defects. After each worker scoops a paddle of beads from the box, the two inspectors count the defects, the inspector of the inspectors inspects the inspectors' count, and the recorder writes down the inspectors' agreed-upon number of defects. Invariably, each worker's scoop contains some red beads. Deming plays the role of the manager by exhorting the workers to produce no defects. When a worker scoops few red beads he may be praised. Scooping many red beads brings criticism and an exhortation to do better, otherwise "we will go out of business." The manager reacts to each scoop of beads as if it had meaning in itself rather than as part of a pattern. Figure 1 shows the number of defective beads each worker produced for four days of work.

Dr. Deming's statistical analysis of the workers' production indicates that the process of producing white beads is in statistical control; that is, the variability of this production system is stable. The near-term prediction about the *pattern*, but not the individual draws, of the system's performance can be made. Near-future draws will yield about an average, over many experiments, of 9.4 red beads. Any one draw may range between one and 18 red beads. In other words, the actual number of red beads scooped by each worker is out of that worker's control. The worker, as Dr. Deming says, "is only delivering the defects." Management, which controls the system, has caused the defects through design of the system. There are a number of insights people draw from this experiment. Walton lists the following:

- Variation is part of any process.
- Planning requires prediction of how things and people will perform. Tests and experiments of past performance can be useful, but not definitive.
- Workers work within a system that—try as they might—is beyond their control. It is the system, not their individual skills, that determines how they perform.
- Only management can change the system.
- Some workers will always be above average, some below.[1]

Name	Day				All 4
	1	2	3	4	
Neil	3	13	8	9	33
Tace	6	9	8	10	33
Tim	13	12	7	10	42
Mike	11	8	10	15	44
Tony	9	13	8	11	41
Richard	12	11	7	15	45
All 6	54	66	48	70	238
Cum $\bar{x}$	9.0	10.0	9.3	9.92	9.92

$$\bar{x} = \frac{238}{6 \times 4} = 9.92$$

$$\bar{p} = \frac{238}{6 \times 4 \times 50} = .198$$

$$\left. \begin{array}{c} \text{UCL} \\ \\ \text{LCL} \end{array} \right\} = \bar{x} \pm 3\sqrt{\bar{x}(1 - \bar{p})}$$

$$= 9.9 \pm 3\sqrt{9.9 \times .802}$$

$$= \begin{cases} 18 \\ 1 \end{cases}$$

Adapted from Deming, p. 347.

Figure 1. Number of defective items by operator, by day.

The red bead experiment illustrates the behavior of systems of stable variability. In Deming's theory, a system is all of the aspects of the organization and environment—employees, managers, equipment, facilities, government, customers, suppliers, shareholders, and so forth—fitted together, with the aim of producing some type of output. Stability implies that the output has regularity to it, so that predictions regarding the output of the system can be made. But man-made systems are inherently unstable. Bringing a system into stability is one of the fundamental managerial activities in the Deming theory.

In Deming's theory, a stable system, that is, a system that shows signs of being in statistical control, behaves in a manner similar to the red bead experiment. In systems, a single datum point is of little use in understanding the causes that influenced the production of that point. It is necessary to withhold judgment about changes in the output of the system until sufficient evidence (additional data points) becomes available to suggest whether or not the system being examined is stable. Statistical theory provides tools to help evaluate the stability of systems. Once a system is stable, its productive capability can be determined; that is, the average output of the system and the spread of variability around that average can be described. This can be used to predict the near-term future behavior of the system.

The inefficiencies inherent in "not knowing what we are doing," that is, in working with systems not in statistical control, might not seem to be that great a competitive penalty if all organizations are similarly out of control. Yet we are beginning to realize that the quality of outputs from organizations that are managed using Deming's theory are many magnitudes beyond what non-Deming organizations have been producing. The differences in quality and productivity can be mind-boggling.

For example, both Walton and Scherkenbach[2] reported that when the Ford Motor Company began using transmissions produced by the Japanese automobile manufacturer, Mazda, Ford found that customers overwhelmingly preferred cars with Mazda transmissions to cars with Ford-manufactured transmissions—because the warranty repairs were ten times lower, and the cars were quieter and shifted more smoothly. When Ford engineers compared their transmissions to the Mazda transmissions, they found that the piece-to-piece variation in the Mazda transmissions was nearly three times less than in the Ford pieces. Both Ford and Mazda conformed to the engineering standards specified by Ford, but Mazda transmissions were far more uniform. More uniform products also cost less to manufacture. With less variability there is less rework and less need for inspection. Only systems in statistical control can begin to reduce variability and thereby improve the quality and quantity of their output. Both authors reported that after Ford began to implement Deming's theory over the last five years, warranty repair frequencies dropped by forty-five percent and "things gone wrong" reports from customers dropped by fifty percent.

14 STEPS MANAGEMENT MUST TAKE

The task of transformation of an entire organization to use the Deming theory becomes an enormous burden for management, and Deming frequently suggests that this process is likely to take a minimum of ten years. The framework for transforming an organization is outlined in the fourteen points (pp. 23–24):

1. Create constancy of purpose toward improvement of product and service, aiming to become competitive, to stay in business, and to provide jobs.
2. Adopt the new philosophy. We are in a new economic age. Western management must awaken to the challenge, must learn their responsibilities, and must take on leadership in order to bring about change.
3. Cease dependence on inspection to achieve quality. Eliminate the need for inspection on a mass basis by building quality into the product in the first place.
4. End the practice of awarding business on the basis of the price tag. Instead, minimize total cost. Move toward a single supplier for any one time and develop long-term relationships of loyalty and trust with that supplier.
5. Improve constantly and forever the systems of production and ser-

vice in order to improve quality and productivity. Thus, one constantly decreases costs.

6. Institute training on the job.
7. Institute leadership. Supervisors should be able to help people to do a better job, and they should use machines and gadgets wisely. Supervision of management and supervision of production workers need to be overhauled.
8. Drive out fear, so that everyone may work effectively for the company.
9. Break down barriers between departments. People in research, design, sales, and production must work as a team. They should foresee production problems and problems that could be encountered when using the product or service.
10. Eliminate slogans, exhortations, and targets that demand zero defects and new levels of productivity. These only create adversarial relationships because the many causes of low quality and low productivity are due to the system, and not the work force.
11a. Eliminate work standards (quotas) on the factory floor. Substitute leadership.
11b. Eliminate management by objectives. Eliminate management by numbers or numerical goals. Substitute leadership.
12a. Remove barriers that rob the hourly worker of his right to pride of workmanship. The responsibility of supervisors must be changed from sheer numbers to quality.
12b. Remove barriers that rob people in management and in engineering of their right to pride of workmanship. This means, inter alia, abolishing the annual or merit rating and management by objectives.
13. Institute a vigorous program of education and self-improvement.
14. Put everybody in the company to work to accomplish the transformation. The transformation is everybody's job.

As mentioned earlier, the fourteen points should not be treated as a list of aphorisms, nor can each of the fourteen points be treated separately without recognizing the interrelationships among them.

CONCLUSIONS

Out of the Crisis is full of examples and ideas, and Deming calls for a radical revision of American management practice. To his credit, Deming constantly recognizes ideas and examples from individuals practicing various aspects of his theory. This constant recognition of other individuals provides a subtle indication that a body of practitioners exists who have had successful experiences applying his 14 steps and other ideas.

A transformation in American management needs to occur, it can take place, and it has begun already in those firms applying Deming's theory. Deming offers a new paradigm for the practice of management that requires a dramatic rethinking and replacement of old methods by those trained in traditional management techniques. In conclusion, Deming recognizes that "it takes courage to admit that you have been doing something wrong, to admit that you have something to learn, that there is a better way" (Walton, 1986, p. 223).

REFERENCES

William B. Gartner and M. James Naughton, "The Deming Theory of Management," *Academy of Management Review,* January 1988, pp. 138–142.

William W. Scherkenbach, *The Deming Route to Quality and Productivity: Roadmaps and Roadblocks,* Milwaukee, WI: ASQC, 1986.

Mary Walton, *The Deming Management Method,* New York: Dodd, Mead, & Company, 1986.

Moments of Truth: New Strategies for Today's Customer-Driven Economy

Jan Carlzon

Summary prepared by Gregory R. Fox

Gregory R. Fox is the Vice Chancellor for Finance and Operations at the University of Minnesota, Duluth (UMD). He earned his master's degree at the University of Washington. He regularly teaches courses in the human resources curriculum in the Management Studies Department at UMD. He consults in the areas of leadership development, supervisory training, and sexual harassment. He has been the recipient of a Bush Mid-Career Leadership Fellowship. He developed instructional materials for Lester Bittel and John Newstrom's book *What Every Supervisor Should Know* (McGraw-Hill, 1990).

The only real assets of a customer-driven company are satisfied customers. Despite the fact that Scandinavian Airlines System (SAS) is the sum total of its aircraft, maintenance bases, offices, and administrative procedures, its customers evaluate their experiences with the company based on the individual contacts that they have with the SAS employees. Each year its customers will come in contact with those employees fifty million times, and the average length of the contact will be fifteen seconds. These individual "moments of truth" eventually determine the success of the company. For that reason, frontline employees need the latitude and responsibility to carry out the ideas, decisions, and actions that will earn satisfied customers.

The customer-driven company needs to turn the traditional corporate structure upside down. The bottom of the traditional pyramid needs to have the power to respond to the individual situations that regularly arise. The organiza-

Jan Carlzon, *Moments of Truth.* New York: Harper & Row, 1987. Hardcover published by Ballinger Publishing Co.

tion will be decentralized and flattened, with power and responsibility being delegated to those persons who come in regular contact with the organization's customers. The changes that are required for an organization to become a customer-oriented company must be initiated by the chief executive officer (CEO), who must become "a true leader, devoted to creating an environment in which employees can accept and execute their responsibilities with confidence and finesse."

In 1974, Jan Carlzon became the president of Vingresor, a 1,400-employee subsidiary of SAS that sold vacation package tours. Here, he acquired a major part of his management philosophy. He began his job by acting the way he thought a boss should act, issuing orders and edicts at every meeting and in every situation. He assumed that everyone wanted him to make all of the decisions. An employee soon confronted him regarding his authoritarian style. This helped him realize that his new role as president did not necessitate a change in his behavior. The job didn't require him to *make* all of the decisions, but rather to "create the right atmosphere, the right conditions for others to do their jobs better."

During his first year at Vingresor the company had its largest profit ever. In 1978 he received an offer to become the president of Linjeflyg, an affiliate of SAS. The company catered to Swedish business executives who wanted to complete their business travel within one day and return to Stockholm in the evening. Fares throughout the country were almost identical. Corporate decisions were based on efficiency, and Carlzon thought the opportunity lacked challenge and excitement. Curt Nicolin, a key Swedish industrialist and member of the Linjeflyg board, convinced Carlzon that Linjeflyg was a troubled company, losing money, and in need of his special talents. Eventually, Carlzon concluded that the job was the perfect challenge to further the development of his leadership skills, and so he accepted the opportunity.

Now the youngest airline president in the world, he invited all staff members throughout the country to assemble on his first day. Meeting with them at Linjeflyg's main hangar, he addressed the problems of the airline, concluding with a plea for them to help Linjeflyg survive by assuming responsibility, and sharing their ideas and experiences. Here again his management philosophy was being shaped by his job and the recognition of the potential within his employees.

The switch from a production-oriented company to one that is customer-driven was to be accomplished through four strategies:

1. Increase the daily utilization of each aircraft.
2. Become "The World's Best Airline" by stressing convenience, timetables, frequent departures, and low prices.
3. Distribute responsibility to more people in the company.
4. Focus on profits by streamlining administrative resources.

By effectively communicating what the company could be, and permitting employees to take responsibility for implementing this vision, Carlzon learned to be a leader rather than simply a manager, and the company's change was a success.

In 1980 Carlzon became the chief operating officer of SAS, which after seventeen years of profit was going to lose a significant amount of money that year. The business strategy that SAS needed was to identify its market and increase its share of the overall market, which at that time was stagnant. They identified businessmen as the only stable part of the airline business. Expenses that would result in better service for frequent business travelers were encouraged.

This focus on service changed employee attitudes in the entire company. Frontline employees had a greater sense of value, all employees received training in providing service, and each person began to feel appreciated and in the limelight. Each of the 20,000 employees received a book entitled *Let's Get in There and Fight,* which outlined, as clearly as possible, the company's vision and goal.

The financial goal had been to increase earnings by $25 million in Year One, and by $50 million in Year Three. In a slumping market in which all other international airlines suffered a total loss of $2 billion, SAS earned $80 million the very first year. In 1983 *Fortune* named SAS the best airline for business travelers, and *Air Transport World* named SAS "airline of the year."

During his first vacation while president of SAS, Carlzon received a continuous stream of telephone calls from subordinates with questions about nearly everything. Within a few days he gave up and returned to work. The following summer, one week prior to his vacation, an interview with him was published in a Swedish newspaper in which he explained that responsibility should be delegated, and employees should use it. He received no calls during his entire four-week holiday—evidence that employees *could* accept responsibility.

Corporations and managers wishing to change or strengthen these customer-driven tendencies can do so by measuring their effectiveness in eight specific areas. As discussed below, these areas include leadership, setting strategy, flattening the organizational pyramid, risk-taking, communication, working with boards and unions, measuring results, and rewarding employees.

LEADERSHIP

The traditional corporate manager expects to know everything and make every decision, while keeping involved in all phases of the operation. The traditional manager assumes that no one else is able to make decisions. The problem with this approach is that such managers think they are taking full responsibility when, in fact, they fail at the most crucial part of their job—"making sure the overall vision of the company was achieved."

Since executives can never investigate each issue, many decisions go unmade. As a result, employees often become passive, believing that their opinions are unimportant or will not be acted upon.

Customer-driven leaders stress the development of a business strategy designed to meet organizational goals. They then communicate this strategy to their corporate boards, unions, and employees, focusing on the importance of creating a secure employment atmosphere. They also encourage their employees to be in regular contact with customers and to accept greater responsibility, encouraging them to work at implementing the vision that has been communicated to them.

Effective performance measures are necessary to ensure that progress is being made. This delegation of responsibility throughout the organization, in some respects, is harder than implementing decisions by yourself. However, by having people closest to the problem involved in the decision-making, you improve the chances that the most effective decisions will be made.

The chief executive doesn't have to have detailed technical knowledge. It is much more important to have good business sense and a broad understanding of how everything fits together, both within the company and with key external groups and individuals.

Another requirement for today's leaders is "helicopter sense." This is a kind of strategic thinking that permits you to see beyond the details to develop a more general understanding of the whole problem and of the steps necessary to implement any changes that are necessary.

In addition to the traditional management responsibility of finance, production, and technology, today's leader must also effectively manage human resources in ways that encourage flexibility and innovation. This requires the new leader to have well-developed skills as a listener, communicator, and educator. Carlzon concludes that oftentimes the leader will appear as an "enlightened dictator—one who is willing to disseminate the vision and goals . . . but who will not brook active dissent to the underlying ideas." If it is not possible for employees to understand or share the vision, they must at least make the commitment of loyalty to those goals. If they are unable to do this, they should not be part of the organization.

The effective leader focuses on results rather than on power or social relationships. Carlzon has been amused by the fact that the press has occasionally leaked information that he was not responsible for all of the ideas that had proven successful at SAS. These revelations reinforce a major piece of his management philosophy: that employee creativity is encouraged through decentralization. At SAS, good ideas come from every division and tend to enhance the organizational vision.

SETTING STRATEGY

By assessing the business climate and remaining constantly aware of the needs of customers, it is possible to develop a business strategy that meets "the customer's needs within the context of the marketplace," and to organize a company to implement that strategy. An examination of the customer's needs and the business climate should be the first order of business, before you devise appropriate goals and strategies. Each company should decide what business it is in from the customer's viewpoint. By determining what service they expect to purchase from you, you will have created a customer orientation that will help you plan an appropriate business strategy.

An example of how determining what customers want can affect your business goals and strategies occurred shortly after Carlzon began working at SAS in 1981. SAS had just accepted the delivery of four Airbuses at a cost of $120 million. These 240-passenger planes were six percent more efficient than the 100-seat DC9s they were to replace. However, no savings could be realized unless the Airbuses were full. The oil crisis, a steady-state market, and the demands of the business traveler led to the inevitable conclusion that the best service to the Scandinavian business traveler would be more frequent, nonstop flights from a variety of cities to the European continent. This could replace the intermediate flights to Copenhagen, and the consolidations to Airbuses for continued, and less frequent, flights to major cities in Europe. As a result, all of the Airbuses were mothballed. Later SAS increased its fleet of DC9s with a new generation of planes.

Frequently, the technological advances of a new fleet of planes—for example, the Boeing 737—did not result in corresponding advances in customer satisfaction. The 737 increased the number of middle seats available on the aircraft despite the fact that few if any airline passengers prefer sitting in the middle of a row of seats. When SAS began planning for its next generation of planes, they began thinking of something they refer to as their Three P plane (Passenger Pleasing Plane), which emphasizes not only technological advances, but also significant improvements in the passenger compartment that would be noticed and appreciated by business travelers.

An important component of any business strategy is recognizing when to say no to ideas that don't meet your overall objectives. At SAS, that meant that ideas helpful to the tourist traveler at the expense of the business traveler had to be rejected. This does not mean that the tourist is ignored. In fact, because of the high percentage of full-fare-paying business travelers, SAS has been able to offer the lowest tourist class fares in Europe, thus increasing overall revenue and, paradoxically, resulting in lower fares for business travelers as well.

FLATTENING THE PYRAMID

The customer-oriented company considers all employees to be managers of their own situation, recognizing that at the "moment of truth" each employee needs "the authority to analyze the situation, determine the appropriate action, and see to it that the action is carried out either alone or with the help of others." As a result, such a company can respond to the customers' needs more quickly and effectively than in the traditional organizational pyramid.

This change in the organization at SAS resulted in one unforeseen problem. The process tended to bypass the middle managers. Confused and frustrated by their loss of power, they became disenchanted and counterproductive. The problem was that they were being asked to play a support role for people who had previously been considered their subordinates. Each promotion had increased the distance between the manager and the customer. Middle managers served the corporation by enforcing regulations, policies, and directives, and by correcting employees who "broke the rules."

The new role of middle managers was to serve their staffs by helping them understand their department's objectives. This required giving them the information and resources required to meet those objectives. Supervisors no longer had the authority to interfere with an employee during a moment of truth. Middle managers learned that they could actually enhance the influence they had in their organization by working *with* their employees to achieve specific results, and then develop their skills by encouraging individual approaches to the achievement of those results. Not only do organizations with flattened pyramids serve their customers better, but they also generate "hidden energy" in employees that results in improved motivation and confidence.

TAKING RISKS

Hierarchical organizations are often run by people who have difficulty making decisions, because no problem is ever fully analyzed. As a result, opportunities frequently pass by them and their organizations. But individual employees and corporations must be willing to take risks. Successful risk takers have courage and conviction, and are willing to act on intuition. Situational analysis, a sound strategy, proper timing, and a desire to move ever forward in the face of uncertainty are critical ingredients for successful leaders and their organizations.

One reason business leaders do not take risks is that they assume that "most things can't be done." Carlzon encourages the elimination of those obstacles with a motto urging employees to "run through walls." While at Vingresor he had assumed that a competing travel firm was earning $20 profit per passenger from selling tour package add-ons like T-shirts and excursions. He challenged his marketing department to match that record. Despite a wide variety of programs and promotions, their profit peaked at $8 per passenger. When checking with the other travel firm to find out what Vingresor was doing wrong, he discovered that he had misinterpreted their original figures and that they had been grossing $20 per head rather than netting that amount. Their competitors' net profit had actually been less than theirs right from the beginning. The misunderstanding, however, had permitted the company to "run through a wall."

In order for frontline employees to be willing to take responsibility for their "moments of truth," they need to feel secure. This security can come from internal and external sources. Internal security can stem from the increased sense of self-worth that accompanies the assumption of greater responsibility. External security is provided by leaders who do not punish employees who take risks. They only use an employee's wrong decision as the basis for guidance and training. This does not mean that an employee has the right to be incompetent, however. Carlzon will not retain managers who do not accept the company's overall strategy, or who are incapable of meeting their objectives.

COMMUNICATING

"A good leader spends more time communicating than doing anything else." Employees need to be informed, persuaded, and inspired. During Carlzon's first year at SAS he spent fifty percent of his time talking with employees. If you want frontline decision makers with discretion to handle individual "moments of truth," you have to be sure your message is understood and absorbed. Be sure the words you choose are straightforward and clear. To Carlzon, "there is no such thing as an 'oversimplified' phrase," and he has stated, "I believe I have successfully conveyed my message if what I said has come across as obvious." Remember that the goal is to persuade and not to show that your knowledge is superior to everybody else's.

Leaders, according to Carlzon, should remember that everything about them has symbolic value. They communicate to employees and customers by their lifestyle and behavior. It should not be surprising that what a leader does is often adopted by others in the company, and that the leader's personality often can be observed throughout the entire organization. Customer-oriented leaders must not, by their actions, suggest that they are superior to their customers, or for that matter, their employees. "Setting a good example is truly the most effective means of communication."

BOARDS AND UNIONS

Successful management teams share the company's overall business strategy with their board of directors. Those managers who are intimidated by their board only share information that will make them look good, and they continually ask their board to approve nearly every decision. Once those decisions are made, they bring them back to the organization and place the full responsibility for the results of their actions on the board. This approach wastes the expertise of the board of directors.

The best way to use a board is to share the firm's business strategy with board members, permitting them to focus on strategic issues rather than small details (which can best be handled in other parts of the company). Carlzon has found it particularly beneficial to keep each of his board chairpersons informed about various business decisions, using them "as a sounding board before approaching the board as a whole."

In 1977, Sweden passed the Co-Determination Act, which "requires companies to provide more information to employees and to consult with the unions on any major changes in the business." Rather than resist the new laws, SAS took full advantage of the change to create an airline council that permitted the labor unions to be involved in strategic planning. Its union adopted three roles:

cooperator, internal auditor, and contract negotiator. In this context, unions can improve corporate success because they have a network of contacts not readily available to management. In the case of both unions and boards of directors, successful relationships are developed most often when involvement with management occurs early and frequently.

MEASURING RESULTS

Service-oriented businesses need to be sure that they are measuring results that are important to their customers. Often, good measurement methods are more important in decentralized companies, because frontline employees have greater responsibility for making the decisions that implement the company's business strategy. Measurements need to focus on the effect of those decisions on customers. When problems are identified, employees should be given the latitude to work on solving the problems in ways they think are best.

REWARDING EMPLOYEES

In December of 1982, every SAS employee received a gold wristwatch, a memo outlining new improved policies concerning free trips for employees, a book entitled *The Fight of the Century,* an invitation to a party, and a letter from Carlzon thanking each of them for the work they had done to turn SAS around.

People, according to Carlzon, need to feel that their contributions are recognized. Praise is important when it is justified, but it will be perceived as insulting when it is clearly unwarranted. Organizations that flatten their pyramids need regularly to "reinforce" the self-worth of individual employees. One reason for this is that many of the former indices of power, such as offices and titles, are less important in the flattened organization. Carlzon believes that empty promotions are less important to an employee than being "awarded well-defined responsibility and trust."

THE SECOND WAVE

By 1984 Carlzon's earlier accomplishments at SAS had made him a prisoner of his success. Significant success having been attained, the sense of working toward common goals was eroding, and employee energy was focusing on more personal objectives. Carlzon's emphasis on a market-oriented company was misunderstood by some employees as an attempt to reduce company concern for safety issues. Other employees began to challenge the entire compensation system. SAS found itself on the defensive. It became clear that new goals were needed to motivate employees. Organizations need to establish long-term as well as short-term goals.

The business strategy developed to meet this challenge first focused on the

95 percent of the things that were working fine at SAS, and second, reaffirmed the "commitment to being the businessman's airline, and the role that each employee had to play to make sure that this objective continued to be primary in the minds of each employee." Employees were also challenged to develop strategies to deal with the potential deregulation of the European airline market. By preparing for deregulation, SAS had once again found an issue to bring the company together. The result was what is now referred to as "The Second Wave" at SAS. Strategies that were proposed included "becoming at least twenty-five percent more efficient; establishment of an improved system of communication, information, and reservations; developing a more competitive system of routes, and improving flight frequency and departure times." The overall goal is that "by 1990 SAS will be the most efficient airline in Europe."

Success at SAS has depended on giving employees real responsibility and authority. At the first (highest) level people establish goals and develop business strategies to reach those goals. The second (middle) level has the responsibility for planning and allocating resources. The third level is at the front line, where "all the specific decisions should be made." At SAS Carlzon has flattened the pyramid and remained true to his goals. His experiences have led him to conclude, "A true leader is one who designs the cathedral and then shares the vision that inspires others to build it."

Reading 3

Service America!

Karl Albrecht and Ron Zemke

Summary prepared by Robert C. Ford

Robert C. Ford is a Professor in the Department of Management at the University of Alabama at Birmingham. Prior to joining UAB, he was a member of the faculty at the University of North Florida. He holds a Ph.D. in management from Arizona State University. In addition to publishing texts on principles of management and organization theory, he has authored or coauthored articles on applied management practices, human resource management, and social responsibility in both practitioner and academic journals. He is an active member of the Academy of Management, the Southern Management Association, and the Society for Human Resource Management.

In 1956, Industrial America became Service America when the workers employed in the service sector of the economy outnumbered those in the industrial area for the first time in history. This trend toward service will continue. It is important, therefore, to understand the challenges of managing in the service sector, how service management differs from industrial management, and what new managerial skills are required. These issues are the focus of Albrecht and Zemke's book, *Service America!*

Defining service is necessary to distinguish those organizations involved in managing services from those in production. However, in reality, every organization has some responsibility for managing service. Even "classic" manufacturing firms like IBM have many employees providing some type of service to the public. It is possible, however, to define three major types of service organizations.

Karl Albrecht and Ron Zemke, *Service America! Doing Business in the New Economy.* Homewood, Ill.: Dow Jones-Irwin, 1985.

SERVICE ORGANIZATIONS AND THE MANAGERIAL CHALLENGE

The first type is the classic "Help Me" service company. These organizations help people do something that they are unable or unwilling to do for themselves. Examples are organizations of tax preparers, bus drivers, real estate salespeople, lawyers, and most of the nonprofit areas of the economy. The second type is the "Fix It" service organization. Examples of this category range from the neighborhood automobile repair shop to repair service sections of a manufacturing organization responsible for ensuring that the product works the way the customer expected.

The third type of service organization is that providing a "Value-Added" service. Of the three types, this is the most difficult one to define. Such organizations provide the intangible extra in the delivery of a product or service that makes a difference between an average commercial transaction and something special. Since this is a value perceived by the customer at the moment the service is received, the responsibility for it falls almost entirely on the frontline person providing the service. Examples would include the computer sales representative who comes back on personal time to show people how to use the new technology, or the bank loan officer who makes the extra effort to treat you like an individual instead of another account number.

These categories of service organization provide today's managers with a major challenge in developing the managerial skills, employee attitudes, and organizational systems that will serve their customers effectively and efficiently. No organization can avoid this challenge if it wishes to stay competitive. This managerial challenge translates directly into the need to develop two new organizational capabilities. One is the ability to build a service orientation through the strategic plan, corporate culture, and vision. The second is the ability to manage systematically the design, development, and delivery of the service.

Developing this second capability is more difficult than the first because it requires the managerial skill of translating the strategic vision of service into work. It means objectively defining the intangible concept of good service. It means spending as much time and management energy on the delivery of the product as is spent on its production. For many organizations, developing these capabilities will mean changing to a very new orientation and a significant shift of managerial focus.

CUSTOMER SERVICE EXAMPLES

Albrecht and Zemke present many examples of how organizations recognized the need to develop a customer orientation and what they have done about putting this important strategic vision of customer service into day-to-day practice. One example is the Scandinavian Airlines System (SAS) which, in 1981, was suffering from a serious economic downturn. A new president, Jan Carlzon, was brought in to turn the airline around. His vision was simple: "Make sure you're selling what the customer wants to buy." On the basis of this, he put in motion a variety of programs, policies, and presentations to remind all employees that every contact with a customer represents a *moment of truth.* SAS needed every employee to recognize the importance of each of the 50,000 moments of truth the company had each day. This management approach led to the creation of the term "service management," and represented the beginning of a major new model of managing uniquely focused on the service sector. In many respects this book was inspired by the teachings of Jan Carlzon, as it organizes and describes what service management is.

THE MANAGEMENT OF SERVICE

Management of service is based on a thorough understanding of the elements of service. The book presents a model that identifies the four components of service and how they relate to each other. Three of the elements are arranged in a triangle (called a *service triangle*) that surrounds the fourth component— The Customer. The three components making up the service triangle are The Service Strategy, The Service System, and The Service People. This model promotes the idea that there are three important characteristics that differentiate outstanding service organizations from the rest.

Service Strategy

Outstanding service firms have a well-conceived *strategy* for focusing the attention of their people toward the real concerns and needs of the customer. This strategy becomes a unifying theme for people throughout the organization, a kind of gospel, and the essence of the message sent to the customer.

The service strategy developed on the basis of a thorough knowledge of the customer is the basis for the action plan an organization develops to deliver to the customer what is wanted in a competitive way. A vision of how the organization believes it can provide service to a customer provides a foundation for a service strategy. The strategy positions the service in the marketplace. Equally important, it sends a strong message to the employees at the front line to let them know what the company believes is important and what level of service quality is expected.

Service System

The second part of the triangle surrounding the customer is the *service system.* The service system logically follows the service strategy to serve the customer. The service system includes all of the physical resources and organizational procedures made available to the service people to help them provide service to the customer. Outstanding firms have customer-friendly systems. The organization designs its physical facilities, policies, procedures, and communication processes to meet consumer needs rather than organizational convenience. Essentially, these systems should be systematically arranged to optimize the customer's contact or experience with the organization. All the organization's systems should deliver what the customer expects and even something more.

Several tools and procedures are available for developing such systems. A simple one is a task analysis chart. A more elaborate approach is a *service blueprint,* developed by Lynn Shostack and presented in a 1984 *Harvard Business Review* article. This blueprint systematically breaks down the entire service delivery into component elements to permit a rigorous analysis of the individual steps, where automation might replace people, where problem areas might arise, and what things make the competition different. In effect, this process creates a level of detailed and rigorous analysis in the service area similar to that found in the production sector.

Service People

The third side of the service triangle represents the *service people,* those who actually deliver the service. Outstanding firms have customer-oriented frontline people. Their leaders have somehow motivated those people who deliver the service to keep focused on the needs of the customer. These frontline people are responsive, attentive, and willing to help, which differentiates the quality of service in the customer's mind.

While many organizations tell their people how important they are, service-oriented managers *reinforce* the message. All too often what a company says and what it rewards are different, and this destroys the service orientation. This is the "last four feet" concept. Even if the customer is well understood, the service strategy perfect, and the service system well executed, the last four feet (distance from employee to customer) is where the service people make the difference. This one moment of truth is where the employee becomes the whole organization to the customer. If the employee doesn't represent the organization well, then all the rest of the effort is wasted. The employee is a vital part of the service management function.

Unfortunately, too often managerial effort takes the form of "brass bands and armbands." Top management creates a big publicity program with all the ribbons and banners, but the employees know this is all smoke. If, on top of this, management sends everyone to training programs to teach them to be nice (smile training), then there is a real problem. Employees know how to be nice and how to smile, and wonder what is wrong with an organization that feels it needs to teach them these things. Instead, those organizations that understand service management provide training focused on developing employee self-esteem, confidence, values, interpersonal skills, stress management, and goal-setting. This training helps people review their personal effectiveness and re-kindles their enthusiasm. People who feel good about themselves are more likely to put creative energy into their jobs.

The critical importance of the frontline people places the selection process high on the list of vital concerns of management. Care must be taken to hire people who can take the pressure of these service roles. Service people need to have an adequate level of maturity and self-esteem. Further, service people need to have adequate social skills and a high level of tolerance for constant social contact. This means that people in the "emotional labor" jobs have to be brought into the firm with the appropriate social skills and emotional stability to deliver the quality service desired.

These three key elements relate to each other, and all relate to the customer. The secret to managing service, then, lies in understanding the component elements, how they relate to one another, and, finally, what management must do to maximize each component.

After developing the components of this four-part model, *Service America!* provides several case examples as illustrations of companies that have paid careful attention to all four elements of the model, successfully developing a service strategy, service systems, and a service orientation in their frontline people to provide quality service to their customers. These illustrations are Deluxe Check Printers in St. Paul, Country Fair Theme park in the Midwest, and British Air in England. Each of these firms was successful in identifying what represented real value to its customers. Each succeeded by developing a simple but focused strategy to allow it to provide that value, establishing the necessary support systems, and getting its people turned on to the vision represented by the strategic plan.

The next to the last chapter, entitled "How to Teach an Elephant to Dance," develops the summary points of this book. On the basis of their observations of highly successful service organizations, the authors report the following nine characteristics.

1. They have a strong, clear, and easily communicated vision of a strategy for service.
2. Their managers visibly do things that show a service commitment.
3. The word "service" is used frequently in organizational communications.
4. They have developed customer-friendly service systems.
5. They balance the use of high technology with high quality personal customer contact.
6. They recruit, hire, train, and reward employees for service.
7. They tell customers of their service commitment as part of their marketing effort.
8. They also tell their own employees of their service commitment as part of their marketing effort.
9. They measure service and tell their frontline people how they are doing through constant feedback.

FIVE STEPS TO SUCCESS

If these are the characteristics, how does an organization achieve this desired state of service orientation? There are five steps to achieving a customer-driven organization.

Step 1—Perform a Service Audit

The organization must develop a thorough understanding of what the customer wants and what he or she thinks about the quality or worth of the service the organization now offers. This involves the systematic collection and analysis of information on the entire process of providing a service and how each point of contact between the firm and the customer is working (or not working). The performance audit allows the identification of where the company is strong and weak in meeting customer needs and expectations.

Step 2—Develop a Strategy

This ideally should occur through a meeting held in a location separate from the day-to-day pressures where involved parties are encouraged to freely express their opinions, be open to new ideas, and have the time to read and reflect on the information discovered in the first step. With the right people, the right atmosphere, and the right problem-solving process, the group can ask and answer the fundamental questions an organization committed to service must address: What is our business? Who is our customer? What does he or she want? How are we going to deliver the service wanted and expected? What specifically do we do next to build on our strengths and eliminate our weaknesses?

Step 3—Preach and Teach the Gospel of Service

If an organization has a culture that is not totally committed to service, then the employees from top to bottom must be informed and trained in this new cultural expectation. Training programs deliver not only a content, but also a message. The program's nature, extent, and materials communicate to all employees that this service orientation is important and must be taken seriously as a corporate value and not just another "be nice and smile but keep the customers moving" program.

Step 4—Release Creativity at the Front Line

The development of quality circle-type group discussions can be an important vehicle for putting the organization's service vision into practice. The people at the point of contact know what happens that customers like and don't like, how they respond to what the company offers, and what good and bad job performance at the front line look like. Bringing this vast pool of knowledge into play through a quality circle can give the people involved a sense of worth, value, importance, and commitment to the organization's service vision. Like any participative management strategy, it allows people to take responsibility for their part of the organization's mission. Since the people represent the moment of truth for nearly all customer points of contact, this step is vital in the development of a service orientation.

Step 5—Keep a Commitment to Service Alive in Organizational Life

Too often, the traditional way of doing something in the organization was developed to make it easy for the organization and not because it was convenient for the customer. Consequently, in many organizations there exists a body of policies, structures, procedures, rituals, work rules, and systems that inhibit enthusiastic, committed, and service-motivated employees from implementing the customer-oriented vision represented by the service strategy. Managers must look closely at what they have created, what they do, and what they reward, to make sure they are keeping everyone's focus on the customer. Further, they need to review constantly what they have created to make sure that everyone and every system stays focused on the customer. Ideally, at some time, attention to these steps, especially the last, will convert the service management program into the corporate way of life.

THREE SERVICE MANAGEMENT MISTAKES

There are mistakes that managers can and do make in implementing service management. The most common is a *short attention span* of top management. Announcing a program, giving a few speeches, and handing out a few awards is not enough. The organization hears what top management says but does not hear what it does not say. If managers do not constantly remind the employees of their commitment to service, the employees will tend to forget and listen, instead, to whatever new is being said.

A second mistake is *misdirected emphasis.* This includes slogans that nobody believes, "brass bands and armbands" that create cynicism instead of commitment by the employees, and "smile training" to teach employees skills and behaviors that the organization should have hired in the first place. Top management sometimes forgets that short-term emphasis on something without continuing evidence of commitment to it is interpreted as "hype" by employees. People who work for organizations are not stupid, and if the organization makes a lot of noise about one vision but rewards something entirely different, they will quickly learn what really is important.

The last mistake is *rigor mortis.* It is terribly easy to over-organize. Creating forms, policies, procedures, and control measures that overregulate can stymie rather than release the creative energy of everyone, especially frontline people, to do their jobs with the desired customer-oriented vision.

SUMMARY

Effective service management is a new and vital issue for the service industry. There is a tremendous need to bring a systematic approach to the rapidly growing service sector equal to that historically seen in the production sector. As services represent an increasingly large part of the gross national product, this need will take on even greater importance. Our future standard of living depends on improving productivity in the service sector through effective service management. Doing this is a massive challenge, and meeting it begins with a systematic development of a service orientation in any organization providing a service. This means, in reality, every organization.

Albrecht and Zemke sum up this whole service management philosophy:

Service management is a top-down, whole-organization approach that starts with the nature of the customer's experience and creates strategies and tactics that maximize the quality of that experience. Service management means turning the whole organization into a customer-driven business entity, which is usually a very tall order (p. 168).

Creating Value for Customers: Designing and Implementing a Total Corporate Strategy

William A. Band

Summary prepared by Susan Rawson Zacur

Susan Rawson Zacur is a Professor of Management in the Robert G. Merrick School of Business at the University of Baltimore where she teaches human resource management and organizational behavior. She received her D.B.A. from the University of Maryland. Dr. Zacur is a management consultant and author, and is active in the Academy of Management.

Contemporary organizations must create value for their customers. Further, they must demonstrate that their value is superior to that of their competitors. Creating value for customers leads to organizational success. To achieve this, organizations must make the transition from the *vision* of being a more customer-driven organization to the reality of continuous customer value improvement. Organizations must adopt a strategy of continually increasing value to customers as their primary focus. With this objective in mind, Band defines the concept of value creation, discusses how to create a value-driven culture, outlines value-creation strategies, and provides suggestions for value-creation improvement.

VALUE CREATION

Value Creation is an essential competitive strategy in today's global economy. It includes all the evolving tools and techniques for quality, service, and customer satisfaction that combine to produce real and perceived customer value.

Portions of this summary appeared in a review for *The Academy of Management Executive*, August, 1991, pp. 99–101, and are used with permission.

In this context, *customer service is a means while value creation is the end.* Value creation integrates the company's functional areas and focuses their efforts toward the common goal of creating and delivering value to customers. Being able to deliver sustainable value to customers profitably means being able to choose and understand the target customer so that the business can offer attractively priced, desired benefits that are, on balance, perceived as superior in value.

The need for value-creation strategic alternatives is supported by research studies that have attempted to quantify the costs of customer dissatisfaction. For example, one study found that sixty-eight percent of customers would change suppliers based upon the indifference of just one employee. Another study reported that the average business never hears from ninety-six percent of its unhappy customers. Of those customers who are unhappy, ninety percent will not buy again. Compounding the problem is the fact that the average customer who has had a problem with an organization tells nine other people about it. Clearly, dissatisfaction is a key issue for the company since lost customers may result from both direct contact with the firm and from "word of mouth" indictment by dissatisfied customers.

Knowing Your Customer and Yourself

In value creation, the definition of the customer is important. The customer is more than just the end user of a product. For the purpose of value creation, the customer is also the distributor, employees, owners, and shareholders. Each of these constituencies will have a perception of value that will be their reality. Organizations must identify who their customers are and let them define what constitutes value. They will clarify what quality factors are important to them if their specific ideas and recommendations are sought. Research suggests that for manufactured items, these factors are likely to be performance, durability, ease of repair, service availability, warranty, ease of use, and price—in that order. Service quality factors include courtesy, promptness, a basic sense that one's needs are being satisfied, and a good attitude on the part of the service provider. Companies that do this kind of research and develop appropriate policies in response to the findings will create streamlined complaint procedures and warranty policies that deliver perceived value. They will work to understand the company's strengths and weaknesses in ability to meet customer desires and then target areas for improvement that will deliver improved value for customers.

CREATING A VALUE-DRIVEN CULTURE

The Vision/Mission Statement

The first step in working toward a customer-value-driven organization is to develop a clear vision (or mission) statement. This will include all of the following: customer satisfaction as the main driving force, impossibly high standards of product and service quality, a long-run profit perspective, cross-functional teams (enabling people from different functional areas to contribute automatically to decision-making), and all employees staying close to the customer. The resulting vision statement must be in harmony with the company's own beliefs and values that influence management behavior. The company must treat its employees (internal customers) as well as it treats its external customers in order for all company representatives to believe in and espouse a customer-value-driven vision.

VALUE CREATION STRATEGIES

Marketing/Measuring Customer Satisfaction

Creating value for customers involves measuring and monitoring value perception. The scope of the traditional marketing research function should be expanded to include an emphasis on understanding the buyer-seller relationship over time with a focus on products as well as the company employees who interact with the customers concerning products. This expanded focus will result in a customer satisfaction research program. Before embarking on such a program, it is useful to define *customer satisfaction,* which is the degree to which customer needs, wants, and expectations are met or exceeded, resulting in repurchase and continuing loyalty. From the company's own working definition of customer satisfaction, various measurement initiatives can be derived. The ingredients for a customer satisfaction research program should include a list of important attributes to measure such as product quality, after-sales support, and aspects of the interaction between employees and customers. Sample research surveys for measuring customer satisfaction should be developed to examine customer needs and wants, previous experience with the company's output, messages received about the company's offering from peers, and advertising initiatives. Data-gathering techniques can range from mail surveys to in-person interviews. The choice of a research method will depend on cost, timing, and the type of data to be collected. *Benchmarking* (understanding what the best of the competition is doing) is a vital part of customer satisfaction research. By comparing their firm with the best of the competition, managers can learn which in-house programs and actions might be developed to close the gap between themselves and the industry leaders.

Managing Customer Relationships

The method of analysis for managing all elements of the customer satisfaction process is *blueprinting*, which means looking at the basic systems and structures of the organization in order to understand better the process of creating satisfied customers. Three frameworks for blueprinting are:

- cycle of service analysis—examining how the customer experiences each point of contact with the organization .
- value-chain analysis—examining each step in the value-adding process,

from production to service maintenance, to uncover opportunities to build customer satisfaction

- story-boarding—examining the hypothetical scenes in which a customer comes in contact with the organization, improving on them, and then building the support processes necessary to make the improved scenes come alive

Once the blueprinting analysis is completed, companies can choose from a host of techniques that range from frequent-patron programs to buyer risk-reduction programs. These eliminate roadblocks and help build lasting customer relationships and trust, based on high product quality and consistent service support.

High-Quality Performance

Managers should strive to achieve high-quality performance by emphasizing compliance with customers' requirements. Corporate or company-wide quality control (CWQC) consists of managerial attention to quality, involvement of all functions and employees, a belief in continuous improvement, and a strong customer focus as the keys to high quality performance. CWQC is achieved through checklists for action, tools for quality control, problem-solving techniques, and quality function deployment (QFD). QFD is a system for designing a product or service based on customer demands and involving all members of the producer or supplier organization.

People as Value Creators

Many firms attempt to treat their external customers with great care and respect. However, they sometimes fail to place the same value on their internal "customers"—their employees. Failure to do so significantly diminishes the success of any customer-value-improvement initiatives, since employees are likely to treat customers the way they are treated by the organization. Organizational audits should be used to monitor employee perceptions on the extent of their organization's customer orientation, understanding of the organization's goals and objectives, quality of intraorganization communication, effectiveness of conflict resolution procedures, and the extent to which employees feel that their ideas are solicited and valued by management. This information should help organization leaders understand corporate culture, plan for their own responsibilities in articulating a customer-focused vision, examine barriers to employee and customer emphasis, and develop strategies for building teamwork as the mechanism for employee commitment to a customer-value-driven mission. In building a customer-oriented work force, management should focus on selecting employees with a customer-oriented attitude and demonstrated ability to work in teams. They should develop job descriptions, training programs, and reward systems to reinforce the importance of a customer focus.

IMPROVING VALUE CREATION

Organization Development

Organization development helps a firm prepare for change by encouraging managers to develop an action plan, implement the plan, and evaluate results. In preparing for and implementing change, managers may take a number of steps to make the vision of excellence a reality. Some of the most important steps are to:

- measure the wants, needs, and expectations of customers
- translate customer requirements into company standards of operation
- develop a value-creation mission statement
- select an appropriate strategy for organization change and commit the necessary resources to the process
- establish a value-creation training program for employees
- change departments, product and/or service features, advertising and marketing strategies, product/service delivery systems as appropriate
- monitor customer feedback regularly
- tell customers to define standards by which they should judge your organization and its offerings in the future
- lock in continuous improvements by creating a recognition system, developing performance measures, and realigning incentive systems and human resource management policies
- track performance in order to ensure gradual, unending improvement over time
- develop a system of effective customer-complaint management
- continuously measure the organization's products, services, and practices against those of the toughest competitors or industry leaders
- create a customer satisfaction index (CSI) to measure the organization's performance against selected product or service attributes that customers judge to be critical to their satisfaction
- assess the effectiveness of the customer-value-improvement process by examining leadership, information and analysis, strategic quality planning, human resource utilization, quality assurance of products and services, and customer satisfaction

These steps help managers instill a value-driven customer focus by unfreezing their organizations, building vision, developing action plans, measuring progress, managing customer complaints, benchmarking, and monitoring organizational performance. Clearly, creating value for customers results in value for the delivering organization, as both internal and external constituencies are considered and accommodated.

Reading 5

Sam Walton: Made in America—My Story

Sam Walton with John Huey

Sam Walton, the guiding architect behind the spectacular success of Wal-Mart Stores and Sam's Club, believed in one basic retailing principle: *give the customers what they want.* This translated into providing wide assortments to choose from, good quality merchandise, low prices, guaranteed satisfaction, friendly, knowledgeable service, convenient hours, and free parking. All of this, asserted Walton, adds up to a pleasant shopping experience, and that will encourage customers to spend more, return again, and tell their neighbors and friends.

Walton searched new store locations from the air, met the competition head on, regularly scouted his competitors for ideas, built stores in smaller market areas, constantly critiqued his own operation, and strove to think and act like a small-town merchant. He worked hard to create a strong corporate culture in each of his stores, while limiting the degree of bureaucracy from the executive suite. The Walton culture stressed listening to customers, communicating with employees, and empowering front-line employees, whom he called "associates." Sam believed in innovation, focusing closely on operating data, controlling inventory shrinkage, praising people when it is deserved, rewarding honesty, and building partnerships with vendors for mutual success. He worked early, late, and hard, and expected the same from his people. And as a pioneer discounter, he discovered that by pricing products lower, the sharply-increased sales volume would boost net profits.

While Walton does not contend that Wal-Mart invented the notion of a strong corporate culture, he worked hard to create one. While people may work hard to achieve important corporate and personal goals, he believed that it is important that they also have fun. He encouraged his managers and associates to do wild things in the store, things that were fun for them and fun for the customer. Walton's venture started out as a partnership with members of his family, and this strong emphasis upon "partnership" spread into the culture of the organization as well. His employees are associates who share in the profits of the store and share in receiving much of the operating data. Walton was convinced that the way management treats its employees strongly influences the way that the employees treat the customers.

Walton summarized his philosophy and practice into 10 Rules for Success. The fundamental guidelines he suggested are:

1. Commit high energy to your business. Work with great passion to make it succeed. Love your work and others will catch a similar spirit.
2. Share profits with associates. Treat them as partners, who can invest in the company. Exercise servant leadership.
3. Motivate associates through goals, competition, job rotation, surprises, and keeping score. Challenge them daily.
4. Communicate with associates, which empowers them to act. Information gives them power, and allows them to care.
5. Demonstrate your appreciation for associates. Praise them sincerely for things they do well.
6. Celebrate success, while having fun and demonstrating your enthusiasm. Look for innovative ways to do this.
7. Listen to employees at all levels, as well as customers. Make ideas bubble up inside the firm.
8. Exceed customer expectations through guaranteed satisfaction. Don't be afraid to apologize for errors or to express appreciation for their business.
9. Control expenses better than your competition. Efficiency allows you to make other mistakes and profit from them.
10. Swim upstream by ignoring conventional wisdom. Find a niche by doing something different.

Walton appeared to agree with the popular Japanese management emphasis on the creation of a team spirit. This sense of teamwork cannot be created in organizations simply through a one-sided, autocratic, management-oriented culture. Good management in the emerging global economy needs to give more responsibility and authority to those who deal with the organization's customers on a day-to-day basis. Good managers, according to Walton, will listen carefully to those on the front line, evaluate, challenge, pool their ideas, and disseminate the successful practices quickly throughout the organization so that others can use them. All of these practices, claims Walton, are embarrassingly simple, amazingly successful, and seldom used.

THIRTEEN

Ethics and Management

Increasingly, reports appear that document unethical activities engaged in by organizations. Simultaneously, the past several years have seen an increase in the number of schools of business that have introduced ethics courses into their curricula. A large number of organizations are discussing ethical behavior, developing codes of conduct or codes of ethics, and making statements about the values of their organizations.

This part of *The Manager's Bookshelf* presents two books that deal with managerial ethics. In *The Power of Ethical Management*, Kenneth Blanchard and Norman Vincent Peale outline three basic questions that guide the exploration of ethical dilemmas that managers may frequently face. They also present the "five Ps of ethical power," which can serve as the core principles leading to ethical behavior. Finally, Blanchard and Peale discuss ethical decision-making, and provide a three-step approach.

R. Edward Freeman and Daniel R. Gilbert, Jr., in their book *Corporate Strategy and the Search for Ethics,* provide a new direction to the search for business ethics. Their book is about the role of values and ethics. According to Freeman and Gilbert, corporate strategy and ethics need to be linked with one another. They believe that excellence in any organization must be based upon ethical reasoning. Their stated purpose is to stimulate thinking about ethics rather than to provide a "cookbook" approach to ethical and unethical corporate behavior.

Reading 1

The Power of Ethical Management

Kenneth Blanchard and Norman Vincent Peale

Summary prepared by Cynthia A. Lengnick-Hall

Cynthia A. Lengnick-Hall is Associate Professor of Strategic Management at Wichita State University. Her articles have appeared in the *Academy of Management Review, Journal of Management, Organizational Studies, Personnel,* and other academic journals. Dr. Lengnick-Hall's current research interests involve examination of the ways in which organizations can gain a distinct competence in innovation without forgoing efficiency, and the strategic management of human resources and technology. She holds a Ph.D. in management policy and strategy from the University of Texas at Austin.

In *The Power of Ethical Management,* the authors use a parable to present an ethical dilemma that has potentially positive competitive outcomes, at least in the short run, but rather reprehensible moral implications in both the short and long run. Both emotional responses and action steps initiated by the protagonist are presented. Several advisors provide contrasting perspectives on his dilemma, illustrating a variety of reference points, personal objectives, and value orientations. The emotional and mental responses to behaviors are separated from potential business outcomes. A contrast is made between not doing something because it is wrong, and not doing something because of a potential for getting caught and, consequently, punished. A basic question is raised: "Is it naive to be ethical in today's complex business world?" The authors' implied response is a resounding NO! Quite the opposite, they argue that in the long run, ethical behavior is likely to lead to competitive, as well as personal, success.

The undercurrent of a protagonist looking for someone to advise him is explored indirectly. Neither authority, nor corporate position, nor training provide sufficiently compelling logic to eliminate a moral dilemma. Moreover, it

Kenneth Blanchard and Norman Vincent Peale, *The Power of Ethical Management.* New York: William Morrow & Company, 1988.

becomes apparent that moral choices are inevitably personal choices that can neither be delegated nor abdicated. In fact, there is actually very little gray area in most moral questions. Further, once a moral issue is considered with sufficient clarity to force a person to choose explicitly a course of action while being fully aware of both direct and indirect consequences, most people *are* able to determine a clear difference between right and wrong. This eliminates an explanation of unethical behavior as acceptable personal differences reflecting an ambiguous and complex set of circumstances. Even highly ethical means can't justify or even mitigate the immorality of unethical ends.

THE ETHICS CHECK

An *ethics check* provides a preliminary tool to aid in the exploration of ethical dilemmas. The ethics check includes three basic questions. First, *is it legal?* This question forces consideration of prevailing external standards of behavior. Specific examples of civil law and company policy are offered. Second, *is it balanced?* This second question triggers consideration of fairness, rationality, and equity. A basic concern is whether the short-term and the long-term consequences of an action are fair to all stakeholders. Highly ethical actions are presumed to promote win-win situations. Many unethical options promote win-lose situations at best, and more frequently result in lose-lose circumstances. The third question in the ethics check is, *how will it make me feel about myself?* This final question focuses on an individual's personal moral code and on his or her emotions. Reactions of pride, self-esteem, and self-worth are seen as the desirable and expected outcomes of ethical actions. Projection to a broader audience of family members, publication in a newspaper, and other avenues for publicity provide a way to evaluate projected emotional responses.

The consideration of all three questions suggests that even if an action is considered acceptable by society's rules, and even though it may be an equitable solution to a problem, it may still be unethical if it violates an individual's personal code of behavior. This third aspect of personal accountability for ethical actions forms the primary theme for the remainder of the book.

Blanchard and Peale argue that the use of the ethics check can become habit-forming. Moreover, managers should recognize that they are not only responsible for ensuring their own ethical behavior, but for providing leadership to their peers and subordinates in resolving ethical dilemmas. It is particularly important to provide leadership by setting a good example. Avoiding direct confrontation of an ethical issue at the least condones unethical behavior, and may even train people to behave unethically, in the worst case. Inaction can be as unethical as active cheating, stealing, or lying if legality, balance, or self-esteem call for an active response but none arises.

Identifying the correct ethical choice is the first step toward ethical behavior. However, *knowing* what is right must be followed by *acting* upon that knowledge if ethical actions are to result. The authors acknowledge that in today's complex world it is unlikely that an ethical choice will receive unanimous support among one's bosses, colleagues, or subordinates. The pressures to act unethically in order to achieve a positive bottom line are examined. Doing what is right is substantially more of a challenge than merely deciding what is right. One benefit of facing ethical challenges is offered: Having freedom of choice and exercising "ethical muscles" in the actions one takes can provide opportunities for moral growth and for developing ethical strength to combat countervailing pressures. Dealing with difficult ethical issues builds character.

One common rationale for avoiding ethical actions is the number or the magnitude of problems an individual must resolve on an ongoing basis. The authors advise that problems should not be viewed as simply negative events to be eliminated as quickly as possible. Rather, problems should be seen as indications that a person is actively engaged in his or her life, and is living fully rather than superficially.

THE FIVE Ps

The "five Ps of ethical power" are advocated as core principles that lead to ethical behavior. These guidelines are also ingredients for a personally successful and highly satisfying life. The first of the five Ps is *purpose*. A sense of purpose is similar to a personal mission, but broader than objectives or goals. Goals or objectives are stopping points along a chosen path of life. Goals are generally tangible—for example, to make money, to gain a promotion, or to have a best-selling novel. Purpose is generally intangible—being trustworthy, or being a responsible citizen. Guilt provides an important test to determine whether or not an individual is true to his or her purpose. If a person is able to sit alone and be deeply introspective without guilt, that individual is behaving in ways that are consistent with his or her life purpose. It is important to take time out from task activities to look into oneself.

The second of the five Ps is *pride*. Pride represents a healthy self-esteem or faith in oneself. This self-confidence is necessary to act upon what one knows is ethical behavior despite various pressures to the contrary. The authors distinguish between self-esteem, false pride, and self-doubt. False pride is self-esteem coupled with excessive egocentricity. False pride often leads to rationalization of behavior and exaggeration of accomplishments. Self-doubt indicates a lack of trust in one's own judgment and a lack of genuine self-liking. People with self-doubt are driven by a desire to be accepted and liked by others. Both false pride and self-doubt can masquerade as arrogance, expediency, or the aggressive forcing of every disagreement into a win-lose situation.

People *learn* self-esteem, implying that false pride or self-doubt can be *unlearned*. Three steps are important in learning self-esteem. First, one should avoid putting negative attributions on one's own behaviors or feelings. Second, one should try to surround oneself with people who are encouraging, and who have self-esteem themselves. Third, one should take an active role in shaping one's own life. Rather than acting like a passive victim, one should take full responsibility for consequences and actively try to change aspects that are undesirable. In the process, it is possible to choose either to feel good and focus on the direction one is trying to follow, or to feel lousy and concentrate on unpleasant aspects of life. An internal locus of control (that is, a belief that one shapes one's own destiny and that events are manageable), coupled with a positive attitude, is essential for self-esteem.

The third principle leading to ethical behavior is *patience.* Patience encompasses both a confidence that events are manageable, and a willingness to wait while an entire process unfolds before passing judgment on a situation. This requires a long-term perspective and a belief in cause-and-effect relationships rather than random events or luck. Faith in a process and faith in one's own judgment are prerequisites for patience. Without patience a person tends to second-guess situations, act erratically, and react to incomplete cues. Patience also includes a willingness to pay a short-term price for a long-term gain.

Persistence is the fourth principle of ethical behavior. Persistence involves a willingness to continue doing what is right, even if the consequences are not what was expected. Persistent ethical behavior can be contrasted with convenient ethical behavior. Persistent ethical behavior is based on commitment, while convenient ethical behavior is based on effort or interest. Persistence implies follow-up and an unwillingness to accept excuses or rationalizations.

The final principle is *perspective.* Perspective provides the integrating element in the five Ps. Perspective comes from concentrating on a non-task-oriented inner self that is thoughtful and reflective. This inner self focuses on meaning and values rather than on accomplishments. Methods for getting in touch with this inner self are personalized and varied to include meditation, prayer, writing, or solitary contemplation. Finding time for reflection requires effective time management and the establishment of appropriate priorities in life. A key to perspective is allowing one's purpose to direct one's life. The five P's are based on the premise that any problem can be solved given time, reflection, and appropriate perspective.

ORGANIZATIONAL BELIEFS VS. PRACTICES

The final section of the book deals with an apparent double standard in many organizations in which there is an articulated belief in fair play and ethical behavior, but where the realities of getting the job done and accomplishing specific goals may overpower these good intentions. Strategies for ethical organizational processes parallel the principles for personal ethical behavior. The pivotal issue is the way in which employees and customers perceive they are being treated by a company and its managers. A firm's purpose and its leadership should be tied to ethical values. Honesty constitutes a primary ingredient. Reliance on attention, appreciation, and praise are important ways to reinforce desirable behaviors. A high level of commitment between employees and managers helps develop trust and integrity in organizations.

Unethical behavior at work may be triggered by negative feelings about an organization. However, organizational pride can counteract negative feelings. This means that people must feel good about what they are doing for the firm and good about themselves as individuals. Building on positive experiences represents a fundamental way to develop both inner strength and organizational pride. The authors suggest that you catch people doing things right and immediately reward them. This idea can be applied upward, downward, and laterally in the organization to change the firm's climate.

This emphasis on positive behaviors should be reflected in a firm's performance-review system. Performance planning, in which specific performance standards and performance objectives are established, forms an essential part of a good performance-review system. Planning should be accompanied by day-to-day coaching in which managers assist employees in accomplishing their goals. Finally, performance evaluation entails a comparison of actual performance with the goals that were set. Most organizations appear to concentrate on the evaluation portion of the system and neglect planning and coaching. As a consequence, employees may feel unnecessarily diminished or unfairly treated. Establishing performance systems with clear goals and measurable standards is one of the best ways to build self-esteem and organizational pride.

Organizational patience is also important. As with individuals, patience involves trusting that the organization's values and processes are right over the long term. This long-term orientation fosters a concern with product quality, customer satisfaction, and the strength of internal and external relationships. The separation of results (such as increased market share) from processes (such as the way a firm treats customers) is emphasized. Patience and faith must be tempered with realism, however. Patience means relying on proven processes, high standards, and ethical values. Patience does not mean waiting for miracles.

The authors link organizational persistence with organizational honesty. Persistence means keeping commitments and holding all employees accountable for their ethical standards and actions. This means that employees must be punished for unethical practices even if their other business-related performance is outstanding. Persistence involves not being willing to compromise on ethical standards.

Perspective means encouraging key organizational members to take the time to reflect on where the organization is, where it is going, and how it plans to get there. In many ways, perspective relates to planning, since planning entails having a specific vision of the future and establishing deliberate activities to achieve that vision. This type of strategic planning should also be coupled with a thorough analysis of current and past performance. Comprehensive analysis accompanied by vision helps keep a firm in balance between planning and implementation.

ETHICAL DECISION MAKING

A three-step approach to decision making is advised. The first step involves information gathering. In this phase, a manager generates as much data about the problem or issue as possible. In the second step, the manager arrives at a consensus regarding the right question to ask. The intent is to frame the problem in such a way that the best possible solution can be developed. In the third step, inward listening, each participant sits quietly for ten minutes and searches for the answer to the right question from within. The authors believe that the results of this procedure are impressive; but even more important are the team-building benefits that improve future communication and problem solving within a group.

What can an individual do if the organizational culture and one's personal ethical standards are inconsistent? There are three courses of action available. The person can choose to *leave the organization* and either undertake an entrepreneurial venture or join a firm with more compatible values. As an alternative, a person can stay with a firm, but *mentally isolate* himself or herself from organizational actions that conflict with a personal sense of right and wrong. This second alternative is both lonely and often very uncomfortable. A third option is to stay in the organization and try to *change the firm's ethical climate.* While this latter alternative is often difficult, it is consistent with setting a good example and with the principles of ethical power discussed earlier. If an individual is committed to high ethical standards for personal actions, often the choice will be among win-win options. In this way, the practice of ethical behavior can lead to personal success as well as high levels of organizational performance if *all* employees behave ethically.

Reading 2

Corporate Strategy and the Search for Ethics

R. Edward Freeman and
Daniel R. Gilbert, Jr.

Summary prepared by Sara A. Morris

Sara A. Morris received her Ph.D. in business policy and strategy from the University of Texas at Austin. Now an Assistant Professor of Management at Old Dominion University in Norfolk, Virginia, her current research is in the use of unethical techniques for obtaining competitor information and in the factors that affect people's attitudes about corporate social responsibility.

Since the publication of *In Search of Excellence,* management thinkers and practitioners have begun to focus on values as a way of understanding corporate strategy. This book explains the role of values and ethics. Freeman and Gilbert argue that the search for excellence really involves a search for ethics. The bases for good strategy are ethical reasoning and a striving for excellence.

The authors provide a word of caution to readers. The purpose of this book is to offer food for thought; the authors express a point of view, but not in cookbook fashion. They present a series of arguments, and ask the reader's patience in following the logic.

PART 1 ETHICS AND STRATEGY: THE REAL REVOLUTION

Part 1 describes how ethics relates to strategy. It answers the critics who claim that moral standards cannot be applied to business, introduces the language and tools of ethics, and proposes the concept of enterprise strategy as a way for managers to link ethics and strategy.

R. E. Freeman and D. R. Gilbert, Jr., *Corporate Strategy and the Search for Ethics,* Englewood Cliffs, N. J.: Prentice-Hall, 1988.

The Revolution in Management

In recent years the American corporation has come under attack on the grounds that large corporations are too powerful, that U.S. business has lost its ability to compete in the global market, and that today's organizations are too impersonal. Strategic managers and planners, once revered, are now scorned. They have tunnel vision, focusing on the grand plan rather than on operations and people, the critics claim. These criticisms are only partly valid. The fallacy in the criticisms is the same as that of most theories and models of corporate strategy: failure to see the intimate connection between ethics and strategy.

The fundamental ethical questions are: "What is a good life?" ("What values are worth pursuing?") and "How should we conduct ourselves to promote a good life for all?" All strategic decisions involve ethics, because they benefit some people while harming others. The growing acceptance of this basic truth is causing a revolution in management. Executives can no longer afford to pretend that strategy can be divorced from ethics.

In order to manage ethically, we must understand values. Two principles and two assumptions are fundamental:

> The Values Principle—People and organizations act as they do in large part because of their values.

> The Interdependence Principle—The firm's stakeholders (groups of people who have a stake in the organization) can affect the firm's success.

> First Axiom of Corporate Strategy—Strategy makers need an understanding of the values of stakeholders.

> Second Axiom of Corporate Strategy—Strategy makers need an understanding of the ethical nature of strategic choice.

From these principles and axioms it is probable that, because they hold different values, stakeholders (as individuals and groups) want to achieve different objectives through their association with the organization. Since stakeholders can affect the firm's success, their values are important for developing a corporate strategy. Ethical problems emerge when sets of values conflict. Since organizations have multiple stakeholders who have competing values claims, managers must decide whose values get priority. Strategy makers must figure out who really counts—owners, managers, employees, customers, regulators, or some other group.

The conventional notion of corporate strategy has been limited to a statement of company mission, objectives, strategy or plan, and the control-feedback loop. The principles and axioms above imply that strategy making is all about the *purposes* of individuals and groups rather than about a company mission statement, quantitative objectives, and the like. Purposes have certain characteristics that make them very unlike our conventional view of strategy. Even though purposes require cooperation from others, a purpose is personal, not corporate. Individuals pursue their purposes through bargaining with others, and ethics provides a framework for such bargaining.

Before the revolution in management can flourish, managers must (1) dispense with the idea that the term "business ethics" is an oxymoron, (2) reject the old excuse that there can be no moral standards applied to business because everything is relative, and (3) become more comfortable with ethical language.

Relativism: "When in Rome . . ."

One real challenge to business ethics is the doctrine of *moral relativism*. According to this theory, we cannot decide in any rational way what is moral, because morality is relative. The kernel of truth in relativism makes it a seductive excuse for managers to ignore the ethical implications of their decisions.

There are several types of moral relativism. If people take the position that padding the expense account is wrong for themselves, but may be understandable for a colleague, depending on the situation, they are engaging in *naive relativism*. According to naive relativism, ethical decisions are so personal, important, and complex that only the decision maker can judge the morality of his or her actions.

Ethics is a conscientious attempt to make sense of life; through the use of reason, people try to define a good life and to determine rules by which everyone can live. Naive relativism shuts down ethical inquiry. Constructive moral argument is impossible with naive relativism, as there can be no answers except individual answers. We need thoughtful moral debate, however. Through scrutiny and criticism we will learn how to make better moral choices.

When people have one set of ethical standards for business decisions and another set for personal decisions, they are practicing *role relativism*. According to role relativism, they are required to put aside personal beliefs and carry out the moral obligations of the roles they occupy. People often use role relativism to justify questionable business actions that they would find unacceptable in personal life. Role relativism leads to the excuse, "I was only doing my job." This presumes that people have no choice in the roles they accept.

People who engage in shady business practices on the grounds that they compete in a cutthroat industry, where "everybody does it," are applying *social group relativism*. This form of relativism, defining morality as accepted practice, is especially prevalent in business. With social group relativism there are no moral leaders, and no one to question accepted practice, but only followers.

A fourth type of relativism is *cultural relativism,* which states that morality is relative to a given culture or society. According to this theory, no one can judge the morality of South Africa, for example; rather, our job would be to understand the moral codes and customs of that society. The business rule is: "When in Rome, do as the Romans do." This would mean discriminating against blacks when doing business in South Africa and discriminating against women in Arab countries. What happens when a society has multiple cultures that clash? Cultural relativism offers no way to deal with this problem.

There is a kernal of good in moral relativism: the tolerance of diversity. Such tolerance is a blessing and a curse, however. The danger is that relativism allows tolerance in the extreme. Moral reasoning is hard work, and relativism gives us an easy way out: Accept all behaviors, regardless of how they affect other people; don't worry about it; assume that the decision maker did what was right for him or her.

Ethical Language and Tools

If business ethics is to be improved, managers must improve their ethical reasoning ability. A good beginning is to learn the language and tools of ethics. *Ethics* can be defined as the inquiry into how decisions affect other people. Ethical decision making requires us to answer questions like:

Who precisely is affected by this decision?

How is each person affected? What are each person's interests and how would this decision harm or benefit those interests?

Who has rights that would be affected here?

What is the decision rule? (The rule might be, "maximize stockholders' wealth," or "keep our largest customer happy," for example.)

Key terms in ethical reasoning are values, rights, duties, and moral rules. A person's *values* are relatively permanent and intrinsically worthwhile; they provide the reason people act as they do. As such, values represent that which people desire. *Rights* are entitlements that give a person the freedom to take a particular action. Rights, like values, are conditional, however. One person cannot ethically interfere with another's rights. Moreover, duties accompany rights. A *duty* is an obligation to do something specific.

Moral rules are guidelines for behavior in situations where competing interests are in conflict. Moral rules prescribe a certain action, generalizable to many situations, if certain conditions exist. Moral rules produce a good or just allocation of benefits, harms, and rights among the parties to a decision. Suppose a competitor of yours has a new technology not yet understood by your firm's R&D staff. Should you hire one of the competitor's scientists to obtain access to the new technology? A moral rule here might be something like:

We should not interfere with another firm's employer-employee relationship, unless all parties agree.

The term *common morality* is used to describe the set of rules that govern everyday ethical situations. Some of the principles of common morality are:

- Promise keeping—Do what you say you will do.
- Nonmalevolence—Do not inflict physical harm to others.
- Mutual aid—Help others in need (if the cost to you is not too great).
- Respect for persons—Treat others as ends in and of themselves, not merely as the means to your own ends.
- Respect for property—Do not use the property of others unless you first obtain their consent.

One noteworthy aspect of common morality is that these rules are conditional. People are expected to follow them most of the time, but there may be exceptional circumstances that would cause an ethical person to break one of the rules. For example, it is ethical for the police to use physical force to subdue criminals.

Society needs to develop a common morality of business. Becoming more familiar and comfortable with ethical terminology is a good starting point.

Enterprise Strategies

The fundamental strategic questions, according to business writers and thinkers of the last twenty years, are: "Where are we going?" or "What business are we in?" and "What business do we want to be in?" If the goal is to connect ethics and strategy, the question should be restated as "What do we stand for?" This new question forces the marriage of values and strategy; in order to answer the question, one must identify exactly what is meant by "we," thereby identifying whose interests the company really serves. Answers to "What do we stand for?" might be excellent customer service, happy employees, or stockholder wealth.

Enterprise strategy, or E-strategy, represents the integration of ethical thinking and strategic thinking. A company's enterprise strategy reveals what the company stands for. Originally conceptualized by Peter Drucker, E-strategy embodies the firm's fundamental reason for being in business. There are at least seven types of enterprise strategies, and each identifies "who holds the trump cards around here." The most common types of E-strategy are:

- *Stockholder E-strategy*
  Company goal: Maximize the interests of stockholders. This strategy is the cornerstone of U.S. business. While commonly espoused, the stockholder E-strategy is seldom practiced. If a company were really stockholder-oriented, managers would be ever vigilant to locate bids for the company that would give stockholders a premium, even if this required the sacrifice of managerial positions.
- *Managerial Prerogative E-Strategy*
  Company goal: Maximize the interests of managers. In a company with this E-strategy, managers would always be trying to figure out what they had to do in order to keep stockholders and other stakeholders satisfied. They would not so much care about the interests of these groups, but would attend to them so that they could continue to use the company to pursue their own objectives.
- *Restricted Stakeholder E-Strategy*
  Company goal: Maximize the interests of a few kinds of stakeholders simultaneously. A common example, portrayed by Tom Peters in his "Excellence" books, is to maximize the interests of customers, employees, and stockholders. These groups become the preferred stakeholders, and other types of stakeholders are treated as second class. A practical

problem with this E-strategy is the inevitable conflicts of interests that will arise.

- *Unrestricted Stakeholder E-strategy*
  Company goal: Maximize the interests of all stakeholders. Managers that adopt this E-strategy, attempting to serve all of the people who have a stake in the firm, often see themselves as advancing the public interest. Some have argued that this E-strategy actually serves to maximize the interests of stockholders. Nevertheless, it takes a wise manager to be able to prioritize and resolve all the conflicting interests here.

- *Personal Projects E-Strategy*
  Company goal: Enable the individual members of the firm to carry out their personal projects. This is the preferred E-strategy from the authors' point of view. The remainder of the book is a justification for the Personal Projects E-Strategy. The basic assumption here is that individual goals are important, not as just means to someone else's ends, and definitely not mere instruments for accomplishing corporate ends. The authors see the corporation as a vehicle for the accomplishment of individual purposes. This is the opposite of how we typically view organizations, as if organization members should subordinate their own goals for the sake of some allegedly more important corporate goals. If managers valued the worth of the individual and personal autonomy, personal projects would guide what organizations do.

The process of deciding on an enterprise strategy is no easy one. It requires a great deal of careful thought and discussion. Stakeholders must be consulted; purposes and values must be identified and incorporated. The reward is *knowing what we stand for.*

PART 2 HOW NOT TO CONNECT ETHICS AND STRATEGY

Part 2 addresses several streams of current literature on strategy and identifies their inadequacies for integrating ethics and strategy.

Corporate Social Responsibility

The term *corporate social responsibility* refers to the idea that business has social as well as economic obligations. This notion has sparked considerable debate over the last twenty-five years. Operationalizing just what those social obligations are has proved to be especially difficult. For example, given limited resources, how could a firm best carry out its social responsibility: by installing additional safety features on the assembly line, lowering prices to customers, or making a charitable contribution?

Frustrated in their attempts to define corporate social responsibility, scholars and managers have more or less abandoned the debate and turned their attention to another concept, *corporate social responsiveness.* This newer approach requires firms to try to anticipate and respond to the demands of society.

Whereas corporate social responsibility calls for companies to be good all-around corporate citizens, corporate social responsiveness requires them to respond to social changes. Neither model requires decision makers to engage in ethical analysis or to understand the role of individuals' values. *Responsiveness* means that corporate decision makers, rather than basing strategies on their own moral principles, merely respond to others. Unfortunately, the objective is to respond adequately to those who can affect you, not because you have an obligation to them, but because they can cause you potential harm.

Strategic Management Models

Strategic management theories have enjoyed widespread popularity in recent years. Examples are portfolio models of corporate strategy and Michael Porter's model of competitive strategy. Portfolio models, like the Boston Consulting Group's (BCG) approach, with its cash cows, stars, dogs, and problem children, apply to diversified firms, where the CEO must decide what combination of businesses to operate, and how to allocate resources among those diverse businesses. Porter's model seeks to answer the question of how to compete in a given industry.

We can judge these models against common morality and against the implicit morality of the market. The implicit morality of the market is the set of rules that firms must follow if we are to have a free enterprise system. The free enterprise system requires managers to strive for perfect competition. The necessary rules include:

- Perfect information—See to it that all parties have perfect information.
- Consultation—Consult stockholders about decisions that significantly affect people.
- Consumer sovereignty—Respond to consumer preferences; do not seek to create consumer demand.
- Price competition—Compete solely on the basis of price, not on unique features.
- Mutual unconcern—Ignore what competitors are doing and focus on the market itself. Do not try to alter the market's allocation of goods and services.
- No externalities—As a seller, make sure that all of the costs and benefits of your product go to the buyer, not to a third party.
- Free entry—Welcome new competitors into the market.

These rules demonstrate that because the price mechanism is expected to resolve all conflicts, and because personal values are ignored, the implicit morality of the market contradicts common morality. Moreover, we can show that strategic management theories violate both the implicit morality of the market and common morality. For example, contrary to common morality, strategic management models tend to treat employees as the means to an end rather than as individuals. Disregarding the implicit morality of the market, the BCG model encourages firms to attain a dominant market share, and Porter's model encourages firms to develop a distinctive competence to protect themselves against competitors. Both approaches eschew consumer sovereignty, mutual unconcern, and free entry. Porter teaches managers how to use information as a resource, rather than nurturing the free flow of information. In an overt attempt to circumvent perfect competition, Porter also describes a differentiation strategy, which enables firms to profit from market segmentation, artificially created consumer demand, premium prices, and the resulting barrier to entry.

Strategic Planning and the Strategy Process

Before strategic management came into vogue, strategic planning and process models described how top executives should engage in strategy formulation and implementation. Strategy formulation entails determining the company purpose and objectives as well as the strategy that will be used to achieve these. Strategy implementation refers to the execution and evaluation of the strategy, with special emphasis on how to get workers committed to carrying out the particular strategy.

Strategic planning is supposed to be a rational, almost mechanical, exercise that produces a predictable result. The fact that *people* populate organizations creates major problems for strategy formulation and implementation. Strategic planning models are based on the following rationale. Top management is responsible for the decision-making process in the organization. The process of organizational decision-making can be structured in such a way that the people in the organization will conform to the desired strategy. The structure should be designed to overcome human limitations (like limited information-processing ability) and to minimize conflicts between personal values and the desired organizational values.

More than corporate social responsibility and strategic management models, strategic planning and process models fail to integrate ethics and strategy. The premises and hypotheses that underlie the planning/process models can be contrasted to the Values Principle. According to the planning/process models, we can substitute organizational structures for individual values as the reason why people act as they do. The values of top management are important, but the values of other organization members are not taken seriously. The decision-making process is to be structured in such a way as to suppress individuals' values. Planning/process models seek to avoid value conflicts and the careful thinking and bargaining that would be required to resolve them.

PART 3 THE SEARCH FOR ETHICS

Part 3 presents the Personal Projects E-Strategy as the authors' solution to how to connect ethics and strategy. Parts 1 and 2 provided a justification for this solution.

The Personal Projects Enterprise Strategy

The Personal Projects E-Strategy, originally outlined in Part 1, is based on personal autonomy and individual rights. As an ideal toward which to strive, this E-strategy can be defended in terms of several moral principles:

- *The principle of personal autonomy*—Individuals have the right to pursue their own projects, unless they violate the rights of others in doing so.
- *The principle of respect for persons*—Individuals have a duty to treat others as ends in and of themselves, not merely as the means to someone else's ends.
- *The principle of voluntary agreements*—Individuals have the right to enter into voluntary agreements with others as they mutually pursue personal projects.
- *The principle of human institutions*—Human institutions, like corporations, exist as vehicles for the accomplishment of the personal projects of institutional members.
- *The principle of corporate membership*—Corporate members (that is, stakeholders such as employees, managers, suppliers, customers, stockholders, and community representatives) have the right to participate in "corporate" decisions that will significantly affect their personal projects.

The authors hope these principles will fuel a continuing debate on business ethics. The principles, and the Personal Projects E-Strategy they support, represent a radical departure from the traditional view of the corporation (where the firm is seen as an end in itself). According to the Personal Projects E-Strategy, in order to pursue their individual projects, persons enter into cooperative agreements with others, and the corporation is merely a collection of voluntary agreements among consenting adults.

Moreover, acceptance of the Personal Projects E-Strategy would make some common notions of management and corporate strategy obsolete. For example, motivation and leadership are irrelevant to such a firm. If individuals voluntarily band together to pursue their own personal projects, they are self-motivated and self-led. They need not be coerced, tricked, inspired, or cajoled into working. The conventional views of strategy formulation and implementation are similarly useless. Under a Personal Projects E-Strategy approach, strategy is not formulated by a small, tight group of senior managers. There are no implementation problems like "creating the right organizational culture to obtain employee commitment to the firm's strategy." Individuals are naturally committed to the accomplishment of their own personal projects.

In conclusion, this book provides a new direction in the search for business ethics. Although the proposed solution can be criticized as impractical, the authors believe that the subject is of utmost importance, and they note that the book is intended as a sketch rather than a finished drawing.

FOURTEEN

Global Dimensions

There are many lessons to be learned by those who manage organizations, as well as by those who legislate the rules that get played in the economic game. The dynamics generated by organizations doing business in the global arena are leading toward the creation of a borderless world.

Several contemporary books focus our attention on global issues that are or should be of managerial interest. In this chapter two books are summarized that address global aspects of organization and management.

William Ouchi, a Professor at the University of California at Los Angeles, shocked the managerial community in the early 1980s with his contention that American businesses have a lot to learn from Japanese corporations. His *Theory Z* book suggests that U. S. firms should create and follow a corporate philosophy that builds upon trust, understanding of personalities, and intimacy at work. Theory Z firms (such as Hewlett-Packard, Dayton-Hudson, Rockwell, Intel, and Eli Lilly) demonstrate their commitment to these values and the employees through vehicles such as quality control (QC) circles.

Kenichi Ohmae attempts to challenge some of the ways that managers have historically viewed the world and the way that business has been conducted. Performance standards are being created by those who buy products in the global marketplace; these standards are no longer being created by those who manufacture or those who regulate the manufacturers. As a consequence, organizations need to adjust their structures so that they are focused on customers, and operate as "insiders" in countries around the globe as opposed to operating as exporters to these countries. Ohmae provides us with insight into how a change in management practices might meet the challenge of the borderless world.

Kenichi Ohmae, the Managing Director of McKinsey and Company, an international consulting firm, has a lesson for managers and governments doing business in the emerging global economy. In his book, *The Borderless World,* Ohmae discusses how companies can win in the new global marketplace.

Theory Z: How American Business Can Meet the Japanese Challenge

William G. Ouchi

Summary prepared by Michael Bisesi

Michael Bisesi is Associate Dean of the College of Business Administration at the University of Houston. He teaches the "Business and Society" course and has research interests involving the business-government-education relationship. His articles have appeared in such journals as *Sloan Management Review, Journal of Policy Analysis and Management,* and the *British Journal of Educational Studies.*

What business phenomenon will be recalled as the hallmark of the 1980s? Some will argue that the "Reagan Revolution," with its emphasis on getting government "off the backs" of business, will be most significant. Others will suggest that past government intervention, such as the Chrysler bailout, will be most memorable. What about mergers and acquisitions, "greenmail," "golden parachutes," and other aspects of what Robert Reich calls "paper entrepreneurialism"? What about trade imbalances, Third World debt, or the deregulation of London's financial markets?

While all of these are important, the most enduring revelation of all is that *Japan is much more interested in effective management than America.* While Americans may have written the dominant management textbooks, the Japanese have actually read them. And while we may have started the trend toward the establishment of global markets, the Japanese have actually mastered them.

The unfair advantages that foreign countries enjoy were the topic of many business conversations in the 1980s. Japan, some said, has a central planning authority in MITI (the Ministry of International Trade and Industry) and thus benefits from government assistance. (These same individuals usually oppose

William Ouchi, *Theory Z: How American Business Can Meet the Japanese Challenge.* Reading, MA.: Addison-Wesley, 1981.

government involvement in the American economy, of course.) Japan, said others, is a homogeneous culture, and what they have will not work here. (These same individuals usually ignore the adaptation of our American practices in Japan and the success of Japanese-managed American plants.)

In *Theory Z*, William Ouchi tells us not about the obvious economic challenge from Japan, but about a more difficult challenge: *refocusing the corporate culture from technology to people.* Ouchi argues that productivity gains are the direct result of an involved work force; that coordinating and organizing people is the most important task of management; and that productivity is a matter of sound social organization.

Just as a nation and a people have a culture, so does an organization. Ouchi's theme is that American organizations can draw on the success of the Japanese without imitating them. Further, there are specific principles of organization that have nothing to do with national cultures and have everything to do with organizational cultures.

More precisely, American managers will have to act in ways that many find publicly uncomfortable. *Trust* is necessary, for both employees and managers. *Subtlety of personalities,* or understanding who works well with whom, must be acknowledged, regardless of bureaucratic rules. *Intimacy* (in the sense of personal concern), an essential ingredient in any healthy society, must become more commonplace at work.

Old plants and equipment are not the cause of the American Problem, Ouchi claims. The cause seems to be how American organizations treat their people. Americans who work for Japanese companies continually marvel at their emphasis on competence, quality, and personal interest. In fact, the contrasts in operating philosophies between Japanese and American organizations are quite revealing.

CHARACTERISTICS OF JAPANESE ORGANIZATIONS

If one characteristic stands out above all others, it is that many Japanese companies are distinguished by their policies of lifetime employment. Companies tend to hire only once a year, usually promote from within, and generally retain employees until the mandatory retirement age of fifty-five years.

Evaluation and promotion of employees is another distinctive feature of Japanese businesses. Two new employees simultaneously entering a typical Japanese firm would receive the same pay raises and promotions for the first *ten years* of their employment. Differentiation would only begin after that point, regardless of prior performance levels. The advantages of such an approach seem to be a reduction of game-playing for short-term gain and a general reduction of colleague competition and backstabbing.

Career development is another interest of Japanese firms. Typical career paths promote the learning of many functions rather than one function. The personnel officer is more important than the financial officer. This emphasis on "people management" builds organizational loyalty instead of a narrowly functional perspective.

Shared experiences and common frames of reference enhance the ability of Japanese employees to communicate effectively. Since overall company philosophies and objectives are already accepted, decision making becomes a participative and collective activity. Discussion is focused on how to reach the goal, and the view is long-term. Responsibility is taken by a team or a group rather than by a single individual.

Finally, there is a holistic concern for people that molds business and social life together. In general, while there may be some variance, all organizations in Japan exhibit the above characteristics to some degree.

THE AMERICAN CONTRAST

American organizations are characterized by comparatively short-term employment. Rapid turnover requires quick evaluation and promotion, with considerable employee unrest if a promotion takes more than three years. Because of the competition for promotions and raises, people tend to work alone rather than collaboratively. Career paths tend to be highly specialized. Standardization is the main method of control, and integration and coordination are almost impossible because of the emphasis on specialization. Decision making and responsibility are individual matters. The organizational concerns tend to be segmented and impersonal rather than holistic.

THE "THEORY Z" ORGANIZATION

Can Japanese management practices work in American business? Ouchi argues that "Theory Z" may be the answer.

A Theory Z organization is one that has a policy of long-term employment, accompanied by an investment in training and a policy of slow evaluation and promotion. It plans career development *across* functional areas. Quantitative analysis *informs* decisions rather than *controlling* them. "Theory Z" organizations are *not* culturally restricted to Japan, as evidenced by successful adaptations in such American corporations as Hewlett-Packard, Dayton-Hudson, Rockwell International, Intel, and Eli Lilly.

A company has to decide to adopt such a style. Value is more than an advertising slogan, because profits will only come to those maintaining high value in products and services and high value in how employees are treated. In fact, the presence of lifetime employment and general trust facilitates the Theory Z organizations. And what is "lost" in terms of professional specialization is gained in terms of group membership.

MAKING "THEORY Z" WORK

Ouchi contends that organizations, like marriages, must be built and maintained. For those who want to implement a Theory Z organization. Ouchi provides a step-by-step guide (*not* a cookbook). The process itself will take patience and time (at least two years). Theory Z must be compared to the current organizational philosophy. The desired philosophy must be defined with the active involvement and support of the top executive. Both organizational structures and motivational incentives will be involved. Interpersonal skills will require more complete development, emphasizing listening and participative decision making, and paying equal attention to the process as well as the content of communication. Questionnaires or other testing devices must be used. Workers (union or otherwise) must be involved, since people support that which they help to create. A system for slow evaluation and promotion must be decided upon, which will really be best for the long-run perspective of the organization. The development of career paths must be broadened, which should enhance employee enthusiasm, effectiveness, and satisfaction. The process must start from the top, and must be organizationally holistic. Such change is gradual, and instant results cannot be expected.

WHY COMPANY PHILOSOPHY IS CRITICAL

None of the above can happen without an awareness and acceptance of organizational values, goals, and philosophy. Moreover, if the stated philosophy is not implemented, the whole exercise becomes meaningless. An organization can use many methods to ensure implementation, ranging from survey-feedback measures to operating procedures. Moreover, there must be a willingness to accept non-quantitative objectives.

A "Theory Z" corporate culture is one based on a tradition and climate in which the commitment to people is the most important organizational philosophy. This commitment is based on trust and teamwork. Ouchi concludes that American organizations will survive, learn from, and prosper from the Japanese challenge if they balance corporate goals with the needs of individual employees.

CASE HISTORIES OF SUCCESSFUL Z COMPANIES

Two appendices add a valuable dimension to this book. Appendix One lists the Company Z philosophies of the five Fortune 500 organizations mentioned above. In each of these firms, the emphasis was on deliberate and gradual change to a new culture.

Hewlett-Packard selects and develops people in a conscious fashion. It recognizes that intelligent ideas can be found at all levels of the organization, and that people need to have latitude in reaching objectives. While profit is the first objective, a customer-oriented approach that has teams of people working on organization-wide problems is one of its distinguishing characteristics. Most important are its people-related objectives: performance-based job security, fostering of initiative and creativity, and recognition of its corporate citizenship responsibilities.

Dayton-Hudson, the diversified retailing firm, has high values for its people and for its products. It is concerned with honesty, integrity, and responsiveness in its retail operations. It is concerned with enhancing the personal and professional development of its employees. While striving to provide shareholders with "an attractive financial return," it also wants "to serve the communities in which we operate."

Rockwell International established a "culture profile" of itself, examining where it was in the mid-1970s, what it has accomplished, where it is now, and what its future direction might be. It assessed itself in a variety of important dimensions, including such Z issues as short- versus long-term environment, organization communication, information sharing, individual orientation, and job security. In all cases, the company decided it should move toward Z attributes.

Intel ties individual and corporate success together. While people are individuals, they are also part of a team. Managers "must be capable of recognizing and accepting their mistakes and to learn from them." Management also is committed to open communication, ethical decisions, employee development, long-term commitments, and teamwork.

Eli Lilly Co. is concerned with fairness, responsibility to the employee, and responsibility to the community.

THE Q-C CIRCLE

Appendix Two is a discussion of the Q-C (quality-control) circle. The Q-C circle is a management-employee group effort for finding and solving production and coordination problems. This form of high worker involvement results in some fifty to sixty implemented suggestions per worker per year in Japan!

A typical Q-C circle has from two to ten employees. All workers are encouraged to become involved in these groups, with the goal of studying any problem that involves the group's work. Whether the issue is product quality, production time, or other related issues, the people closest to the problem—the workers—systematically study it and make recommendations. American firms should accept the fact that "a firm can realize the full potential of its employees only if it both invests in their training and then shares with them the power to influence decisions."

CONCLUSION

Ouchi effectively refutes those arguments that suggest that a Theory Z approach is culture-bound to Japan tradition. *Theory Z* provides a rich resource of information and illustrations for those who want to do further study on the subject of Japanese management and its adaptation to American firms. For many American managers, the Japanese challenge is one that will require substantial reexamination and reorientation of some comfortable ways of thinking.

Reading 2

The Borderless World

Kenichi Ohmae

Summary prepared by Robert Wharton

Robert Wharton is an Assistant Professor of Management Studies at the University of Minnesota, Duluth, where he teaches courses in strategic management and business and society. He received his Ph.D. from Rutgers University and is a member of several professional associations, including the Academy of Management.

"An isle is emerging that is bigger than a continent—the Interlinked Economy (ILE) of the Triad (the United States, Europe, and Japan)" (p. xi). Joined by aggressive economies in Taiwan, Hong Kong, and Singapore, the ILE has grown so powerful that it is destroying the old national borders that once defined consumer groups and corporate identities.

The emergence of the ILE has resulted in a great deal of confusion, both for managers and for economic policy makers. Old theories that compared one nation against others simply do not work anymore. When the economy grows stronger, jobs are created abroad and not at home, disappointing the experts. If the government raises interest rates to control inflation, cheaper money rushes in from other countries in the ILE. Statistics on the balance of trade become meaningless when corporations spread their production and distribution functions throughout the ILE. Any managers or politicians who do not understand this new reality risk isolating their companies, or their citizens, from the dynamic economy of the borderless world.

The Borderless World is organized into three parts. First, the strategy and organization of companies operating in the new international environment are discussed. Second, government bureaucrats who are causing great problems for their citizens are attacked, even as these officials are becoming powerless and irrelevant. Finally, Ohmae's vision of the economic world into which we are moving is presented.

STRATEGIES FOR INTERNATIONAL COMPANIES

An Inside-Out View of Macroeconomics

In a borderless world, strategic managers need to understand, and master, five concerns in order to operate effectively in an interlinked economy. Striking the correct balance among these *five Cs* is essential to any successful business.

Customers Managers must understand the growing power of consumers around the globe. Customers throughout the Triad have few national allegiances; they are only interested in buying the products that offer them value— the best quality at the best price. Lack of allegiances gives consumers their power, and as news of product performance becomes harder to suppress, consumer power grows greater still. The critical objective for a company, therefore, is to find new ways to create new value for its customers.

Competition Products on the market today require so many different technologies, and the technologies change so rapidly, that no company can maintain a lead in all of them. Fifty years ago, General Motors could keep in house all the technology involved in building a car. But today, consider what has made the IBM Personal Computer such a success. Lotus, along with many other companies, wrote the application software for an operating system designed by Microsoft. Microsoft wrote the operating system for a microprocessor designed by Intel. Today, no single company can simultaneously master all of the technologies essential to making a product successful. And because companies are forced to cooperate, no technology stays secret for long. Therefore, operating globally means finding partners, some of whom may also be competitors.

Company A fundamental change has taken place in business over the last ten or fifteen years. Automation has nearly eliminated the labor component of manufacturing a product, so production is increasingly a fixed-cost activity. Because new technologies are so critical and change so rapidly, research and development (R&D) is also becoming a fixed-cost activity. And because maintaining brand recognition for powerful customers is essential, marketing and advertising become fixed costs as well. Managers can no longer boost profits by reducing wages or labor hours or other variable costs. For companies with large fixed costs, the only way to defray their investment is to find more customers and increase sales. This means rising fixed costs are driving companies toward globalization.

Currency In a borderless world, currency exchange rates are much more volatile than they were just a few years ago. In order to neutralize the effect of currency, managers of global companies are forced to become strong in all areas of the Triad. Then, if currency becomes a negative in one area, positives in another area cancel it out.

Country   Companies move into a country as they seek to neutralize the impact of currency fluctuations. To serve them well, though, they have to move deeply into those countries to get as close to their customers as possible. Managers have to find a way for their companies to benefit from world-scale operations. But at the same time, they must know and serve their customers as well as any local company from the same country. Coca-Cola's success in Japan, for example, is partly a result of introducing unique products for Japanese consumers.

Changes in the five Cs have forced companies to spread out across national borders, but the changes have been so rapid that managers have not always been able to make the necessary adjustments in the way they organize their companies, in the way they think about strategy, or in their assumptions about how to do business.

The Equidistant Manager

Most managers are nearsighted, with their vision dominated by customers in their home countries. Too few try to plan and build companies as if all key customers were equidistant from the corporate headquarters. Honda, for example, has divisions throughout the Triad, but its managers do not act as if the company were divided into Japanese and overseas operations. In fact, the word "overseas" has no place at Honda. The first rule of equidistance is to *see and think globally*.

National boundaries may still be clear on a map, but for managers those boundaries have largely disappeared. With the persistent flow of information around the world, people quickly learn what products are available, and what level of quality they can expect. People have become genuinely global consumers. For managers, this flow of information puts a priority on learning to meet the demands of a borderless world.

This may mean becoming an *insider*, replicating a complete business in every country or key market in which your company does business. Managers cannot hope to run every business in every market around the world from corporate headquarters. They have to become a true *insider* in each market so they can respond to competitors and provide the value local consumers demand.

Managing effectively in the borderless world means paying central attention to delivering value to customers, and to developing an equidistant perspective on who they are and what they want. First and most important is the strategic need to *see your customers clearly*.

Getting Back to Strategy

For many managers, strategy still means beating the competition. It means doing what your competition does, only better. This belief is wrong, since strategy should first be a process of responding to the needs of customers and delivering value to those customers. Indeed, strategy should include an effort to *avoid* competition whenever possible.

Many Japanese managers have failed to learn this lesson. As these firms went global, they concentrated on differentiating their products from those of their competitors. Today, though, many find themselves trapped between competing customer needs. On the one hand, German companies, such as Mercedes or BMW in automobiles, command high prices by serving the quality end of the market. On the other hand, companies like Korea's Hyundai have tried to satisfy price-conscious consumers on the low end of the market. The result, for Japanese firms, is a painful squeeze caused by their focus on competitors, rather than on customer needs.

How should a manager respond to this squeeze? Consider the strategy of Yamaha, a Japanese maker of pianos. The piano market is in decline, as people simply are not buying many new pianos today, and most of the existing ones are sitting around gathering dust. Yamaha decided to take a hard look at its customers and the product. What they found was fewer and fewer people with the time to play the piano, or even to learn how to play the piano. How does one provide value for these customers? Yamaha worked hard on new electronic technology that could turn existing pianos into sophisticated player-pianos. Now, for $2,500, customers can turn their idle pianos into useful instruments. And instead of a dying market, Yamaha now has the prospect of a $2,500 sale to retrofit up to forty million old pianos.

Like Yamaha, many Japanese companies are talented value-adders. Many others are so intent on beating the competition that whole industries have suffered as a consequence. In the blind pursuit of *companyism* (the desire to beat the competition by *doing more better*), Japanese shipbuilders and producers of semiconductors, color TVs, and watches have relentlessly overbuilt and overproduced in an effort to beat their competitors. Now, these industries are flooded with overcapacity and all companies are robbed of an opportunity to make a profit.

Companyism is not entirely a bad thing, of course. Many American companies suffer from too little company orientation. Japanese firms build loyalty, in part, by nurturing a sense of equal participation throughout the company. In most firms, for example, the total compensation of most Japanese CEOs is no more than ten times that of a factory worker. By contrast, Lee Iacocca of Chrysler had an income that was roughly one thousand times greater than that of one of his factory workers.

What is critical, however, is that managers not be so blinded by company loyalty that they forget to ask whether the system needs to be the way it is. Managers in a borderless world need a certain mindset. They need the freedom to rethink their products and ask whether there is a better way to serve their customers. In a changeable world, very few solutions will work forever.

The China Mentality

In product development, one remedy for companyism is to create multiple product teams, each with the same general direction, and then set these teams free to find their own approaches to a single problem. Managers will then not only have multiple solutions from which they may choose, but they will also be able to offer their customers several solutions to the same problem. At the same time, their companies keep churning out new or improved products at regular intervals. NEC, for example, introduces something new to the market every month. Its competitors do so only once every year or two.

What is necessary for world-class product development is the freedom to keep asking the question "Why?" when attempting to meet customer needs. Unfortunately, too many managers lack the *China Mentality* (China, literally translated, means "center of the universe"). Too many managers fail to believe they are the center of the universe, and hence lack the inner confidence that they can change the world. Lacking this confidence, managers do not allow themselves to be led to answers that deviate far from the company norm. For global players, however, confidence to act on their knowledge of key markets is the secret to success in a borderless world.

Getting Rid of the Headquarters Mentality

Company headquarters often becomes another problem for managers as they begin the process of globalization. Overeager and overanxious corporate managers have frequently destroyed profitable businesses by trying to supervise from a distance. No company can operate globally by centralizing all key decisions at the corporate headquarters. Rather, *decomposing* the corporate center into several regional headquarters is becoming an essential ingredient in the strategy of effective global competitors.

The real challenge in decomposing the corporate center, what Akio Morita of Sony terms *global localization,* is not organizational. The real challenge is psychological, a matter of values. When the mother-country identity of the old corporate headquarters disappears, it must be replaced by a commitment to a single, unified global identity. When managers overcome their headquarters mentality, when they come to believe that they may work *in* different nations but they are *of* the global corporation, then the company will have taken the last step toward true global status. Managers will then be free to decide how best to run their business in their particular market.

The Global Logic of Strategic Alliances

For most managers, management means control. Alliances, though, mean sharing control. So it's not surprising that managers have been slow to experiment with genuine strategic alliances. But in a borderless world, in a world of rapidly changing technologies and escalating fixed costs, true alliances become an essential component of strategy.

Glaxo, the British pharmaceutical company, did not want to establish an extensive sales and service network in every country in which it did business. It could not afford to, given its costly commitment to R&D. So Glaxo decided to develop alliances with major pharmaceutical companies in Japan, trade its best drugs with each partner, and focus its own resources on its base in Europe. Now, for each alliance, Glaxo has two profitable drugs to market without any increase in its fixed investment in R&D or marketing.

True alliances are marriages of equals. They avoid the problems of equity ownership and parental control that have plagued so many joint ventures. Instead, alliances help global companies address the common problem of fixed costs. Nissan distributes for Volkswagen in Japan, and Volkswagen reciprocates in Europe. Ford and Mazda swap cars throughout the Triad. Unless an organization is committed to building a fixed investment in every region of the world, it makes sense to cooperate with someone who already has that force in place.

GOVERNMENTS AND BUREAUCRATS

"Lies, Damned Lies, and Statistics"

The charges are familiar. The United States has an enormous trade deficit, especially with Japan. And while the value of the dollar falls, selfish consumers save virtually none of their incomes. Worse, they insist on buying products manufactured abroad. The country is on an irresponsible binge, in the process of being destroyed by selfishness and short-term thinking.

The charges are familiar, but a different picture can be painted. The United States does not have a trade deficit. In fact, because dollars are the settlement currency in foreign trade, the United States does not have any "foreign" trade at all. Unlike Brazil or France, or even Japan, the United States never has to earn foreign currency to purchase something from abroad. All it has to do is expand its domestic economy across the borders of its trading partners. Because the money used to buy foreign goods is always in dollars, buying cars from Japan is no different than buying PCs from Texas or oranges from California.

Government trade statistics measure goods that cross the national border, but in a borderless world the figures they report are completely meaningless. We act as if they really mean something, when in fact they bear no relation to the real flows of economic activity in the world. Most American corporations have developed a local insider presence in countries around the world, and this is the biggest reason why United States exports have declined statistically. The products they sell to global markets are made in those markets. In fact, any goods they ship back home are recorded as Japanese or European exports to the United States.

The trade deficit is an illusion, created by a system that only measures goods crossing national borders. Consider that in 1985, Japanese purchases of American goods (regardless of where those goods were produced) averaged $580 per person. American per capita purchases of Japanese goods averaged just $298.

Americans also assume that the Japanese have a much higher savings rate. Yet these savings statistics are just as flawed and misleading. A closer examination of the assumptions behind these statistics suggests that there is little or no difference in the savings habits of American and Japanese consumers. In fact, if one looks at the assets we collect rather than the income we put away, Americans may actually be far *better* savers than the Japanese.

Americans worry that the United States has become a debtor nation, that we have mortgaged our future and put ourselves in debt to the rest of the world. But there is no reason to be concerned with most of these "liabilities." The United States is an attractive place for foreigners to invest their money, so foreign investment pours into the country. Most of these investments (the purchase of companies or real estate, for example) carry no interest charges, so the United States incurs no financial obligations. But most foreign investments are recorded at the national border as "external liabilities," so people worry.

Development in a Borderless World

Politicians and policy makers, misled by official statistics and not fully understanding the nature of the borderless world, continue to intervene in the economy with disastrous results. Attempts are made to weaken the value of the dollar in order to make American goods more competitive. But officials succeed only in frightening new investments away. Governments try to "manage" the foreign exchange markets, but accomplish little more than to punish their own domestic companies and consumers.

Perhaps the most murderous effects of confused government policy result from the folly of protectionism. Nations that have been successful at development efforts have made the determination to open the door to the global economy. They have decided to become a part of the global marketplace. Those that fail still harbor the illusion that participation in the interlinked economy is not important.

In a borderless world, the role of a responsible government is to give its people as much choice as possible, and to keep its people well informed. The government of India does not do this. Their domestic auto industry is highly protected against foreign products. But cars in India are miserable vehicles, and the auto industry is still sick. Hong Kong, by contrast, has no natural resources and a tiny population. Yet, with a "free port" approach, the people of Hong Kong have achieved a per capita GNP that rivals Great Britain's.

VISION OF THE FUTURE

We need to accept the fact that information and knowledge, not natural resources, are the key to wealth and economic growth. National borders mean little for the real flows of economic activity, and national governments no longer have the ability to produce economic wealth based on what's under the soil, or on what can be taxed, or on the strength of their military. Instead, *wealth emerges from the hard work of well-educated people.*

Given this new reality, what is the role of a modern government? It must educate its people, and guarantee them as much information and as much choice as possible. In the interlinked economy, it does not matter who builds this factory or who owns that office building. What is important is that the global corporations that do business in an area give people good work to do and an opportunity to buy the products they want.

It makes no sense for politicians and journalists to be concerned about national industrial competitiveness. Nations are no longer in competition. The only thing that matters is that IBM is in global competition with DEC and Fujitsu, or that Toyota competes worldwide with Honda and Ford. No government should be in the business of dictating choices for their citizens in order to protect domestic firms. In a borderless world, the best companies will be organized on a global scale. Companies that will not, or cannot, compete globally are simply not worth saving.

How close is the ILE to becoming a truly borderless world? Perhaps closer than we think. Certainly, there are still problems. Many companies still suffer from a headquarters mentality. Too few are ready to take advantage of genuine strategic alliances. National borders are still controlled, and domestic markets are still protected. But more and more corporations are not committed to globalization, and they have benefitted from that commitment. And daily, the information age makes consumers more knowledgeable and more demanding. As these trends continue, government leaders may soon realize that their role is not one of dictating choices to their citizens. Governments may provide guidance on such issues as safety and minimum levels of service. But they must step back and allow people the freedom to vote with their pocketbooks.

FIFTEEN

Epilogue

*Jon L. Pierce and John W. Newstrom, with
L. L. Cummings*

EPILOGUE

This concluding section provides our reflections upon management (both the body of knowledge and its practice), as well as upon the wave of management books that have become part of the popular press. We hope it will provide some degree of closure, and point you in some new directions.

Management can be defined as the skillful application of a body of knowledge to a particular organizational situation. This definition suggests to us that management is an art form as well as a science. That is, there is a body of knowledge that has to be applied with the fine touch and instinctive sense of the master artist. Execution of the management role and performance of the managerial functions are more complex than the simple application of a few management concepts. The development of effective management, therefore, requires the development of an in-depth understanding of organizational and management concepts, as well as the capacity to grasp when and how to apply this knowledge.

The organizational arena presents today's manager with a number of challenges. The past few decades have been marked by a rapid growth of knowledge about organizations and management systems. As a consequence of this growth in management information, we strongly believe that it is important for today's manager to engage in *lifelong learning,* by continually remaining a student of management. It is also clear to us that our understanding of organizations and management systems is still in the early stages of development. That is, there remain many unanswered questions that pertain to the effective management of organizations.

Many observers of the perils facing today's organizations have charged that the crises facing American organizations are largely a function of "bad management." Similarly, Tom Peters and Bob Waterman have observed that the growth of our society during the earlier part of this century was so rapid that almost any management approach appeared to work and work well. The real test of effective management systems did not appear until the recent decades, when competitive, economic, political, and social pressures created a form of environmental turbulence that pushed existing managerial tactics beyond their limits. Not only are students of management challenged to learn about effective management principles, but they are also confronted with the need to develop the skills and intuitive sense to apply that management knowledge.

Fortunately, there are many organizations in our society that they can learn from, and there is a wealth of knowledge that has been created that focuses on effective organizational management. There are, at least, two literatures that provide rich opportunities for regular reading. First, there is the traditional management literature that is found in management and organization textbooks and academic journals (e.g., *Academy of Management Journal, Administrative Science Quarterly,* and *California Management Review*). Second, this past decade has seen the emergence of a nontraditional management literature written by management practitioners and management consultants who are describing their organizational experiences and providing a number of other management themes. Knowledge about effective and ineffective management systems can be gleaned by listening to the management scholar, philosopher, and practitioner.

Since not all that is published in the academic journals or in the popular press meets combined tests of scientific rigor and practicality, it is important that motivated readers immerse themselves in *both* of these literatures. Yet, neither source should be approached and subsequently consumed without engaging in critical thinking.

CRITICAL THINKING AND CAUTIOUS CONSUMPTION

We believe that the ideas promoted in these best-sellers should not be blindly integrated into any organization. Each should be subjected to careful scrutiny in order to identify its inherent strengths and weaknesses; each should be examined within the context of the unique organizational setting in which it may be implemented; and modifications and fine-tuning of the technique may be required in order to tailor it to a specific organizational setting and management philosophy. Finally, the process that is used to implement the management technique may be as important to its success as the technique itself.

This is an era of an information-knowledge explosion. Perhaps consumers of that information need to be reminded of the relevance of the "caveat emptor" from the product domain, because there are both good and questionable informational products on the market. Fortunately, advisory services like *Consumer Reports* exist to advise us on the consumption of consumer goods. There is, however, no similar guide for our consumption of information in the pop-management press. Just because something has been a best-seller or widely promoted does not mean that the information contained therein is worthy of direct consumption. It may be a best-seller because it presents an optimistic message, it is enjoyable reading, or because it has been successfully marketed to the public!

The information in all management literature should be approached with caution; it should be examined and questioned. The pop-management literature should not be substituted for more scientific-based knowledge about effective management. In addition, this knowledge should be compared and contrasted with what we know about organizations and management systems from other sources—the opinions of other experts, the academic management literature, and our own prior organizational experiences.

We invite you to question this literature. In the process there are a myriad of questions that should be asked. For example: What are the author's credentials, and are they relevant to the book? Has the author remained an objective observer of the reported events? Why did the author write this book? What kind of information is being presented (e.g., opinion, values, facts)? How reliable and valid is the information that is being presented? Does this information make sense when it is placed into previously developed theories (e.g., from a historical context)? Could I take this information and apply it to another situation at a different point in time and in a different place, or was it unique to the author's experience? These and similar questions should be part of the information screening process.

INTERVIEW WITH PROFESSOR L. L. CUMMINGS[1]

As we became increasingly familiar with the "best-sellers" through our roles as editors, we found ourselves asking a number of questions about this type of literature. For example,

1. Is this material "intellectual pornography," as some have claimed?
2. Do we want our students to read this material?

---

[1] Larry L. Cummings is the Carlson Professor of Management in the Carlson School of Management at the University of Minnesota. Formerly, he served as the J. L. Kellogg Distinguished Research Professor of Organizational Behavior at Northwestern University and was the Slichter Research Professor, H. I. Romnes Faculty Fellow, and Director of the Center for the Study of Organizational Performance in the Graduate School of Business, University of Wisconsin, Madison. In addition, he has also taught at Columbia University, Indiana University, and the University of British Columbia. Professor Cummings has published more than eighty journal articles and has authored, coauthored, or edited sixteen books. In addition, he has been an active member of several professional associa-

3. Should managers of today's organizations be encouraged to read this material and take it seriously?
4. What contributions to management education and development come from this collection of management books?
5. How should this management literature be approached?

As a part of our reflection upon the currently popular literature, we talked with a distinguished management scholar, organization and management consultant, and educator of MBA and Ph.D. students: Professor L. L. Cummings. Following are excerpts from that interview:

Question   Larry, during the past decade we have witnessed an explosion in the number and type of books that have been written on management and organizations for the trade market. Many of these books have found themselves on the "best-sellers" list. What, in your opinion, has been the impact of these publications? What is the nature of their contribution?

Answer   Quite frankly, I think these books have made a number of subtle contributions, most of which have not been labeled or identified by either the business press or the academic press. In addition, many of their contributions have been misappropriately or inaccurately labeled.

Permit me to elaborate. I think it is generally true that a number of these very popular "best-seller list" books, as you put it, have been thought to be reasonably accurate translations or interpretations of successful organizational practice. While this is not the way that these books have been reviewed in the academic press, my interactions with managers, business practitioners, and MBA students reveal that many of these books are viewed as describing organizational structure, practices, and cultures that are thought to contribute to excellence.

On the other hand, when I evaluate the books myself and when I pay careful attention to the reviews by respected, well-trained, balanced academicians, it is my opinion that these books offer very little, if anything, in the way of *generalizable* knowledge about successful organizational practice. As organizational case studies, they are the most dangerous of the lot, in that the data (information) presented has not been systematically, carefully, and cautiously collected and interpreted. Of course, that criticism is common for case studies. Cases were never meant to be contributions to scientific knowledge. Even the best ones are primarily pedagogical aids.

The reason I describe the cases presented in books like *When Giants Learn to Dance* and *In Search of Excellence* as frequently among the most dangerous is because they are so well done (i.e., well done in a marketing and journalistic sense), and therefore, they are easily read, and so believable. They are likely to influence the naive, those who consume them without critically evaluating their content. They epitomize the glamour and the action orientation, and even the machoism of American management practice; that is, they represent the epitome of competition, control, and order as dominant interpersonal and organizational values.

Rather, I think the contributions of these books, in general, have been to provide an apology, a rationale, or a positioning, if you like, of American management as something that is not *just* on the defensive with regard to other world competitors. Instead, they have highlighted American management as having many good things to offer: a sense of spirit, a sense of identification, a sense of clear caricature. This has served to fill a very important need. In American management thought there has emerged a lack of self-confidence and a lack of belief that what we are doing is proactive, effective, and correct. From this perspective these books have served a useful role in trying to present an upbeat, optimistic characterization.

Question In addition to a large volume of sales, surveys reveal that many of these books have been purchased and presumably read by those who are managing today's organizations. Does this trouble you? More specifically, are there any concerns that you have, given the extreme popularity of these types of books?

Answer I am of two minds with regard to this question. First, I think that the sales of these books are not an accurate reflection of either the degree, the extent, nor the carefulness with which they have been read. Nor do I believe that the sales volumes tell us anything about the pervasiveness of their impact. Like many popular items (fads), many of these books have been purchased for desktop dressing. In many cases, the preface, the introduction, and the conclusion (maybe the summary on the dust jacket) have been read such that the essence of the book is picked up so that it can become a part of managerial and social conversation.

Obviously, this characterization does not accurately describe everyone in significant positions of management who has purchased these books. There are obviously many managers who make sincere attempts to follow the management literature thoroughly and to evaluate it critically. I think that most of the people that I come in contact with in management circles, both in training for management and in actual management positions, who have carefully read the books are not deceived by them. They are able to put them in the perspective of representations or characterizations of a fairly dramatic sort. As a consequence, I am not too concerned about the books being overly persuasive in some dangerous, Machiavellian, or subterranean sense.

On the other hand, I do have a concern of a different nature concerning these books. That concern focuses upon the possibility that the experiences they describe will be taken as legitimate bases or legitimate directions for the study of management processes. These books represent discourse by the method of emphasizing the extremes, in particular the extremes of success. I think a much more fruitful approach to studying and developing prescriptions for management thought and management action is to use the *method of differences* rather than the *method of extremes*.

The method of differences would require us to study the conditions which gave rise to success at Chrysler, or which gave rise to success at McDonald's, or which currently gives rise to success at Merck, or any of the other best-managed companies. However, through this method we would also contrast these companies with firms in the same industries which are not as successful. The method of contrast (differences) is likely to lead to empirical results which are much less dramatic, much less exciting, much less subject to journalistic account (i.e., they're likely to be more boring to read), but it is much more likely to lead to observations that are more generalizable across managerial situations, as well as being generative in terms of ideas for further management research.

Thus, the issue is based on the fundamental method that underlies these characterizations. My concern is not only from a methodological perspective. It also centers on our ethical and professional obligations to make sure that the knowledge we transmit does not lead people to overgeneralize. Rather, it should provide them with information which is diagnostic rather than purely prescriptive.

The method of extremes does not lead to a diagnostic frame of mind. It does not lead to a frame of mind which questions why did that happen, under what conditions will it happen, or under what conditions will it not happen. The method of differences is much more likely to lead to the discovery of the conditional nature of knowledge and the conditional nature of prescriptions.

Question   A CEO or middle manager is about to take a sabbatical and has on his/her agenda the reading of a number of these "best-sellers." What advice would you like to offer?

Answer   Let me make the assumption that the CEO's sabbatical is for three months. My first advice would be to make an absolute public commitment to spend not more than one month of the sabbatical (i.e., not more than one third of it) reading these best-sellers. That would be the absolute maximum! Because of the lack of generalizability and validity of much of this information, any more time than this would be poorly spent. A crash course of one month, supplemented by perhaps video and audio tapes, would be sufficient to get the manager up to the place where he or she knows basically what is in these books. At this point the manager would have a working knowledge of the material as well as be capable of carrying on a reasonable conversation about the contents of the books.

Far more important, and worthy of at least two thirds of the time, would be reading of a different sort. Reading and study of the classics, both the intellectual and the philosophical classics, as well as the spiritual classics and historical classics would be of significant value.

I think one of the most important disciplines for the study of management, particularly for an experienced manager on sabbatical, is the study of history—the study of the development and decline of nation states and religious empires. They should look at history from a strategic perspective (i.e., what things did important nations and leaders take into consideration and what did they fail to take into consideration; what were their points of vulnerability and how could that have been prevented). It seems to me that this kind of knowledge is far more likely to lead to the discovery of useful diagnostics than the knowledge that is likely to be gained from reading the "best-seller" list.

CONCLUSION

We hope that you have enjoyed reading the views of management scholar Professor Cummings and this sampling of recent popular management books. In addition, we hope that these readings have served to stimulate your thinking about effective and ineffective practices of management. We reiterate that there is no single universally applicable practice of management, for management is the skillful application of a body of knowledge to a particular situation. We invite you to continue expanding your understanding of new and developing management concepts. In a friendly sort of way, we challenge you to develop the skills to know when and how to apply this knowledge in the practice of management.

Glossary of Terms

amicitia An alliance in which members agree to protect each other's interests. (Zaleznik)

asset rationalization Meeting competitive pressures by equating human and physical assets with current economics. (Beer, et al.)

assumption analysis A process of categorizing the assumptions that underlie conclusions in light of their certainty and importance. (Kilmann)

benchmarking A method by which organizations monitor the performance of the best of their competitors to use as a standard for their own performance. (Band)

blueprinting A method of analysis for managing all elements of the customer satisfaction process which looks at the basic systems and structures of the organization in order to understand better the process of creating satisfied customers. (Band)

bridge team Group developed from the key stakeholders to monitor the status of revitalization and to resolve issues beyond the scope of the team structure. (Beer, et al.)

charismatic leader One who senses unexploited opportunities, formulates and communicates an idealized vision, builds trust in oneself and support for the vision, and provides the means to achieve the vision. (Conger)

China mentality The conviction that one *can* change the world, motivating one to reject the usual answers and examine old problems in a new light. (Ohmae)

commitment gap A reluctance on the part of organizational members to commit themselves to their work or to their employer. (Bennis)

companyism An excessive concern for, or loyalty to, one's company, which leads to the inability to examine company strategy or past ways of doing business critically. (Ohmae)

competitive advantage An advantage that a firm creates for itself by providing more value for customers than competitors provide. Firms can achieve a cost advantage or a differentiation advantage. (Porter)

contention Tension that results in constructive conflict; it arises from inevitable contradictions that are an outgrowth of embracing organizational attributes which appear to be in opposition. (Pascale)

cost advantage A competitive advantage that a firm achieves by providing equivalent benefits at a lower price than competitors charge. (Porter)

creative imitation A strategy in which the entrepreneur does something somebody else has already done, yet applies it better than the original innovator. (Drucker)

creative problem making A heuristic used to enhance a decision maker's or leader's creativity in identifying organizational problems. (Leavitt)

critical path The various stages that an organization must follow (allowing overlap across them) to develop an organization which naturally continues to revitalize itself. (Beer, et al)

culture A system of attitudes, actions, and artifacts that endures over time and that operates to produce among its members a relatively unique common psychology. (Vaill)

culture track The first step in an organizational improvement program that emphasizes establishing trust, information sharing, and adaptiveness. (Kilmann)

cultural paradigm A set of interrelated assumptions that form a coherent pattern regarding culture. (Schein)

culture clash Conflict over basic values that occurs between groups of people with different core identities. (Loden and Rosener)

customer satisfaction The state in which customer needs, wants, and expectations, through the transaction cycle, are met or exceeded, resulting in repurchase and continuing loyalty. (Band)

deadly diseases A set of chronic ailments that can plague any organization and prevent its success. (Deming)

defensive reasoning Reasoning that occurs when individuals (1) firmly hold premises of questionable validity yet think they are unassailable; (2) make inferences that do not necessarily follow from the premises yet they think they do; and (3) reach conclusions that they believe they have tested carefully yet they have not because the way they have been framed make them untestable. (Argyris)

Deming Management Theory A set of 14 steps that managers are advised to take to transform their organizations into more successful systems. (Deming)

dependent actors Workers, customers, clients, suppliers, community members, and others who are dependent on the organization for wages, benefits, business, taxes, etc. (Meyer & Zucker)

dialexia The compulsion to examine all issues dialectically and to assume that in all cases those issues are not as they seem. (Vaill)

differentiation advantage A competitive advantage that a firm achieves by providing greater benefits than competitors provide at a higher price than competitors charge. The value of the benefits exceeds the price differential between the firm's products and competitor's products. (Porter)

differently abled A term used to focus on a person's abilities while still acknowledging physical and/or developmental differences. (Loden and Rosener)

discontinuity The break in progress created by moving from the old to the new (restructured) organization. (Kanter)

disorder The confusion created as a restructured organization rebuilds itself. (Kanter)

distraction The shift of focus and energy from an accent on running the business to solving immediate problems. (Kanter)

diversity Those human qualities that are different from our own and outside the groups to which we belong, yet present in other individuals and groups. (Loden and Rosener)

double-loop learning Learning that focuses on the values governing the actions that produced the errors. (Argyris)

dynamic synthesis A conflict solution which relies on neither static either-or choices nor splitting the difference, but rather a seemingly paradoxical embrace of both positions. (Pascale)

effective managers Managers who manage themselves and others so that both employees and the organization benefit. (Blanchard and Johnson)

empowerment Helping employees take ownership of their jobs so that they take personal interest in improving the performance of the organization. (Kanter)

enterprise web A group of symbolic analysts who combine their skills so that the group's ability to innovate is something more than the simple sum of its parts. (Reich)

entrepreneurial judo A strategy in which a business moves into a territory held by an already established leader. Such established leaders fail to defend, or defend only halfheartedly, their territory out of a belief that "the market" is really theirs and they cannot be threatened. (Drucker)

espoused theories The beliefs and values people hold about how to manage their lives. (Argyris)

ethics check A set of three questions used to explore ethical dilemmas—"Is it legal? Is it balanced? How will it make me feel about myself?" (Blanchard and Peale)

fancy footwork Actions that permit individuals to be blind to inconsistencies in their actions, to deny that these inconsistencies exist, or to blame other people for their actions. (Argyris)

feedback Information regarding results of one's efforts (how well one is performing). (Blanchard and Johnson)

first-order errors Errors that are caused by not knowing. (Argyris)

five Ps of ethical power Core principles leading to ethical behavior, including purpose, pride, patience, persistence, and perspective. (Blanchard and Peale)

fixed costs Costs that are based on commitments from previous budgets and cannot be altered quickly. (Ohmae)

frame A schema, map, image, metaphor, tool, or perspective that presents a unique image of organizations and allows managers to gather information, make judgments, and determine how to take action from its vantage point. The four frames are the structural, human resources, political, and symbolic. (Bolman and Deal)

fustest with the mostest A strategy in which the entrepreneur aims at leadership, if not dominance, in a new market or new industry. (Drucker)

gainsharing System of financial rewards in which employee bonuses are based on organizational performance. (Lawler)

glass ceiling Invisible organizational barriers or roadblocks that may prevent women from reaching top-level executive jobs. (Morrison, et al)

global localization The capacity to operate on a global scale while retaining the ability to serve local customers and markets. (Ohmae)

global web An enterprise web of a high-value enterprise which spans across national borders. (Reich)

globalization The standardization of product design and advertising strategy throughout the world. (Ohmae)

goal-setting The establishment of targets (goals) for employee performance that facilitate the conscious intentions of employees to perform. (Blanchard and Johnson)

Greatest Management Principle (GMP) Concept based on reinforcement theory suggesting that "the things that get rewarded get done." (LeBoeuf)

group dynamics Patterns of interaction that occur within groups that help or hinder the accomplishment of tasks. (Loden and Rosener)

helicopter sense Strategic thinking in which a manager rises above details to develop a more general understanding of whole problems and possible solutions. (Carlzon)

Icarus Paradox Overconfident, complacent executives extend the very factors that contributed to success to the point where they cause organizational decline. (Miller)

integration Creating conditions at work such that individuals can *best* achieve their own goals by directing their efforts toward the success of the enterprise. (McGregor)

interlinked economy The open and deregulated global economy that is currently emerging, encompassing Japan, Europe, the United States, and other aggressive economies. (Ohmae)

job enrichment Creating jobs in which individuals can be responsible for an entire product or service. (Lawler)

leadership A process by which an individual or team induces a group to pursue objectives held by the leader or shared by the leader and his or her followers. (Gardner)

learning disability A way of thinking in organizations which keeps managers and others from making necessary changes and adapting to environmental needs. (Senge)

loyalists Employees who choose to remain in a declining firm rather than leave, because they believe that their best efforts will still lead to improvement. (Meyer and Zucker)

management of attention The ability of effective leaders to be able to draw others to them, and to communicate a vision and a focus of commitment. (Bennis)

management of meaning The ability of a leader to communicate effectively a vision or ideas across great distances (e.g., across multiple levels in the organizational hierarchy). (Bennis)

management skills track The second step in an organizational improvement program that emphasizes development of conceptual, analytic, administrative, social, and interpersonal skills. (Kilmann)

managerial competency A definable and trainable skill alleged to have an impact on overall managerial performance. (Vaill)

managerial mystique An outdated belief that solid methods (relying heavily on structure and process to control behavior) will produce success in organizations. (Zaleznik)

managers People in organizations who do things right. (Bennis)

master managers Individuals who recognize the pervasiveness of change in their environments, and learn to use contradictory and paradoxical value frameworks to achieve excellence. (Quinn)

MBWA (Managing By Wandering Around) The process of having managers spend a substantial portion of their time meeting with customers, vendors, and employees to learn their needs. (Peters and Waterman)

mental models Deeply ingrained generalizations, assumptions, or pictures which influence how people see the world. (Senge)

moment of truth That instant in which an employee comes in contact with a customer and has the opportunity to make a good or bad impression on the customer. (Carlzon)

new-design plants Organization-wide approaches to participative management, in which group members participate in selection decisions, layout facilitates work group tasks, job design revolves around teams, pay systems are egalitarian, etc. (Lawler)

newstreams Future products and services. (Kanter)

nichemanship An organizational strategy of fulfilling a segment of unmet demand in a larger market. (Belasco)

organizational culture The pattern of basic assumptions that a given group has invented, discovered, or developed in learning to cope with its problems of external adaptation and internal integration, and that have worked well enough to be considered valid and, therefore, to be taught to new members as the correct way to perceive, think, and feel in relation to those problems. (Schein)

organizational defensive routines Actions or policies that protect individuals or segments of the organization from experiencing embarrassment or threat. (Argyris)

others People who are different from us along one or several dimensions such as age, ethnicity, gender, race, sexual/affectional orientation, and so on. (Loden and Rosener)

paradigm A mental model or mindset which reflects the natural human tendency to perceive patterns. Paradigms are the fundamental assumptions which guide management decision-making. (Pascale)

paradox A statement whose parts may seem contradictory but may actually be true. (Vaill)

participative goal-setting A process during which employees have the opportunity to play an active role in developing their own goals. (LeBoeuf)

participative leadership A type of leadership that emphasizes empowerment and increased employee involvement in problem solving. (Loden and Rosener)

pathfinding One part of the managerial process that relies on a leader's vision, clear values, and determination level to guide organizational activities effectively. (Leavitt)

permanent failure The outcome of divergent preferences between owners and dependent actors; persistence or survival of an organization which has a sustained record of low performance. (Meyer and Zucker)

permanent white water The condition of continuous chaos and complexity characteristic of contemporary business environments. (Vaill)

personal freedom norms Organizational norms which reflect the organization's position on self-expression, the exercise of personal discretion, and self-satisfaction. (Kilmann)

personal time inventory A record of daily activities and the absolute and relative amounts of time spent on each activity. (LeBoeuf)

Pinocchio Effect When an actual consequence fails to resemble the original intention as a result of inadequate expression (communication) of meaning. (Bennis)

planned playfulness A method of generating creativity by the periodic, conscious, and temporary relaxation of analytic problem-solving rules, which enables the exercise of imagination without fear of criticism or requirements of consistency or hard evidence. (Leavitt)

pluralistic leadership A type of leadership that assumes that organization culture must change in order to attain diversity, employee empowerment, and involvement. (Loden and Rosener)

power economics strategies Methods of maintaining and enhancing one's personal political base by using dependency reversal, power enhancement, and personal investments. (Zaleznik)

powershift The idea that knowledge (the K-factor) will dominate brute force and wealth as the driving force in future global struggles for power. (Toffler)

praise Verbal reinforcement (e.g., compliment) for desirable employee behavior and performance. (Blanchard and Johnson)

primary dimensions Immutable human differences that are inborn and/or that exert an important impact on early socialization or throughout life. Examples of primary dimensions are age, ethnicity, gender, physical abilities, race, and sexual/affectional orientation. (Loden and Rosener)

problem The difference between what is actually happening and what you want to happen. (Blanchard and Johnson)

problem-identifier Person who has the skills required to help customers understand their needs and how those needs can best be met by customized products and to identify new problems and possibilities to which the customized product might be applicable. (Reich)

problem-solver Person who has the skills required to put things together in unique ways and continually searches for new applications, combinations, and refinements capable of solving all sorts of emerging problems. (Reich)

productivity Employee output in terms of the quantity and quality of work completed. (Blanchard and Johnson)

Program Management Organization (PMO) A diverse collection of organizational members from varying levels and areas in an organization who spend part of their time away from their formal responsibilities in order to address complex organizational issues. (Kilmann)

programmatic change Change made in how a corporation functions, based on human resource issues. This directly opposes asset rationalization. (Beer, et al.)

protectionism The attempt to defend domestic companies from trade or competition with foreign industries. (Ohmae)

psychology of commitment The act of increasing public commitment to a cause or organization even after its repeated failures. (Meyer and Zucker)

purposing Continuous leadership actions to induce clarity, consensus, and commitment regarding the organization's basic purposes. (Vaill)

reinforcement Anything a manager does or applies that subsequently improves the behavior of an employee. (LeBoeuf)

reprimand Negative verbal feedback provided when undesirable employee behavior and performance occur. (Blanchard and Johnson)

revitalization Enhancing the abilities of the individuals and the organization to cope with an increasingly competitive environment. (Beer, et al.)

reward Anything positive, whether tangible or intangible, that is presented to employees in order to increase productive behavior. (LeBoeuf)

reward system track The fifth step in an organizational improvement program that develops a performance-based reward system. (Kilmann)

Sapp A force that drains energy from people. (Byham)

Satchmo's Paradox The inability of the expert to explain his/her area of expertise to the novice (e.g., "If you have to explain what jazz is, you'll never know."). (Vaill)

schismogenic thinking Choosing one value over another so as to eliminate contradiction, while also eliminating competing positive values from consideration. (Quinn)

second-order errors Errors that humans actively design and produce. (Argyris)

secondary dimensions Mutable human differences that are acquired, discarded, and/or modified throughout life. Examples of secondary dimensions are educational background, income, marital status, military status, religious beliefs, and work experience. (Loden and Rosener)

selective adaptation Choice of a method or action that accommodates identified conditions rather than ignoring or going against those facts. (McGregor)

self-managed work team A group of employees that is assigned significant, interdependent pieces of work and managed in a way such that each member learns and participates in all aspects of the job. (LeBoeuf)

semiautonomous teams Small groups of employees who manage many dimensions of their own work affairs. (Byham)

service audit Systematic collection and analysis of information on the entire process of providing a service so as to gain a thorough understanding of what the customers want and what the quality or worth of that service is perceived to be. (Albrecht and Zemke)

service system All of the physical resources and organizational procedures made available to service people to help them provide service to the customer. (Albrecht and Zemke)

shadow track A steering committee responsible for monitoring and coordinating a comprehensive organizational improvement program that integrates culture, management skills, reward systems, strategy-structure, and team-building. (Kilmann)

shared vision The capacity to hold a shared picture of the future. (Senge)

single-loop learning Learning that focuses on the presenting problem (symptom) and ignores the causes of the problem. (Argyris)

social relationship norms Organizational norms which suggest the extent to which socializing and mixing work with pleasure are condoned or even encouraged. (Kilmann)

spin-in partnership An enterprise web where strategic brokers in headquarters purchase the best of good ideas bubbling up outside the firm from independent groups of problem-identifiers and problem-solvers, and then produce, distribute, and market the ideas under the firm's own well-known trademark. (Reich)

spin-off partnership An enterprise web where strategic brokers in headquarters act as venture capitalists and midwives, nurturing good ideas that bubble up from groups of problem-solvers and problem-identifiers and then spinning the groups off as independent businesses in which the strategic brokers at headquarters retain a partial stake. (Reich)

strategic alliance A mutually beneficial, long-term, and cooperative relationship with another firm. (Ohmae)

strategic broker Person who has the skills necessary to link problem-solvers and problem-identifiers, and to manage ideas. (Reich)

strategic management The process by which top management teams identify the unit of interest and determine the mission for that unit via thorough analysis of organizational strengths/weaknesses and environmental threats and opportunities. (Vaill)

strategy-structure track The fourth step in an organizational improvement program which focuses on aligning objectives, tasks, and people. (Kilmann)

superficial man A rather bland, composite, unreal individual that most behavioral science theories attempt to describe and explain. (Vaill)

symbolic analytic services Services typically provided by people who trade worldwide the manipulations of symbols—data, words, and oral and visual representations. (Reich)

symbolic analyst Person who provides symbolic-analytic services, generally the problem-solver, problem-identifier, and the strategic broker. (Reich)

synergy Creating a whole that is greater than the sum of its parts. (Kanter)

systems thinking The ability to look at the whole and how one part affects another. (Senge)

task alignment Balancing the organization's behavioral and business concerns and focusing on the core tasks rather than on the organizational structure. (Beer, et al.)

task-driven organization An organization in which roles and responsibilities are assigned based on the task, rather than on an established hierarchy. (Beer, et al.)

task innovation norms Organizational norms which focus on creativity and innovation and reflect the organization's stance on status quo versus change. (Kilmann)

task support norms Organizational norms which focus on information sharing, helping other work groups, and efficiency concerns. (Kilmann)

team-building track The third step in an organizational improvement program that emphasizes managing troublemakers, team buildings, and inter-team building. (Kilmann)

team gaps The difference between actual and desired dimensions of work-group functioning. (Kilmann)

technoholic One who believes all of the world's problems can be solved by the rational development of a plan and the application of appropriate technologies. (Vaill)

theories in use The actual rules or master programs that individuals use to achieve control. (Argyris)

Theory X A set of assumptions that explains some human behavior and has influenced conventional principles of management. It assumes that workers want to avoid work and must be controlled and coerced to accept responsibility and exert effort toward organizational objectives. (McGregor)

Theory Y A set of assumptions offered as an alternative to Theory X. Theory Y assumes that work is a natural activity, and given the right conditions, people will seek responsibility and apply their capacities to organizational objectives without coercion. (McGregor)

transcendent management The higher order of complexity which is necessary to manage organizational renewal successfully; it is based on the belief that the management of disequilibrium is a preferred strategy for successful adaptation. (Pascale)

transformational cycle A dynamic sequence of phases through which a master manager journeys toward excellent performance, encompassing initiation, uncertainty, transformation, and routinization. (Quinn)

transitional stages of growth The phases through which organizations move across time as they emphasize different values—entrepreneurial, collectivity, formalization, and elaboration of structure. (Quinn)

triad The combined market of the industrialized world (Japan, Europe, and the United States). (Ohmae)

value chain The network of discrete activities that comprise an organization's product design, logistics, marketing, production, distribution, and service activities. (Porter)

value creation Combining all the tools and techniques for quality, service, and customer satisfaction into a program that will create and deliver value to customers. (Band)

variable costs Costs that are closely associated with the volume of the business. (Ohmae)

vision A pathfinder's capacity to envision alternative futures proactively and focus others toward an organizational mission. (Leavitt)

vision A mental image or a dream of a highly desirable future state for the organization. (Conger)

Wallenda Factor The capacity to concentrate on one's intention, task, and decision. (Bennis)

work simplification The process of eliminating those tasks that are unnecessary and unrelated to performance or task completion. (LeBoeuf)

work teams Groups of employees who are given considerable responsibility to decide how the group will operate. (Lawler)

wu-wei An element of Taoism that suggests that more can be accomplished in the world by nonaction than by forcing action. (Vaill)

Zapp A force that energizes people, enabling them to seek and obtain continuous improvement in their jobs. (Byham)

Index